THE WORLD'S CLASSICS

606

ELIZABETHAN
HISTORY PLAYS

Oxford University Press, Amen House, London E.C. 4

GLASGOW NEW YORK TORONTO MELBOURNE WELLINGTON
BOMBAY CALCUTTA MADRAS KARACHI LAHORE DACCA
CAPE TOWN SALISBURY NAIROBI IBADAN
KUALA LUMPUR HONG KONG

ELIZABETHAN
HISTORY PLAYS

Edited with an Introduction and
Glossary by

WILLIAM A. ARMSTRONG

LONDON
OXFORD UNIVERSITY PRESS
NEW YORK   TORONTO
1965

This volume of Elizabethan History Plays
was first published in The World's Classics
in 1965

Selection, Introduction, and Glossary
© *Oxford University Press* 1965

PRINTED IN GREAT BRITAIN

CONTENTS

INTRODUCTION

GREAT enterprises often have unexpected origins. The creative process which culminated in Shakespeare's history plays was probably set in motion by William Tyndale's terse but pointed criticism of Catholic chroniclers in *The Obedience of a Christian Man* (1528): 'Consider the story of King John, where I doubt not but they have put the best and fairest for themselves, and the worst of King John: for I suppose they make the chronicles themselves.' This hint no doubt prompted John Bale to rehabilitate John by making him the hero of the first English history play a few years later. Imbued with the doctrines of reform propagated by Wyclif and Tyndale, Bale was a strong supporter of Henry VIII in his quarrel with the Papacy, and *King John* is the most important of a series of polemical plays that he wrote in the royal cause. The first version was probably written by 1534, a second was completed in 1538, and further revisions appear in the unique manuscript of the play, which dates from about 1561.

In conception, *King John* was a highly original play. The medieval morality play had dramatized a conflict between personified forces of good and evil for the possession of man's soul, showing how its salvation depended on the doctrines and sacraments of the Church. A significant shift of interest is shown in John Skelton's morality, *Magnificence* (written about 1519), in which the main character is a king, not Everyman, in which the personifications of good and evil are wise or wicked counsellors, and in which the central issue is the welfare of the state. Bale's innovations were even more radical. He combines historical with allegorical personages and reinterprets the conflict between King John and Pope Innocent III, presenting John as a martyr who upheld doctrines soundly based on the Bible, who surrendered to the Papacy to save his kingdom from being ravaged by war, and who died from a poisonous draught administered by a traitorous monk. As Bale's Interpreter observes at the end of Act I, this 'mirror' of past events throws reflections on the recent struggle between Henry VIII and the Pope. This interconnexion of past and present is systematically developed in Act II, where Sedition, the chief agent of John's downfall, is brought low by Verity and Imperial Majesty, who clearly represents Henry himself, for he is given titles—'supreme head of the church' and 'true defender' of the Christian faith —borne by Henry VIII. Underlying Bale's interpretation of history is the Protestant doctrine of kingship and obedience which had been eloquently expounded by Tyndale in *The Obedience of a Christian Man*. Basing his arguments on Biblical texts in the approved Protestant fashion, John asserts that kings are appointed by God, that 'God speaketh in their lips' when they give judgement, that only God may sit in judgement on kings, that it is a sin for their subjects to resist them, and that rebels will come to the same bad end as Dathan and Abiram, who defied Moses and were swallowed up by the earth.

Much of *King John* is thus more homiletic than dramatic, but Bale has some theatrical skill. He has arranged his dialogue so that the nineteen roles can be performed by nine actors and extracts dramatic irony from this economy by directing the actors who play Usurped Power, Private Wealth, and Sedition to appear also as the Pope, Cardinal Pandulphus, and a Monk respectively. He dresses England in widow's weeds as a visual reminder of how the wicked clergy have exiled her husband, God. England's son, Commonalty, is blind for want of knowledge of the Gospels and has to grope his way on and off the stage. There is another shrewd piece of stagecraft when Sedition is carried in by Usurped Power, Private Wealth, and Dissimulation. But what Bale bequeathed to later writers of history plays was not a settled dramatic form but a set of potentialities. He showed how chronicle material could be adapted to illustrate the new theories of kingship, commonweal, and obedience, how it could reveal the general working of divine justice in human affairs, and how it could be linked with particular matters of moment in contemporary politics by the use of 'mirror' scenes.

Bale's *King John* emphasizes most of all the obedience which subjects owe to their divinely appointed monarchs. By persistently enforcing the same lesson, later homilists and historians obliged thoughtful men to consider its corollary, namely, the duty owed by kings to their subjects, the commonweal, divine law, natural law, and civil law. Various forms of literature were used to enjoin this duty on kings. Prose treatises like Sir Thomas Elyot's *The Governor* offered monarchs precepts and examples of good rule. Verse narratives like *The Mirror for Magistrates* showed, among other things, how God favoured virtuous kings and punished tyrants. Some writers of history plays also treated these matters in detail and thus kept drama in contact with one of the most vital political issues of the day. Among the most distinguished of these writers were the anonymous authors of *Edward III* and *Woodstock*. Some critics have been puzzled by the structure of *Edward III*. Act I is based mainly on Holinshed's chronicle and shows Edward verifying his right to the throne of France and relieving the castle of Roxborough, which has been treacherously attacked by the treaty-breaking king of Scotland, David. Act II, however, derives mainly from William Painter's adaptation of an Italian *novella* in his *Palace of Pleasure*, and shows Edward first trying to seduce the Countess of Salisbury then bringing his passions under control. In the succeeding three acts, the playwright reverts to historical materials and deals with the English campaigns in France, but his attention seems divided between Edward and the Black Prince, his son. Once it is appreciated, however, that the basic themes of the play are the education of princes and the illustration of king-becoming virtues, its various episodes assume a meaningful relationship. The education comes especially through learning to respect those covenants on which honour and civilization depend. The eloquent Countess of Salisbury convinces Edward that his passions have put him in danger of committing 'high treason against the King of Heaven', who instituted the marriage bond before He appointed kings. Similarly, Villiers convinces Charles of Normandy that princes cannot counter-mand the parole given by a soldier. Later, when King John of France would revoke the safe-conduct which Charles has given to Salisbury, he, too, is taught that kings must not abuse their powers. The kingly virtues are illustrated by Edward's care in ensuring that war against France would be just, by the fortitude displayed by the Black Prince at Crecy and Poitiers, and by Edward's clemency towards the six burghers of Calais. Contrasts are used to throw these themes into relief; David of Scotland is a breaker of cove-nants, and when John uses Frenchmen to fight for his usurped crown, he is represented as a tyrant, a 'thirsty tiger' tearing the entrails of the realm.

The rich vocabulary, iterative imagery, and fine eloquence of *Edward III* have led some critics to suggest that it was written or revised by Shakespeare. Completed in the early fifteen–nineties, it certainly anticipates Shakespeare's por-trayal of the education of Prince Hal in the two parts of *Henry IV* and of his ideal kingship in *Henry V*. *Woodstock*, written between 1591 and 1595, was well known to Shake-speare, whose *Richard II* is in some respects a sequel to it. The author of *Woodstock* drastically altered the historical characters and events described by Holinshed and Stowe in order to present a tragic conflict between a king and his counsellors. In the chronicles, Thomas of Woodstock, Duke of Gloucester and uncle to Richard II, is a man of self-centred ambition who is murdered for plotting treason and war; in the play, on the other hand, Woodstock is an honest and altruistic patriot who serves his nephew loyally despite great provocation. Richard is a flawed but complex character. Anxious at times to emulate the greatness of his father, the Black Prince, and ever conscious of his position as 'the highest God's anointed deputy', he is fatally deficient in the quality which Tudor moralists defined as 'affability', i.e. the capacity for accepting good counsel. When Richard re-nounces the Protectorship of Woodstock and the counsel of York, Lancaster, Surrey, and Arundel, he severs contact with the ideals of order, degree, and justice upheld by these patriotic aristocrats, with their endorsement of hereditary rights and responsibilities and their desire to give every social class its due. In their place Richard sets the upstart lawyer, Tresilian, and a faction of flattering, luxury-loving courtiers—Greene, Bagot, Bushy, and Scroope. Swayed by these pernicious guides, Richard becomes the enemy of order and equity, rack-renting the common people to feast and clothe his minions, elevating Tresilian to the position of Lord Chief Justice, extorting money by compelling men of substance to sign and seal blank charters, and farming out his revenues to his favourites in return for a monthly stipend of £7,000. His tyranny reaches its nadir when he has Woodstock kidnapped, deported, and murdered in Calais.

Tyrannical though he is, Richard has succeeded to his throne by hereditary right. A king of this kind, according to orthodox Elizabethan political theory, was not to be resisted but endured as a divine visitation on the collective sins of the nation and left to the judgement of heaven. Woodstock professes this doctrine and is eventually a martyr to it, but he adheres to it with difficulty, and his creator finds so much justification for the rebellion against Richard after the killing of Woodstock that his play is rather a challenge to orthodoxy than a confirmation of it. The imaginative power as well as the intellectual independence of *Woodstock* make it one of the finest of Elizabethan history plays. This imaginative power is especially apparent in the coherence and balance of the plot, in the clarity and force of the language, in the controlled irony of the humorous passages, in the illuminating images drawn from bird and animal life, and in the economic but telling use of special costumes and stage spectacle. The plain frieze dress worn by Woodstock contrasts with the luxurious and highly coloured attire of Richard's favourites, but the playwright's purposes go deeper than allegorical antitheses, and the complexity of his art is seen at its best in Act IV, Scene ii, where pathos, irony, spectacle, and foreboding images of disorder are blended as Woodstock characteristically interprets his wife's dream as a premonition of the destruction of England, not of himself, and then welcomes the armed masquers while warning them that he will not join in any plot against the king, not realizing that they are his enemies in disguise, led by Richard himself.

Tudor historians and playwrights were profoundly interested in the sequence of events which followed the death of Woodstock. Most of them regarded the Wars of the Roses as a consequence of the deposition of Richard II, and the victory of Henry Tudor at Bosworth as the beginning of a period of peace and order. After the death of Elizabeth I, the history play became less popular, but Bacon's *History of King Henry the Seventh* (1622) encouraged John Ford to dramatize in *Perkin Warbeck* certain events of the period immediately after that of Shakespeare's *Richard III*. Ford elaborates contrasts between two legitimate kings, Henry VII of England and James IV of Scotland, and Perkin Warbeck, pretender to the English throne. He makes Henry better and James worse than Bacon had done in his biography. Ford's Henry, indeed, exhibits most of the virtues of the ideal kings described by contemporary writers of *specula principum*. He is introduced as the physician of the state who has healed the wounds of civil war and has brought hopes of lasting peace by marrying Elizabeth of York. In domestic matters, he is thrifty, eschewing luxury and favourites. In foreign affairs, he accepts the wise counsel of the Bishop of Durham, and Hialas, the Spanish ambassador. In war, he tempers justice with clemency; when Warbeck and followers are overcome, he treats the pretender's wife with meticulous courtesy. James, by comparison, is capricious, imperious, and reckless. Dazzled by Warbeck's stately language and regal bearing, he accepts him as a true Plantagenet without proper proofs. He invades England, but suddenly grows sceptical of Warbeck's claims, and renounces them entirely when offered the hand of Henry's daughter.

As a statesman, Henry is manifestly superior to James, and most Elizabethan playwrights using Ford's source-materials would have made Henry the hero of the play with Warbeck as its villain, damned as upstart, rebel, and would-be usurper. Not so Ford, however; here, as elsewhere, his sympathies go out to the character who defies conventional standards, and he almost vindicates Warbeck by the ideality of the passion with which he invests him. In the chronicles, Warbeck is reduced to confessing the falseness of his claims, whereas Ford's quixotic hero never falters in his belief that he is Richard of York, and his *folie de grandeur* is transfigured by a vision of magnanimity which gives him an infallible command of the kingly gesture in every crisis. When James abandons him, he majestically comments, 'I am my father's son still'. When Henry captures him, he begs for mercy for his followers, but not for himself; Henry may break his neck, but not his heart, which

> Will mount till every drop of blood be frozen
> By death's perpetual winter

and he goes to execution in this exalted spirit, happy in the knowledge that his wife, Dalyell, and his low-born counsellors have remained loyal to him.

Like Shelley's Prometheus, Warbeck is capable of aspiring 'till Hope creates from its own wreck the thing it contemplates', and the element of romantic individualism which he brings into the history play challenges the ideal of hereditary right and fixed social hierarchies which it so often endorses. Written in the early sixteen-thirties about the same time as *Perkin Warbeck*, Robert Davenport's *King John and Matilda* also combines old and new themes. Eschewing chronicles, Davenport takes most of his source-materials from a play by Henry Chettle and Anthony Munday, *The Downfall of Robert, Earl of Huntington* (1601). His plotting and characterization are much influenced by John Fletcher and his followers. The fortunes of King John are made to rise and fall in every act to provide the maximum of suspense and excitement. Far from being the pioneer of Protestant virtues, Davenport's John is a lustful tyrant who neglects the commonweal to pursue Matilda Fitzwater, daughter of one of the barons with whom he has quarrelled. His worst crime is to have her poisoned after she has entered a monastery to escape from him. A Jacobean interest in lust is also apparent in the sub-plot, which shows how Brand, a jailor, starves Lady Bruce and her son to death when she will not submit to his demands.

Despite these sensational elements, *King John and Matilda* is a history play and not a febrile excursion into Fletcherian tragedy. Its political ideas are solid and consistent, and are firmly based on Elizabethan foundations. In its treatment of illicit passion and the covenants that kings must respect, it has much in common with *Edward III*. By pursuing Matilda, John ignores her vow to die a maid, which he has sworn to respect. Only after her death does he repent and acknowledge that 'Whilst passion holds the helm, reason and honour Do suffer wrack'. Correspondingly, John is at odds with Fitzwater and his followers because he has not kept the covenants made in the Magna Carta. Blunt in utterance and plain in dress, Fitzwater is modelled on Woodstock in the earlier history play. Like Woodstock, he reverences 'the high calling of a king', but claims the right of 'modest admonition', opposing exactions for private coffers and exorbitant concessions to the Papacy. Once John becomes a man of his word, Fitzwater renounces the French allies of the barons and forgives the murder of his daughter in the interests of national unity. 'We will be all one soul again', he exclaims, and in this ecstatic phrase, more so than in any other in the play, the Elizabethan vision of the harmony of king and subject within the nation-state as an almost sacramental concord is memorably affirmed. *King John and Matilda* has been neglected and underestimated; like *Edward III*, *Woodstock*, and *Perkin Warbeck*, it is among the most stageworthy of Elizabethan history plays, and all four merit revival in the theatre.

The texts in this volume are based on the following editions: *King Johan* (ed. J. H. P. Pafford, Malone Society Reprints, Oxford, 1931), *The Raigne of King Edward the Third* (London, 1596, 1599), *The First Part of the Reign of King Richard the Second or Thomas of Woodstock* (ed. W. P. Frijlinck, Malone Society Reprints, Oxford, 1929), *Perkin*

Warbeck (London, 1634), and *King John and Matilda* (London, 1655, 1662). In accordance with the policy of the World's Classics series, modern spelling and punctuation have been adopted. Particular care has been taken to preserve the original stage directions and all additions to the original texts are enclosed in square brackets. In the modernizing of the texts, I owe much to the following editions: A. J. S. Farmer's *The Dramatic Writings of John Bale* (London, 1907), G. C. Moore Smith's *Edward III* (London, 1897), A. P. Rossiter's *Woodstock* (London, 1946), and A. Dyce's revision of W. Gifford's *The Works of John Ford* (3 vols., London, 1869). Thanks to Pafford's excellent edition of the manuscripts of Bale's *King John*, my text includes a lengthy passage not given by Farmer. In *Woodstock*, I have adopted the title given to the play by Rossiter, and his method of indicating by indentation and a line-edge those passages marked for cutting by the writer of the manuscript of the text, but I have employed a more modern system of punctuation than his. To the best of my knowledge, mine is the first modernized text of *King John and Matilda* to be published. I am deeply grateful to my friends, Professor Arthur Brown of University College, London, and Professor W. S. Maguinness of King's College, London, for helping me to solve some of the problems presented by a modernization of Bale's manuscript. In literary parlance, the term 'Elizabethan' is applied to plays written between 1559 and 1642. As Bale completed his final version of *King John* after 1559 (possibly for a performance before Elizabeth herself), my chosen plays fall within this period, and this volume can be conveniently styled *Elizabethan History Plays*.

WILLIAM A. ARMSTRONG

ACKNOWLEDGEMENTS

Grateful acknowledgement is made of the kind permission given by the Malone Society to make use of its editions of *The First Part of the Reign of King Richard the Second or Thomas of Woodstock* (ed. W. P. Frijlinck, Oxford, 1929) and of *King Johan* (ed. J. H. P. Pafford, Oxford, 1931), and by Messrs. Chatto & Windus to make use of their edition of *Woodstock, A Moral History* (ed. A. P. Rossiter, London, 1946), in the preparation of this volume.

KING JOHN

by

JOHN BALE

[DRAMATIS PERSONAE:

KING JOHN
WIDOW ENGLAND
CLERGY
} By one Player

SEDITION
CIVIL ORDER
STEPHEN LANGTON
COMMONALTY
} By one Player

NOBILITY
CARDINAL PANDULPHUS
PRIVATE WEALTH
} By one Player

DISSIMULATION
RAYMUNDUS
SIMON OF SWINSETT
} By one Player

USURPED POWER
THE POPE
} By one Player

INTERPRETER
TREASON
VERITY
IMPERIAL MAJESTY

(N.B. Stage directions require the doubling of roles indicated above.)]

KING JOHN

King John. To declare the powers, and their force to
  enlarge,
The Scripture of God doth flow in most abundance;
And of sophisters, the cautels to discharge,
Both Peter and Paul maketh plenteous utterance.
How that all people should show their true allegiance
To their lawful king, Christ Jesu doth consent;
Which to the high powers was ever obedient.
To show what I am, I think it convenient:
John, King of England, the chronicles doth me call.
My grandfather was an emperor excellent;
My father a king by succession lineal;
A king my brother, like as to him did fall—
Richard Cœur de Lion they called him in France,
Which had over enemies most fortunable chance.
By the will of God and High high ordinance,
In Ireland and Wales, in Anjou and Normandy,
In England also, I have had the governance,
I have worn the crown and wrought victoriously;
And now do purpose, by practice and by study,
To reform the laws and set men in good order;
That true justice may be had in every border.
 England vidua.[1] Then I trust your grace will weigh a poor
  widow's cause,
Ungodly used, as ye shall know in short clause.
 K. John. Yea, that I will swear, if it be true and just.
 Eng. Like as it beareth truth, so let it be discussed.
 K. John. Then, gentle widow! tell me what the matter is.
 Eng. Alas! your clergy hath done very sore amiss
In misusing me against all right and justice;
And, for my more grief thereto, they other entice.
 K. John. Whom do they entice for to do thee injury?
 Eng. Such as hath entered by false hypocrisy,

[1] 'Widow England'.

Much worse fruits having than hath the thorns unpleasant;
For they are the trees that God did never plant;
And, as Christ doth say, blind leaders of the blind.

    K. John. Tell me whom thou meanest, to satisfy my
        mind.

    Eng. Such lubbers as hath disguised heads in their hoods,
Which in idleness do live by other men's goods—
Monks, canons, and nuns, in divers colour and shape;
Both white, black, and pied: God send their increase ill hap!

    K. John. Let me know thy name or I go further with thee.

    Eng. England, sir! England my name is; ye may trust me!

    K. John. I marvel right sore how thou comest changed
        thus.   *[Enter Sedition.]*

    Sedition. What, you two alone? I will tell tales, by Jesus!
And say that I see you fall here to bitchery.

    K. John. Avoid, lewd person! for thy words are ungodly.

    Sedit. I cry you mercy, sir! pray you be not angry.
By my faith and truth! I came hither to be merry.

    K. John. Thou canst with thy mirth in no wise discontent
        me,
So that thou powder it with wisdom and honesty.

    Sedit. I am no spicer; by the mass! ye may believe me.

    K. John. I speak of no spice, but of civil honesty.

    Sedit. Ye spake of powder, by the Holy Trinity!

    K. John. Not as thou takest it, of a gross capacity;
But as Saint Paul meaneth unto the Colossians plain:
So season your speech that it be without disdain.
Now, England, to thee; go thou forth with thy tale,
And show the cause why thou lookest so wan and pale.

    Eng. I told you before the fault was in the clergy
That I, a widow, appear to you so barely.

    Sedit. Ye are a wily wat, and wander here full warely.

    K. John. Why in the clergy? do me to understand!

    Eng. For they take from me my cattle, house and land
My woods and pastures, with other commodities—
Like as Christ did say to the wicked Pharisees:
Poor widows' houses ye gross up by long prayers—
In side-coats wandering like most disguised players.

Sedit. They are well at ease that hath such soothsayers.

K. John. They are thy childern, thou oughtest to say
then good.

Eng. Nay, bastards they are; unnatural, by the rood!
Since their beginning they were never good to me.
The wild boar of Rome—God let him never to the[e]!—
Like pigs they follow in fantasies, dreams and lies;
And ever are fed with his vile ceremonies.

Sedit. Nay, sometime they eat both flauns and pigeon pies.

K. John. By the boar of Rome, I trow, thou meanest the
Pope?

Eng. I mean none other but him; God give him a rope!

K. John. And why dost thou thus compare him to a
swine?

Eng. For that he and his to such beastliness incline.
They forsake God's word, which is most pure and clean,
And unto the laws of sinful men they lean;
Like as the vile swine the most vile meats desire,
And hath great pleasure to wallow themselves in mire,
So hath this wild boar with his church universal;
His sow, with her pigs and monsters bestial,
Delight in men's draff and covetous lucre all;
Yea, *aper de silva*[1] the prophet did him call.

Sedit. Hold your peace, ye whore! or else, by mass!
I trow
I shall cause the Pope to curse thee as black as a crow.

K. John. What art thou, fellow! that seem so bragging
bold?

Sedit. I am Sedition, that with the Pope will hold
So long as I have a hole within my breech.

Eng. Command this fellow to avoid, I you beseech;
For doubtless he hath done me great injury.

K. John. Avoid, lewd fellow! or thou shalt rue it truly.

Sedit. I will not away for that same wedred witch;
She shall rather kiss whereas it doth not itch.
Quodcunque ligaveris,[2] I trow, will play such a part,

[1] 'The boar out of the wood' (Psalms lxxx. 13).
[2] 'Whatsoever thou shalt bind' (Matthew xvi. 19).

That I shall abide in England, maugre your heart.
Tush! the Pope ableth me to subdue both king and kaiser.
    K. John. Of that, thou and I will common more at leisure.
    Eng. Truly, of the devil they are that do any thing
To the subduing of any Christian king;
For, be he good or bad, he is of God's appointing:
The good for the good; the bad is for ill doing.
    K. John. Of that we shall talk hereafter: say forth thy
       mind now,
And show me how thou art thus become a widow.
    Eng. These vile popish swine hath clean exiled my
       husband.
    K. John. Who is thy husband? tell me, good, gentle
       England.
    Eng. Forsooth! God himself, the spouse of every sort
That seek Him in faith to the soul's health and comfort.
    Sedit. He is scant honest that so many wives will have.
    K. John. I say, hold your peace; and stand aside like a
       knave!
Is God exiled out of this region? tell me!
    Eng. Yea, that He is, sir! it is the much more pity.
    K. John. How cometh it to pass that He is thus abused?
    Eng. Ye know He abideth not where His word is refused;
For God is His word, like as Saint John doth tell
In the beginning of his most blessed gospel.
The Pope's pigs may not abide this word to be heard,
Nor known of people, or had in any regard:
Their eyes are so sore they may not abide the light,
And that bread so hard their gall'd gums may it not bite.
I, knowing your grace to have here the governance,
By the gift of God, do knowledge my allegiance,
Desiring your grace to weigh such injuries
As I daily suffer by these same subtle spies,
And let me have right, as ye are a rightful king
Appointed of God to have such matter in doing.
For God willeth you to help the poor widow's cause,
As He, by Esaye, protesteth in this same clause:
Querite judicium, subvenite oppresso,

Judicate pupillo, defendite viduam:[1]
Seek right to poor, to the weak and fat[h]erless;
Defend the widow when she is in distress.

    Sedit. I tell ye, the woman is in great heaviness.

    K. John. I may not in no wise leave thy right undiscussed;
For God hath set me, by His appointment just,
To further thy cause, to maintain thy right;
And, therefore, I will support thee day and night:
So long as my simple life shall here endure
I will see thee have no wrong, be fast and sure.
I will, first of all, call my nobility—
Dukes, earls, and lords—each one in their degree;
Next them the clergy, or fathers spiritual—
Archbishops, bishops, abbots, and priors all;
Then the great judges and lawyers every one,
So openi[n]g to them thy cause and pitiful moan,
By the means whereof I shall their minds understand:
If they help thee not, myself will take it in hand,
And set such a way as shall be to thy comfort.

    Eng. Then, for an answer, I will shortly again resort.

    K. John. Do, England, hardly! and thou shalt have remedy.

    Eng. God reward your grace, I beseech Him heartily,
And send you long days to govern this realm in peace!

    K. John. Gramercy, England! and send thee plenteous increase!

        Go out England, and dress for Clergy.

    Sedit. Of babbling matters, I trow, it is time to cease.

    K. John. Why dost thou call them babbling matters? tell me!

    Sedit. For they are not worth the shaking of a pear-tree
When the pears are gone: they are but dibble-dabble—
I marvel ye can abide such bibble-babble.

    K. John. Thou seemest to be a man of simple discretion.

    Sedit. Alas, that ye are not a priest to hear confession!

    K. John. Why for confession? let me know thy fantasy.

---

[1] 'Seek judgement, relieve the oppressed, judge the fatherless, plead for the widow' (Isaiah i. 17).

Sedit. Because that ye are a man so full of mercy;
Namely, to women that weep with a heavy heart
When they in the church hath let but a little fart.

    K. John. I perceive well now thou speakest all this in
        mockage,
Because I take part with England's rightful heritage.
Say thou what thou wilt, her matters shall not perish.

    Sedit. It is joy of him that women so can cherish.

    K. John. God hath me ordained, in this same princely
        estate,
For that I should help such as be desolate.

    Sedit. It is as great pity to see a woman weep
As it is to see a silly dodman creep;
Or, as ye would say, a silly goose go barefoot.

    K. John. Thou seemest, by thy words, to have no more
        wit than a coot.
I marvel thou art to England so unnatural,
Being her own child: thou art worse than a beast brutal.

    Sedit. I am not her child; I defy her, by the mass!
I her son? quoth he! I had rather she were headless.
Though I sometime be in England for my pastance,
Yet was I neither born here, in Spain, nor in France;
But under the Pope, in the holy city of Rome;
And there will I dwell unto the day of doom.

    K. John. But what is thy name? tell me yet once again!

    Sedit. As I said afore; I am Sedition plain:
In every religion and monkish sect I reign,
Having you princes in scorn, hate, and disdain.

    K. John. I pray thee, good friend! tell me what is thy
        fashion.

    Sedit. Search! and ye shall find in every congregation
That long to the Pope; for, they are to me full sure,
And will be so long as they last and endure.

    K. John. If thou be a cloisterer, tell of what order thou
        art.

    Sedit. In every estate of the clergy I play a part.
Sometime I can be a monk in a long side cowl;
Sometime I can be a nun, and look like an owl;

Sometime a canon in a surplice fair and white;
A chapterhouse monk sometime I appear in sight.
I am our Sir John, sometime, with a new shaven crown;
Sometime the parson, and sweep the streets with a side
    gown;
Sometime the bishop with a mitre and a cope;
A grey friar sometime with cut shoes and a rope;
Sometime I can play the white monk, sometime the friar,
The purgatory priest, and every man's wife desire.
This company hath provided for me mortmain,
For that I might ever among their sort remain.
Yea, to go farther, sometime I am a cardinal;
Yea, sometime a pope; and then am I lord over all,
Both in heaven and earth and also in purgatory,
And do wear three crowns when I am in my glory.
    K. John. But what dost thou here in England? tell me
      shortly!
    Sedit. I hold up the Pope, as in other places many;
For his ambassador I am continually—
In Sycell, in Naples, in Venice and Italy;
In Pole, Spruse, and Berne, in Denmark and Lombardy;
In Aragon, in Spain, in France, and in Germany;
In England, in Scotland, and in other regions else—
For his holy cause I maintain traitors and rebels,
That no prince can have his people's obedience
Except it doth stand with the Pope's pre-eminence.
    K. John. Get thee hence, thou knave, and most pre-
      sumptuous wretch!
Or, as I am true king, thou shalt an halter stretch.
We will thou know it, our power is of God;
And, therefore, we will so execute the rod
That no lewd priest shall be able to maintain thee.
I see now they be at too much liberty:
We will short their horns, if God send time and space.
    Sedit. Then I, in England, am like to have no place?
    K. John. No, that thou art not; and, therefore, avoid
      apace!
    Sedit. By the holy mass! I must laugh to hear your grace.

Ye suppose and think that ye could me subdue:
Ye shall never find your supposition true,
Though ye were as strong as Hector and Diomedes;
Or as valiant as ever was Achilles.
Ye are well content that bishops continue still?

    K. John. We are so, indeed, if they their duty fulfil.

    Sedit. Nay then, good enough! your authority and power
Shall pass as they will; they have sauce both sweet and sour.

    K. John. What meanest thou by that? show me thy
        intent this hour.

    Sedit. They are God's vicars, they can both save and
        loose.

    K. John. Ah! thy meaning is that they may a prince
        depose.

    Sedit. By the rood! they may; and that will appear by
        you.

    K. John. By the help of God we shall see to that well enou'!

    Sedit. Nay, ye cannot, though ye had Argus eyes—
In abbeys they have so many subtle spies;
For once in the year they have secret visitations,
And if any prince reform their ungodly fashions,
Then two of the monks must forth to Rome, by and by,
With secret letters to avenge their injury.
For a thousand pound they shrink not in such matter;
And yet, for the time, the prince to his face they flatter.
I am evermore their guide and their advocate.

    K. John. Then with the bishops and monks thou art
        check mate?

    Sedit. I dwell among them and am one of their sort.

    K. John. For thy sake they shall of me have but small
        comfort.
Look! where I find thee, that place will I put down.

    Sedit. What if ye do chance to find me in every town
Whereas is founded any sect monastical?

    K. John. I pray God I sink if I destroy them not all!

    Sedit. Well, if ye so do, yet know I where to dwell.

    K. John. Thou art not skoymose thy fantasy for to tell.

    Sedit. Guess! at a venture ye may chance the mark to hit.

K. John. Thy falsehood to show, no man than thyself
    more fit.

Sedit. Marry! in confession underneath *Benedicite.*

K. John. Nay, tell it again, that I may understand thee.

Sedit. I say I can dwell, when all other places fail me,
In ear-confession underneath *Benedicite;*[1]
And, when I am there, the priest may not bewray me.

K. John. Why will ear-confession such a secret traitor be?

Sedit. When all other fail, he is so sure as steel.
Offend Holy Church, and I warrant ye shall it feel;
For, by confession, the Holy Father knoweth
Throughout all Christendom what to his Holiness groweth.

K. John. Oh, where is Nobility, that he might know this
    falsehood?

Sedit. Nay, he is become a maintainer of our godhead.
I know that he will do Holy Church no wrong;
For I am his ghostly father and teacher among.
He believeth nothing but as Holy Church doth tell.

K. John. Why, giveth he no credence to Christ's holy
    gospel?

Sedit. No, sir, by the mass! but he calleth them heretics
That preach the gospel, and seditious schismatics;
He 'tach them, vex them, from prison to prison he turn
    them;
He inditeth them, judge them; and, in conclusion, he burn
    them.

K. John. We rue to hear this of our nobility.
But in this behalf what sayst of the spirituality?

Sedit. Of this I am sure to them to be no stranger,
And specially when their honour is in danger.

K. John. We trust our lawyers have no such wicked
    minds.

Sedit. Yes, they many times are my most secret friends.
With faithful preachers they can play legerdemain,
And with false colours procure them to be slain.

K. John. I perceive this world is full of iniquity.
As God would have it here cometh Nobility.

    [1] 'Bless thee': the blessing given at confession.

Sedit. Doth he so indeed? by our Lord! then will I
  hence.

K. John. Thou saidest thou wouldst dwell where he
  keepeth residence.

Sedit. Yea, but first of all I must change mine apparel
Unto a bishop, to maintain with my quarrel;
To a monk or priest, or to some holy friar.
I should never else accomplish my desire.

K. John. Why art thou going? nay, brother, thou shalt
  not hence.

Sedit. I would not be seen as I am for forty pence.
When I am religious I will return again.

K. John. Thou shalt tarry here, or I must put thee to
  pain.

Sedit. I have a great mind to be a lecherous man:
A vengeance take it! I would say, a religious man.
I will go and come so fast as ever I can.

K. John. Tush! dally not with me. I say thou shalt abide.

Sedit. Ween you to hold me that I shall not slip aside?

K. John. Make no more prating, for I say thou shalt
  abide.

Sedit. Stop not my passage! I must over sea at the next
  tide.

K. John. I will ordain so, I trow, thou shalt not over.

Sedit. Tush, tush! I am sure of ready passage at Dover.

K. John. The devil go with him! the unthrifty knave is
  gone.

Here go out Sedition and dress for Civil Order.

                              [*Enter Nobility.*]

Nobility. Trouble not yourself with no such dissolute
  person;
For ye know, full well, very little honesty
Is got at their hands in every commonalty.

K. John. This is but dalliance: ye do not speak as ye
  think.

Nob. By my troth I do, or else I would I should sink!

K. John. Then must I marvel at you, of all men living.

Nob. Why marvel at me? tell me your very meaning.

K. John. For no man living is in more familiarity
With that wicked wreten, if it be true that he told me.

Nob. What wretch speak ye of? for Jesus' love, intimate!

K. John. Of that presumptuous wretch that was with me
here of late,
Whom you willed not to vex myself withal.

Nob. I know him not, I, by the way that my soul to shall!

K. John. Make it not so strange, for ye know him well
enou'.

Nob. Believe me if ye will! I know him not, I assure you.

K. John. Were ye never yet acquainted with Sedition?

Nob. Since I was a child, both him and his condition
I ever hated for his iniquity.

K. John. A clear token that is of true nobility:
But I pray to God we find it not otherwise.
It was never well since the clergy wrought by practice,
And left the scripture for men's imaginations,
Dividing themselves in so many congregations
Of monks, canons and friars, of divers colours and fashions.

[*Enter Clergy.*]

The Clergy. I do trust your grace will be as loving now
As your predecessors have been to us before you.

K. John. I will sure weigh my love with your behaviours;
Like as ye deserve, so will I bear you favours.
Clergy, mark it well! I have more to you to say
Than, as the saying is, the priest did speak a Sunday.

Clergy. Ye will do us no wrong, I hope, nor injury.

K. John. No, I will do you right in seeing you do your
duty.
We know the cautels of your subtle company.

Clergy. If ye do us wrong we shall seek remedy.

K. John. Yea, that is the cast of all your company.
When kings correct you for your acts most ungodly,
To the Pope, sitting in the chair of pestilence,
Ye run to remain in your concupiscence.
Thus set ye at nought all princely pre-eminence;
Subduing the order of due obedience.
But, within a while, I shall so abate your pride

That, to your Pope, ye shall neither run nor ride;
But ye shall be glad to seek to me, your prince,
For all such matters as shall be within this province,
Like as God willeth you by His scripture evident.

   Nob. To the church, I trust, ye will be obedient.

   K. John. No matter to you whether I be so or no.

   Nob. Yes, marry! is it; for I am sworn thereunto.
I took a great oath when I was dubbed a knight.
Ever to defend the Holy Church's right.

   Clergy. Yea, and in her quarrel ye ought unto death to
     fight.

   K. John. Like bats, in the dark ye always take your flight,
Flittering in fancies, and ever abhor the light.
I rue it in heart that you, Nobility,
Should thus bind yourself to the great captivity
Of bloody Babylon, the ground and mother of whoredom—
The Romish Church I mean—more vile than ever was
    Sodom;
And, to say the truth, a meet spouse for the fiend.

   Clergy. Your grace is far gone: God send you a better
mind!

   K. John. Hold your peace! I say; ye are a little too fat;
In a while, I hope, you shall be leaner somewhat.

                          [Civil Order enters.]
We shall look to you and to Civil Order also;
Ye walk not so secret but we know whereabout ye go.

   Civil Order. Why, your grace hath no cause with me to
     be displeased.

   K. John. All things considered, we have small cause to be
     pleased.

   C. Order. I beseech your grace to grant me a word or
     two.

   K. John. Speak on your pleasure, and your whole mind
     also.

   C. Order. Ye know very well, to set all things in order,
I have much adó, and many things pass fro me
For your commonwealth; and that in every border—
For offices, for lands, for law and for liberty;

And for transgressors I appoint the penalty;
That cities and towns may stand in quietous peace,
That all theft and murder, with other vice, may cease.
If I have chanced, for want of circumspection,
To pass the limits of right and equity,
I submit myself until your grace's correction,
Desiring pardon of your benignity.
I wot I may fall through my fragility;
Therefore, I pray you, tell me what the matter is,
And amends shall be whereas I have done amiss.

   K. John. Against amendment no reasonable man can be.
   Nob. That sentence riseth out of an high charity.
   K. John. Now that ye are here assembled all together,
Amongst other things ye shall first of all consider
That my displeasure reboun[d]eth on to you all.
   Clergy. To you none of us is prejudicial.
   K. John. I shall prove it; yes! how have ye used England?
   Nob. But as it becometh us, so far as I understand.
   K. John. Yes! the poor woman complaineth here
grievously,
And not without a cause, for she hath great injury.
I must see to it—there is no remedy—
For it is a charge given me from God almighty—
How say ye, Clergy, appeareth it not so to you?
   Clergy. If it liketh your grace, all we know that well enou'.
   K. John. Then you, Nobility, will affirm it, I am sure.
   Nob. Yea, that I will, sir! so long as my life endure.
   K. John. And you, Civil Order, I think will grant the
same?
   C. Order. Undoubted, sir! yea! else were it to me great
shame.
   K. John. Then, for England's cause, I will be somewhat
plain.
It is you, Clergy, that hath her in disdain;
With your Latin hours, sermons, and poppetly plays:
In her, more and more, God's holy word decays;
And, them to maintain, unreasonable is the spoil
Of her lands, her goods, and of her poor childers' toil.

Reckon first your tithes, your devotions, and your offerings,
Mortuaries, pardons, bequests, and other things;
Besides that ye catch for hallowed bells and purgatory;
For jewels, for relics, confession, and courts of bawdry;
For legacies, trentals, with scalacely masses,
Whereby ye have made the people very asses.
And, over all this, ye have brought in a rabble
Of Latin mummers, and sects deceivable,
Even to devour her and eat her up at once.

 Clergy. You would have no church, I ween, by these
  sacred bones!
 K. John. Yes, I would have a church, not of disguised
  shavelings,
But of faithful hearts and charitable doings;
For when Christ's church was in her highest glory
She knew neither these sects nor their hypocrisy.
 Clergy. Yes, I will prove it by David substantially:
Astitit Regina a dextris tuis in vestitu
Deaurato, circumdata varietate—[1]
A queen, saith David, on thy right hand, Lord, I see;
Apparelled with gold, and compassed with diversity.
 K. John. What is your meaning by that same scripture?
  tell me!
 Clergy. This queen is the church, which through all
  Christian regions
Is beautiful, decked with many holy religions—
Monks, canons, and friars, most excellent divines:
As Grandmontensers and other Benedictines,
Premonstratensians, Bernards, and Gilbertines,
Jacobites, Minors, White Carmes, and Augustines,
Sanbenets, Cluniacs, with holy Carthusians,
Hermits and Anchors, with most mighty Rhodians;
Crucifers, Lucifers, Bridgets, Ambrosians,
Stellifers, Ensifers, with Purgatorians,
Sophians, Indians and Camaldulensers,
Clarines and Columbines, Templars, New Ninevites,

 [1] 'At thy right hand stood the Queen in a vesture of gold'
(Psalms xlv. 9).

Rufianes, Tertians, Lorettes and Lazarites,
Hungaries, Teutonics, Hospitalers, Honofrines,
Basils and Bonhams, Solanons and Celestines,
Paulines, Jeronimites, and Monks of J'osaphat's Valley,
Fuligines, Flamines, with Brethern of the Black Alley,
Donates and Dimisines, with Canons of Saint Mark,
Vestals and Monials—a world to hear them bark—
Abbots and doctors, with bishops and cardinals,
Archdeacons and priests, as to their fortune falls.

  C. Order. Methinketh your first text standeth nothing
    with your reason;
For, in David's time, were no such sects of religion.

  K. John. David meaneth virtues by the same diversity,
As, in the said psalm, it is evident to see,
And not monkish sects; but, it is ever your cast,
For your advancement, the scriptures for to wrast.

  Clergy. Of our Holy Father, in this, I take my ground,
Which hath authority the Scriptures to expound.

  K. John. Nay, he presumeth the Scriptures to confound.
Neither thou nor the Pope shall do poor England wrong,
I being governor and king her people among:
While you, for lucre, set forth your popish laws
Yourselves to advance, ye would make us pick straws.
Nay, hypocrites, nay! we will not be scorned so
Of a sort of knaves; we shall look you otherwise too.

  Nob. Sir! your spirits are moved, I perceive, by your
    language.

  K. John. I wonder that you, for such vain popish
    baggage.
Can suffer England to be impoverished
And made a beggar: you are very ill advised.

  Nob. I marvel greatly that ye say thus to me.

  K. John. For doubtless ye do not as becometh Nobility.
Ye spare neither lands nor goods, but all ye give
To these cormorants: it would any good man grieve
To see your madness, as I would God should save me.

  Nob. Sir! I suppose it good to build a perpetuity
For me and my friends, to be prayed for evermore.

K. John. Tush! it is madness all to despair in God so sore,
And to think Christ's death to be unsufficient.

Nob. Sir! that I have done was of a good intent.

K. John. The intent is nought which hath no sure ground.

Clergy. If you continue, ye will Holy Church confound.

K. John. Nay, no Holy Church, nor faithful congregation,
But an heap of adders of Antichrist's generation.

C. Order. It pityeth me much that ye are to them so hard.

K. John. It pityeth me more than ye them so much
        regard.
They destroy men's souls with damnable superstition,
And decay all realms by maintenance of sedition—
Ye would wonder to know what proof I have of this.

Nob. Well, amendment shall be where anything is amiss;
For, undoubted, God doth open such things to princes
As to none other men in the Christian provinces;
And, therefore, we will not, in this, with your grace contend.

C. Order. No, but with God's grace we shall our mis-
        deeds amend.

Clergy. For all such forfeits as your princely majesty,
For your own person or realm, can prove by me,
I submit myself to you, both body and goods.

                                                    Kneel.

K. John. We pity you now, considering your repentant
        moods,
And our gracious pardon we grant you upon amendment.

Clergy. God preserve your grace and majesty excellent!

K. John. Arise, Clergy, arise! and ever be obedient;
And, as God commandeth you, take us for your governor.

Clergy. By the grace of God the Pope shall be my ruler.

K. John. What say ye, Clergy, who is your governor?

Clergy. Ha! did I stumble? I said my prince is my ruler.

K. John. I pray to our Lord this obedience may endure.

Clergy. I will not break it, ye may be fast and sure.

K. John. Then, come hither, all three: ye shall know
        more of my mind.

Clergy. Our king to obey, the Scripture doth us bind.

K. John. Ye shall first be sworn, to God and to the crown

To be true and just in every city and town;
And this to perform set hand and kiss the book.

   C. Order. With the wife of Lot we will not backward look,
Nor turn from our oath, but ever obey your grace.

   K. John. Then will I give you your charges here in place,
And accept you all to be of our high council.

   Clergy, Nob., and *C. Order.* To be faithful, then, ye us
    more straitly compel.

   K. John. For the love of God, look to the state of
    England!
Let none enemy hold her in miserable bond;
See you defend her as it becometh Nobility;
See you instruct her according to your degree;
Furnish her you with a civil honesty;
Thus shall she flourish in honour and great plenty.
With godly wisdom your matters so convey
That the commonalty the powers may obey;
And ever beware of that false thief, Sedition,
Which poisoneth all realms and bring them to perdition.

   Nob. Sir! for such wretches we will be so circumspect
That neither their falsehood nor guile shall us infect.

   Clergy. I warrant you, sir, no! and that shall well appear.

   C. Order. We will so provide, if any of them come here
To disturb the realm, they shall be full glad to flee.

   K. John. Well, your promise includeth no small difficulty;
But, I put the case that this false thief, Sedition,
Should come to you three, and call himself Religion—
Might he not under the pretence of holiness
Cause you to consent to much ungodliness?

   Nob. He shall never be able to do it, verily!

   K. John. God grant ye be not deceived by hypocrisy.
I say no more, I: in sheep's apparel some walk
And seem religious that deceivably can calk.
Beware of such hypocrites as the kingdom of heaven from
    man
Do hide for advantage, for they deceive now and then.
Well, I leave you here: each man consider his duty.

   Nob. With God's leave, no fault shall be in this company.

K. John. Come, Civil Order! ye shall go hence with me.

C. Order. At your commandment! I will gladly wait upon ye.

  Here King John and Civil Order go out, and Civil
          Order dress him for Sedition.

Nob. Methink the king is a man of a wonderful wit.

Clergy. Nay, say that he is of a vengeable crafty wit;
Then shall ye be sure the truth of the thing to hit.
Heard ye not how he of the Holy Church did rail?
His extreme threatenings shall little him avail:
I will work such ways that he shall of his purpose fail.

 Nob. It is meet a prince to say somewhat for his pleasure.

 Clergy. Yea, but it is too much to rail so without measure.

 Nob. Well, let every man speak like as he hath a cause.

 Clergy. Why, do ye say so? it is time for me, then, to pause.

 Nob. This will I say, sir! that he is so noble a prince
As this day reigneth in any Christian province.

 Clergy. Marry! it appeareth well by that he won in France.

 Nob. Well, he lost not there so much, by martial chance,
But he gat much more in Scotland, Ireland, and Wales.

 Clergy. Yea, God speed us well! Christmas songs are merry tales.

 Nob. Ye disdain such matter, as ye know, full evident.
Are not both Ireland and Wales to him obedient?
Yes, he holdeth them both in peaceable possession;
And, because I will not from your tale make digression,
For his land in France he giveth but little force,
Having to England all his love and remorse;
And Anjou he gave to Arthur, his nevy, in change.

 Clergy. Our changes are such that an abbey turneth to a grange:
We are so handled we have scarce either horse or male.

 Nob. He that doth hate me the worse will tell my tale.
It is your fashion such kings to discommend
As your abuses reform or reprehend.
You priests are the cause that chronicles doth defame
So many princes and men of notable name;

For you take upon you to write them evermore;
And, therefore, King John is like to rue it sore
When ye write his time, for vexing of the clergy.

   Clergy. I marvel ye take his part so earnestly.

   Nob. It becometh Nobility his prince's fame to preserve.

   Clergy. If he continue, we are like in a while to starve—
He demandeth of us the tenth part of our living.

   Nob. I think it is then for some necessary thing.

   Clergy. Marry! to recover that he hath lost in France;
As Normandy dukedom, and his land beyond Orleans.

   Nob. And think ye not that a matter necessary?

   Clergy. No, sir! by my troth! he taking it of the clergy.

   Nob. Ye could be content that he should take it of us?

   Clergy. Yea, so that he would spare the clergy, by sweet
Jesus!
This taking of us might soon grow to a custom,
And then Holy Church might so be brought to thraldom,
Which hath been ever from temporal princes free,
As touching tribute or other captivity.

   Nob. He that defendeth you ought to have part of your
goods.

   Clergy. He hath the prayers of all them that hath hoods.

   Nob. Why, is that enough to help him in his war?

   Clergy. The Church he may not of liberty debar.

   Nob. Did not Christ Himself pay tribute unto Cæsar?
If He paid tribute, so ought His holy vicar.

   Clergy. To hear ye reason so indiscreetly I wonder!
Ye must consider that Christ, that time, was under,
But his vicar, now, is above the princes all;
Therefore, beware ye do not to heresy fall.
Ye ought to believe as Holy Church doth teach you,
And not to reason in such high matters now.

   Nob. I am unlearned: my wits are soon confounded.

   Clergy. Then leave such matters to men more deeply
grounded.

   Nob. But how will ye do for the oath that ye have take?

   Clergy. The keys of the Church can all such matters
off-shake.

Nob. What call ye those keys? I pray you heartily tell me!
Clergy. Our Holy Father's power, and his high authority.
Nob. Well, I can no more say; ye are too well learned for
me.
My business is such that here now I must leave ye.
  Clergy. I must hence also so fast as ever may be
To sue unto Rome for the Church's liberty.

                    Go out Nobility and Clergy.
                    Here Sedition cometh in.
  Sedit. Have in once again! in spite of all my enemies!
For they cannot drive me from all men's companies;
And though it were so that all men would forsake me,
Yet doubt I it not but some good women would take me.
I look for fellows that here should make some sport:
I marvel it is so long ere they hither resort.
By the mass! I ween the knaves are in the briars;
Or else they are fallen into some order of friars.
Nay! shall I guess right? they are gone into the stews;
I hold ye my neck, anon we shall hear news.

            [A voice heard] saying the Litany.
List, for God's passion! I trow here cometh some hogherd
Calling for his pigs. Such a noise I never heard.

    Here come Dissimulation singing of the Litany.
  Dissim. (*sing.*). *Sancte Dominice, ora pro nobis!*[1]
  Sedit. (*sing.*). *Sancte pyld monache, I beshrow vobis!*[2]
  Dissim. (*sing.*). *Sancte Francisse, ora pro nobis!*[3]
  Sedit. Hear ye not? Cock's soul! what meaneth this
    hypocrite knave?
  Dissim. *Pater noster,*[4] I pray God bring him soon to his
    grave,
Qui es in celis,[5] with a vengeable *sanctificetur,*[6]
Or else Holy Church shall never thrive, by Saint Peter!
  Sedit. Tell me, good fellow! makest thou this prayer
    for me?

_____
[1] 'Holy Dominicans, pray for us.'
[2] 'Holy bald-pated monk, I beshrew thee.'
[3] 'Holy Franciscans, pray for us.'   [4] 'Our Father.'
[5] 'Who art in heaven.'   [6] 'Hallowed be.'

Dissim. Ye are as fierce as though ye had broke your
    nose at the buttery.

I meddle not with thee, but here to good saints I pray
Against such enemies as will Holy Church decay.

Here sing this.

A Johanne Rege iniquo, libera nos, domine.[1]

Sedit. Leave, I say! or, by the mass! I will make you
    groan.

Dissim. If thou be gentle, I pray thee, let me alone;
For, within a while, my devotion will be gone.

Sedit. And wherefore dost thou pray here so bitterly,
Mumbling thy paternoster and chanting the litany?

Dissim. For that Holy Church might save her patrimony,
And to have of King John a triumphant victory.

Sedit. And why of King John? doth he vex you so sore?

Dissim. Both churches and abbeys he oppresseth more
    and more,
And take of the clergy—it is unreasonable to tell.

Sedit. Out with the Pope's bulls then, and curse him
    down to hell!

Dissim. Tush, man! we have done so, but all will not help:
He regardeth no more the Pope than he doth a whelp.

Sedit. Well, let him alone; for that will I give him a
    skelp—
But what art thou called of thine own monkish nation?

Dissim. Keep it in counsel, Dane Davy Dissimulation.

Sedit. What, Dissimulation! Cock's soul! mine old
    acquaintance!

Par me faye, mon amye, Je [suis] tote ad voutre plesaunce.[2]

Dissim. Gramercies, good friend! with all my very heart:
I trust we shall talk more freely or we depart.

Sedit. Why, villain whoreson! knowest not thy cousin
    Sedition?

Dissim. I have ever loved both thee and thy condition.

Sedit. Thou must needs, I trow, for we come of two
    brethren:

    [1] 'From wicked King John deliver us, O Lord.'
    [2] 'By my faith, my friend, I am entirely at your service.'

If thou remember, our fathers were one man's childern—
Thou comest of Falsehood, and I of Privy Treason.

Dissim. Then Infidelity our grandfather is, by reason.

Sedit. Marry! that is true; and his beginner Antichrist,
The great Pope of Rome, or first vain popish priest.

Dissim. Now welcome, cousin! by the way that my soul
 shall to.

Sedit. Gramercy, cousin! by the holy bishop Benno!
Thou keepest thy old wont; thou art still an abbey man.

Dissim. To hold all things up I play my part now and
 than.

Sedit. Why, what manner of office hast thou within the
 abbey?

Dissim. Of all religions I keep the church-door key.

Sedit. Then, of a likelihood, thou art their general porter?

Dissim. Nay, of monks and canons I am the subtle sorter.
While some talk with Besse, the residue keep silence:
Though we play the knaves we must show a good pretence.
Wheresoever some eat, a certain keep the froiter;
Wheresoever some sleep, some must needs keep the dorter.
Didst thou never know the manner of our senys?

Sedit. I was never with them acquainted, by Saint
 Denys!

Dissim. Then never knewest thou the knavery of our
 menys—
If I should tell all, I could say more than that.

Sedit. Now of good fellowship, I beseech thee, show me
 what.

Dissim. The profitable lucre cometh ever in by me.

Sedit. But, by what mean? tell me, I heartily pray thee!

Dissim. To win the people, I appoint each man his place—
Some to sing Latin, and some to duck at grace;
Some to go mumming, and some to bear the cross;
Some to stoop downward as the[ir] heads were stopped with
 moss;
Some read the Epistle and Gospel at high mass;
Some sing at the lectern with long ears like an ass;
The pavement of the church the ancient fathers treads,

Some time with a portasse, sometime with a pair of beads;
And this exceedingly draw'th people to devotion,
Specially when they do see so good religion.
Then have we images of Saint Spirit and Saint Saviour—
Much is the seeking of them to get their favour:
Young women barefoot, and old men seek them breechless.
The miracles wrought there I can, in no wise, express.
We lack neither gold nor silver, girdles nor rings,
Candles nor tapers, nor other customed offerings.
Though I seem a sheep, I can play the subtle fox:
I can make Latin to bring this gear to the box.
Tush! Latin is alone to bring such matter to pass:
There is no English that can such sleights compass;
And, therefore, we will no service to be sung,
Gospel nor 'Pistle, but all in Latin tongue.
Of our subtle drifts many more points are behind;
If I told you all we should never have an end.

    Sedit. In nomine Patris,[1] of all that ever I heard
Thou art alone yet of such a dreaming buzzard!

    Dissim. Nay, dost thou not see how I in my colours jet?
To blind the people I have yet a farther set.
This is for Bernard, and this is for Benet,
This is for Gilbard, and this is for Jhenet:
For Francis this is, and this is for Dominic,
For Austin and Elen, and this is for Saint Patrick.
We have many rules, but never one we keep:
When we sing full loud our hearts be fast asleep.
We resemble saints in grey, white, black, and blue;
Yet unto princes not one of our number true:
And that shall King John prove shortly, by the rood!

    Sedit. But, in the meantime, yourselves get little good.
Your abbeys go down, I hear say, everywhere.

    Dissim. Yea, friend Sedition, but thou must see to that gear.

    Sedit. Then must I have help, by sweet Saint Benet's cup!

    Dissim. Thou shalt have a child of mine own bringing up.

    Sedit. Of thy bringing up? Cock's soul! what knave is
      that?

        [1] 'In the name of the Father.'

Dissim. Marry! Private Wealth; now have I told thee
　　what.
I made him a monk and a perfect cloisterer,
And in the abbey he began first cellarer;
Then prior, then abbot of a thousand pound land—no worse;
Now he is a bishop and rideth with a hundred horse;
And, as I hear say, he is like to be a cardinal.

Sedit. Is he so, indeed? by the mass! then have at all!

Dissim. Nay, first Private Wealth shall bring in Usurped
　　Power
With his authority, and then the game is o'er.

Sedit. Tush! Usurped Power doth favour me of all men;
For, in his troubles, I ease his heart now and then.
When princes rebel against his authority,
I make their commons against them for to be.
Twenty thousand men are but a morning breakfast
To be slain for him, he taking his repast.

Dissim. Thou hast, I perceive, a very subtle cast.

Sedit. I am for the Pope, as for the ship the mast.

Dissim. Then help, Sedition! I may still in England be:
King John hath threatened that I shall over sea.

Sedit. Well, if thou wilt of me have remedy this hour,
Go fetch Private Wealth and also Usurped Power!

Dissim. I can bring but one, by Mary, Jesus' mother!

Sedit. Bring thou in the one, and let him bring in the
　　other.

　　　　　　　　　　　*Here come in Usurped Power and
　　　　　　　　　　　　Private Wealth, singing one after another.*

*Usurped Power sing this. Super flumina Babylonis sus-
　　pendimus organa nostra.*[1]

*Private Wealth sing this. Quomodo cantabimus canticum
　　bonum in terra aliena?*[2]

Sedit. By the mass! methink they are singing of *placebo.*[3]

[1] 'By the waters of Babylon we hung up our harps' (Psalms
cxxxvii. 1–2).

[2] 'How shall we sing a good song in a strange land?' (Ibid.
cxxxvii. 4).

[3] 'placebo', i.e. Vespers in the Office for the Dead.

Dissim. Peace! for with my spectacles *vadam et videbo*![1]
Cock's soul! it is they: at the last I have smelled them out.
> *Here go and bring them.*

Sedit. Thou mayest be a sow, if thou hast so good a
    snout—
Sirs, mark well this gear! for, now, it beginneth to work.
False Dissimulation doth bring in Private Wealth;
And Usurped Power, which is more fierce than a Turk,
Cometh in by him to decay all spiritual health;
Than I by them both, as clear experience tell'th.
We four, by our crafts, King John will so subdue,
That for three hundred years all England shall it rue.

Dissim. Of the clergy, friends! report like as ye see;
That their Private Wealth cometh ever in by me.

Sedit. But, by whom comest thou? by the mass! even
    by the devil;
For the ground thou art of the Christian people's evil.

Dissim. And what are you, sir? I pray you say good by me.

Sedit. By my troth! I come by thee and thy affinity.

Dissim. Fetch thou in thy fellow, so fast as ever thou can.

P. Wealth. I trow, thou shalt see me now play the pretty
    man.
Of me, Private Wealth, came first Usurped Power:
Ye may perceive it, in pageant here, this hour.

Sedit. Now welcome, fellows, by all these bones and
    nails!

Us. Power. Among companions good fellowship never
    fails.

Sedit. Nay, Usurped Power! thou must go back again;
For I must also put thee to a little pain.

Us. Power. Why, fellow Sedition! what wilt thou have
    me do?

Sedit. To bear me on thy back, and bring me in also,
That it may be said that, first, Dissimulation
Brought in Private Wealth to every Christian nation!
And that Private Wealth brought in Usurped Power;
And he Sedition, in city, town, and tower:

[1] 'I shall go and see' (Genesis xlv. 28).

That some man may know the fetch of all our sort.

Us. Power. Come on thy ways, then, that thou mayest make thee fort.

Dissim. Nay, Usurped Power, we shall bear him all three, Thyself, he and I, if ye will be ruled by me—

For there is none of us but in him hath a stroke.

P. Wealth. The whoreson knave weigheth and it were a crooked oak.

> *Here they shall bear him in, and Sedition saith—*

Sedit. Yea, thus it should be; marry! now I am aloft—

I will beshite you all if ye set me not down soft.

In my opinion, by sweet Saint Antony!

Here is now gathered a full honest company.

Here is neither Austin, Ambrose, Jerome, nor Gregory;

But here is a sort of companions much more merry.

They of the Church, then, were four holy doctors;

We of the Church, now, are the four general proctors.

Here is, first of all, good father Dissimulation,

The first beginner of this same congregation;

Here is Private Wealth, which hath the Church infect

With all abusions, and brought it to a sinful sect;

Here is Usurped Power, that all kings doth subdue

With such authority as is neither good nor true;

And I, last of all, am even sance pere[1] Sedition.

Us. Power. Under heaven is not a more knave in condition.

Whereas thou dost come, that commonwealth cannot thrive:

By Our Lord! I marvel that thou art yet alive.

P. Wealth. Where herbs are plucked up the weeds many time remain.

Dissim. No man can utter an evidence more plain.

Sedit. Yea, ye think so, you? now God's blessing break your head!

I can do but laugh to hear you, by this bread!

I am so merry that we are met, by Saint John!

I feel not the ground that I do go upon—

---

[1] 'Without peer.'

For the love of God let us have some merry song.

    Us. Power. Begin thyself then, and we shall leap in
        among.   *Here sing.*

    Sedit. I would ever dwell here to have such merry sport.

    P. Wealth. Thou mayst have it, man! if thou wilt hither
        resort;

For the Holy Father is as good a fellow as we.

    Dissim. The Holy Father! why, pray thee which is he?

    P. Wealth. Usurped Power here; which, though he
        apparent be

In this apparel, yet hath he authority

Both in heaven and earth, in purgatory and in hell.

    Us. Power. Mark well his sayings! for a true tale he doth
        tell.

    Sedit. What, Usurped Power? Cock's soul! ye are our
        Pope?

Where is your three crowns, your cross keys, and your cope?

What meaneth this matter? methink ye walk astray.

    Us. Power. Thou knowest I must have some dalliance
        and play;

For I am a man, like as another is;

Sometime I must hunt, sometime I must Alison kiss.

I am bold of you; I take ye for no strangers;

We are as spiritual, I doubt in you no dangers.

    Dissim. I ought to consider your Holy Fatherhood:

From my first infancy ye have been to me so good.

For God's sake! witsave to give me your blessing here—
                              Kneel

A pena et culpa[1]—that I may stand this day clear.

    Sedit. From making cuckolds? marry! that were no
        merry cheer.

    Dissim. A pena et culpa: I trow thou canst not hear.

    Sedit. Yea, with a cuckold's wife ye have drunk double
        beer.

    Dissim. I pray thee, Sedition, my patience no more stere—

A pena et culpa I desire to be clear,

And then all the devils of hell I would not fear.

             [1] 'From penalty and fault.'

Us. Power. But tell me one thing: dost thou not preach
    the Gospel?

Dissim. No, I promise you, I defy it to the devil of hell.

Us. Power. If I knew thou didst, thou shouldst have none
    absolution.

Dissim. If I do, abjure me or put me to execution.

P. Wealth. I dare say he breaketh no popish constitution.

Us. Power. Such men are worthy to have our contribu-
    tion—

I assoil thee here, behind and also beforne:

Now art thou as clear as that day thou wert born.

Rise, Dissimulation! and stand up like a bold knight;

Doubt not of my power, though my apparel be light.

Sedit. A man, by the mass! cannot know you from a
    knave;

Ye look so like him, as I would God should me save.

P. Wealth. Thou art very lewd our father so to deprave.

Though he, for his pleasure, such light apparel have.

It is now summer, and the heat is without measure,

And among us he may go light at his own pleasure.

Fellow Sedition! though thou dost mock and scoff,

We have other matters than this to be commoned of.

Friend Dissimulation! why dost thou not thy message,

And show, out of England, the cause of thy far passage?

Tush! blemish not, whoreson! for I shall ever assist thee.

Sedit. The knave is white-livered, by the Holy Trinity!

Us. Power. Why so, Private Wealth, what is the matter?
    tell me!

P. Wealth. Dissimulation is a messenger for the clergy;

I must speak for him, there is no remedy.

The clergy of England, which is your special friend,

And of a long time hath borne you very good mind,

Filling your coffers with many a thousand pound,

If ye set not to hand, he is like to fall to the ground.

I do promise you truly, his heart is in his hose:

King John so useth him that he reckoneth all to lose.

Us. Power. Tell, Dissimulation, why art thou so ashamed

To show thy message? thou art much to be blamed.

Let me see those writings: tush, man! I pray thee come near.

    Dissim. Your Horrible Holiness putt'th me in wonderful fear.

    Us. Power. Tush! let me see them, I pray thee heartily!

    Here Dissimulation shall deliver the writings to Usurped
                                Power.

I perceive it well, thou wilt lose no ceremony.

    Sedit. Yet is he no less than a false knave, verily!

I would thou hadst kissed his arse, for that is holy.

    P. Wealth. How dost thou prove me that his arse is holy
      now?

    Sedit. For it hath an hole, even fit for the nose of you!

    P. Wealth. Your part is not else but for to play the knave,

And so ye must still continue to your grave.

    Us. Power. I say, leave your gauds, and attend to me this
      hour—

The bishops writeth here to me, Usurped Power,

Desiring assistance of mine authority

To save and support the Church's liberty.

They report King John, to them, to be very hard,

And to have the Church in no price nor regard.

In his parliament he demandeth of the clergy,

For his wars, the tent[h] of the Church's patrimony.

    P. Wealth. Ye will not consent to that, I trow, by Saint
      Mary!

    Sedit. No! draw to you still; but let none from you carry!

    Us. Power. Ye know it is clean against our holy decrees

That princes should thus contemn our liberties.

He taketh upon him to reform the tithes and offerings,

And intermeddleth with other spiritual things.

    P. Wealth. Ye must sequester him, or else that will mar all.

    Us. Power. Nay! besides all this, before judges temporal,

He conventeth clerks of causes criminal.

    P. Wealth. If ye see not to that, the Church will have a fall.

    Sedit. By the mass! then priests are like to have a pang;

For treason, murder and theft, they are like to hang.

By cock's soul! then I am like to walk for treason

If I be taken—look to it, therefore, in season!

P. Wealth. Marry! God forbid that ever your holy
anointed
For treason or theft should be hanged, racked or jointed;
Like the rascal sort of the profane laity.

Us. Power. Nay, I shall otherwise look to it, ye may trust
me!
Before himself, also, the bishops he doth convent,
To the derogation of their dignity excellent;
And will suffer none to the Court of Rome to appeal.

Dissim. No, he contemneth your authority and seal;
And saith, in his land, he will be lord and king;
No priest so hardy to enterprise anything.
For the which, of late, with him were at variance
Four of the bishops, and, in manner, at defiance—
William of London, and Eustace Bishop of Ely,
Walter of Winchester, and Giles of Hertford, truly.
By your authority they have him excommunicate.

Us. Power. Then have they done well; for he is a repro-
bate:
To that I admit he is always contrary.
I made this fellow here the Archbishop of Canterbury,
And he will agree thereto in no condition.

P. Wealth. Then, hath he knowledge that his name is
Sedition?

Dissim. Doubtless he hath so; and that drowneth his
opinion.

Us. Power. Why do ye not say his name is Steven Langton?

Dissim. Tush! we have done so; but that helpeth not the
matter:
The Bishop of Norwich for that cause doth him flatter.

Us. Power. Stick thou to it fast, we have once admitted
thee.

Sedit. I will not one jot from my admission flee:
The best of them all shall know that I am he—
Nay! in such matters let men beware of me.

Us. Power. The monks of Canterbury did more, at my
request,

Than they would at his, concerning that election.
They chase Sedition, as it is now manifest,
In spite of his heart: then he, for their rebellion,
Exiled them all, and took their whole possession
Into his own hands, them sending over sea
Their livings to seek in extreme poverty.
This custom also he hath, as it is told me:
When prelates depart—yea, bishop, abbot, or curate—
He entereth their lands without my liberty,
Taking the profits till the next be consecrate,
Institute, stalled, induct, or enthronisate;
And of the pied monks he intendeth to take a dime—
All will be marred if I look not to it in time.

    Dissim. It is taken, sir! the sum is unreasonable—
A nine thousand mark—to live they are not able:
His suggestion was to subdue the Irish men.

    P. Wealth. Yea, that same people doth ease the Church,
      now and then—
For that enterprise they would be looked upon.

    Us. Power. They get no money, but they shall have clean
      remission;
For those Irish men are ever good to the Church:
When kings disobey it, then they begin to worch.

    P. Wealth. And all that they do is for indulgence and
      pardon.

    Sedit. By the mass! and that is not worth a rotten warden.

    Us. Power. What care we for that? to them it is venison.

    P. Wealth. Then let them have it, a God's dear benison!

    Us. Power. Now, how shall we do for this same wicked
      king?

    Sedit. Suspend him, and curse him, both with your word
      and writing.
If that will not help, then interdict his land
With extreme cruelness; and if that will not stand,
Cause other princes to revenge the Church's wrong—
It will profit you to set them a-work among.
For clean remission, one king will subdue another;
Yea, the child sometime will slay both father and mother.

Us. Power. This counsel is good: I will now follow it plain.

Tarry thou still here till we return again.

> *Here go out Usurped Power and Private Wealth and
> Sedition: Usurped Power shall dress for the Pope:
> Private Wealth for a Cardinal; and Sedition for a
> Monk. The Cardinal shall bring in the cross, and
> Steven Langton the book, bell, and candle.*

Dissim. This Usurped Power, which now is gone from hence,

For the Holy Church will make such ordinance,

That all men shall be under his obedience;

Yea, kings will be glad to give him their allegiance;

And then shall we priests live here without disturbance.

As God's own vicar, anon, ye shall see him sit,

His flock to advance by his most politic wit.

He shall make prelates, both bishop and cardinal,

Doctors and prebends with furred hoods and side gowns.

He will also create the orders monastical—

Monks, canons, and friars with grey coats and shaven crowns;

And build them places to corrupt cities and towns.

The dead saints shall show both visions and miracles;

With images and relics he shall work sterracles.

He will make matins, hours, mass, and evensong,

To drown the Scriptures, for doubt of heresy;

He will send pardons to save men's souls among,

Latin devotions with the holy rosary.

He will appoint fastings, and pluck down matrimony;

Holy water and bread shall drive away the devil;

Blessings with black beads will help in every evil.

King John of England, because he hath rebelled

Against Holy Church, using it worse than a stable,

To give up his crown shall shortly be compelled;

And the Albigenes, like heretics detestable,

Shall be brent because against our father they babble.

Through Dominic's preaching an eighteen thousand are slain,

To teach them how they shall Holy Church disdain.
All this to perform he will cause a general council
Of all Christendom, to the Church of Laternense.
His intent shall be for to suppress the Gospel,
Yet will he glose it with a very good pretence—
To subdue the Turks by a Christian violence.
Under this colour he shall ground there many things,
Which will, at the last, be Christian men's undoings.
The Pope's power shall be above the powers all,
And ear-confession a matter necessary;
Ceremonies will be the rites ecclesiastical.
He shall set up there both pardons and purgatory.
The Gospel preaching will be an heresy.
By this provision, and by such other kinds,
We shall be full sure always to have our minds.

> [*Enter Usurp. Power as the Pope, Priv. Wealth as a
> Cardinal, Sedition as a Monk.*]

The Pope. Ah! ye are a blab; I perceive ye will tell all:
I left ye not here to be so liberal.

Dissim. Mea culpa, mea culpa, gravissima mea culpa![1]
Give me your blessing, *pro Deo et sancta Maria!*[2]

> *Kneel and knock on the breast.*

Pope. Thou hast my blessing. Arise now, and stand aside!
Dissim. My skin is so thick, it will not through glide.
Pope. Let us go about our other matters now.
Say this all three. We wait here upon the great holiness
of you.

Pope. Forasmuch as King John doth Holy Church so
handle,
Here I do curse him with cross, book, bell, and candle,
Like as this same rood turneth now from me his face,
So God I require to sequester him of His grace.
As this book doth spear by my work manual,
I will God to close up from him his benefits all.
As this burning flame goeth from this candle in sight,
I will God to put him from His eternal light.

[1] 'My fault, my fault, my most heinous fault.'
[2] 'For God and Holy Mary.'

I take him from Christ, and, after the sound of this bell,
Both body and soul I give him to the devil of hell.
I take from him baptism, with the other sacraments
And suffrages of the Church, both Ember days and Lents.
Here I take from him both penance and confession,
Mass of the Five Wounds, with censing and procession.
Here I take from him holy water and holy bread,
And never will them to stand him in any stead.
This thing to publish I constitute you three,
Giving you my power and my full authority.

 Say this all three. With the grace of God we shall perform it then.

 Pope. Then get you forward, so fast as ever ye can,
Upon a bon voyage: yet let us sing merrily.

 Sedit. Then begin the song, and we shall follow gladly.
          Here they shall sing.

 Pope. To colour this thing thou shalt be called Pandul-
  phus;
Thou, Steven Langton, thy name shall be Raymundus.
First thou, Pandulphus, shall openly him suspend
With book, bell, and candle: if he will not so amend,
Interdict his land, and the churches all up-spear.

 P. Wealth. I have my message; to do it I will not fear.
      Here go out and dress for Nobility.

 Pope. And thou, Steven Langton! command the bishops
  all,
So many to curse as are to him beneficial—
Dukes, earls, and lords—whereby they may forsake him.

 Sedit. Sir, I will do it, and that, I trow, shall shake him.

 Pope. Raymundus! go thou forth to the Christian princes
  all:
Bid them, in my name, that they upon him fall,
Both with fire and sword, that the Church may him conquer.

 Dissim. Your pleasure I will no longer time defer.

 Pope. Say this to them also: Pope Innocent the Third
Remission of sins to so many men hath granted
As will do their best to slay him, if they may.

 Dissim. Sir! it shall be done without any longer delay.

Pope. In the mean season I shall such gear advance
As will be to us a perpetual furtherance.
First ear-confession, then pardons, then purgatory;
Saints-worshipping then, then seeking of imagery;
Then Latin service, with the ceremonies many,
Whereby our bishops and abbots shall get money.
I will make a law to burn all heretics;
And kings to depose when they are schismatics.
I will also raise up the four begging orders
That they may preach lies, in all the Christian borders.
For this and other, I will call a General Council
To ratify them, in like strength, with the Gospel.

THE INTERPRETER

In this present act we have to you declared,
As in a mirror, the beginning of King John:
How he was, of God, a magistrate appointed
To the governance of this same noble region,
To see maintained the true faith and religion;
But Satan the Devil, which that time was at large,
Had so great a sway that he could it not discharge.

Upon a good zeal he attempted very far,
For wealth of this realm, to provide reformation
In the Church thereof; but they did him debar
Of that good purpose; for, by excommunication,
The space of seven years, they interdict thi[s] nation.
These blood-suppers thus, of cruelty and spite,
Subdued this good king for executing right.

In the second act this will appear more plain:
Wherein Pandulphus shall him excommunicate
Within this his land, and depose him from his reign.
All other princes they shall move him to hate,
And to persecute after most cruel rate.
They will him poison in their malignity,
And cause ill report of him always to be.

This noble King John, as a faithful Moses,
Withstood proud Pharaoh for his poor Israel;
Minding to bring it out of the land of darkness.
But the Egyptians did against him so rebel
That his poor people did still in the desert dwell,
Till that Duke Josue, which was our late King Henry,
Clearly brought us into the land of milk and honey.

As a strong David, at the voice of verity,
Great Golie, the Pope, he strake down with his sling;
Restoring again to a Christian liberty
His land and people, like a most victorious king;
To her first beauty intending the Church to bring,
From ceremonies dead to the living word of the Lord—
This the second act will plenteously record.

FINIT ACTUS PRIMUS. [INCIPIT ACTUS SECUNDUS.]

*Here the Pope go out, and Sedition and Nobility come in
and say:—*

Nob. It pitieth my heart to see the controversy
That nowadays reigneth between the king and the clergy.
All Canterbury monks are now the realm exiled;
The priests and bishops continually reviled;
The Cist'ian monks are in such perplexity
That, out of England, they reckon all to flee—
I lament the chance, as I would God should me save!

Sedit. It is graciously said; God's blessing might ye have!
Blessed is that man that will grant or condescend
To help religion, or Holy Church defend.

Nob. For their maintenance I have given lands full fair;
I have disherited many a lawful heir.

Sedit. Well, it is your own good: God shall reward you
for it;
And in heaven, full high, for such good works shall ye sit.

Nob. Your habit showeth ye to be a man of religion.

Sedit. I am no worse, sir! my name is Good Perfection.

Nob. I am the more glad to be acquainted with ye.

Sedit. Ye show yourself here like a nobleman, as ye be.
I perceive right well your name is Nobility.

Nob. Your servant and umfrey! of truth, father! I am he.

Sedit. From Innocent, the Pope, I am come from Rome,
even now:

A thousand times, I ween, he commendeth him unto you,

And sent you clean remission to take the Church's part.

Nob. I thank his Holiness; I shall do it with all my heart.

If ye would take pains for hearing my confession

I would, out of hand, receive this clean remission.

Sedit. Marry! with all my heart I will be full glad to do it.

Nob. Put on your stole then, and I pray you in God's
name sit.

> *Here sit down, and Nobility shall say Benedicite.*

Nob. Benedicite![1]

Sedit. D[o]m[i]n[u]s: *In nomine Domini Pape, amen!*[2]

Say forth your mind in God's name.

Nob. I have sinned against God; I 'knowledge myself to
blame—

In the seven deadly sins I have offended sore:

God's ten commandments I have broken evermore:

My five bodily wits I have ungodly kept:

The works of charity, in manner, I have outslept.

Sedit. I trust ye believe as Holy Church doth teach ye;

And from the new learning ye are willing for to flee.

Nob. From the new learning? Marry, God of heaven
save me!

I never loved it of a child, so mote I thee.

Sedit. Ye can say your creed, and your Latin Ave Mary?

Nob. Yea, and dirge also, with seven psalms and litany.

Sedit. Do ye not believe in purgatory and holy bread?

Nob. Yes, and that good prayers shall stand my soul in
stead.

Sedit. Well then, good enough! I warrant my soul for your.

Nob. Then execute on me the Holy Father's power.

Sedit. Nay, while I have you here, underneath *benedicite,*[3]

---

[1] 'Bless thee!'

[2] 'Lord: in the name of our Lord the Pope, Amen!'

[3] i.e. confession.

In the Pope's behalf I must move other things to ye.

Nob. In the name of God, say here what ye will to me.

Sedit. Ye know that King John is a very wicked man;
And, to Holy Church, a continual adversary.
The Pope willeth you to do the best ye can
To his subduing for his cruel tyranny;
And, for that purpose, this privilege graciously
Of clean remission he hath sent you this time,
Clean to release you of all your sin and crime.

Nob. It is clean against the nature of Nobility
To subdue his King without God's authority;
For his princely estate and power is of God.
I would gladly do it, but I fear His rightful rod.

Sedit. God's holy vicar gave me his whole authority—
Lo! it is here, man; believe it! I beseech thee,
Or else thou wilt fall in danger of damnation.

Nob. Then I submit me to the Church's reformation.

Sedit. I assoil thee here from the King's obedience,
By the authority of the Pope's magnificence.
Auctoritate Roma in pontificis ego absolvo te[1]
From all possessions given to the spirituality,
In nomine Domini Pape, amen![2]
Keep all things secret, I pray you heartily.

                                        Go out Nobility.

Nob. Yes, that I will, sir, and come again hither shortly.
            *Here enter Clergy and Civil Order together, and
                  Sedition shall go up and down a pretty while.*

Clergy. Is not your fatherhood Archbishop of Canter-
      bury?

Sedit. I am Steven Langton. Why make ye here inquiry?
            [Clergy and Civil Order] kneel and say both.
Ye are right welcome to this same region truly.

Sedit. Stand up, I pray you: I trow, thou art the Clergy.

Clergy. I am the same, sir! and this is Civil Order.

Sedit. If a man might axe you, what make you in this
      border?

[1] 'By Roman authority in matters pontifical, I absolve thee.'
[2] 'In the name of our Lord the Pope, Amen!'

Clergy. I heard tell yesterday ye were come into the land:
I thought for to see you, some news to understand.

Sedit. In faith! thou art welcome: is Civil Order thy
friend?

Clergy. He is a good man, and beareth the Church good
mind.

C. Order. Right sorry I am of the great controversy
Between him and the king, if I might it remedy.

Sedit. Well, Civil Order, for thy good will, gramercy!
That matter will be of another fashion shortly.
First, to begin with, we shall interdict the land.

C. Order. Marry! God forbid we should be in such bond.
But who shall do it, I pray you heartily?

Sedit. Pandulphus and I: we have it in our legacy—
He went to the king for that cause yesterday;
And I will follow so fast as ever I may.
Lo! here is the bull of mine authority.

Clergy. I pray God to save the Pope's holy majesty.

Sedit. Sit down on your knees, and ye shall have absolution

A pena et culpa,[1] with a thousand days of pardon.
Here is first a bone of the blessed Trinity,
A dram of the turd of sweet Saint Barnaby.
Here is a feather of good Saint Michael's wing,
A tooth of Saint Twyde, a piece of David's harp string,
The good blood of Hales, and our blessed Lady's milk;
A louse of Saint Francis in this same crimson silk.
A scab of Saint Job, a nail of Adam's toe,
A maggot of Moses, with a fart of Saint Fandigo.
Here is a fig-leaf and a grape of Noe's vineyard,
A bead of Saint Blythe, with the bracelet of a bearward.
The devil that was hatched in Master John Shorn's boot,
That the tree of Jesse did pluck up by the root.
Here is the latchet of sweet Saint Thomas' shoe,
A rib of Saint Rabart, with the huckle bone of a Jew;
Here is a joint of Darvel Gathiron,
Besides other bones and relics many one.

---

[1] 'From penalty and fault.'

In nomine Domini ·Pape, amen![1]

Arise now, like men, and stand upon your feet,
For here ye have caught an holy and a blessed heat.
Ye are now as clean as that day ye were born,
And like to have increase of childern, cattle and corn.

    C. Order. Childern? he can have none, for he is not of that
       load.

    Sedit. Tush! though he hath none at home, he may have
       some abroad.

Now, Clergy, my friend! this must thou do for the Pope,
And for Holy Church: thou must men's conscience grope;
And, as thou feelest them, so cause them for to work:
Let them show King John no more favour than a Turk;
Everywhere stir them to make an insurrection.

    Clergy. All that shall I do; and, to provoke them more,
This interdiction I will lament very sore
In all my preachings, and say, through his occasion,
All we are under the danger of damnation.
And this will move people to help to put him down;
Or else compel him to give up sceptre and crown.
Yea, and that will make those kings that shall succeed
Of the Holy Church to stand evermore in dread.
And, besides all this, the church doors I will upseal,
And close up the bells that they ring never a peal;
I will spear up the chalice, chrismatory, cross, and all,
That mass they shall have none, baptism nor burial:
And this, I know well, will make the people mad.

    Sedit. Marry! that it will; such sauce he never had—
And what wilt thou do for Holy Church, Civil Order?

    C. Order. For the clergy's sake I will, in every border,
Provoke the great men to take the common's part.
With cautels of the law I will so tickle their heart
They shall think all good that they shall pass upon;
And so shall we come to our full intent anon:
For if the Church thrive, then do we lawyers thrive;
And if they decay our wealth is not alive.
Therefore, we must help your state, masters! to uphold;

    [1] 'In the name of our Lord the Pope, Amen!'

Or else our profits will catch a winter cold.
I never knew lawyer which had any crafty learning
That ever escaped you without a plenteous living;
Therefore, we may not leave Holy Church's quarrel,
But ever help it, for their fall is our parel.

   Sedit. God's blessing have ye! this gear then will work,
     I trust.

   C. Order. Or else some of us are like to lie in the dust.

   Sedit. Let us all avoid! by the mass! the king cometh
     here.

   Clergy. I would hide myself for a time, if I wist where.

   C. Order. Go we hence apace, for I have spied a corner.

           Here go out all, and King John cometh in.

   K. John. For none other cause God hath kings constitute,
And given them the sword, but for to correct all vice.
I have attempted this thing to execute
Upon transgressors, according unto justice;
And because I will not be partial in mine office
For theft and murder, to persons spiritual,
I have against me the priests and the bishops all.
A like displeasure in my father's time did fall,
Forty years ago, for punishment of a clerk:
No counsel might them to reformation call,
In their opinion they were so sturdy and stark,
But against their prince to the Pope they did so bark,
That here, in England, in every city and town
Excommunications as thunderbolts came down.
For this their captain had after a pared crown,
And died upon it without the king's consent.
Then interdictions were sent from the Pope's renown,
Which never left him till he was penitent,
And fully agreed unto the Pope's appointment,
In England to stand with the Church's liberty;
And suffer the priests to Rome for appeals to flee.
They bound him also to help Jerusalem city
With two hundred men the space of a year, and more;
And three year after to maintain battle free
Against the Saracens, which vexed the Spaniards sore.

Since my father's time I have borne them grudge, therefore,
Considering the pride and the captious disdain
That they have to kings which ought over them to reign.

Private Wealth come in like a cardinal.

God save you, sir King, in your princely majesty!

    K. John. Friend, ye be welcome! what is your pleasure
       with me?

    P. Wealth. From the Holy Father, Pope Innocent the
       Third,
As a messenger I am to you directed;
To reform the peace between Holy Church and you;
And, in his behalf, I advertise you here, now,
Of the Church's goods to make full restitution,
And to accept also the Pope's hely constitution
For Steven Langton, Archbishop of Canterbury;
And so admit him to his state and primacy:
The monks exiled ye shall restore again
To their places and lands, and nothing of theirs retain.
Our Holy Father's mind is that ye shall again restore
All that ye have ravished from Holy Church, with the more.

    K. John. I reckon your Father will never be so hard,
But he will my cause, as well as theirs, regard.
I have done nothing but that I may do well;
And, as for their tax, I have for me the Gospel.

    P. Wealth. Tush! Gospel or no, ye must make a recom-
      pense.

    K. John. Your Father is sharp, and very quick in sentence,
If he weigheth the word of God no more than so;
But, I shall tell you in this what I shall do.
I am well content to receive the monks again
Upon amendment; but, as for Steven Langton, plain,
He shall not come here; for I know his disposition—
He is much inclined to sturdiness and sedition.
There shall no man rule in the land where I am king
Without my consent, for no man's pleasure living.
Nevertheless, yet, upon a new behaviour,
At the Pope's request hereafter I may him favour,
And grant him to have some other benefice.

P. Wealth. By this, I perceive, ye bear him grudge and
   malice.
Well, this will I say, because ye are so blunt,
A prelate to discharge, Holy Church was never wont;
But her custom is to minister punishment
To kings and princes being disobedient.

   K. John. Avaunt, peevish priest! what, dost thou
      threaten me?
I defy the worst both of thy Pope and thee!
The power of princes is given from God above;
And, as saith Solomon, their hearts the Lord doth move.
God speaketh in their lips when they give judgment;
The laws that they make are by the Lord's appointment.
Christ willed not his the princes to correct,
But to their precepts rather to be subject.
The office of you is not to bear the sword,
But to give counsel according to God's word.
He never taught his to wear neither sword nor sallett,
But to preach abroad without staff, scrip, or wallet;
Yet are ye become such mighty lords, this hour,
That ye are able to subdue all princes' power.
I cannot perceive but ye are become Bel's priests,
Living by idols; yea, the very Antichrists!

   P. Wealth. Ye have said your mind; now will I say mine
      also.
Here I curse you for the wrongs that ye have do
Unto Holy Church, with cross, book, bell, and candle;
And, besides all this, I must you otherwise handle.
Of contumacy the Pope hath you convict:
From this day forward your land stand interdict.
The Bishop of Norwich and the Bishop of Winchester
Hath full authority to spread it in England here.
The Bishop of Salisbury and the Bishop of Rochester
Shall execute it in Scotland everywhere.
The Bishop of Llandaff, Saint Asaph, and Saint Davy,
In Wales and in Ireland shall publish it openly.
Throughout all Christendom the bishops shall suspend
All such as to you any maintenance pretend;

And I curse all them that give to you their heart—
Dukes, earls, and lords—so many as take your part:
And I assoil your people from your obedience;
That they shall owe you neither fewte nor reverence.
By the Pope's authority I charge them with you to fight
As with a tyrant against Holy Church's right;
And, by the Pope's authority, I give them absolution
A pena et culpa,[1] and also clean remission.
Sedition extra locum.[2] Alarum! Alarum! tro ro ro ro ro!
    tro ro ro ro! tro ro ro ro ro!
Thump, thump, thump! down, down, down! to go, to go,
    to go!

    K. John. What a noise is this that without the door is
    made?

    P. Wealth. Such enemies are up as will your realm
    invade.

    K. John. Ye could do no more and ye came from the
    devil of hell
Than ye go about here to work by your wicked counsel.
Is this the charity of that ye call the Church?
God grant Christian men not after your ways to worch!
I set not by your curses the shaking of a rod;
For, I know they are of the devil, and not of God.
Your curses we have that we never yet demanded,
But we cannot have that God hath you commanded.

    P. Wealth. What ye mean by that I would ye should
    openly tell.

    K. John. Why, know ye it not? the preaching of the
    Gospel.
Take to ye your trash, your ringing, sin[g]i[n]g, piping,
So that we may have the Scriptures opening—
But that we cannot have, it standeth not with your advantage.

    P. Wealth. Ah! now I tell you, for this heretical language
I think neither you, nor any of yours, I wis—
We will so provide—shall wear the crown after this.

               Go out and dress for Nobility.

---

[1] 'From penalty and fault.'
[2] i.e. off-stage.

K. John. It become not thee, God's secret works to deem—
Get thee hence! or else we shall teach thee to blaspheme.
Oh, Lord! how wicked is that same generation
That never will come to a godly reformation.
The priests report me to be a wicked tyrant
Because I correct their acts and life unpleasant.
Of thy prince, saith God, thou shalt report none ill,
But thyself apply his pleasure to fulfil.
The birds of the air shall speak to their great shame,
As saith Ecclesiastes, that will a prince defame.
The powers are of God, I wot Paul hath such sentence—
He that resist them, against God maketh resistance.
Mary and Joseph, at Cyrin's appointment,
In the description to Cæsar were obedient.
Christ did pay tribute for Himself and Peter too,
For a law prescribing the same unto priests also.
To profane princes he obeyed unto death;
So did John Baptist so long as he had breath.
Peter, John, and Paul, with the other apostles all,
                                    [*Enter Civil Order.*]
Did never withstand the powers imperial.
Priests are so wicked they will obey no power,
But seek to subdue their princes day and hour,
As they would do me; but I shall make them smart
If that Nobility and Law will take my part.

   C. Order. Doubtless we cannot till ye be reconciled
Unto Holy Church, for ye are a man defiled.

   K. John. How am I defiled? tell me, good gentle mate!

   C. Order. By the Pope's high power ye are excommunicate.

   K. John. By the word of God, I pray thee, what power
hath he?

   C. Order. I spake not with him; and, therefore, I cannot
tell ye.

   K. John. With whom spake ye not? let me know your
intent.

   C. Order. Marry! not with God since the latter week of
Lent.

K. John. Oh merciful God! what an unwise clause is this
                        [Enter Clergy.]
Of him that should see that nothing were amiss.
That sentence or curse that Scripture doth not direct,
In my opinion, shall be of none effect.

    Clergy. Is that your belief? Marry! God save me from
        you!

    K. John. Prove it by Scripture, and then will I it allow—
But this know I well: when Balaam gave the curse
Upon God's people they were never a whit the worse.

    Clergy. I pass not on the Scripture; that is enou' for me
Which the Holy Father approveth by his authority.

    K. John. Now, alas, alas! what wretched people ye are;
And how ignorant your own words doth declare.
Woe is that people which hath so wicked teachers!

    Clergy. Nay! woe is that people that hath so cruel rulers!
                      [Enter Nobility.]
Our Holy Father, I trow, could do no less,
Considering the facts of your outrageousness.

    Nob. Come away, for shame! and make no more ado:
Ye are in great danger for commoning with him so.
He is accursed; I marvel ye do not weigh it.

    Clergy. I hear by his words that he will not obey it.

    Nob. Whether he will or no, I will not with him talk
Till he be assoiled. Come on, my friends! will ye walk?

    K. John. Oh, this is no token of true Nobility,
To flee from your king in his extremity!

    Nob. I shall desire you, as now, to pardon me:
I have much rather do against God, verily!
Than to Holy Church to do any injury.

    K. John. What blindness is this? On this people, Lord,
        have mercy!
Ye speak of defiling, but ye are corrupted all
With pestilent doctrine, or leaven pharisaical.
God to faithful Susan said that it was much better
To fall in danger of men than do the gretter,
As to leave God's law, which is His word most pure.

    Clergy. Ye have nothing, you, to allege to us but Scripture—

Ye shall fare the worse for that, ye may be sure.

K. John. What should I allege else, thou wicked Pharisee?
To your false learning no faithful man will agree.
Doth not the Lord say, *nunc reges intellige*:[1]
The kings of the earth that worldly causes judge—
Seek to the Scripture, let that be your refuge?

C. Order. Have ye nothing else but this? then God be
with ye!

K. John. One question more, yet; ere ye depart from me
I will first demand of you, Nobility!
Why leave ye your prince and cleave to the Pope so sore?

Nob. For I took an oath to defend the Church evermore.

K. John. Clergy! I am sure then your quarrel is not small.

Clergy. I am professed to the rights ecclesiastical.

K. John. And you, Civil Order, oweth her some office
of duty?

C. Order. I am her feed man: who should defend her
but I?

K. John. Of all three parties it is spoken reasonably:
Ye may not obey because of the oath ye made;
Your strong profession maketh you of that same trade;
Your fee provoketh you to do as these men do—
Great things to cause men from God to the devil to go!
Your oath is grounded first upon foolishness;
And your profession upon much peevishness;
Your fee, last of all, riseth out of covetousness—
And these are the causes of your rebelliousness!

Clergy. Come, Civil Order! let us depart from hence.

K. John. Then are ye at a point for your obedience?

C. Order. We will in no wise be partakers of your ill.

*Here go out Clergy and dress for England, and Civil
Order for Commonalty.*

K. John. As ye have been ever, so ye will continue still—
Though they be gone, tarry you with me awhile:
The presence of a prince to you should never be vile.

Nob. Sir, nothing grieveth me but your excommunication.

[1] 'Be wise, therefore, O kings' (Psalms ii. 10).

K. John. That is but a fantasy in your imagination.
The Lord refuse not such as hath His great curse,
But call them to grace, and favour them never the worse.
Saint Paul willeth you, when ye are among such sort,
Not to abhor them, but give them words of comfort.
Why should ye then flee from me your lawful king,
For pleasure of such as ought to do no such thing?
The Church's abusions, as holy Saint Paul do say,
By the prince's power ought for to be taken away—
He bareth not the sword without a cause (saith he).
In this neither bishop nor spiritual man is free;
Offending the law they are under the powers all.

Nob. How will ye prove me that the fathers spiritual
Were under the princes ever continually?

K. John. By the acts of kings I will prove it by and by.
David and Solomon the priests did constitute,
Commanding the offices that they should execute.
J'osaphat, the king, the ministers did appoint;
So did King Ezekias whom God himself did anoint.
Divers of the princes, for the priests, did make decrees;
Like as it is plain in the first of Maccabees.
Our priests are risen, through liberty of kings,
By riches to pride and other unlawful doings;
And that is the cause that they so oft disobey.

Nob. Good Lord, what a craft have you these things to
        convey!

K. John. Now, alas, that the false pretence of superstition
Should cause you to be a maintainer of Sedition!
Some thinketh nobility in nature to consist,
Or in parentage; their thought is but a mist;
Where habundance is of virtue, faith, and grace,
With knowledge of the Lord, nobility is there in place;
And not whereas is the wilful contempt of things
Pertaining to God in the obedience of kings.
Beware ye sink not with Dathan and Abiron
For disobeying the power and dominion.

Nob. Nay, bid me be aware I do not sink with you here,
Being accursed; of truth, ye put me in fear.

K. John. Why, are ye gone hence and will ye no longer tarry?

Nob. Nowhere as you are in place, by sweet Saint Mary!
Here Nobility go out and dress for the Cardinal. Here enter England and Commonalty.

K. John. Blessed Lord of Heaven! what is the wretched-
ness
Of this wicked world? An evil of all evils, doubtless!
Perceive ye not here how the clergy hath reject
Their true allegiance, to maintain the popish sect?
See ye not how light the lawyers set the power,
Whom God commandeth them to obey each day and hour?
Nobility also, which ought his prince to assist,
Is vanished away, as it we[re] a winter mist.
All they are from me: I am now left alone,
And, Got wot! know not to whom to make my moan.
Oh, yet would I fain know the mind of my Commonalty,
Whether he will go with them or abide with me.

Eng. He is here at hand, a simple creature as may be.

K. John. Come hither, my friend! stand near! is thyself
he?

[*Enter Commonalty.*]

Commonalty. If it like your grace, I am your poor
Commonalty.

K. John. Thou art poor enough; if that be good, God
help thee!
Methink thou art blind—tell me, friend! canst thou not see?

Eng. He is blind indeed; it is the more ruth and pity.

K. John. How comest thou so blind? I pray thee, good
fellow, tell me!

Com. For want of knowledge in Christ's lively verity.

Eng. This spiritual blindness bringeth men out of the
way,
And cause them ofttimes their kings to disobey.

K. John. How sayst thou, Commonalty? wilt not thou
take my part?

Com. To that I could be contented with all my heart;
But, alas! in me are two great impediments.

K. John. I pray thee show me what are those impediments.

Com. The first is blindness; whereby, I might take with
   the Pope

Sooner than with you; for, alas! I can but grope;

And ye know full well there are many naughty guides.

The next is poverty; which cleave so hard to my sides,

And punish me so sore, that my power is little or none.

K. John. In God's name tell me how cometh thy substance gone!

Com. By priests, canons, and monks, which do but fill
   their belly

With my sweat and labour for their popish purgatory.

Eng. Your grace promised me that I should have remedy

In that same matter when I was last here, truly!

K. John. Doubtless I did so; but, alas! it will not be—

In heart I lament this great infelicity.

Eng. Let me have my spouse and my lands at liberty,

And I promise you my son here, your Commonalty,

I will make able to do ye dutiful service.

K. John. I would I were able to do to thee that office;

But, alas! I am not; for why? my Nobility,

My Lawyers, and Clergy hath cowardly forsake me;

And now, last of all, to my most anguish of mind,

My Commonalty here I find both poor and blind.

Eng. Rest upon this, sir! for my governor ye shall be

So long as ye live: God hath so appointed me.

His outward blindness is but a signification

Of blindness in soul, for lack of information

In the word of God; which is the original ground

Of disobedience, which all realms doth confound.

If your grace would cause God's word to be taught sincerely,

And subdue those priests that will not preach it truly,

The people should know to their prince their lawful duty;

But, if ye permit continuance of hypocrisy

In monks, canons, and priests, and ministers of the clergy,

Your realm shall never be without much traitory.

K. John. All that I perceive; and, therefore, I keep out
   friars

Lest they should bring thee much farther into the briars.
They have made labour to inhabit this same region:
They shall, for my time, not enter my dominion.
We have too many of such vain louts already—
I beshrew their hearts! they have made you two full needy.

    Here enter Pandulphus, the Cardinal, and saith:

Pand. What, Commonalty, is this the covenant keeping?
Thou toldest me thou wouldst take him no more for thy
  king.

Com. Peccavi, mea culpa![1] I submit me to your holiness.

Pand. Get thee hence then shortly! and go about thy
  business—
Wait on thy captains, Nobility and the Clergy,
With Civil Order, and the other company.
Blow out your trumpets and set forth manfully:
The French King Philippe, by sea, doth hither apply,
With the power of France, to subdue this heretic.

K. John. I defy both him and thee, lewd schismatic!
Why wilt thou forsake thy prince or thy prince leave thee?

Com. I must needs obey when Holy Church commandeth
  me.   *Go out Commonalty.*

Eng. If thou leave thy king, take me never for thy mother.

Pand. Tush! care not thou for that; I shall provide thee
  another—
It were fitter for you to be in another place.

Eng. It shall become me to wait upon his grace,
And do him service whereas he is resident;
For I was given him of the Lord omnipotent.

Pand. Thou mayst not abide here; for why? we have him
  cursed.

Eng. I beshrew your hearts! so have ye me unpursed.
If he be accursed, then are we a meet couple,
For I am interdict: no salve that sore can supple.

Pand. I say, get thee hence! and make me no more
  prating.

Eng. I will not away from mine own lawful king,
Appointed of God, till death shall us depart.

       [1] 'I have sinned, my fault!'

Pand. Will ye not, indeed? well then, ye are like to smart.

Eng. I smart already through your most subtle practice;
And am clean undone by your false merchandise,
Your pardons, your bulls, your purgatory pick-purse,
Your Lent fasts, your shrifts, that I pray God give you his
     curse!

Pand. Thou shalt smart better or we have done with thee;
For we have, this hour, great navies upon the sea,
In every quarter, with this Loller here to fight,
And to conquer him for the Holy Church's right.
We have, on the north, Alexander, the King of Scots,
With an army of men that for their towns cast lots.
On the south side we have the French king with his power,
Which will slay and burn till he come to London Tower.
In the west parts we have King Alfonso with the Spaniards,
With ships full of gunpowder now coming hither towards;
And on the east side we have Esterlings, Danes, and Nor-
     ways,
With such power landing as can be resisted no ways.

K. John. All that is not true that you have here expressed.

Pand. By the mass! so true as I have now confessed.

K. John. And what do ye mean by such an hurly-burly?

Pand. For the Church's right to subdue ye ma[n]fully.

Sedit. To all that will fight I proclaim a jubilee
Of clean remission, this tyrant here to slee;
Destroy his people, burn up both city and town,
That the Pope of Rome may have his sceptre and crown!
In the Church's cause to die, this day, be bold!
Your souls shall to heaven ere your flesh and bones be cold.

K. John. Most merciful God! as my trust is in thee,
So comfort me now in this extremity!
As thou helpe[d]st David in his most heaviness,
So help me this hour, of thy grace, mercy, and goodness!

Pand. This outward remorse, that ye show here evident
Is a great likelihood and token of amendment.
How say ye, King John? can ye find now in your heart
To obey Holy Church and give over your froward part?

K. John. Were it so possible to hold these enemies back,

That my sweet England perish not in this shipwrack!

Pand. Possible, quoth he! yea, they should go back indeed,
And their great armies to some other quarters lead;
Or else they have not so many good blessings now,
But as many cursings they shall have, I make God avow!
I promise you, sir! ye shall have special favour
If ye will submit yourself to Holy Church here.

K. John. I trust then ye will grant some deliberation
To have an answer of this your protestation.

Sedit. Tush! give up the crown, and make no more ado!

K. John. Your spiritual charity will be better to me than so—
The crown of a realm is a matter of great weight;
In giving it up we may not be too slaight.

Sedit. I say, give it up! let us have no more ado!

Pand. Yea, and in our wars we will no farther go.

K. John. Ye will give me leave to talk first with my Clergy?

Sedit. With them ye need not: they are at a point already.

K. John. Then with my lawyers, to hear what they will tell?

Sedit. Ye shall ever have them as the Clergy give them counsel.

K. John. Then will I common with my Nobility.

Sedit. We have him so juggled he will not to you agree.

K. John. Yet shall I be content to do as he counsel me.

Pand. Then be not too long from hence, I will advise ye.

[*Exit with England.*]

Sedit. Is not this a sport? by the mass! it is, I trow!
What wealth and pleasure will now to our kingdom grow!
England is our own, which is the most pleasant ground
In all the round world: now may we realms confound.
Our Holy Father may now live at his pleasure,
And have habundaunce of wenches, wines, and treasure.
He is now able to keep down Christ and His Gospel,
True faith to exile, and all virtues to expel.
Now shall we ruffle it in velvets, gold, and silk;

With shaven crowns, side-gowns, and rochets white as milk.
By the mass, Pandulphus! now may we sing *cantate*,[1]
And crow *confitebor*[2] with a joyful *jubilate*.[3]
Hold me! or else for laughing I must burst.

    Pand. Hold thy peace, whoreson!—I ween thou art
accursed—
Keep a sad countenance: a very vengeance take thee!

    Sedit. I cannot do it, by the mass! and thou shouldst
      hang me.
If Solon were here, I reckon that he would laugh
Which never laughed yet; yea, like a whelp he would waugh.
Ha, ha, ha! laugh, quoth he? yea, laugh and laugh again:
We had never cause to laugh more free, I am plain.

    Pand. I pray thee, no more! for here come the king again.
Ye are at a point whereto ye intend to stand.

                  [*Enter K. John and England.*]

    Sedit. Yea, hardly, sir, give up the crown of England.

    K. John [*to England*]. If I should not grant, here would
be a wonderful spoil;
Everywhere the enemies would ruffle and turmoil;
The loss of [the] people sticketh most unto my heart.

    Eng. Do as ye think best; each way is to my smart.

    Pand. [*to K. John*]. Ye are at a point whereto ye intend
to stand?

    K. John. I have cast in my mind the great displeasures
of war;
The dangers, the losses, the decays both near and far;
The burning of towns, the throwing down of buildings,
Destruction of corn and cattle, with other things;
Defiling of maids, and shedding of Christian blood,
With such like outrages, neither honest, true, nor good—
These things considered, I am compelled this hour
To resign up here both crown and regal power.

    Eng. For the love of God yet take some better advisement!

    Sedit. Hold your tongue, ye whore! or, by the mass!
ye shall repent.
Down on your marybones, and make no more ado!

    [1] 'Sing ye.'   [2] 'I will confess.'   [3] 'Be joyful.'

Eng. If ye love me, sir, for God's sake do never so!

K. John. O England, England! show now thyself a
    mother;

Thy people will else be slain here without number.

As God shall judge me, I do not this of cowardness,

But of compassion in this extreme heaviness.

Shall my people shed their blood in such habundaunce?

Nay! I shall rather give up my whole governance.

Sedit. Come off apace then, and make an end of it
    shortly!

Eng. The most pitiful chance that hath been hitherto,
    surely!

K. John. Here I submit me to Pope Innocent the Third,

Desiring mercy of his Holy Fatherhood.

Pand. Give up the crown then, it shall be the better for
    ye:

He will unto you the more favourable be.

       Here the King deliver the crown to the Cardinal.

K. John. To him I resign here the sceptre and the crown

Of England and Ireland, with the power and renown,

And put me wholly to his merciful ordinance.

Pand. I may say this day the Church hath a full great
    chance:

This five days I will keep this crown in mine own hand,

In the Pope's behalf, upseizing England and Ireland.

In the mean season ye shall make an obligation

For you and your heirs in this signification:

To receive your crown of the Pope for evermore

In manner of fe[off]-farm; and, for a token therefore,

Ye shall every year pay him a thousand mark

With the Peter Pence, and not against it bark.

Ye shall also give to the Bishop of Canterbury

A three thousand mark for his great injury.

To the Church, besides, for the great scath ye have done,

Forty thousand mark ye shall deliver soon.

K. John. Sir! the tax that I had of the whole realm of
    England

Amounted to no more but unto thirty thousand—

Why should I then pay so much unto the clergy?

   Pand. Ye shall give it them: there is no remedy.

   K. John. Shall they pay no tribute if the realm stand in rerage?

   Pand. Sir! they shall pay none: we will have no such bondage.

   K. John. The Pope had at once three hundred thousand mark.

   Pand. What is that to you? ah, still ye will be stark!

Ye shall pay it, sir: there is no remedy!

   K. John. It shall be performed as ye will have it, truly.

   Eng. So noble a realm to stand tributary, alas,

To the devil's vicar! such fortune never was!

   Sedit. Out with this harlot! Cock's soul! she hath let a fart.

   Eng. Like a wretch, thou liest! Thy report is like as thou art.

   Pand. Ye shall suffer the monks and canons to make re-entry

Into their abbeys, and to dwell there peaceably;

Ye shall see also to my great labour and charge:

For other things else we shall common more at large.

   K. John. Sir, in every point I shall fulfil your pleasure.

   Pand. Then ply it apace, and let us have the treasure!

   Eng. Alack, for pity, that e'er ye granted this!

For me, poor England, ye have done sore amiss;

Of a free woman ye have now made a bondmaid:

Yourself and your heirs ye have fore'er decay'd.

Alas, I had rather be underneath the Turk

Than under the wing of such a thief to lurk.

   K. John. Content thee, England, for there is no remedy.

   Eng. If you be pleased then I must consent gladly.

   K. John. If I should not grant, here would be a wonderful spoil;

Everywhere the enemies would ruffle and turmoil.

The loss of people sticketh most unto my heart.

   Eng. Do as ye think best: each way is to my smart.

   Pand. Are ye at a point with the same obligation?

K. John. It is here ready at your interrogation.

    Here King John shall deliver the obligation.

Pand. Where is the money for your full restitution?

K. John. Here, sir, according to your last constitution.

Pand. Come hither, my lord; by the Pope's authority,
Assoil this man here of irregularity.

    Here the bishop, Stephen Langton, comes in.

K. John. Methink[s] this bishop resembleth much Sedition.

Pand. I counsel you yet to be ware of wrong suspicion:
This is Stephen Langton, your metropolitan.

K. John. Then do the office of the good Samaritan,
And pour oil and wine in my old fester'd wound;
Release me of sin that it doth not me confound.

*Confiteor domino pape et omnibus cardinalibus eius et vobis quia
    peccavi nimis exigendo ab ecclesia tributum; mea culpa.
Ideo precor sanctissimum dominum papam et omnes prelatos
    eius et vos orare pro me.*

*S. Langton. Misereatur tui omnipotens papa et dimittat
    tibi omnes erratus tuos liberetque te ab suspencione excomi-
    nicacione et interdicto et restituat te in regnum tuum.*

K. John. Amen.

*S. Langton. Dominus papa noster te absolvat et ego absol-
    vote auctoritate eius et apostolorum petri et pauli. In
    hac parte mihi com[m]issa ab omnibus impietatibus tuis
    et restituo te corone et regno in nomine domini pape, amen.*[1]

[1] [John] 'I confess to our lord the Pope and all his cardinals
and you that I have sinned in exacting excessive tribute from
the Church; the fault is mine, so I beg our most holy lord
the Pope and all his prelates and you to pray for me.'

[Langton] 'May the all-powerful Pope have pity on you and
forgive you all your sins, and deliver you from suspension,
excommunication, and interdiction, and restore you to your
throne.'

[John] 'Amen.'

[Langton] 'May our lord the Pope absolve you [as] I absolve
you, on his authority and that of the apostles Peter and Paul
herein entrusted to me, from all your impieties, and restore
you to your crown and throne in the name of our lord the
Pope, Amen.'

Pand. Ye are well content to take this man for your
    primate?

K. John. Yea, and to use him according to his estate.
I am right sorry that ever I you offended.

Sedit. And I am full glad ye are so well amended.
Unto Holy Church ye are now an obedient child,
Where ye were afore with heresy much defiled.

Eng. Sir! yonder is a clerk which is condemned for
    treason.
The shrives would fain know what to do with him this
season.

K. John. Come hither, fellow! What, methink thou art
    a priest.   [*Enter Treason.*]

Treason. He hath ofter guessed that of the truth have missed!

K. John. A priest and a traitor? how may that well agree?

Treas. Yes, yes, well enough! underneath *benedicite.*
Myself hath played it; and, therefore, I know it the better:
Among crafty coiners there hath not been a greater.

K. John. Tell some of thy feats; thou mayst the better
    escape.

Sedit. Hem! not too bold yet: for a mouse the cat will
    gape.

Treas. Twenty thousand traitor[s] I have made in my
    time
Under *benedicite,* between high mass and prime.
I have made Nobility to be obedient
To the Church of Rome, which most kings may repent.
I have so conveyed that neither priest nor lawyer
Will obey God's word, nor yet the Gospel favour.
In the place of Christ I have set up superstitions;
For preachings, ceremonies; for God's word, men's tradi-
tions.
Come to the temple and there Christ hath no place;
Moses and the pagans doth utterly him deface!

Eng. Mark well, sir! tell what we have of Moses.

Treas. All your ceremonies, your copes, and your censers,
    doubtless;
Your fires, your waters, your oils, your altars, your ashes,

Your candlesticks, your cruets, your salt, with such like
          trashes—
Ye lack but the blood of a goat, or else a calf.

 Eng. Let us hear somewhat also in the pagan's behalf.

 Treas. Of the pagans ye have your gilded images all,
In your necessities upon them for to call;
With crouchings, with kissings, and setting up of lights,
Bearing them in procession, and fastings upon their nights;
Some for the toothache, some for the pestilence and pox;
With images of wax to bring money to the box.

 Eng. What have they of Christ in the Church? I pray
          thee, tell!

 Treas. Marry! nothing at all but the epistle and the
          gospel,
And that is in Latin that no man should it know!

 Sedit. Peace, naughty whoreson, peace! thou playest the
          knave, I trow.

 K. John. Hast thou known such ways, and sought no
          reformation?

 [*Treas.*] It is the living of our whole congregation.
If superstitions and ceremonies from us fall,
Farewell monk and canon, priest, friar, bishop, and all!
Our conveyance is such that we have both money and
          ware.

 Sedit. Our occupation thou wilt mar; God give thee care!

 Eng. Very few of ye will Peter's office take.

 Treas. Yes, the more part of us our Master hath forsake.

 Eng. I mean for preaching—I pray God thou be cursed!

 Treas. No, no! with Judas we love well to be pursed:
We sell our Maker so soon as we have Him made;
And, as for preaching, we meddle not with that trade
Lest Annas, Caiaphas, and the lawyers should us blame;
Calling us to reckoning for preaching in that name.

 K. John. But tell to me, person! why wert thou cast in
          prison?

 [*Treas.*] For no great matter; but a little petty treason:
For conjuring, calking, and coining of new groats;
For clipping of nobles, with such like pretty motes.

Eng. This is high treason, and hath been evermore.

K. John. It is such treason as he shall sure hang for.

Treas. I have holy orders: by the mass! I defy your worst.
Ye cannot touch me but ye must be accurst.

K. John. We will not touch thee; the halter shall do it
    alone—
Curse the rope, therefore, when thou beginnest to groan.

Treas. And set ye no more by the holy order of priest-
    hood?
Ye will prove yourself an heretic, by the rood!

K. John. Come hither, England! and hear what I say
    to thee.

Eng. I am all ready to do as ye command me.

K. John. For so much as he hath falsified our coin,
As he is worthy, let him with an halter join:
Thou shalt hang no priest, nor yet none honest man;
But a traitor, a thief, and one that little good can.

Pand. What, yet against the Church? get me book, bell,
    and candle!
As I am true priest, I shall ye yet better handle!
Ye neither regard his crown nor anointed fingers,
The office of a priest, nor the grace that therein lingers.

Sedit. Sir, patient yourself! and all thing shall be well.
Fie, man! to the Church that ye should be still a rebel!

Eng. I account him no priest that work such heinous
    treason.

Sedit. It is a world to hear a foolish woman reason!

Pand. After this manner ye used Peter Pomfret:
A good simple man, and, as they say, a prophet.

K. John. Sir, I did prove him a very superstitious wretch,
And blasphemous liar; therefore, did the law him upstretch.
He prophesied first I should reign but fourteen years,
Making the people to believe he could bind bears;
And I have reigned a seventeen years, and more.
And anon after he grudged at me very sore,
And said I should be exiled out of my realm
Before the Ascension, which was turned to a fantastical
    dream,

Saying he would hang if his prophecy were not true:
Thus his own decay his foolishness did brew.

    Pand. Ye should not hang him which is a friend to the
    Church.

    K. John. Alack! that ye should count them friends of the
    Church
That against all truth so hypocritically lurch—
An ill Church is it that hath such friends, indeed!

    Eng. Of Master Morris such another fable we read,
That in Morgan's field the soul of a knight made verses,
Appearing unto him, and this one he rehearses:
Destruat hoc regnum Rex regum duplici plaga,[1]
Which is true, as God spake with the Ape at Praga.
The souls departed from this heavy mortal pain
To the hands of God returneth never again—
A marvellous thing that ye thus delight in lies!

    Sedit. This queen doth not else but mock the blessed
    stories:
That Peter angered ye when he called ye a devil incarnate.

    K. John. He is now full sure no more so uncomely to
    prate—
Well, as for this man, because that he is a priest
I give him to ye: do with him what ye list!

    Pand. In the Pope's behalf I will somewhat take upon
    me—
Here I deliver him to the Church's liberty,
In spite of your heart: make of it what ye list!

    K. John. I am pleased, I say, because he is priest.

    Pand. Whether ye be or no, it shall not greatly force—
Let me see those cheanes: go thy way and have remorse.

    Treas. God save your lordships! I trust I shall amend,
And do no more so; or else, sir, God defend!

    Sedit. I shall make thee, I trow, to keep thy benefice.
By the Mary mass! the knave will never be wise.

    Eng. Like lord, like chaplain; neither barrel better
    herring.

[1] 'The King of Kings will destroy this kingdom with a double
stroke.'

Sedit. Still she must trattle: that tongue is always
   stirring—
A word or two, sir, I must tell you in your ear.
   Pand. Of some advantage I would very gladly hear.
   Sedit. Release not England of the general interdiction
Till the king hath granted the dowry and the pension
Of Julyane, the wife of King Richard Cœur-de-lion:
Ye know very well she beareth the Church good mind.
Tush! we must have all, man! that she shall leave behind:
As the saying is, he findeth that surely bind.
It were but folly such loose ends for to lose:
The land and the money will make well for our purpose.
Tush! lay yokes upon him, more than he is able to bear;
Of Holy Church so he will stand ever in fear;
Such a shrew as he it is good to keep under awe.
   Eng. Woe is that person which is underneath your law!
Ye may see, good people! what these same merchants are:
Their secret knaveries their open facts declare.
   Sedit. Hold thy peace, callet! God give thee sorrow and
   care!
   Pand. Ere I release you of the interdiction here,
In the which your realm continued hath this seven year,
Ye shall make Julyane, your sister-in-law, this band:
To give her the third part of England and of Ireland.
   K. John. All the world knoweth, sir! I owe her no such
   duty.
   Pand. Ye shall give it to her; there is no remedy—
Will ye still withstand our Holy Father's precept?
   Sedit. In pain of damnation his commandment must be
   kept.
   K. John. Oh, ye undo me, considering my great pay-
   ments!
   Eng. Sir, discomfort not! for God hath sent debatements.
Your merciful Maker hath showed upon ye His power,
From this heavy yoke delivering you this hour—
The woman is dead: such news are hither brought.
   K. John. For me a sinner this miracle hath God wrought.
In most high perils He ever me preserved;

And in this danger He hath not from me swerved.

In genua procumbens Deum adorat, dicens:[1]

As David saith: Lord! Thou dost not leave Thy servant
That will trust in Thee, and in Thy blessed covenant.

Sedit. A vengeance take it! by the mass! it is unhappy
She is dead so soon. Now is it past remedy:
So must we lose all now that she is clearly gone.
If that prey had been ours, oh, it had been alone!
The chance being such, by my troth! even let it go:
No groat, no paternoster; no penny, no *placebo*—[2]
The devil go with it, seeing it will be no better!

Eng. Their minds are all set upon the filthy lucre.

Pand. Then here I release you of your interdictions all,
And straitly command you, upon dangers that may fall,
No more to meddle with the Church's reformation,
Nor hold men from Rome when they make appellation—
By God and by all the contents of this book.

K. John. Against Holy Church I will no more speak nor
   look.

Sedit. Go, open the church doors, and let the bells be
   rung;
And throughout the realm see that *Te Deum* be sung.
Prick up your candles before Saint Loy and Saint Legard:
Let Saint Antony's hog be had in some regard.
If your ale be sour, and your bread mould, certain
Now will they wax sweet, for the Pope hath blessed ye again.

Eng. Then within a while I trust ye will preach the
   Gospel.

Sedit. That shall I tell thee, keep thou it in secret counsel:
It shall neither come in church nor yet in chancel.

Pand. Go your ways apace, and see our pleasure be done!

K. John. As ye have commanded, all shall be performed
   soon.   [*Exeunt K. John and Eng.*]

Pand. By the mass! I laugh to see this clean conveyance:
He is now full glad, as our pipe goeth, to dance.
By cock's soul! he is now become a good parish clerk.

───────────

[1] 'Falling on his knees, he worships God, saying . . .'.
[2] i.e. Vespers in the Office of the Dead.

    Sedit. Ha, ha! wily whoreson! dost that so busily mark?
I hope, in a while, we will make him so to rave
That he shall become, unto us, a common slave;
And shall do nothing but as we bid him do.
If we bid him slay, I trow he will do so;
If we bid him burn such as believe in Christ,
He shall not say nay to the bidding of a priest.
But yet, it is hard to trust what he will be;
He is so crabbed: by the Holy Trinity!
To save all things up, I hold best we make him more sure,
And give him a sauce that he no longer endure.
Now that I remember we shall not leave him thus.

    Pand. Why, what shall we do to him else? in the name of
        Jesus!

    Sedit. Marry! fetch in Louis, King Philippe's son, of
        France,
To fall upon him with his men and ordnance;
With wildfire, gunpowder, and such like merry tricks;
To drive him to hold and search him in the quicks:
I will not leave him till I bring him to his end.

    Pand. Well, farewell, Sedition, do as shall lie in thy
        mind.   [*Exit.*]

    Sedit. I marvel greatly where Dissimulation is.

    Dissim. I will come anon, if thou tarry till I piss.
                           [*Enter Dissimulation.*]

    Sedit. I beshrew your heart! where have ye been so long?

    Dissim. In the garden, man! the herbs and weeds among;
And there have I got the poison of toad:
I hope in a while to work some feat abroad.

    Sedit. I was wont sometime of thy privy council to be:
Am I nowadays become a stranger to thee?

    Dissim. I will tell thee all, underneath *benedicite*,[1]
What I mind to do, in case thou wilt assoil me.

    Sedit. Thou shalt be assoiled by the most Holy Father's
        authority.

    Dissim. Shall I so indeed? by the mass! then now have at
        thee!

               [1] i.e. under confession, secretly.

Benedicite![1]

Sedit. In nomine Papæ, amen![2]

Dissim. Sir, this is my mind: I will give King John this poison,
So making him sure that he shall never have foison;
And this must thou say to colour with the thing:
That a penny loaf he would have brought to a shilling.

Sedit. Nay, that is such a lie as easily will be felt.

Dissim. Tush, man! among fools it never will be out-smelt.
Though it be a foul lie, set upon it a good face;
And that will cause men believe it in every place.

Sedit. I am sure, then, thou wilt give it him in a drink.

Dissim. Marry! that I will, and the one half with him swink,
To encourage him to drink the bottom off.

Sedit. If thou drink the half, thou shalt find it no scoff:
Of terrible death thou wilt stacker in the plashes.

Dissim. Tush! though I die, man, there will rise more of my ashes!
I am sure the monks will pray for me so bitterly,
That I shall not come in hell, nor in purgatory.
In the Pope's kitchen the scullions shall not brawl
Nor fight for my grease. If the priests would for me yawl,
And grunt a good pace *placebo*[3] with requiem mass,
Without much tarriance I should to Paradise pass,
Where I might be sure to make good cheer and be merry,
For I cannot away with that whoreson purgatory.

Sedit. To keep thee from thence thou shalt have five monks singing
In Swinsett Abbey, so long as the world is during:
They will daily pray for the soul of father Simon,
A Cist'ian monk which poisoned King John.

Dissim. When the world is done, what help shall I have than?

Sedit. Then shift for thyself so well as ever thou can.

[1] 'Bless thee.'   [2] 'In the name of the Pope, Amen.'
[3] i.e. Vespers in the Office of the Dead.

Dissim. Cock's soul! he cometh here. Assoil me that I
    were gone then.
Sedit. Ego absolvo te in nomine Papæ, amen![1]
                        [*Exeunt. Enter K. John and England.*]
    K. John. No prince in the world in such captivity
As I am this hour, and all for righteousness.
Against me I have both the lords and commonalty,
Bishops and lawyers; which, in their cruel madness,
Hath brought in hither the French King's eldest son Louis.
The chance unto me is not so dolorous,
But my life, this day, is much more tedious.
More of compassion for shedding of Christian blood
Than anything else, my sceptre I gave up lately
To the Pope of Rome, which hath no title good
Of jurisdiction, but of usurpation only:
And now to Thee, Lord! I would resign up gladly
                            Flectit genua[2]
Both my crown and life; for Thine own right it is,
If it would please Thee to take my soul to Thy bliss.
    Eng. Sir! discomfort ye not! in the honour of Christ Jesu
God will never fail you, intending not else but virtue.
    K. John. The anguish of spirit so pangeth me everywhere
That, incessantly, I thirst till I be there.
    Eng. Sir! be of good cheer, for the Pope hath sent a legate,
Whose name is Gualo, your foes to excommunicate;
Not only Louis, which hath won Rochester,
Windsor and London, Reading and Winchester;
But so many else as against ye have rebelled,
He hath suspended and openly accursed.
    K. John. They are all false knaves; all men of them,
    beware!
They never left me till they had me in their snare.
Now have they Otto, the emperor, so well as me,
And the French king, Philippe, under their captivity.
All Christian princes they will have in their hands:
The Pope and his priests are poisoners of all lands.

    [1] 'I absolve thee in the name of the Pope, Amen.'
    [2] 'He bends his knee.'

All Christian people, beware of traitorous priests!
For, of truth, they are the pernicious Antichrists.

 Eng. This same Gualo, sir! in your cause doth stoutly
  bark.
 K. John. They are all nought, England! so many as wear
  that mark.
From this habitation, sweet Lord! deliver me,
And preserve this realm of Thy benignity!
          [Dissimulation from without.]

 Dissim. Wassail! wassail! out of the milk-pail,
Wassail! wassail! as white as my nail;
Wassail! wassail! in snow, frost, and hail;
Wassail! wassail! with partridge and rail;
Wassail! wassail! that much doth avail;
Wassail! wassail! that never will fail.

 K. John. Who is that, England? I pray thee step forth
  and see.
 Eng. He doth seem afar some religious man to be.
            [Enter Dissimulation.]

 Dissim. Now Jesus preserve your worthy and excellent
  grace!
For, doubtless, there is a very angelic face.
Now forsooth, and God! I would think myself in heaven
If I might remain with you but years eleven—
I would covet here none other felicity.

 K. John. A loving person thou mayest seem for to be.
 Dissim. I am as gentle a worm as ever ye see.
 K. John. But what is thy name, good friend? I pray thee,
  tell me!
 Dissim. Simon of Swinsett my very name is, perdee!
I am taken of men for monastical devotion;
And here have I brought you a marvellous good potion,
For I heard ye say that ye were very dry.

 K. John. Indeed, I would gladly drink. I pray thee,
  come nigh!
 Dissim. The days of your life never felt ye such a cup,
So good and so wholesome, if ye would drink it up:
It passeth malmsey, capric, tyre, or hippocras—

By my faith! I think a better drink never was.

   K. John. Begin, gentle monk! I pray thee, drink half to
      me!

   Dissim. If ye drank all up, it were the better for ye;

It would slake your thirst and also quicken your brain:

A better drink is not in Portugal nor Spain;

Therefore, sup it off, and make an end of it, quickly!

   K. John. Nay, thou shalt drink half: there is no remedy.

   Dissim. Good luck to ye, then! have at it, by and bye!

Half will I consume if there be no remedy.

   K. John. God saint thee, good monk, with all my very
      heart!

   Dissim. I have brought ye half; convey me that for your
      part.   *[He goes aside.]*

Where art thou, Sedition? by the mass! I die, I die!

Help now at a pinch! Alas, man! come away shortly.

   Sedit. Come hither, apace! and get thee to the farmery;

I have provided for thee, by sweet Saint Paul!

Five monks that shall sing continually for thy soul,

That, I warrant thee, thou shalt not come in hell.

   Dissim. To send me to heaven go ring the holy bell;

And sing for my soul a mass of Scala Cœli,

That I may climb up aloft with Enoch and Heli—

I do not doubt it but I shall be a saint.

Provide a gilder mine image for to paint;

I die for the Church with Thomas of Canterbury—

Ye shall fast my vigil, and upon my day be merry.

No doubt but I shall do miracles in a while;

And, therefore, let me be shrined in the north aisle.

   Sedit. To thee, then, will offer both cripple, halt, and
      blind,

Madmen and mesels, with such as are woe behind.

                                  Exeunt.

   K. John. My body me vexeth: I doubt much of a
      timpany.

   Eng. Now, alas, alas! your grace is betrayed cowardly.

   K. John. Where became the monk that was here with me
      lately?

Eng. He is poisoned, sir, and lieth a-dying surely!

K. John. It cannot be so, for he was here even now.

Eng. Doubtless, sir, it is so true as I have told you!
A false Judas kiss he hath given and is gone.
The halt, sore, and lame this pitiful case will moan:
Never prince was there that made, to poor people's uses,
So many masendewes, hospitals, and spital houses,
As your grace hath done, yet since the world began.

    K. John. Of priests, and of monks, I am counted a wicked
      man
For that I never built church nor monastery;
But my pleasure was to help such as were needy.

    Eng. The more grace was yours; for, at the day of judg-
      ment,
Christ will reward them which hath done His command-
      ment.
There is no promise for voluntary works,
No more than there is for sacrifice of the Turks.

    K. John. Doubtless, I do feel much grievance in my body.

    Eng. As the Lord well knoweth, for that I am full sorry.

    K. John. There is no malice to the malice of the clergy:
Well, the Lord God of heaven on me and them have mercy!
For doing justice they have ever hated me.
They caused my land to be excommunicate;
And me to resign both crown and princely dignity,
From my obedience assoiling every estate;
And now, last of all, they have me intoxicate.
I perceive right well their malice hath none end:
I desire not else but that they may soon amend.
I have sore hungered and thirsted [for] righteousness
For the office' sake that God hath me appointed;
But now I perceive that sin and wickedness
In this wretched world, like as Christ prophesied,
Have the overhand: in me it is verified.
Pray for me, good people! I beseech you heartily;
That the Lord above on my poor soul have mercy.
Farewell, noblemen! with the clergy spiritual;
Farewell, men of law! with the whole commonalty.

Your disobedience I do forgive you all,
And desire God to pardon your iniquity.
Farewell, sweet England! now, last of all, to thee!
I am right sorry I could do for thee no more.
Farewell, once again, yea, farewell for evermore!
   Eng. With the leave of God I will not leave ye thus;
But still be with ye till He do take you from us;
And then will I keep your body for a memorial.
   K. John. Then ply it, England! and provide for my
      burial.
A widow's office it is to bury the dead.
   Eng. Alas, sweet master! ye weigh so heavy as lead.
Oh, horrible case! that ever so noble a king
Should thus be destroyed, and lost for righteous doing,
By a cruel sort of disguised blood-suppers;
Unmerciful murderers, all drunk in the blood of martyrs!
Report what they will, in their most furious madness,
Of this noble king much was the godliness.

                                        Exeunt.
      [*Enter Verity, Nobility, Clergy, and Civil Order.*]
   Verity. I assure ye, friends, let men write what they will,
King John was a man both valiant and godly.
What though Polydorus reporteth him very ill
At the suggestions of the malicious clergy?
Think you a Roman with the Romans cannot lie?
Yes! therefore, Leland, out of thy slumber awake,
And witness a truth for thine own country's sake!
For his valiantness many excellent writers make:
As Sigbertus, Vincentius, and also Nauclerus;
Giraldus and Matthew Paris with his noble virtues take;
Yea, Paulus Phrigio, John Major, and Hector Boethius.
Nothing is allowed in his life, of Polydorus;
Which discommendeth his punishments for traitory;
Advancing very sore high treason in the clergy.
Of his godliness thus much report will I:
Gracious provision for sore, sick, halt, and lame
He made in his time; he made both in town and city,
Granting great liberties for maintenance of the same,

By markets and fairs in places of notable name.
Great monuments are in Ipswich, Dunwich, and Bury,
Which noteth him to be a man of notable mercy.
The city of London, through his mere grant and premye,
Was first privileged to have both mayor and shrive;
Where, before his time, it had but bailiffs only;
In his days the bridge the citizens did contrive.
Though he now be dead, his noble acts are alive;
His zeal is declared, as touching Christ's religion,
In that he exiled the Jews out of this region.

    Nob. Whom speak ye of, sir? I beseech ye, heartily.

    Verity. I talk of King John, of late your prince most
        worthy.

    Nob. Sir, he was a man of a very wicked sort.

    Verity. Ye are much to blame your prince so to report.
How can ye presume to be called Nobility,
Defaming a prince in your malignity?
Ecclesiastes saith: If thou with an hateful heart
Misnamest a king, thou playest such a wicked part
As birds of air to God will represent,
To thy great peril and exceeding punishment.
Saint Jerome saith also, that he is of no renown,
But a vile traitor, that rebelleth against the crown.

    Clergy. He speaketh not against the crown, but the man,
        perdee!

    Verity. Oh! where is the spirit which ought to reign in
        thee?
The crown of itself, without the man, is nothing.
Learn of the Scriptures to have better understanding.
The heart of a king is in the hands of the Lord;
And He directeth it, wise Solomon to record—
They are abominable that use him wickedly.

    Clergy. He was never good to us, the sanctified clergy.

    Verity. Will ye know the cause, before this worshipful
        company?
Your conversation and lives are very ungodly.
King Solomon saith: Who hath a pure mind,
Therein delighting, shall have a king to friend.

On this word *cleros*,[1] which signifieth a lot—
Or a sorting out into a most godly knot—
Ye do take your name; for that ye are the Lord's
Select; of His word to be the special records.
As of Saint Mathias we have a singular mention,
That they chose him out anon after Christ's ascension.
Thus do ye reckon: but, I fear ye come of *clerus*,[2]
A very noiful worm, as Aristotle showeth us;
By whom are destroyed the honeycombs of bees—
For, poor widows ye rob, as did the Pharisees.

   C. Order. I promise you, it is uncharitably spoken.

   Verity. Truth engendereth hate: ye show thereof a token.
Ye are such a man as ought everywhere to see
A godly order; but ye loose each commonalty.
Plato thought always that no higher love could be
Than a man to pain himself for his own country.
David, for their sake, the proud Philistine slew:
Ehud made Eglon his wickedness to rue.
Esdras, from Persia, for his own country's sake,
Came to Jerusalem, their strongholds up to make.
But you, like wretches, cast over both country and king:
All manhood shameth to see your unnatural doing.
Ye wicked rulers! God doth abhor ye all;
As Mantuan reporteth, in his Eclogues pastoral:
Ye feed not the sheep, but ever ye pill the flock;
And clip them so nigh that scarcely ye leave one lock.
Your judgements are such that ye call to God in vain
So long as ye have your princes in disdain.
Chrysostom reporteth that nobility of friends
Availeth nothing, except ye have godly minds.
What profiteth it you to be called spiritual
Whilst you, for lucre, from all good virtues fall?
What praise is it to you to be called Civility
If you from obedience and godly order flee?
Anneus Seneca hath this most provable sentence:
The gentle, free heart goeth never from obedience.

---

      [1] 'clergymen'.   [2] A worm like a spider.

C. Order. Sir! my brethern and I would gladly know
    your name.

Verity. I am Veritas, that come hither, you to blame
For casting away of [y]our most lawful king:
Both God and the world detesteth your damnable doing.
How have ye used King John here now, of late?
I shame to rehearse the corruptions of your state.
Ye were never well till ye had him cruelly slain;
And now, being dead, ye have him still in disdain.
Ye have raised up of him most shameless lies;
Both by your reports, and by your written stories.
He that slew Saul, through fierceness violent,
Was slain soon after at David's just commandment;
For because that Saul was anointed of the Lord—
The Second of Kings of this beareth plenteous record—
He was, in those days, esteemed worthy to die
On a 'nointed King that laid hands violently.
Ye are not ashamed to find five priests to sing
For that same traitor that slew your natural king.
A traitorous knave ye can set up for a saint,
And a righteous king like an odious tyrant paint.
I could show the place where you, most spitefully,
Put out your torches upon his phys'nomy.
In your glass windows ye whip your natural kings—
As I said afore, I abhor to show your doings:
The Turks, I dare say, are a thousand times better than you.

    Nob. For God's love, no more! Alas! ye have said enough.

    Clergy. All the world doth know that we have done sore
        amiss.

    C. Order. Forgive it us, so that we never hear more of
        this.

    Verity. But are ye sorry for this ungodly work?

    Nob. I pray to God else I be damned, like a Turk.

    Verity. And make true promise ye will never more do so?

    Clergy. Sir! never more shall I from true obedience go.

    Verity. What say you, brother? I must have also your
        sentence.

    C. Order. I will ever give to my prince due reverence.

Verity. Well then, I doubt not but the Lord will con-
   descend
To forgive you all, so that ye mind to amend.
Adieu to ye all! for now I must be gone.

                   [Enter Imperial Majesty.]

Imperial Majesty. Abide, Verity! ye shall not depart so
   soon—
Have ye done all things as we commanded you?

Verity. Yea, most gravious prince! I concluded the
   whole, even now.

Imp. Maj. And how do they like the customs they have
   used
With our predecessors, whom they have so abused,
Specially King John? think they they have done well?

Verity. They repent that ever they followed seditious
   counsel;
And have made promise they will amend all faults.

Imp. Maj. And forsake the Pope with all his cruel assaults?

Verity [*to Nobility, Clergy, and Civil Order*].
Why do ye not bow to Imperial Majesty?
Kneel, and ask pardon for your great enormity!

Nob. Most godly governor! we ask your gracious pardon,
Promising nevermore to maintain false Sedition.

Clergy. Neither Private Wealth, nor yet Usurped Power
Shall cause me disobey my prince, from this same hour.
False Dissimulation shall never me beguile;
Where I shall meet him I will ever him revile.

Imp. Maj. I perceive, Verity! ye have done well your part,
Reforming these men: gramercies, with all my heart!
I pray you take pains to call our Commonalty
To true obedience, as ye are God's Verity.

Verity. I will do it, sir! yet shall I have much ado.
With your popish prelates; they will hunt me to and fro.

Imp. Maj. So long as I live they shall do you no wrong.

Verity. Then will I go preach God's word your commons
   among—
But, first, I desire you their stubborn facts to remit.

Imp. Maj. I forgive you all, and pardon your froward wit.

Omnes una. The heavenly Governor reward your goodness for it!

Verity. For God's sake obey, like as doth you befall;
For, in his own realm, a king is judge over all
By God's appointment; and none may him judge again
But the Lord Himself: in this the Scripture is plain.
He that condemneth a king, condemneth God, without doubt;
He that harmeth a king, to harm God goeth about.
He that a prince resisteth, doth damn God's ordinance;
And resisteth God in withdrawing his affiance.
All subjects offending are under the king's judgment:
A king is reserved to the Lord omnipotent.
He is a minister immediate under God,
Of His righteousness to execute the rod.
I charge you, therefore, as God hath charge[d] me,
To give to your king his due supremity;
And exile the Pope this realm for evermore.

Omnes una. We shall gladly do according to your lore.

Verity. Your grace is content I show your people the same?

Imp. Maj. Yea, gentle Verity! show them their duty, in
God's name!

To confirm the tale that Verity had now,
The Second of Kings is evident to you:
The young man, that brought the crown and bracelet
Of Saul to David, saying that he had him slain,
David commanded, as though he had done the forfeit,
Straightway to be slain: God's spirit did him constrain
To show what it is a king's blood to distain.
So did he those two that in the field him met,
And unto him brought the head of Is[h]bos[h]et.
Consider that Christ was under the obedience
Of worldly princes, so long as He was here;
And always used them with a lowly reverence;
Paying them tribute, all his true servants to stere
To obey them, love them, and have them in reverent fear.
Damnation it is to him that an order break
Appointed of God, like as the Apostle spake.
No man is exempt from this, God's ordinance—

Bishop, monk, canon, priest, cardinal, nor Pope:
All they, by God's law, to kings owe their allegiance.
This will be well known in this same realm, I hope.
Of Verity's words the sincere meaning I grope:
He saith that a king is of God immediately;
Then shall never Pope rule more in this monarchy.

   Clergy. If it be your pleasure we will exile him clean,
That he, in this realm, shall nevermore be seen;
And your grace shall be the supreme head of the Church—
To bring this to pass ye shall see how we will wurch.

   Imp. Maj. Here is a nice tale! he saith: if it be my
      pleasure
He will do this act to the Pope's most high displeasure.
As who saith: I would, for pleasure of my person,
And not for God's truth, have such an enterprise done.
Full wisely conveyed! the crow will not change her hue—
It is marvel to me and ever ye be true.
I will the authority of God's holy word to do it,
And it not to arise of your vain, slipper wit:
That Scripture doth not is but a light fantasy.

   Clergy. Both Daniel and Paul calleth him God's adver-
      sary;
And, therefore, ye ought, as a devil, him to expel.

   Imp. Maj. Knew ye this afore, and would it never tell?
Ye should repent it had we not now forgiven ye.
Nobility! what say you? Will ye to this agree?

   Nob. I can no less, sir! for he is worse than the Turk,
Which none other ways but by tyranny doth work.
This bloody butcher, with his pernicious bait,
Oppress Christian princes by fraud, craft, and deceit,
Till he compel them to kiss his pestilent feet,
Like a leviathan sitting in Moses' seat.
I think we can do unto God no sacrifice
That is more accept, nor more agreeing to justice,
Than to slay that beast and slaughterman of the devil,
That Babylon boar, which hath done so much evil.

   Imp. Maj. It is a clear sign of a true Nobility,
To the Word of God when your conscience doth agree;

For, as Christ did say to Peter: *Caro et sanguis*
Non revelavit tibi, sed Pater meus celestis:[1]
Ye have not this gift of carnal generation,
Nor of noble blood, but by God's own demonstration—
Of you, Civil Order, one sentence would I hear.

   C. Order. I rue it that ever any heart I did him bear.
I think he hath sprung out of the bottomless pit;
And, in men's conscience, in the stead of God doth sit;
Blowing forth a swarm of grasshoppers and flies—
Monks, friars, and priests—that all truth putrefies.
Of the Christian faith, play now the true defender!
Exile this monster and ravenous devourer!
With his venom worms, his adders, whelps, and snakes,
His cucculled vermin that unto all mischief wakes.

   Imp. Maj. Then, in this purpose, ye are all of one mind?

   Clergy. We detest the Pope, and abhor him to the fiend.

   Imp. Maj. And ye are well content to disobey his pride?

   Nob. Yea, and his lousy laws and decrees to set aside.

   Imp. Maj. Then must ye be sworn to take me for your
   head.

   C. Order. We will obey you, as our governor, in God's
   stead.

   Imp. Maj. Now that ye are sworn unto me, your principal,
I charge ye to regard the word of God over all;
And, in that, alone to rule, to speak and to judge,
As ye will have me your succour and refuge.

   Clergy. If ye will make sure, ye must exile Sedition,
False Dissimulation, with all vain superstition;
And put Private Wealth out of the monasteries;
Then, Usurped Power may go a-birding for flies.

   Imp. Maj. Take you it in hand, and do your true diligence:
Each man for his part; ye shall want no assistance.

   Clergy. I promise you here to exile Usurped Power,
And your supremacy to defend each day and hour.

   Nob. I promise also out of the monasteries
To put Private Wealth, and detect his mysteries.

   [1] 'Flesh and blood hath not revealed it unto thee, but my Father
which is in heaven' (Matthew xvi. 17).

C. Order. False Dissimulation I will hang up in Smith-
    field,
With such superstition as your people hath beguiled.

Imp. Maj. Then I trust we are at a very good conclusion—
Virtue to have place, and vice to have confusion.
Take Verity with ye for every act ye do;
So shall ye be sure not out of the way to go.

Sedition intrat.[1]

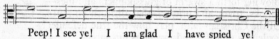

    Peep! I see ye!   I am glad I have spied ye!

Nob. There is Sedition: stand you aside awhile;
Ye shall see how we shall catch him by a wile.

Sedit. No noise among ye? where is the merry cheer
That was wont to be, with quaffing of double beer?
The world is not yet as some men would it have;
I have been abroad, and I think I have played the knave.

C. Order. Thou canst do none other, except thou change
    thy wont.

Sedit. What mischief ail ye that ye are to me so blunt?
I have seen the day ye have favoured me, Perfection.

Clergy. Thyself is not he, thou art of another com-
    plexion—
Sir! this is the thief that first subdued King John,
Vexing other princes that since have ruled this region;
And now he doth prate he hath so played the knave,
That the world is not yet as some men would it have—
It would be known, sir! what he hath done of late.

Imp. Maj. What is thy name, friend? to us here intimate!

Sedit. A sanct'ary! a sanct'ary! for God's dear passion,
    a sanct'ary!
Is there none will hold me? and I have made so many!

Imp. Maj. Tell me what thy name is! Thou playest the
    knave, I trow!

Sedit. I am windless, good man! I have much pain to
    blow.

               [1] 'Sedition enters.'

Imp. Maj. I say, tell thy name, or the rack shall thee constrain!

Sedit. Holy Perfection my godmother called me, plain!

Nob. It is Sedition; God give him a very mischief!

C. Order. Under heaven is not a more detestable thief.

Sedit. By the mass, ye lie! I see well ye do not know me.

Imp. Maj. Ah, brother! art thou come? I am right glad we have thee.

Sedit. By body, blood, bones, and soul! I am not he!

Clergy. If swearing might help he would do we[ll] enough.

Imp. Maj. He 'scape not our hands so lightly, I warrant you!

Clergy. This is that thief, sir! that all Christendom hath troubled;
And the Pope of Rome against all kings maintained.

Nob. Now that ye have him, no more! but hang him up!

C. Order. If ye so be content, it shall be done ere I sup.

Imp. Maj. Lo! the Clergy accuseth thee; Nobility condemneth thee;
And the Law will hang thee. What sayst now to me?

Sedit. I would I were now at Rome at the Sign of the Cup;
For heaviness is dry. Alas! must I needs climb up?
Pardon my life, and I shall tell ye all;
Both that is past, and that will hereafter fall.

Imp. Maj. Arise! I pardon thee, so that thou tell the truth.

Sedit. I will tell to you such treason as ensueth—
Yet a ghostly father ought not to bewray confession.

Imp. Maj. No confession is but ought to discover treason.

Sedit. I think it may keep all thing, save heresy.

Imp. Maj. It may hold no treason, I tell thee verily!
And, therefore, tell the whole matter by and by.
Thou saidst now of late that thou hadst played the knave,
And that the world was not as some men would it have.

Sedit. I could play Pasquil, but I fear to have rebuke.

Imp. Maj. For uttering the truth, fear neither bishop nor duke!

Sedit. Ye gave injunctions that God's word might be
　　taught;
But who observe them? full many a time have I laught
To see the conveyance that prelates and priests can find.

　　Imp. Maj. And why do they bear God's word no better
　　mind?

　　Sedit. For, if that were known, then would the people
　　regard
No head but their prince: with the Church then were it hard;
Then should I lack help to maintain their estate,
As I attempted, in the North, but now of late;
And since that same time in other places, beside,
Till my setters-on were of their purpose wide.
A vengeance take it! it was never well with me
Since the coming hither of that same Verity!
Yet do the bishops for my sake vex him among.

　　Imp. Maj. Do they so indeed? well! they shall not do so
　　long.

　　Sedit. In your parliament, command you what ye will,
The Pope's ceremonies shall drown the Gospel still.
Some of the bishops at your injunctions sleep;
Some laugh, and go by; and some can play bo-peep.
Some of them do nought but search for heretics
Whilst their priests abroad do play the schismatics.
Tell me! in London, how many their oaths discharge
Of the curates there? yet is it much worse at large.
If your true subjects impugn their treacheries,
They can fetch them in anon for Sacramentaries,
Or Anabaptists: thus find they a subtle shift
To prop up their kingdom: such is their wily drift.
Get they false witnesses, they force not of whence they be—
Be they of Newgate, or be they of the Marshalsea.
Peradventure, a thousand are in one bishop's book;
And, against a day, are ready to the hook.

　　Imp. Maj. Are those matters true that thou hast spoken
　　here?

　　Sedit. What can, in the world, more evident witness
　　bear?

First of all, consider the prelates do not preach;
But persecute those that the holy Scriptures teach:
And, mark me this well! they never punish for popery,
But the Gospel-readers they handle very coarsely;
For, on them, they lay by hundred pounds of iron,
And will suffer none with them once for to common.
Sit they never so long, nothing by them cometh forth
To the truth's furtherance that anything is worth.
In some bishops' house ye shall not find a Testament;
But each man ready to devour the innocent.
We linger a time, and look but for a day
To set up the Pope, if the Gospel would decay.

 Clergy. Of that he hath told hisself is the very ground.

 Imp. Maj. Art thou of counsel in this that thou hast
  spoken?

 Sedit. Yea, and in more than that, if all secrets might be
  broken:
For the Pope I make so much as ever I may do.

 Imp. Maj. I pray thee, heartily, tell me why thou dost so?

 Sedit. For I perceive well the Pope is a jolly fellow,
A trim fellow, a rich fellow; yea, and merry fellow.

 Imp. Maj. A jolly fellow! how dost thou prove the Pope?

 Sedit. For he hath crosskeys with a triple crown and a
  cope,
Trim as a trencher, having his shoes of gold;
Rich in his royalty, and angelic to behold.

 Imp. Maj. How dost thou prove him to be a fellow mirry?

 Sedit. He hath pipes and bells, with Kyrie! kyrie! kyrie!
Of him ye may buy both salt, cream, oil, and wax;
And, after High Mass, ye may learn to bear the pax.

 Imp. Maj. Yea! and nothing hear of the 'pistle and the
  gospel?

 Sedit. No, sir, by the mass! he will give no such counsel.

 Imp. Maj. When thou art abroad, where dost thou
  lodging take?

 Sedit. Among such people as God did never make:
Not only cuckolds, but such as follow the Pope's laws
In disguised coats, with bald crowns like jack daws.

Imp. Maj. Then everywhere thou art the Pope's altogether.

Sedit. Ye had proved it ere this if I had not chanced
hither.
I sought to have served you like as I did King John,
But that Verity stopped me—the devil him poison!

Nob. He is worthy to die and there were men no more.

C. Order. Hang up the vile knave, and keep him no
longer in store!

Imp. Maj. Draw him to Tyburn: let him be hanged and
quartered!

Sedit. Why, of late days, ye said I should not be so
martyred—
Where is the pardon that ye did promise me?

Imp. Maj. For doing more harm thou shalt soon pardoned
be.
Have him forth, Civil Order! and hang him till he be dead;
And, on London Bridge, look ye bestow his head.

C. Order. I shall see it done and return to you again.

Sedit. I beshrew your heart for taking so much pain!
Some man tell the Pope, I beseech ye, with all my heart:
How I am ordered for taking the Church's part,
That I may be put in the holy litany
With Thomas Becket, for I think I am as worthy.
Pray to me with candles, for I am a saint already.
O blessed Saint Patrick! I see thee, I, verily!

[Exit.]

Imp. Maj. I see by this wretch there hath been much
fault in ye:
Show yourselves hereafter more sober and wise to be!
King John ye subdued, for that he punished treason,
Rape, theft and murder, in the holy spiritualty:
But Thomas Becket ye exalted without reason,
Because that he died for the Church's wanton liberty,
That the priests might do all kinds of iniquity,
And be unpunished. Mark now the judgment
Of your idle brains; and, for God's love, repent!

Nob. As God shall judge me I repent me of my rudeness.

Clergy. I am ashamed of my most vain foolishness.

Nob. I consider now that God hath for Sedition
Sent punishments great: examples we have in Brute,
In Catiline, in Cassius, and fair Absalom;
Whom, of their purpose, God always destitute;
And terrible plagues on them did execute
For their rebellion. And, therefore, I will beware
Lest His great vengeance trap me in suchlike snare.

Clergy. I ponder also that, since the time of Adam,
The Lord evermore the governors preserved:
Examples we find in Noe and in Abraham,
In Moses and David, from whom God never swerved.
I will, therefore, obey lest He be with me displeased.
Homerus doth say that God putteth forth His shield
The prince to defend when he is in the field.

C. Order. This also I mark: when the priests had govern-
    ance
Over the Hebrews, the sects did first arise:
As Pharisees, Sadducees, and Esse[n]es, which wrought much
    grievance
Among the people by their most devilish practice;
Till destructions the princes did devise,
To the quietness of their faithful commons all,
As your grace hath done with the sects papistical.

Imp. Maj. That point hath, in time, fallen to your mem-
    ories.
The Anabaptists, a sect new risen of late,
The Scriptures poisoneth with their subtle allegories,
The heads to subdue after a seditious rate—
The city of Münster was lost through their debate.
They have here begun their pestilent seeds to sow;
But, we trust in God, to increase they shall not grow.

Clergy. God forbid they should! for they might do much
    harm.

C. Order. We shall cut them short if they do hither
    swarm.

Imp. Maj. The administration of a prince's governance.
Is the gift of God, and His high ordinance;

Whom, with all your power, you three ought to support
In the laws of God, to all his people's comfort.
First you, the Clergy, in preaching of God's word;
Then you, Nobility, defending with the sword;
You, Civil Order, in executing justice.
Thus, I trust, we shall seclude all manner of vice;
And, after we have established our kingdom
In peace of the Lord and in His godly freedom,
We will confirm it with wholesome laws and decrees,
To the full suppressing of Antichrist's vanities.

                      Hic omnes rex osculatur.[1]

Farewell to ye all! first to you, Nobility!
Then to you, Clergy! then to you, Civility!
And above all things remember our injunction!
Omnes una.[2] By the help of God each one shall do his
    function!

                        [*Exit Imp. Majesty.*]

   Nob. By this example ye may see, with your eyes,
How Antichrist's whelps have noble princes used.
Again, ye may see how they, with prodigious lies,
And crafts uncomely, their mischiefs have excused:
Both nature, manhood, and grace they have abused,
Defiling the law and blinding Nobility—
No Christian region from their abusions free.

   Clergy. Mark well the damnable bestowing of their
    masses,
With their foundations for poisoning of their king!
Their confession-drifts all other traitory passes:
A saint the[y] can make of the most knave this day living,
Helping their market; and, to promote the thing,
He shall do miracles; but he that blemish their glory
Shall be sent to hell without any remedy!

   C. Order. Here was to be seen what riseth of Sedition;
And how he doth take his maintenance and ground
Of idle persons, brought up in superstition;
Whose daily practice is always to confound

                [1] 'Here the King kisses them all.'
                [2] 'All in unison.'

Such as mindeth virtue and to them will not be bound.
Expedient it is to know their pestilent ways,
Considering they were so busy now of late days.

   Nob. England hath a Queen, thanks to the Lord above!
Which may be a light to other princes all,
For the godly ways whom she doth daily move
To her liege people, through God's word special.
She is that angel, as Saint John doth him call,
That with the Lord's seal doth mark out His true servants,
Printing in their hearts His holy words and covenants.

   Clergy. In Daniel's spirit she hath subdued the papists,
With all the offspring of Antichrist's generation;
And now, of late days, the sect of Anabaptists
She seeketh to suppress for their pestiferous fashion.
She vanquisheth also the great abomination
Of superstitions, witchcrafts, and idolatry,
Restoring God's honour to His first force and beauty.

   C. Order. Pray unto the Lord that her grace may continue
The days of Nestor, to our souls' consolation;
And that her offspring may live also to subdue
The great Antichrist, with his whole generation,
In Helias' spirit to the comfort of this nation:
Also to preserve her most honourable Council,
To the praise of God and glory of the Gospel!

PRETIUM XX^s.

THUS ENDETH THE TWO PLAYS OF KING JOHN.

THE
RAIGNE OF
KING EDVVARD
the third:

As it hath bin sundrie times plaied about
the Citie of London.

LONDON,
Printed for Cuthbert Burby.
1596.

[DRAMATIS PERSONÆ

EDWARD THE THIRD, King of England
EDWARD, Prince of Wales, his Son
EARL OF WARWICK
EARL OF DERBY
EARL OF SALISBURY
LORD AUDLEY
LORD PERCY
LODWICK, Edward's Confidant
SIR WILLIAM MOUNTAGUE
SIR JOHN COPLAND
Two Esquires, and a Herald, English
ROBERT, styling himself Earl, of Artois
LORD MOUNTFORD (or MONTFORT)
GOBIN DE GREY
JOHN, King of France
CHARLES, } his Sons
PHILIP,
DUKE OF LORRAINE
VILLIERS, a French Lord
King of Bohemia } Aids to King John
A Polish Captain
Two Citizens of Calais
A Captain, and a poor Inhabitant, of the same
Another Captain; a Mariner
Three Heralds, and four other Frenchmen
DAVID, King of Scotland
EARL DOUGLAS
Two Messengers, Scotch
PHILIP, Edward's Queen
COUNTESS OF SALISBURY
A French Woman

    Lords, and divers other Attendants; Heralds
        Officers, Soldiers, etc.

SCENE—Dispersed; in ENGLAND, FLANDERS, and FRANCE]

THE REIGN OF KING EDWARD
THE THIRD

[ACT I

SCENE I

London. A Room of State in the Palace.]

*Enter King Edward, Derby, Prince Edward, Audley, and
Artois.*

K. Ed. Robert of Artois, banish'd though thou be
From France, thy native country, yet with us
Thou shalt retain as great a signiory;
For we create thee Earl of Richmond here.
And now go forwards with our pedigree;
Who next succeeded Philip Le Beau?
Art. Three sons of his; which all, successively,
Did sit upon their father's regal throne,
Yet died and left no issue of their loins.
K. Ed. But was my mother sister unto those?
Art. She was, my lord; and only Isabel
Was all the daughters that this Philip had:
Whom afterward your father took to wife;
And, from the fragrant garden of her womb,
Your gracious self, the flower of Europe's hope,
Derived is inheritor to France.
But note the rancour of rebellious minds.
When thus the lineage of Le Beau was out,
The French obscur'd your mother's privilege;
And, though she were the next of blood, proclaim'd
John, of the house of Valois, now their king:
The reason was, they say, the realm of France,
Replete with princes of great parentage,
Ought not admit a governor to rule
Except he be descended of the male;

And that's the special ground of their contempt
Wherewith they study to exclude your grace:
But they shall find that forged ground of theirs
To be but dusty heaps of brittle sand.
Perhaps it will be thought a heinous thing
That I, a Frenchman, should discover this:
But Heaven I call to record of my vows;
It is not hate nor any private wrong,
But love unto my country and the right,
Provokes my tongue thus lavish in report:
You are the lineal watchman of our peace,
And John of Valois indirectly climbs:
What then should subjects, but embrace their king?
Ah, wherein may our duty more be seen,
Than striving to rebate a tyrant's pride
And place the true shepherd of our commonwealth?

K. Ed. This counsel, Artois, like to fruitful showers,
Hath added growth unto my dignity:
And, by the fiery vigour of thy words,
Hot courage is engenderd in my breast,
Which heretofore was rack'd in ignorance,
But now doth mount with golden wings of fame,
And will approve fair Isabel's descent
Able to yoke their stubborn necks with steel
That spurn against my sov'reignty in France.—

Sound a horn.

A messenger?—Lord Audley, know from whence.

Enter a messenger, Lorraine

Aud. The Duke of Lorraine, having cross'd the seas,
Entreats he may have conference with your highness.

K. Ed. Admit him, lords, that we may hear the news.—
Say, Duke of Lorraine, wherefore art thou come?

Lor. The most renowned prince, K[ing] John of France,
Doth greet thee, Edward: and by me commands,
That, for so much as by his liberal gift
The Guyenne dukedom is entail'd to thee,
Thou do him lowly homage for the same:

And, for that purpose, here I summon thee
Repair to France within these forty days,
That there, according as the custom is,
Thou may'st be sworn true liegeman to our king;
Or, else thy title in that province dies,
And he himself will repossess the place.

K. Ed. See, how occasion laughs me in the face!
No sooner minded to prepare for France,
But straight I am invited, nay, with threats,
Upon a penalty, enjoin'd to come:
'Twere but a childish part to say him nay.—
Lorraine, return this answer to thy lord:
I mean to visit him, as he requests;
But how? not servilely dispos'd to bend,
But like a conqueror, to make him bow.
His lame unpolish'd shifts are come to light,
And truth hath pull'd the vizard from his face
That set a gloss upon his arrogance.
Dare he command a fealty in me?
Tell him, the crown, that he usurps, is mine,
And where he sets his foot, he ought to kneel:
'Tis not a petty dukedom that I claim,
But all the whole dominions of the realm;
Which if with grudging he refuse to yield,
I'll take away those borrow'd plumes of his
And send him naked to the wilderness.

Lor. Then, Edward, here, in spite of all thy lords,
I do pronounce defiance to thy face.

Pr. Ed. Defiance, Frenchman? we rebound it back,
Even to the bottom of thy master's throat:
And,—be it spoke with reverence of the king
My gracious father, and these other lords,—
I hold thy message but as scurrilous,
And him that sent thee, like the lazy drone
Crept up by stealth unto the eagle's nest;
From whence we'll shake him with so rough a
    storm,
As others shall be warned by his harm.

War. Bid him leave off the lion's case he wears,
    Lest, meeting with the lion in the field,
    He chance to tear him piecemeal for his pride.
Art. The soundest counsel I can give his grace
    Is to surrender ere he be constrain'd.
    A voluntary mischief hath less scorn,
    Than when reproach with violence is borne.
Lor. Degenerate traitor, viper to the place
    Where thou wast foster'd in thine infancy,
    Bear'st thou a part in this conspiracy? *He draws his sword.*
K. Ed. Lorraine, behold the sharpness of this steel:
                                        [*Drawing his.*]
    Fervent desire, that sits against my heart,
    Is far more thorny-pricking than this blade;
    That, with the nightingale, I shall be scar'd,
    As oft as I dispose myself to rest,
    Until my colours be display'd in France.
    This is thy final answer; so be gone.
Lor. It is not that, nor any English brave,
    Afflicts me so, as doth his poison'd view,
    That is most false, should most of all be true.
                                        [*Exeunt Lorraine.*]
K. Ed. Now, Lord, our fleeting bark is under sail;
    Our gage is thrown, and war is soon begun,
    But not so quickly brought unto an end.—

                    Enter Mountague.

    But wherefore comes Sir William Mountague?
    How stands the league between the Scot and us?
Moun. Crack'd and dissever'd, my renowned lord.
    The treacherous king no sooner was inform'd
    Of your withdrawing of your army back,
    But straight, forgetting of his former oath,
    He made invasion on the bordering towns.
    Berwick is won; Newcastle spoil'd and lost;
    And now the tyrant hath begirt with siege
    The castle of Roxborough, where enclos'd
    The Countess Salisbury is like to perish.

K. Ed. That is thy daughter, Warwick—is it not?—
　Whose husband hath in Britain serv'd so long,
　About the planting of Lord Mountford there?
War. It is, my lord.
K. Ed. Ignoble David! hast thou none to grieve,
　But silly ladies, with thy threat'ning arms?
　But I will make you shrink your snaily horns.—
　First, therefore, Audley, this shall be thy charge;
　Go levy footmen for our wars in France:
　And, Ned, take muster of our men at arms:
　In every shire elect a several band.
　Let them be soldiers of a lusty spirit,
　Such as dread nothing but dishonour's blot:
　Be wary therefore; since we do commence
　A famous war and with so mighty a nation.
　Derby, be thou ambassador for us.
　Unto our father-in-law, the Earl of Hainault:
　Make him acquainted with our enterprise;
　And likewise will him, with our own allies
　That are in Flanders, to solicit to
　The Emperor of Almaine in our name.
　Myself, whilst you are jointly thus employ'd,
　Will, with these forces that I have at hand,
　March and once more repulse the trait'rous Scot.
　But, sirs, be resolute; we shall have wars
　On every side: and, Ned, thou must begin
　Now to forget thy study and thy books
　And ure thy shoulders to an armour's weight.
Pr. Ed. As cheerful sounding to my youthful spleen
　This tumult is of war's increasing broils,
　As at the coronation of a king
　The joyful clamours of the people are
　When, 'Ave, Cæsar!' they pronounce aloud.
　Within this school of honour I shall learn,
　Either to sacrifice my foes to death
　Or in a rightful quarrel spend my breath.
　Then cheerfully forward, each a several way;
　In great affairs 'tis naught to use delay.　　　*Exeunt.*

[SCENE II

Roxborough. Before the Castle.]

Enter the Countess [above].

[*Count.*] Alas, how much in vain my poor eyes gaze
 For succour that my sovereign should send!
 Ah, cousin Mountague, I fear, thou want'st
 The lively spirit sharply to solicit
 With vehement suit the king in my behalf:
 Thou dost not tell him, what a grief it is
 To be the scornful captive to a Scot;
 Either to be woo'd with broad untuned oaths,
 Or forc'd by rough insulting barbarism:
 Thou dost not tell him, if he here prevail,
 How much they will deride us in the north;
 And, in their wild, uncivil, skipping jigs,
 Bray forth their conquest and our overthrow,
 Even in the barren, bleak, and fruitless air.

Enter David and Douglas, Lorraine.

I must withdraw; the everlasting foe
 Comes to the wall: I'll closely step aside,
 And list their babble, blunt and full of pride.
K. *Dav.* My Lord of Lorraine, to our brother of
  France
 Commend us, as the man in Christendom
 Whom we most reverence and entirely love.
 Touching your embassage, return and say
 That we with England will not enter parley
 Nor never make fair weather or take truce,
 But burn their neighbour towns, and so persist
 With eager rods beyond their city York.
 And never shall our bonny riders rest,
 Nor rusting canker have the time to eat
 Their light-borne snaffles nor their nimble spurs;
 Nor lay aside their jacks of gymold mail;
 Nor hang their staves of grained Scottish ash

In peaceful wise upon their city walls;
Nor from their button'd tawny leathern belts
Dismiss their biting whinyards, till your king
Cry out, 'Enough; spare England now for pity.'
Farewell, and tell him, that you leave us here
Before this castle; say, you came from us
Even when we had that yielded to our hands.

Lor. I take my leave, and fairly will return
Your acceptable greeting to my king.

Exit Lor.

K. Dav. Now, Douglas, to our former task again,
For the division of this certain spoil.

Doug. My liege, I crave the lady, and no more.

K. Dav. Nay, soft ye, sir, first I must make my choice;
And first I do bespeak her for myself.

Doug. Why, then, my liege, let me enjoy her jewels.

K. Dav. Those are her own, still liable to her,
And, who inherits her, hath those withal.

Enter a Scot in haste.

Mess. My liege, as we were pricking on the hills,
To fetch in booty, marching hitherward
We might descry a mighty host of men;
The sun, reflecting on the armour, show'd
A field of plate, a wood of pikes advanc'd.
Bethink your highness speedily herein:
An easy march within four hours will bring
The hindmost rank unto this place, my liege.

K. Dav. Dislodge, dislodge, it is the King of England.

Doug. Jemmy my man, saddle my bonny black.

K. Dav. Mean'st thou to fight, Douglas? We are too
weak.

Doug. I know it well, my liege, and therefore fly.

Count. My lords of Scotland, will ye stay and drink?

K. Dav. She mocks at us; Douglas, I can't endure it.

Count. Say, good my lord, which is he, must have the
lady,
And which, her jewels? I am sure, my lords,

Ye will not hence, till you have shar'd the spoils.
K. Dav. She heard the messenger and heard our talk;
And now that comfort makes her scorn at us.

Another messenger.

Mess. Arm, my good lord! O, we are all surpris'd!
[*Count.*] After the French ambassador, my liege,
And tell him that you dare not ride to York;
Excuse it, that your bonny horse is lame.
K. Dav. She heard that too; intolerable grief!—
Woman, farewell: although I do not stay,—

Exeunt Scots.

Count. 'Tis not for fear, and yet you run away.—
O happy comfort, welcome to our house!
The confident and boist'rous boasting Scot,—
That swore before my walls, they would not back
For all the armed power of this land,—
With faceless fear that ever turns his back,
Turn'd hence again the blasting north-east wind
Upon the bare report and name of arms.

Enter Mountague.

O summer's day! see where my cousin comes.
Moun. How fares my aunt? we are not Scots;
Why do you shut your gates against your friends?
Count. Well may I give a welcome, cousin, to thee,
For thou com'st well to chase my foes from hence.
Moun. The king himself is come in person hither;
Dear aunt, descend, and gratulate his highness.
Count. How may I entertain his majesty,
To show my duty and his dignity?

[*Exit, from above.*]

Enter King Edward, Warwick, Artois, with others.

K. Ed. What, are the stealing foxes fled and gone
Before we could uncouple at their heels?
War. They are, my liege; but, with a cheerful cry,
Hot hounds and hardy chase them at the heels.

Enter Countess.

K. Ed. This is the countess, Warwick, is it not?

War. Even she, my liege; whose beauty tyrant's fear,
  As a May blossom with pernicious winds,
  Hath sullied, wither'd, overcast, and done.

K. Ed. Hath she been fairer, Warwick, than she is?

War. My gracious king, fair is she not at all,
  If that herself were by to stain herself,
  As I have seen her when she was herself.

K. Ed. What strange enchantment lurk'd in those her eyes
  When they excell'd this excellence they have,
  That now her dim decline hath power to draw
  My subject eyes from piercing majesty
  To gaze on her with doting admiration?

Count. In duty lower than the ground I kneel
  And for my dull knees bow my feeling heart,
  To witness my obedience to your highness;
  With many millions of a subject's thanks
  For this your royal presence, whose approach
  Hath driven war and danger from my gate.

K. Ed. Lady, stand up: I come to bring thee peace,
  However thereby I have purchas'd war.

Count. No war to you, my liege; the Scots are gone,
  And gallop home toward Scotland with their hate.

[*K. Ed.*] Lest yielding here I pine in shameful love,
  Come, we'll pursue the Scots;—Artois, away!

Count. A little while, my gracious sovereign, stay
  And let the power of a mighty king
  Honour our roof; my husband in the wars,
  When he shall hear it, will triumph for joy:
  Then, dear my liege, now niggard not thy state;
  Being at the wall, enter our homely gate.

K. Ed. Pardon me, countess, I will come no[t] near;
  I dream'd to-night of treason, and I fear.

Count. Far from this place let ugly treason lie!

K. Ed. No farther off than her conspiring eye,
  Which shoots infected poison in my heart

Beyond repulse of wit or cure of art.
Now in the sun alone it doth not lie
With light to take light from a mortal eye;
For here two day-stars, that mine eyes would see,
More than the sun, steals mine own light from me.
Contemplative desire! desire to be
In contemplation, that may master thee!
Warwick, Artois, to horse, and let's away!

Count. What might I speak, to make my sovereign stay?

K. Ed. What needs a tongue to such a speaking eye
That more persuades than winning oratory?

Count. Let not thy presence, like the April sun,
Flatter our earth and suddenly be done.
More happy do not make our outward wall.
Than thou wilt grace our inner house withal.
Our house, my liege, is like a country swain,
Whose habit rude and manners blunt and plain
Presageth nought, yet inly beautified
With bounty's riches and fair hidden pride:
For, where the golden ore doth buried lie,
The ground, undeck'd with nature's tapestry,
Seems barren, sere, unfertile, fruitless, dry;
And where the upper turf of earth doth boast
His pride, perfumes and parti-colour'd cost,
Delve there, and find this issue and their pride
To spring from ordure and corruption's side.
But, to make up my all too long compare,
These ragged walls no testimony are
What is within; but, like a cloak, doth hide,
From weather's waste, the under-garnish'd pride.
More gracious than my terms can let thee be,
Intreat thyself to stay a while with me.

K. Ed. As wise as fair; what fond fit can be heard
When wisdom keeps the gate as beauty's guard?—
Countess, albeit my business urgeth me,
It shall attend while I attend on thee.—
Come on, my lords, here will I host to-night.

Exeunt.

[ACT II

SCENE I

The same. Gardens of the Castle.]

[Enter Lodwick.]

Lod. I might perceive his eye in her eye lost,
　　His ear to drink her sweet tongue's utterance;
　　And changing passion, like inconstant clouds
　　That rack upon the carriage of the winds,
　　Increase and die in his disturbed cheeks.
　　Lo, when she blush'd, even then did he look pale,
　　As if her cheeks, by some enchanted power,
　　Attracted had the cherry blood from his:
　　Anon, with reverent fear when she grew pale,
　　His cheeks put on their scarlet ornaments,
　　But no more like her oriental red,
　　Than brick to coral or live things to dead.
　　Why did he then thus counterfeit her looks?
　　If she did blush, 'twas tender modest shame,
　　Being in the sacred presence of a king;
　　If he did blush, 'twas red immodest shame,
　　To vail his eyes amiss, being a king:
　　If she look'd pale, 'twas silly woman's fear,
　　To bear herself in presence of a king;
　　If he look'd pale, it was with guilty fear,
　　To dote amiss, being a mighty king:
　　Then, Scottish wars, farewell! I fear, 'twill prove
　　A ling'ring English siege of peevish love.
　　Here comes his highness, walking all alone.

Enter King Edward.

K. Ed. She is grown more fairer far since I came hither;
　　Her voice more silver every word than other,
　　Her wit more fluent: what a strange discourse
　　Unfolded she of David and his Scots!

'Even thus,' quoth she, 'he spake,'—and then spoke
  broad,
With epithets and accents of the Scot;
But somewhat better than the Scot could speak:
'And thus,' quoth she,—and answer'd then herself;
For who could speak like her? but she herself
Breathes from the wall an angel's note from heaven
Of sweet defiance to her barbarous foes.
When she would talk of peace, methinks, her tongue
Commanded war to prison; when of war,
It waken'd Cæsar from his Roman grave,
To hear war beautified by her discourse.
Wisdom is foolishness, but in her tongue,
Beauty a slander, but in her fair face:
There is no summer, but in her cheerful looks,
Nor frosty winter, but in her disdain.
I cannot blame the Scots that did besiege her,
For she is all the treasure of our land;
But call them cowards, that they ran away,
Having so rich and fair a cause to stay.—
Art thou there, Lodwick? give me ink and paper.
Lod. I will, my liege.
K. Ed. And bid the lords hold on their play at chess,
  For we will walk and meditate alone.
Lod. I will, my sovereign.   [*Exit.*]
K. Ed. This fellow is well read in poetry
  And hath a lusty and persuasive spirit:
  I will acquaint him with my passion;
  Which he shall shadow with a veil of lawn,
  Through which the queen of beauty's queens shall
    see.
  Herself the ground of my infirmity.—

Enter Lodwick.

Hast thou pen, ink, and paper ready, Lodwick?
Lod. Ready, my liege.
K. Ed. Then in the summer arbour sit by me,
  Make it our council-house, or cabinet;

Since green our thoughts, green be the conventicle
Where we will ease us by disburd'ning them.
Now, Lodwick, invocate some golden muse
To bring thee hither an enchanted pen
That may, for sighs, set down true sighs indeed;
Talking of grief, to make thee ready groan;
And, when thou writ'st of tears, encouch the word,
Before and after, with such sweet laments,
That it may raise drops in a Tartar's eye,
And make a flint-heart Scythian pitiful:
For so much moving hath a poet's pen;
Then, if thou be a poet, move thou so,
And be enriched by thy sovereign's love.
For, if the touch of sweet concordant strings
Could force attendance in the ears of hell;
How much more shall the strains of poet's wit
Beguile and ravish soft and human minds?

Lod. To whom, my lord, shall I direct my style?

K. Ed. To one that shames the fair and sots the wise;
   Whose body is an abstract or a brief,
   Contains each general virtue in the world.
   Better than beautiful, thou must begin;
   Devise for fair a fairer word than fair;
   And every ornament, that thou wouldst praise,
   Fly it a pitch above the soar of praise:
   For flattery fear thou not to be convicted;
   For, were thy admiration ten times more,
   Ten times ten thousand more the worth exceeds,
   Of that thou art to praise, thy praise's worth.
   Begin, I will to contemplate the while:
   Forget not to set down, how passionate,
   How heart-sick, and how full of languishment,
   Her beauty makes me.

Lod.   Write I to a woman?

K. Ed. What beauty else could triumph over me;
   Or who, but women, do our love-lays greet?
   What, think'st thou I did bid thee praise a horse?

Lod. Of what condition or estate she is,

'Twere requisite that I should know, my lord.

K. Ed. Of such estate, that hers is as a throne,
And my estate the footstool where she treads:
Then may'st thou judge what her condition is,
By the proportion of her mightiness.
Write on, while I peruse her in my thoughts.
Her voice to music, or the nightingale:
To music every summer-leaping swain
Compares his sun-burnt lover when she speaks:
And why should I speak of the nightingale?
The nightingale sings of adulterate wrong;
And that, compar'd, is too satirical:
For sin, though sin, would not be so esteem'd;
But, rather, virtue sin, sin virtue deem'd.
Her hair, far softer than the silkworm's twist,
Like to a flattering glass, doth make more fair
The yellow amber: 'like a flattering glass'
Comes in too soon; for, writing of her eyes,
I'll say, that like a glass they catch the sun,
And thence the hot reflection doth rebound
Against my breast, and burns my heart within.
Ah, what a world of descant makes my soul
Upon this voluntary ground of love!—
Come, Lodwick, hast thou turn'd thy ink to gold?
If not, write but in letters capital
My mistress' name, and it will gild thy paper.
Read, lord, read;
Fill thou the empty hollows of mine ears
With the sweet hearing of thy poetry.

Lod. I have not to a period brought her praise.

K. Ed. Her praise is as my love, both infinite,
Which apprehend such violent extremes
That they disdain an ending period.
Her beauty hath no match but my affection;
Hers more than most, mine most, and more than
    more:
Hers more to praise than tell the sea by drops;
Nay, more, than drop the massy earth by sands,

And, sand by sand, print them in memory:
Then wherefore talk'st thou of a period,
To that which craves unended admiration?
Read, let us hear.

Lod. 'More fair and chaste than is the queen of
  shades,'—

K. Ed. That line hath two faults, gross and palpable:
Compar'st thou her to the pale queen of night,
Who, being set in dark, seems therefore light?
What is she, when the sun lifts up his head,
But like a fading taper, dim and dead?
My love shall brave the eye of heaven at noon,
And, being unmask'd, outshine the golden sun.

Lod. What is the other fault, my sovereign lord?

K. Ed. Read o'er the line again.

Lod.   'More fair and chaste,'—

K. Ed. I did not bid thee talk of chastity,
To ransack so the treasure of her mind;
For I had rather have her chas'd, than chaste.
Out with the moon-line, I will none of it,
And let me have her liken'd to the sun:
Say, she hath thrice more splendour than the sun,
That her perfections emulates the sun,
That she breeds sweets as plenteous as the sun,
That she doth thaw cold winter like the sun,
That she doth cheer fresh summer like the sun,
That she doth dazzle gazers like the sun:
And, in this application to the sun,
Bid her be free and general as the sun;
Who smiles upon the basest weed that grows,
As lovingly as on the fragrant rose.
Let's see what follows that same moon-light line.

Lod. 'More fair and chaste than is the queen of shades;
More bold in constancy'—

K. Ed. In constancy! than who?

Lod.   —'than Judith was.'

K. Ed. O monstrous line! Put in the next a sword,
And I shall woo her to cut off my head.

Blot, blot, good Lodwick! Let us hear the next.

Lod. There's all that yet is done.

K. Ed. I thank thee then, thou hast done little ill;
But what is done, is passing passing ill.
No, let the captain talk of boist'rous war;
The prisoner, of immured dark constraint;
The sick man best sets down the pangs of death;
The man that starves, the sweetness of a feast;
The frozen soul, the benefit of fire;
And every grief, his happy opposite:
Love cannot sound well, but in lovers' tongues;
Give me the pen and paper, I will write.—

Enter Countess.

But, soft, here comes the treasurer of my spirit.—
Lodwick, thou know'st not how to draw a battle;
These wings, these flankers, and these squadrons
Argue in thee defective discipline:
Thou shouldst have plac'd this here, this other here.

Count. Pardon my boldness, my thrice-gracious lords;
Let my intrusion here be call'd my duty,
That comes to see my sovereign how he fares.

K. Ed. Go, draw the same, I tell thee in what form.

Lod. I go.   [*Exit.*]

Count. Sorry I am, to see my liege so sad:
What may thy subject do, to drive from thee
Thy gloomy consort, sullen melancholy?

K. Ed. Ah, lady, I am blunt, and cannot straw
The flowers of solace in a ground of shame:
Since I came hither, countess, I am wrong'd.

Count. Now, God forbid, that any in my house
Should think my sovereign wrong! Thrice-gentle king,
Acquaint me with your cause of discontent.

K. Ed. How near then shall I be to remedy?

Count. As near, my liege, as all my woman's power
Can pawn itself to buy thy remedy.

K. Ed. If thou speak'st true, then have I my redress:

Engage thy power to redeem my joys,
And I am joyful, countess; else, I die.

Count. I will, my liege.

K. Ed. Swear, countess, that thou wilt.

Count.   By Heaven, I will.

K. Ed. Then take thyself a little way aside,
And tell thyself, a king doth dote on thee:
Say that within thy power [it] doth lie
To make him happy, and that thou hast sworn
To give him all the joy within thy power:
Do this; and tell me, when I shall be happy.

Count. All this is done, my thrice-dread sovereign:
That power of love, that I have power to give,
Thou hast with all devout obedience;
Employ me how thou wilt in proof thereof.

K. Ed. Thou hear'st me say, that I do dote on thee.

Count. If on my beauty, take it if thou canst;
Though little, I do prize it ten times less:
If on my virtue, take it if thou canst;
For virtue's store by giving doth augment:
Be it on what it will, that I can give
And thou canst take away, inherit it.

K. Ed. It is thy beauty that I would enjoy.

Count. O, were it painted, I would wipe it off
And dispossess myself, to give it thee.
But, sovereign, it is solder'd to my life;
Take one, and both; for, like an humble shadow,
It haunts the sunshine of my summer's life.

K. Ed. But thou may'st leave it me, to sport withal.

Count. As easy may my intellectual soul
Be lent away, and yet my body live,
As lend my body, palace to my soul,
Away from her, and yet retain my soul.
My body is her bower, her court, her abbey,
And she an angel, pure, divine, unspotted;
If I should leave her house, my lord, to thee,
I kill my poor soul, and my poor soul me.

K. Ed. Didst thou not swear, to give me what I would?

Count. I did, my liege; so, what you would, I could.

K. Ed. I wish no more of thee than thou may'st give,
    Nor beg I do not, but I rather buy;
    That is, thy love; and, for that love of thine,
    In rich exchange, I tender to thee mine.

Count. But that your lips were sacred, my lord,
    You would profane the holy name of love.
    That love, you offer me, you cannot give,
    For Cæsar owes that tribute to his queen:
    That love, you beg of me, I cannot give,
    For Sara owes that duty to her lord.
    He that doth clip or counterfeit your stamp
    Shall die, my lord: and will your sacred self
    Commit high treason against the King of Heaven,
    To stamp his image in forbidden metal,
    Forgetting your allegiance and your oath?
    In violating marriage' sacred law,
    You break a greater honour than yourself:
    To be a king, is of a younger house
    Than to be married; your progenitor,
    Sole-reigning Adam on the universe,
    By God was honour'd for a married man,
    But not by him anointed for a king.
    It is a penalty to break your statutes,
    Though not enacted with your highness' hand:
    How much more, to infringe the holy act
    Made by the mouth of God, seal'd with his hand?
    I know, my sovereign—in my husband's love,
    Who now doth loyal service in his wars—
    Doth but to try the wife of Salisbury,
    Whether she will hear a wanton's tale, or no;
    Lest being therein guilty by my stay,
    From that, not from my liege, I turn away.

                        Exit.

K. Ed. Whether is her beauty by her words divine,
    Or are her words sweet chaplains to her beauty?
    Like as the wind doth beautify a sail,
    And as a sail becomes the unseen wind,

So do her words her beauty, beauty words.
O, that I were a honey-gathering bee,
To bear the comb of virtue from his flower;
And not a poison-sucking envious spider,
To turn the juice I take to deadly venom!
Religion is austere, and beauty gentle;
Too strict a guardian for so fair a ward.
O, that she were, as is the air, to me!
Why, so she is; for, when I would embrace her,
This do I, and catch nothing but myself.
I must enjoy her; for I cannot beat,
With reason and reproof, fond love away.

Enter Warwick.

Here comes her father: I will work with him,
To bear my colours in this field of love.
War. How is it, that my sovereign is so sad?
   May I with pardon know your highness' grief,
   And that my old endeavour will remove it,
   It shall not cumber long your majesty.
K. Ed. A kind and voluntary gift thou proffer'st,
   That I was forward to have begg'd of thee.
   But, O thou world, great nurse of flattery,
   Why dost thou tip men's tongues with golden
      words
   And peise their deeds with weight of heavy lead,
   That fair performance cannot follow promise?
   O, that a man might hold the heart's close book,
   And choke the lavish tongue when it doth utter
   The breath of falsehood not character'd there!
War. Far be it from the honour of my age
   That I should owe bright gold and render lead!
   Age is a cynic, not a flatterer:
   I say again, that, if I knew your grief,
   And that by me it may be lessened,
   My proper harm should buy your highness' good.
K. Ed. These are the vulgar tenders of false men,
   That never pay the duty of their words.

Thou wilt not stick to swear what thou hast said;
But, when thou know'st my grief's condition,
This rash-disgorged vomit of thy word
Thou wilt eat up again, and leave me helpless.

War. By Heaven, I will not, though your majesty
Did bid me run upon your sword and die.

[*K. Ed.*] Say, that my grief is no way med'cinable,
But by the loss and bruising of thine honour?

War. If nothing but that loss may vantage you,
I would account that loss my vantage too.

K. Ed. Think'st that thou canst unswear thy oath
again?

War. I cannot; nor I would not, if I could.

K. Ed. But, if thou dost, what shall I say to thee?

War. What may be said to any perjur'd villain
That breaks the sacred warrant of an oath.

K. Ed. What wilt thou say to one that breaks an oath?

War. That he hath broke his faith with God and man
And from them both stands excommunicate.

K. Ed. What office were it to suggest a man
To break a lawful and religious vow?

War. An office for the devil, not for man.

K. Ed. That devil's office must thou do for me;
Or break thy oath or cancel all the bonds
Of love and duty 'twixt thyself and me.
And therefore, Warwick, if thou art thyself,
The lord and master of thy word and oath,
Go to thy daughter, and in my behalf
Command her, woo her, win her any ways,
To be my mistress and my secret love.
I will not stand to hear thee make reply;
Thy oath breaks hers, or let thy sovereign die.

Exit.

War. O doting king! O detestable office!
Well may I tempt myself to wrong myself,
When he hath sworn me by the name of God
To break a vow made by the name of God.
What if I swear by this right hand of mine

To cut this right hand off? the better way
Were to profane the idol than confound it:
But neither will I do; I'll keep mine oath
And to my daughter make a recantation
Of all the virtue I have preach'd to her.
I'll say, she must forget her husband Salisbury,
If she remember to embrace the king;
I'll say, an oath may easily be broken,
But not so easily pardon'd, being broken;
I'll say, it is true charity to love,
But not true love to be so charitable;
I'll say, his greatness may bear out the shame,
But not his kingdom can buy out the sin;
I'll say, it is my duty to persuade,
But not her honesty to give consent.

Enter Countess

See, where she comes: was never father, had
Against his child an embassage so bad.
Count. My lord and father, I have sought for you:
My mother and the peers importune you
To keep in presence of his majesty
And do your best to make his highness merry.
War. How shall I enter in this graceless errand?
I must not call her child; for where's the father
That will, in such a suit, seduce his child?
Then, 'Wife of Salisbury',—shall I so begin?
No, he's my friend; and where is found the friend,
That will do friendship such endamagement?—
[*To the Countess.*] Neither my daughter, nor my dear
    friend's wife,
I am not Warwick, as thou think'st I am,
But an attorney from the court of hell;
That thus have hous'd my spirit in his form,
To do a message to thee from the king.
The mighty King of England dotes on thee:
He hath power to take away thy life
Hath power to take thine honour; then consent

To pawn thine honour, rather than thy life:
Honour is often lost and got again;
But life, once gone, hath no recovery.
The sun, that withers hay, doth nourish grass;
The king that would distain thee will advance thee.
The poets write that great Achilles' spear
Could heal the wound it made: the moral is,
What mighty men misdo, they can amend.
The lion doth become his bloody jaws
And grace his foragement, by being mild
When vassal fear lies trembling at his feet.
The king will in his glory hide thy shame;
And those that gaze on him to find out thee
Will lose their eyesight, looking in the sun.
What can one drop of poison harm the sea,
Whose hugy vastures can digest the ill
And make it lose his operation?
The king's great name will temper thy misdeeds,
And give the bitter potion of reproach
A sugar'd-sweet and most delicious taste:
Besides, it is no harm, to do the thing
Which without shame could not be left undone.
Thus have I, in his majesty's behalf,
Apparell'd sin in virtuous sentences,
And dwell upon thy answer in his suit.
Count. Unnatural besiege! Woe me unhappy,
    To have escap'd the danger of my foes
    And to be ten times worse envir'd by friends!
    Hath he no means to stain my honest blood,
    But to corrupt the author of my blood
    To be his scandalous and vile solicitor?
    No marvel, though the branches be then infected,
    When poison hath encompassed the root:
    No marvel, though the leprous infant die,
    When the stern dam envenometh the dug.
    Why then, give sin a passport to offend,
    And youth the dangerous rein of liberty:
    Blot out the strict forbidding of the law;

And cancel every canon, that prescribes
A shame for shame or penance for offence.
No, let me die, if this too boist'rous will
Will have it so, before I will consent
To be an actor in his graceless lust.

War. Why, now thou speak'st as I would have thee
    speak:
And mark how I unsay my words again.
An honourable grave is more esteem'd,
Than the polluted closet of a king:
The greater man, the greater is the thing,
Be it good or bad, that he shall undertake:
An unreputed mote, flying in the sun,
Presents a greater substance than it is:
The freshest summer's day both soonest taint
The loathed carrion that it seems to kiss:
Deep are the blows made with a mighty axe:
That sin doth ten times aggravate itself,
That is committed in a holy place:
An evil deed, done by authority,
Is sin and subornation: deck an ape
In tissue, and the beauty of the robe
Adds but the greater scorn unto the beast.
A spacious field of reasons could I urge
Between his glory, daughter, and thy shame:
That poison shows worst in a golden cup;
Dark night seems darker by the lightning-flash;
Lilies that fester smell far worse than weeds;
And every glory that inclines to sin,
The shame is treble by the opposite.
So leave I, with my blessing in thy bosom;
Which then convert to a most heavy curse,
When thou convert'st from honour's golden name
To the black faction of bed-blotting shame!

Count. I'll follow thee; and, when my mind turns so,
My body sink my soul in endless woe!

                        Exeunt.

[SCENE II

The same. A room in the castle.]

Enter at one door Derby from France: at another door Audley with a drum.

Der. Thrice-noble Audley, well encounter'd here:
　How is it with our sovereign and his peers?
Aud. 'Tis full a fortnight since I saw his highness,
　What time he sent me forth to muster men;
　Which I accordingly have done, and bring them
　　hither
　In fair array before his majesty.
　What news, my Lord of Derby, from the Emperor?
Der. As good as we desire: the Emperor
　Hath yielded to his highness friendly aid;
　And makes our king lieutenant-general
　In all his lands and large dominions:
　Then *via* for the spacious bounds of France!
Aud. What, doth his highness leap to hear these news?
Der. I have not yet found time to open them;
　The king is in his closet, malcontent,
　For what, I know not, but he gave in charge,
　Till after dinner, none should interrupt him:
　The Countess Salisbury, and her father Warwick,
　Artois, and all, look underneath the brows.
Aud. Undoubtedly then something is amiss.
　　　　　　　　　　　　　　[*Trumpet within.*]
Der. The trumpets sound; the king is now abroad.

Enter the King

Aud. Here comes his highness.
Der. Befall my sovereign all my sovereign's wish!
K. Ed. Ah, that thou wert a witch, to make it so!
Der. The emperor greeteth you:
K. Ed.　　　　　　　Would it were the countess!
Der. And hath accorded to your highness' suit.

K. Ed. Thou liest, she hath not; but I would, she had!

Aud. All love and duty to my lord the king!

K. Ed. Well, all but one is none:—what news with you?

Aud. I have, my liege, levied those horse and foot,
According to your charge, and brought them hither.

K. Ed. Then let those foot trudge hence upon those
    horse,
According to our discharge, and be gone.—
Derby,
I'll look upon the countess' mind anon.

Der. The countess' mind, my liege?

K. Ed. I mean the emperor: leave me alone.

Aud. What's in his mind?

Der.   Let's leave him to his humour.
                                        Exeunt.

K. Ed. Thus from the heart's abundance speaks the
    tongue;
Countess for emperor: and, indeed, why not?
She is as imperator over me;
And I to her
Am as a kneeling vassal that observes
The pleasure or displeasure of her eye.—

Enter Lodwick.

What says the more than Cleopatra's match
To Cæsar now?

Lod.   That yet, my liege, ere night
She will resolve your majesty.   [*Drum within.*]

K. Ed. What drum is this, that thunders forth this march,
To start the tender Cupid in my bosom?
Poor sheep-skin, how it brawls with him that beateth
    it!
Go, break the thund'ring parchment-bottom out,
And I will teach it to conduct sweet lines
Unto the bosom of a heavenly nymph:
For I will use it as my writing-paper:
And so reduce him, from a scolding drum,
To be the herald and dear counsel-bearer

Betwixt a goddess and a mighty king.
Go, bid the drummer learn to touch the lute,
Or hang him in the braces of his drum;
For now we think it an uncivil thing,
To trouble heaven with such harsh resounds:
Away.—   *Exit [Lodwick.]*
The quarrel, that I have, requires no arms
But these of mine; and these shall meet my foe
In a deep march of penetrable groans:
My eyes shall be my arrows; and my sighs
Shall serve me as the vantage of the wind,
To whirl away my sweet'st artillery:
Ah but, alas, she wins the sun of me,
For that is she herself; and thence it comes
That poets term the wanton warrior blind;
But love hath eyes as judgment to his steps,
Till too-much-loved glory dazzles them.—

Enter Lodwick.

How now?
Lod. My liege, the drum that struck the lusty march
    Stands with Prince Edward, your thrice-valiant son.
                                                [*Exit.*]

Enter Prince Edward.

K. Ed. I see the boy. O, how his mother's face,
    Modell'd in his, corrects my stray'd desire
    And rates my heart and chides my thievish eye;
    Who being rich enough in seeing her,
    Yet seeks elsewhere: and basest theft is that,
    Which cannot cloak itself on poverty.—
    Now, boy, what news?
Pr. Ed. I have assembled, my dear lord and father,
    The choicest buds of all our English blood
    For our affairs in France; and here we come,
    To take direction from your majesty.
K. Ed. Still do I see in him delineate
    His mother's visage; those his eyes are hers,
    Who looking wistly on me make me blush;

For faults against themselves give evidence:
Lust is a fire, and men, like lanthorns, show
Light lust within themselves, even through themselves.
Away, loose silks of wavering vanity!
Shall the large limit of fair Brittany
By me be overthrown? and shall I not
Master this little mansion of myself?
Give me an armour of eternal steel;
I go to conquer kings; and shall I not then
Subdue myself and be my enemy's friend?
It must not be.—Come, boy, forward, advance!
Let's with our colours sweet the air of France.

Enter Lodwick.

Lod. My liege, the countess with a smiling cheer
Desires access unto your majesty.

K. Ed. Why, there it goes! that very smile of hers
Hath ransom'd captive France, and set the king,
The Dauphin, and the peers, at liberty.—
Go, leave me, Ned, and revel with thy friends.

Exit Prince.

Thy mother is but black; and thou, like her,
Dost put into my mind how foul she is.—
Go, fetch the countess hither in thy hand
And let her chase away those winter clouds;
For she gives beauty both to heaven and earth.

Exit Lodwick.

The sin is more to hack and hew poor men,
Than to embrace in an unlawful bed
The register of all rarities
Since leathern Adam till this youngest hour.

Enter Countess [and Lodwick].

Go, Lodwick, put thy hand into my purse,
Play, spend, give, riot, waste; do what thou wilt,
So thou wilt hence a while and leave me here.

[Exit Lodwick.]

Now, my soul's playfellow! art thou come,

To speak the more than heavenly word of *yea*
To my objection in thy beauteous love?

Count. My father on his blessing hath commanded—

K. Ed. That thou shalt yield to me.

Count. Ay, dear my liege, your due.

K. Ed. And that, my dearest love, can be no less
Than right for right and tender love for love.

Count. Than wrong for wrong and endless hate for
hate.
But,—sith I see your majesty so bent,
That my unwillingness, my husband's love,
Your high estate, nor no respect respected
Can be my help, but that your mightiness
Will overbear and awe these dear regards,—
I bind my discontent to my content,
And, what I would not, I'll compel I will;
Provided that yourself remove those lets
That stand between your highness' love and mine.

K. Ed. Name them, fair countess, and, by Heaven, I
will.

Count. It is their lives, that stand between our love,
That I would have chok'd up, my sovereign.

K. Ed. Whose lives, my lady?

Count.   My thrice-loving liege,
Your queen, and Salisbury my wedded husband;
Who living have that title in our love
That we can not bestow but by their death.

K. Ed. Thy opposition is beyond our law.

Count. So is your desire: if the law
Can hinder you to execute the one,
Let it forbid you to attempt the other:
I cannot think you love me as you say
Unless you do make good what you have sworn.

K. Ed. No more; thy husband and the queen shall die.
Fairer thou art by far than Hero was;
Beardless Leander not so strong as I:
He swum an easy current for his love;
But I will through a Hellespont of blood

To arrive at Sestos where my Hero lies.

Count. Nay, you'll do more; you'll make the river, too,
 With their heart-bloods that keep our love asunder,
 Of which my husband and your wife are twain.

K. Ed. Thy beauty makes them guilty of their death
 And gives in evidence that they shall die;
 Upon which verdict, I, their judge, condemn them.

Count. O perjur'd beauty! more corrupted judge!
 When to the great star-chamber o'er our heads
 The universal sessions calls to count
 This packing evil, we both shall tremble for it.

K. Ed. What says my fair love? is she resolute?

Count. Resolute to be dissolv'd; and, therefore, this,—
 Keep but thy word, great king, and I am thine.
 Stand where thou dost, I'll part a little from thee,
 And see how I will yield me to thy hands.
 Here by my side doth hang my wedding knives:
 Take thou the one and with it kill thy queen
 And learn by me to find her where she lies;
 And with this other I'll despatch my love,
 Which now lies fast asleep within my heart:
 When they are gone, then I'll consent to love.
 Stir not, lascivious king, to hinder me;
 My resolution is more nimbler far
 Than thy prevention can be in my rescue,
 And, if thou stir, I strike: therefore stand still,
 And hear the choice that I will put thee to:
 Either swear to leave thy most unholy suit,
 And never henceforth to solicit me;
 Or else, by Heaven, this sharp-pointed knife
 Shall stain thy earth with that which thou wouldst stain,
 My poor chaste blood. Swear, Edward, swear,
 Or I will strike and die before thee here.

K. Ed. Even by that Power I swear, that gives me now
 The power to be ashamed of myself,
 I never mean to part my lips again

In any words that tends to such a suit.
Arise, true English lady, whom our isle
May better boast of, than e'er Roman might
Of her, whose ransack'd treasury hath task'd
The vain endeavour of so many pens:
Arise; and be my fault thy honour's fame,
Which after-ages shall enrich thee with.
I am awaked from this idle dream;—
Warwick, my son, Derby, Artois, and Audley,
Brave warriors all, where are you all this while?

Enter all.

Warwick, I make thee Warden of the North:—
Thou, Prince of Wales, and Audley, straight to sea;
Scour to Newhaven; some there stay for me:—
Myself, Artois, and Derby, will through Flanders
To greet our friends there and to crave their aid:
This night will scarce suffice me, to discover
My folly's siege against a faithful lover;
For, ere the sun shall guide the eastern sky,
We'll wake him with our martial harmony.

Exeunt.

[ACT III

SCENE I

Flanders. The French Camp.]

*Enter King John of France; his two Sons, Charles
of Normandy, and Philip; Duke of Lorraine.*

K. *John.* Here, till our navy of a thousand sail
Have made a breakfast to our foe by sea,
Let us encamp to wait their happy speed.—
Lorraine, what readiness is Edward in?
How hast thou heard that he provided is
Of martial furniture for this exploit?
Lor. To lay aside unnecessary soothing

And not to spend the time in circumstance,
'Tis bruited for a certainty, my lord,
That he's exceeding strongly fortified;
His subjects flock as willingly to war
As if unto a triumph they were led.

Char. England was wont to harbour malcontents,
Bloodthirsty and seditious Catilines,
Spendthrifts, and such as gape for nothing else
But changing and alteration of the state;
And is it possible,
That they are now so loyal in themselves?

Lor. All but the Scot; who solemnly protests,
As heretofore I have inform'd his grace,
Never to sheathe his sword, or take a truce.

K. John. Ah, that's the anch'rage of some better hope!
But, on the other side, to think what friends
King Edward hath retain'd in Netherland,
Among those ever-bibbing Epicures,
Those frothy Dutchmen, puff'd with double beer,
That drink and swill in every place they come,
Doth not a little aggravate mine ire:
Besides, we hear, the Emperor conjoins,
And stalls him in his own authority:
But, all the mightier that their number is,
The greater glory reaps the victory.
Some friends have we beside domestic power;
The stern Polonian, and the warlike Dane,
The King of Bohemia and of Sicily,
Are all become confederates with us,
And, as I think, are marching hither apace.

[*Drum within.*]

But, soft, I hear the music of their drums,
By which I guess that their approach is near.

*Enter the King of Bohemia, with Danes, and a Polonian
captain, with other soldiers, another way.*

K. Boh. King John of France, as league and neighbour-
hood

Requires when friends are anyway distress'd,
I come to aid thee with my country's force.

Pole. And from great Moscow, fearful to the Turk,
And lofty Poland, nurse of hardy men,
I bring these servitors to fight for thee
Who willingly will venture in thy cause.

K. John. Welcome, Bohemian king; and welcome, all:
This your great kindness I will not forget.
Besides your plentiful rewards in crowns,
That from our treasury ye shall receive,
There comes a hare-brain'd nation, deck'd in pride,
The spoil of whom will be a treble game.
And now my hope is full, my joy complete:
At sea, we are as puissant as the force
Of Agamemnon in the haven of Troy;
By land, with Xerxes we compare of strength
Whose soldiers drank up rivers in their thirst:
Then, Bayard-like, blind over-weening Ned,
To reach at our imperial diadem
Is either to be swallow'd of the waves
Or hack'd a-pieces when thou com'st ashore.

Enter [Mariner].

Mar. Near to the coast I have descried, my lord,
As I was busy in my watchful charge,
The proud Armado of King Edward's ships:
Which at the first, far off when I did ken,
Seem'd as it were a grove of wither'd pines;
But, drawing near, their glorious bright aspect,
Their streaming ensigns wrought of colour'd silk,
Like to a meadow full of sundry flowers,
Adorns the naked bosom of the earth.
Majestical the order of their course,
Figuring the horned circle of the moon:
And on the top-gallant of the admiral,
And likewise all the handmaids of his train,
The arms of England and of France unite
Are quarter'd equally by herald's art.

Thus, tightly carried with a merry gale,
They plough the ocean hitherward amain.
[*K. John.*] Dare he already crop the flower-de-luce?
I hope, the honey being gather'd thence,
He, with the spider, afterward approach'd,
Shall suck forth deadly venom from the leaves.—
But where's our navy? how are they prepar'd
To wing themselves against this flight of ravens?
Mar. They, having knowledge brought them by the
　　scouts,
Did break from anchor straight; and, puff'd with rage
No otherwise than were their sails with wind,
Made forth, as when the empty eagle flies
To satisfy his hungry griping maw.
K. John. There's for thy news. Return unto thy bark;
And, if thou scape the bloody stroke of war
And do survive the conflict, come again
And let us hear the manner of the fight.—

　　　　　　　　　　　　　　　　Exit [*Mariner*].

Mean space, my lords, 'tis best we be dispers'd
To several places, lest they chance to land:
First, you, my lord, with your Bohemian troops,
Shall pitch your battles on the lower hand;
My eldest son, the Duke of Normandy,
Together with this aid of Muscovites,
Shall climb the higher ground another way;
Here in the middle coast, betwixt you both,
Philip, my youngest boy, and I will lodge.
So, lords, be gone, and look unto your charge;
You stand for France, an empire fair and large.—

　　　　　　　　　　　　　　　　　　Exeunt.

Now tell me, Philip, what is thy conceit,
Touching the challenge that the English make?
Phil. I say, my lord, claim Edward what he can,
And bring he ne'er so plain a pedigree,
'Tis you are in possession of the crown,
And that's the surest point of all the law:
But, were it not, yet, ere he should prevail,

I'll make a conduit of my dearest blood
Or chase those straggling upstarts home again.
K. John. Well said, young Philip! Call for bread and wine,
That we may cheer our stomachs with repast,
To look our foes more sternly in the face.

The battle heard afar off

Now is begun the heavy day at sea.
Fight, Frenchmen, fight; be like the field of bears,
When they defend their younglings in their caves!
Steer, angry Nemesis, the happy helm;
That with the sulphur battles of your rage
The English fleet may be dispers'd and sunk!

Shot.

Phil. O, father, how this echoing cannon-shot,
Like sweet harmony, disgests my cates!
K. John. Now, boy, thou hear'st what thund'ring terror
  'tis,
To buckle for a kingdom's sovereignty.
The earth, with giddy trembling when it shakes,
Or when the exhalations of the air
Breaks in extremity of lightning flash,
Affrights not more than kings when they dispose
To show the rancour of their high-swoln hearts.

Retreat.

Retreat is sounded; one side hath the worse:
O, if it be the French!—Sweet Fortune, turn;
And, in thy turning, change the forward winds,
That, with advantage of a favouring sky,
Our men may vanquish and the other fly!

Enter Mariner.

My heart misgives:— say, mirror of pale death,
To whom belongs the honour of this day?
Relate, I pray thee, if thy breath will serve,
The sad discourse of this discomfiture.
Mar. I will, my lord.
My gracious sovereign, France hath ta'en the foil,

And boasting Edward triumphs with success.
These iron-hearted navies,
When last I was reporter to your grace,
Both full of angry spleen, of hope and fear,
Hasting to meet each other in the face,
At last conjoin'd, and by their admiral
Our admiral encounter'd many shot.
By this, the other, that beheld these twain
Give earnest-penny of a further wrack,
Like fiery dragons took their haughty flight;
And, likewise meeting, from their smoky wombs
Sent many grim ambassadors of death.
Then gan the day to turn to gloomy night;
And darkness did as well enclose the quick
As those that were but newly reft of life.
No leisure serv'd for friends to bid farewell;
And, if it had, the hideous noise was such,
As each to other seemed deaf and dumb.
Purple the sea; whose channel fill'd as fast
With streaming gore that from the maimed fell
As did her gushing moisture break into
The crannied cleftures of the through-shot planks.
Here flew a head, dissever'd from the trunk;
There mangled arms and legs were toss'd aloft,
As when a whirlwind takes the summer dust
And scatters it in middle of the air.
Then might ye see the reeling vessels split
And tottering sink into the ruthless flood
Until their lofty tops were seen no more.
All shifts were tried both for defence and hurt.
And now the effect of valour and of force,
Of resolution and of cowardice,
We lively pictur'd; how the one for fame,
The other by compulsion laid about.
Much did the Nonpareille, that brave ship;
So did the Black-snake of Bullen, than which
A bonnier vessel never yet spread sail:
But all in vain; both sun, the wind and tide

Revolted all unto our foemen's side,
That we perforce were fain to give them way,
And they are landed: thus my tale is done;
We have untimely lost, and they have won.

K. John. Then rests there nothing, but with present
speed
To join our several forces all in one,
And bid them battle ere they range too far.—
Come, gentle Philip, let us hence depart;
This soldier's words have pierc'd thy father's heart.

Exeunt.

[SCENE II

Picardy. Fields near Cressy.]

*Enter two Frenchmen; a woman and two little children meet
them, and other citizens.*

1 [*Fr.*] Well met, my masters: how now? what's the
news?
And wherefore are ye laden thus with stuff?
What, is it quarter-day, that you remove
And carry bag and baggage too?

[1 *cit.*] Quarter-day? ay, and quartering day, I fear:
Have ye not heard the news that flies abroad?

1 [*Fr.*] What news?

[2 *cit.*] How the French navy is destroy'd at sea
And that the English army is arriv'd.

1 [*Fr.*] What then?

[1 *cit.*] What then, quoth you? why, is't not time to fly,
When envy and destruction is so nigh?

1 [*Fr.*] Content thee, man; they are far enough from
hence;
And will be met, I warrant ye, to their cost,
Before they break so far into the realm.

[1 *cit.*] Ay, so the grasshopper doth spend the time
In mirthful jollity, till winter come;
And then too late he would redeem his time

When frozen cold hath nipp'd his careless head.
He, that no sooner will provide a cloak
Than when he sees it doth begin to rain,
May, peradventure, for his negligence,
Be throughly wash'd when he suspects it not.
We that have charge and such a train as this
Must look in time to look for them and us,
Lest, when we would, we cannot be reliev'd.

1 [*Fr.*] Belike, you then despair of all success
And think your country will be subjugate.

[2 *cit.*] We cannot tell; 'tis good to fear the worst.

1 [*Fr.*] Yet rather fight, than like unnatural sons
Forsake your loving parents in distress.

[1 *cit.*] Tush, they that have already taken arms
Are many fearful millions in respect
Of that small handful of our enemies.
But 'tis a rightful quarrel must prevail;
Edward is son unto our late king's sister,
Where John Valois is three degrees remov'd.

Wom. Besides, there goes a prophecy abroad,
Publish'd by one that was a friar once
Whose oracles have many times prov'd true;
And now he says, 'The time will shortly come,
When as a lion, roused in the west,
Shall carry hence the flower-de-luce of France':
These, I can tell ye, and such-like surmises
Strike many Frenchmen cold unto the heart.

Enter a Frenchman.

[3 *Fr.*] Fly, countrymen and citizens of France!
Sweet-flow'ring peace, the root of happy life,
Is quite abandon'd and expuls'd the land:
Instead of whom, ransack-constraining war
Sits like to ravens upon your houses' tops;
Slaughter and mischief walk within your streets,
And, unrestrain'd, make havoc as they pass:
The form whereof even now myself beheld,
Upon this fair mountain, whence I came.

For so far off as I directed mine eyes,
I might perceive five cities all on fire,
Corn-fields and vineyards burning like an oven;
And, as the reeking vapour in the wind
Turn'd but aside, I likewise might discern
The poor inhabitants, escap'd the flame,
Fall numberless upon the soldiers' pikes.
Three ways these dreadful ministers of wrath
Do tread the measures of their tragic march.
Upon the right hand comes the conquering king,
Upon the left his hot unbridled son,
And in the midst our nation's glittering host;
All which, though distant, yet conspire in one
To leave a desolation where they come.
Fly, therefore, citizens, if you be wise,
Seek out some habitation further off.
Here if you stay, your wives will be abus'd,
Your treasure shar'd before your weeping eyes.
Shelter you yourselves, for now the storm doth rise.
Away, away! methinks, I hear their drums.
Ah, wretched France, I greatly fear thy fall;
Thy glory shaketh like a tottering wall.   *Exeunt.*

[SCENE III

The Same.]

*Enter King Edward, and the Earl of Derby, with soldiers and
Gobin de Grey.*

  K. Ed. Where's the Frenchman, by whose cunning guide
    We found the shallow of this river Somme,
    And had direction how to pass the sea?

  Gob. Here, my good lord.

  K. Ed. How art thou called? tell me thy name.

  Gob. Gobin de Grey, if please your excellence.

  K. Ed. Then, Gobin, for the service thou hast done,
    We here enlarge and give thee liberty;

And, for recompense, beside this good,
Thou shalt receive five hundred marks in gold.—
I know not how we should have met our son,
Whom now in heart I wish I might behold.

Enter Artois.

Art. Good news, my lord; the prince is hard at hand,
    And with him comes Lord Audley and the rest,
    Whom since our landing we could never meet.

Enter Prince Edward, Lord Audley, and soldiers.

K. Ed. Welcome, fair prince! How hast thou sped, my
        son,
    Since thy arrival on the coast of France?
Pr. Ed. Successfully, I thank the gracious heavens:
    Some of their strongest cities we have won,
    As Harflew, Lo, Crotaye, and Carentine,
    And others wasted; leaving at our heels
    A wide apparent field and beaten path
    For solitariness to progress in:
    Yet, those that would submit, we kindly pardon'd;
    But who in scorn refus'd our proffer'd peace,
    Endur'd the penalty of sharp revenge.
K. Ed. Ah, France, why shouldst thou be thus obstinate
    Against the kind embracement of thy friends?
    How gently had we thought to touch thy breast
    And set our foot upon thy tender mould,
    But that in froward and disdainful pride
    Thou, like a skittish and untamed colt,
    Dost start aside and strike us with thy heels?—
    But tell me, Ned, in all thy warlike course
    Hast thou not seen the usurping King of France?
Pr. Ed. Yes, my good lord, and not two hours ago,
    With full a hundred thousand fighting men,
    Upon the one side of the river's bank,
    And on the other both his multitudes.
    I fear'd he would have cropp'd our smaller power:
    But, happily, perceiving your approach

He hath withdrawn himself to Cressy plains;
Where, as it seemeth by his good array,
He means to bid us battle presently.

K. Ed. He shall be welcome, that's the thing we crave.

Enter King John, Dukes of Normandy and Lorraine, King of Bohemia, young Philip, and soldiers.

K. John. Edward, know, that John, the true King of France,—
Musing thou shouldst encroach upon his land,
And, in thy tyrannous proceeding, slay
His faithful subjects and subvert his towns,—
Spits in thy face; and in this manner following
Upbraids thee with thine arrogant intrusion.
First, I condemn thee for a fugitive,
A thievish pirate, and a needy mate;
One, that hath either no abiding place,
Or else, inhabiting some barren soil,
Where neither herb nor fruitful grain is had,
Dost altogether live by pilfering:
Next,—insomuch thou hast infring'd thy faith,
Broke league and solemn covenant made with me,—
I hold thee for a false pernicious wretch:
And last of all,—although I scorn to cope
With one so much inferior to myself;
Yet, in respect thy thirst is all for gold,
Thy labour rather to be fear'd than lov'd,—
To satisfy thy lust in either part,
Here am I come, and with me have I brought
Exceeding store of treasure, pearl and coin.
Leave therefore now to persecute the weak;
And, armed ent'ring conflict with the arm'd,
Let it be seen, 'mongst other petty thefts,
How thou canst win this pillage manfully.

K. Ed. If gall or wormwood have a pleasant taste,
Then is thy salutation honey-sweet:
But as the one hath no such property,
So is the other most satirical.

Yet wot how I regard thy worthless taunts;—
If thou have utter'd them to foil my fame
Or dim the reputation of my birth,
Know that thy wolvish barking cannot hurt:
If slily to insinuate with the world,
And with a strumpet's artificial line
To paint thy vicious and deformed cause,
Be well assur'd the counterfeit will fade
And in the end thy foul defects be seen:
But if thou didst it to provoke me on,—
As who should say, I were but timorous,
Or coldly negligent did need a spur,—
Bethink thyself how slack I was at sea;
How, since my landing, I have won no towns,
Enter'd no further but upon the coast,
And there have ever since securely slept.
But if I have been otherwise employ'd,
Imagine, Valois, whether I intend
To skirmish, not for pillage, but for the crown
Which thou dost wear; and that I vow to have,
Or one of us shall fall into his grave.

Pr. Ed. Look not for cross invectives at our hands
Or railing execrations of despite:
Let creeping serpents hid in hollow banks
Sting with their tongues; we have remorseless swords,
And they shall plead for us and our affairs.
Yet thus much, briefly, by my father's leave:
As all the immodest poison of thy throat
Is scandalous and most notorious lies,
And our pretended quarrel is truly just,
So end the battle when we meet to-day;
May either of us prosper and prevail
Or, luckless curst, receive eternal shame!

K. Ed. That needs no further question, and, I know,
His conscience witnesseth, it is my right.—
Therefore, Valois, say, wilt thou yet resign,
Before the sickle's thrust into the corn
Or that enkindled fury turn to flame?

K. John. Edward, I know what right thou hast in France;
    And ere I basely will resign my crown,
    This champion field shall be a pool of blood
    And all our prospect as a slaughter-house.
Pr. Ed. Ay, that approves thee, tyrant, what thou art:
    No father, king or shepherd of thy realm;
    But one that tears her entrails with thy hands
    And, like a thirsty tiger, suck'st her blood.
Aud. You peers of France, why do you follow him
    That is so prodigal to spend your lives?
Char. Whom should they follow, aged impotent,
    But he that is their true-born sovereign?
K. Ed. Upbraid'st thou him, because within his face
    Time hath engrav'd deep characters of age?
    Know that these grave scholars of experience,
    Like stiff-grown oaks, will stand immovable,
    When whirlwind quickly turns up younger trees.
Der. Was ever any of thy father's house
    King, but thyself, before this present time?
    Edward's great lineage, by the mother's side,
    Five hundred years hath held the sceptre up:—
    Judge then, conspirators, by this descent,
    Which is the true-born sovereign, this, or that.
Phil. Father, range your battles, prate no more;
    These English fain would spend the time in words,
    That, night approaching, they might escape unfought.
K. John. Lords and my loving subjects, now's the time
    That your intended force must bide the touch:
    Therefore, my friends, consider this in brief,—
    He that you fight for is your natural king;
    He against whom you fight, a foreigner:
    He that you fight for, rules in clemency
    And reins you with a mild and gentle bit;
    He against whom you fight, if he prevail,
    Will straight enthrone himself in tyranny,
    Make slaves of you, and with a heavy hand
    Curtail and curb your sweetest liberty.
    Then, to protect your country and your king,

Let but the haughty courage of your hearts
Answer the number of your able hands,
And we shall quickly chase these fugitives.
For what's this Edward but a belly-god,
A tender and lascivious wantonness,
That th' other day was almost dead for love?
And what, I pray you, is his goodly guard?
Such as, but scant them of their chines of beef
And take away their downy feather-beds,
And, presently, they are as resty-stiff
As 'twere a many over-ridden jades.
Then, Frenchmen, scorn that such should be your lords,
And rather bind ye them in captive bands.

French. Vive le Roy! God save King John of France!

K. John. Now on this plain of Cressy spread yourselves,—
And, Edward, when thou dar'st, begin the fight.

> [*Exeunt King John, Charles, Philip,*
> *Lorraine, Bohemia, and Forces.*]

K. Ed. We presently will meet thee, John of France:—
And, English lords, let us resolve to-day
Either to clear us of that scandalous crime
Or be entombed in our innocence.—
And, Ned, because this battle is the first
That ever yet thou fought'st in pitched field,
As ancient custom is of martialists,
To dub thee with the type of chivalry,
In solemn manner we will give thee arms:—
Come, therefore, heralds, orderly bring forth
A strong attirement for the prince my son.—

> *Enter four Heralds, bringing in a coat-*
> *armour, a helmet, a lance, and a shield.*

Edward Plantagenet, in the name of God,
As with this armour I impall thy breast,
So be thy noble unrelenting heart
Wall'd in with flint of matchless fortitude
That never base affections enter there;
Fight and be valiant, conquer where thou com'st!—

Now follow, lords, and do him honour too.

Der. [*Receiving the helmet.*]
Edward Plantagenet, Prince of Wales,
As I do set this helmet on thy head,
Wherewith the chamber of thy brain is fenc'd,
So may thy temples, with Bellona's hand,
Be still adorn'd with laurel victory;
Fight and be valiant, conquer where thou com'st!

Aud. [*Receiving the lance.*]
Edward Plantagenet, Prince of Wales,
Receive this lance into thy manly hand;
Use it in fashion of a brazen pen
To draw forth bloody stratagems in France
And print thy valiant deeds in honour's books;
Fight and be valiant, conquer where thou com'st!

Art. [*Receiving the shield.*]
Edward Plantagenet, Prince of Wales,
Hold, take this target, wear it on thy arm;
And may the view thereof, like Perseus' shield,
Astonish and transform thy gazing foes
To senseless images of meagre death;
Fight and be valiant, conquer where thou com'st!

K. Ed. Now wants there nought but knighthood; which deferr'd
We leave till thou hast won it in the field.

[*Pr. Ed.*] My gracious father, and ye forward peers,
This honour, you have done me, animates
And cheers my green yet-scarce-appearing strength
With comfortable good-presaging signs,
No otherwise than did old Jacob's words
When as he breath'd his blessings on his sons.
These hallow'd gifts of yours when I profane,
Or use them not to glory of my God,
To patronage the fatherless and poor,
Or for the benefit of England's peace,
Be numb my joints! wax feeble both mine arms!
Wither my heart! that, like a sapless tree,
I may remain the map of infamy.

K. Ed. Then thus our steeled battles shall be rang'd;—
    The leading of the vaward, Ned, is thine;
    To dignify whose lusty spirit the more,
    We temper it with Audley's gravity;
    That, courage and experience join'd in one,
    Your manage may be second unto none:
    For the main battles, I will guide myself;
    And, Derby, in the rearward march behind.
    That orderly dispos'd and set in 'ray,
    Let us to horse; and God grant us the day!

                                Exeunt.

[SCENE IV

The Same.]

Alarum. Enter a many Frenchmen fleeing. After them Prince Edward, running. Then enter King John and Duke of Lorraine.

K. John. O Lorraine, say, what mean our men to fly?
    Our number is far greater than our foes.
Lor. The garrison of Genoese, my lord,
    That came from Paris, weary with their march,
    Grudging to be suddenly employ'd,
    No sooner in the fore-front took their place,
    But, straight retiring, so dismay'd the rest
    As likewise they betook themselves to flight;
    In which, for haste to make a safe escape,
    More in the clust'ring throng are press'd to death,
    Than by the enemy, a thousand-fold.
K. John. O hapless fortune! Let us yet assay
    If we can counsel some of them to stay.

                               [Exeunt.]

        Enter King Edward and Audley.

K. Ed. Lord Audley, whiles our son is in the chase,
    Withdraw your powers unto this little hill,
    And here a season let us breathe ourselves.
Aud. I will, my lord.   *Exit. Sound Retreat.*

K. Ed. Just-dooming Heaven, whose secret providence
　　To our gross judgment is inscrutable,
　　How are we bound to praise thy wondrous works,
　　That hast this day giv'n way unto the right
　　And made the wicked stumble at themselves!

Enter Artois.

[*Art.*] Rescue, King Edward! rescue for thy son!
K. Ed. Rescue, Artois? what, is he prisoner?
　　Or by violence fell beside his horse?
Art. Neither, my lord; but narrowly beset
　　With turning Frenchmen whom he did pursue,
　　As 'tis impossible that he should scape
　　Except your highness presently descend.
K. Ed. Tut, let him fight; we gave him arms to-day,
　　And he is labouring for a knighthood, man.

Enter Derby.

Der. The prince, my lord, the prince! O, succour him;
　　He's close encompass'd with a world of odds!
K. Ed. Then will he win a world of honour too
　　If he by valour can redeem him thence:
　　If not, what remedy? we have more sons
　　Than one, to comfort our declining age.

Enter Audley.

Aud. Renowned Edward, give me leave, I pray,
　　To lead my soldiers where I may relieve
　　Your grace's son, in danger to be slain.
　　The snares of French, like emmets on a bank,
　　Muster about him; whilst he, lion-like,
　　Entangled in the net of their assaults,
　　Frantic'ly rends and bites the woven toil:
　　But all in vain, he cannot free himself.
K. Ed. Audley, content; I will not have a man,
　　On pain of death, sent forth to succour him:
　　This is the day ordain'd by destiny
　　To season his courage with those grievous thoughts,

That, if he break out, Nestor's years on earth,
Will make him savour still of this exploit.
Der. Ah, but he shall not live to see those days.
K. Ed. Why, then his epitaph is lasting praise.
Aud. Yet, good my lord, 'tis too much wilfulness,
To let his blood be spilt that may be sav'd.
K. Ed. Exclaim no more; for none of you can tell
Whether a borrow'd aid will serve or no.
Perhaps, he is already slain or ta'en:
And dare a falcon when she's in her flight,
And ever after she'll be haggard-like:
Let Edward be deliver'd by our hands,
And still in danger he'll expect the like;
But if himself himself redeem from thence,
He will have vanquish'd, cheerful, death and fear,
And ever after dread their force no more
Than if they were but babes or captive slaves.
Aud. O cruel father!—Farewell, Edward, then!
Der. Farewell, sweet prince, the hope of chivalry!
Art. O, would my life might ransom him from death!
K. Ed. But, soft; methinks I hear   [*Retreat sounded.*]
The dismal charge of trumpets' loud retreat:
All are not slain, I hope, that went with him;
Some will return with tidings, good or bad.

*Enter Prince Edward in triumph, bearing in his hand his
shivered lance, and the King of Bohemia, borne before
wrapped in the colours. They run and embrace him.*

Aud. O joyful sight! victorious Edward lives!
Der. Welcome, brave prince!
K. Ed. Welcome, Plantagenet!
Pr. Ed. First having done my duty, as beseem'd,
                              Kneels, and kisses his father's hand.
Lords, I regreet you all with hearty thanks.
And now, behold,—after my winter's toil,
My painful voyage on the boist'rous sea
Of war's devouring gulfs and steely rocks,—
I bring my fraught unto the wished port,

My summer's hope, my travel's sweet reward:
And here with humble duty I present
This sacrifice, this firstfruit of my sword,
Cropp'd and cut down even at the gate of death,
The King of Boheme, father, whom I slew;
Whose thousands had intrench'd me round about,
And lay as thick upon my batter'd crest
As on an anvil with their pond'rous glaives:
Yet marble courage still did underprop;
And when my weary arms with often blows,
Like the continual-lab'ring woodman's axe
That is enjoin'd to fell a load of oaks,
Began to falter, straight I would remember
My gifts you gave me and my zealous vow,
And then new courage made me fresh again;
That, in despite, I carv'd my passage forth
And put the multitude to speedy flight.
Lo, thus hath Edward's hand fill'd your request,
And done, I hope, the duty of a knight.

K. Ed. Ay, well thou hast deserv'd a knighthood, Ned!
And, therefore, with thy sword, yet reeking warm
       His sword borne by a soldier.
With blood of those that fought to be thy bane,
Arise, Prince Edward, trusty knight at arms:
This day thou hast confounded me with joy
And proved thyself fit heir unto a king.

Pr. Ed. Here is a note, my gracious lord, of those
That in this conflict of our foes were slain:
Eleven princes of esteem; fourscore
Barons; a hundred and twenty knights;
And thirty thousand common soldiers;
And, of our men, a thousand.

[*K. Ed.*] Our God be praised! Now, John of France, I
    hope,
Thou know'st King Edward for no wantonness,
No love-sick cockney; nor his soldiers, jades.—
But which way is the fearful king escap'd?

Pr. Ed. Towards Poiters, noble father, and his sons.

K. Ed. Ned, thou and Audley shall pursue them still;
Myself and Derby will to Calice straight,
And there begirt that haven-town with siege:
Now lies it on an upshot; therefore strike,
And wistly follow while the game's on foot.
What picture's this? *[Pointing to the colours.]*
Pr. Ed. A pelican, my lord,
Wounding her bosom with her crooked beak
That so her nest of young ones may be fed
With drops of blood that issue from her heart;
The motto, '*Sic et vos*,' 'And so should you.'

Exeunt.

[ACT IV

SCENE I

Brittany. Camp of the English.]

*Enter Lord Mountford with a coronet in his hand; with him the
Earl of Salisbury.*

Mount. My Lord of Salisbury, since by your aid
Mine enemy Sir Charles of Blois is slain,
And I again am quietly possess'd
In Britain's dukedom, know that I resolve,
For this kind furth'rance of your king and you,
To swear allegiance to his majesty:
In sign whereof, receive this coronet,
Bear it unto him, and withal mine oath,
Never to be but Edward's faithful friend.
Sal. I take it, Mountford: thus, I hope, ere long
The whole dominions of the realm of France
Will be surrender'd to his conquering hand.

Exit Mountford.

Now, if I knew but safely how to pass,
I would at Calice gladly meet his grace,
Whither I am by letters certified
That he intends to have his host remov'd.

It shall be so: this policy will serve:—
Ho, who's within? Bring Villiers to me.—

Enter Villiers.

Villiers, thou know'st, thou art my prisoner,
And that I might for ransom, if I would,
Require of thee a hundred thousand franks,
Or else retain and keep thee captive still:
But so it is, that for a smaller charge
Thou may'st be quit, an if thou wilt thyself;
And this it is, procure me but a passport
Of Charles the Duke of Normandy, that I
Without restraint may have recourse to Calice
Through all the countries where he hath to do,
(Which thou may'st easily obtain, I think,
By reason I have often heard thee say,
He and thou were students once together)
And then thou shalt be set at liberty.
How say'st thou? wilt thou undertake to do it?

Vil. I will, my lord; but I must speak with him.

Sal. Why, so thou shalt; take horse, and post from hence:
Only, before thou go'st, swear by thy faith
That, if thou canst not compass my desire,
Thou wilt return my prisoner back again;
And that shall be sufficient warrant for me.

Vil. To that condition I agree, my lord,
And will unfeignedly perform the same.   *Exit.*

Sal. Farewell, Villiers.—
This once I mean to try a Frenchman's faith.

                                              Exit.

[SCENE II

Picardy. The English Camp before Calais.]

Enter King Edward and Derby, with Soldiers.

K. Ed. Since they refuse our proffer'd league, my lord,
And will not ope their gates and let us in,

We will intrench ourselves on every side,
That neither victuals nor supply of men
May come to succour this accursed town;
Famine shall combat where our swords are stopp'd.

Der. The promis'd aid that made them stand aloof
Is now retir'd and gone another way;
It will repent them of their stubborn will.

Enter six poor Frenchmen.

But what are these poor ragged slaves, my lord?

K. Ed. Ask what they are; it seems, they come from
Calice.

Der. You wretched patterns of despair and woe,
What are you? living men, or gliding ghosts,
Crept from your graves to walk upon the earth?

First Fr. No ghosts, my lord, but men that breathe a life
Far worse than is the quiet sleep of death:
We are distressed poor inhabitants
That long have been diseased, sick and lame;
And now, because we are not fit to serve,
The captain of the town hath thrust us forth
That so expense of victuals may be sav'd.

K. Ed. A charitable deed, no doubt, and worthy praise.—
But how do you imagine then to speed?
We are your enemies; in such a case
We can no less but put you to the sword,
Since, when we proffer'd truce, it was refus'd.

First Fr. An if your grace no otherwise vouchsafe,
As welcome death is unto us as life.

K. Ed. Poor silly men, much wrong'd and more dis-
tress'd!—
Go, Derby, go, and see they be reliev'd;
Command that victuals be appointed them
And give to every one five crowns a-piece:—

[*Exeunt Derby and Frenchmen.*]

The lion scorns to touch the yielding prey,
And Edward's sword must flesh itself in such
As wilful stubbornness hath made perverse.—

Enter Lord Percy.

Lord Percy! welcome: what's the news in England?
Per. The queen, my lord, comes here to your grace;
  And from her highness and the lord vicegerent
  I bring this happy tidings of success:
  David of Scotland, lately up in arms,
  (Thinking, belike, he soonest should prevail,
  Your highness being absent from the realm)
  Is, by the fruitful service of your peers
  And painful travel of the queen herself
  That, big with child, was every day in arms,
  Vanquish'd, subdu'd and taken prisoner.
K. Ed. Thanks, Percy, for thy news, with all my heart!
  What was he, took him prisoner in the field?
Per. A squire, my lord; John Copland is his name:
  Who since, entreated by her majesty,
  Denies to make surrender of his prize
  To any but unto your grace alone;
  Whereat the queen is grievously displeas'd.
K. Ed. Well, then we'll have a pursuivant despatch'd
  To summon Copland hither out of hand,
  And with him he shall bring his prisoner king.
Per. The queen's, my lord, herself by this at sea,
  And purposeth, as soon as wind will serve,
  To land at Calice and to visit you.
K. Ed. She shall be welcome; and, to wait her coming
  I'll pitch my tent near to the sandy shore.

Enter a [French] Captain.

[*Cap.*] The burgesses of Calice, mighty king,
  Have, by a council, willingly decreed
  To yield the town and castle to your hands,
  Upon condition it will please your grace
  To grant them benefit of life and goods.
K. Ed. They will so! then, belike, they may command,
  Dispose, elect, and govern as they list.
  No, sirrah, tell them, since they did refuse

Our princely clemency at first proclaim'd,
They shall not have it now, although they would;
[I] will accept of nought but fire and sword,
Except, within these two days, six of them,
That are the wealthiest merchants in the town,
Come naked, all but for their linen shirts,
With each a halter hang'd about his neck,
And prostrate yield themselves, upon their knees,
To be afflicted, hang'd, or what I please;
And so you may inform their masterships.   *Exeunt.*
Cap. Why, this it is to trust a broken staff.
Had we not been persuaded, John our king
Would with his army have reliev'd the town,
We had not stood upon defiance so.
But now 'tis past that no man can recall,
And better some do go to wrack, than all.   *Exit.*

[SCENE III

Poitou. Fields near Poitiers. The French Camp.]

Enter Charles of Normandy and Villiers.

Char. I wonder, Villiers, thou shouldst importune me
    For one that is our deadly enemy.
Vil. Not for his sake, my gracious lord, so much
    Am I become an earnest advocate
    As that thereby my ransom will be quit.
Char. Thy ransom, man! why need'st thou talk of
        that?
    Art thou not free? and are not all occasions,
    That happen for advantage of our foes,
    To be accepted of and stood upon?
Vil. No, good, my lord, except the same be just;
    For profit must with honour be comix'd
    Or else our actions are but scandalous:
    But, letting pass these intricate objections,
    Will't please your highness to subscribe, or no?

Char. Villiers, I will not nor I cannot do it;
   Salisbury shall not have his will so much,
   To claim a passport how it please himself.
Vil. Why, then I know the extremity, my lord:
   I must return to prison whence I came.
Char. Return! I hope, thou wilt not.
   What bird that hath escap'd the fowler's gin
   Will not beware how she's ensnar'd again?
   Or what is he so senseless and secure,
   That, having hardly pass'd a dangerous gulf,
   Will put himself in peril there again?
Vil. Ah, but it is mine oath, my gracious lord,
   Which I in conscience may not violate,
   Or else a kingdom should not draw me hence.
Char. Thine oath! why, that doth bind thee to abide:
   Hast thou not sworn obedience to thy prince?
Vil. In all things that uprightly he commands.
   But either to persuade or threaten me
   Not to perform the covenant of my word
   Is lawless and I need not to obey.
Char. Why, is it lawful for a man to kill
   And not to break a promise with his foe?
Vil. To kill, my lord, when war is once proclaim'd,
   So that our quarrel be for wrongs receiv'd,
   No doubt, is lawfully permitted us:
   But, in an oath, we must be well advis'd
   How we do swear, and, when we once have sworn,
   Not to infringe it, though we die therefore.
   Therefore, my lord, as willing I return
   As if I were to fly to paradise.
Char. Stay, my Villiers; thine honourable mind
   Deserves to be eternally admir'd.
   Thy suit shall be no longer thus deferr'd;
   Give me the paper, I'll subscribe to it:
   And, wheretofore I lov'd thee as Villiers,
   Hereafter I'll embrace thee as myself;
   Stay, and be still in favour with thy lord.
Vil. I humbly thank your grace, I must despatch

And send this passport first unto the earl,
And then I will attend your highness' pleasure.
Char. Do so, Villiers;—and Charles, when he hath need,
Be such his soldiers, howsoe'er he speed!

Exit Villiers.

Enter King John.

K. John. Come, Charles, and arm thee; Edward is
entrapp'd,
The Prince of Wales is fall'n into our hands,
And we have compass'd him, he cannot scape.
Char. But will your highness fight to-day?
K. John. What else, my son? he's scarce eight thousand
strong,
And we are threescore thousand at the least.
Char. I have a prophecy, my gracious lord,
Wherein is written what success is like
To happen us in this outrageous war;
It was deliver'd me at Cressy's field
By one that is an aged hermit there.   [*Reads.*]

'When feather'd fowl shall make thine army tremble,
    And flint-stones rise, and break the battle 'ray,
Then think on him that doth not now dissemble,
    For that shall be the hapless dreadful day:
Yet in the end thy foot thou shalt advance
As far in England as thy foe in France.'

K. John. By this it seems we shall be fortunate:
For as it is impossible that stones
Should ever rise and break the battle 'ray,
Or airy fowl make men in arms to quake,
So is it like, we shall not be subdu'd:
Or, say this might be true, yet, in the end,
Since he doth promise we shall drive him hence
And forage their country as they have done ours,
By this revenge that loss will seem the less.
But all are frivolous fancies, toys and dreams:
Once we are sure we have ensnar'd the son,
Catch we the father after how we can.   *Exeunt.*

[SCENE IV

The Same. The English Camp.]

Enter Prince Edward, Audley, and others.

Pr. Ed. Audley, the arms of death embrace us round,
　　And comfort have we none, save that to die
　　We pay sour earnest for a sweeter life.
　　At Cressy field our clouds of warlike smoke
　　Chok'd up those French mouths and dissever'd them:
　　But now their multitudes of millions hide,
　　Masking as 'twere, the beauteous-burning sun;
　　Leaving no hope to us but sullen dark
　　And eyeless terror of all-ending night.
Aud. This sudden, mighty and expedient head,
　　That they have made, fair prince, is wonderful.
　　Before us in the valley lies the king,
　　Vantag'd with all that heaven and earth can yield;
　　His party stronger battled than our whole:
　　His son, the braving Duke of Normandy,
　　Hath trimm'd the mountain on our right hand up
　　In shining plate, that now the aspiring hill
　　Shows like a silver quarry or an orb;
　　Aloft the which, the banners, bannerets,
　　And new-replenish'd pendants cuff the air,
　　And beat the winds, that for their gaudiness
　　Struggles to kiss them: on our left hand lies
　　Philip, the younger issue of the king,
　　Coting the other hill in such array
　　That all his gilded upright pikes do seem
　　Straight trees of gold, the pendant[s] leaves,
　　And their device of antique heraldry,
　　Quarter'd in colours seeming sundry fruits,
　　Makes it the orchard of the Hesperides:
　　Behind us too the hill doth bear his height,
　　For, like a half-moon, op'ning but one way,
　　It rounds us in; there at our backs are lodg'd
　　The fatal cross-bows, and the battle there

Is govern'd by the rough Chatillion.
Then thus it stands,—the valley for our flight
The king binds in; the hills on either hand
Are proudly royalized by his sons;
And on the hill behind stands certain death,
In pay and service with Chatillion.

Pr. Ed. Death's name is much more mighty than his
    deeds;—
Thy parcelling this power hath made it more.
As many sands as these my hands can hold
Are but my handful of so many sands;
Then, all the world,—and call it but a power,—
Easily ta'en up and quickly thrown away:
But, if I stand to count them sand by sand,
The number would confound my memory
And make a thousand millions of a task
Which, briefly, is no more, indeed, than one.
These quarters, squadrons, and these regiments,
Before, behind us, and on either hand,
Are but a power: when we name a man,
His hand, his foot, his head, hath several strengths;
And being all but one self instant strength,
Why, all this many, Audley, is but one,
And we can call it all but one man's strength.
He, that hath far to go, tells it by miles;
If he should tell the steps, it kills his heart:
The drops are infinite that make a flood,
And yet, thou know'st, we call it but a rain.
There is but one France, one King of France,
That France hath no more kings; and that same
    king
Hath but the puissant legion of one king;
And we have one: then apprehend no odds,
For one to one is fair equality.—

Enter a Herald from King John.

What tidings, messenger? be plain, and brief.
Her. The King of France, my sovereign lord and master,

Greets by me his foe the Prince of Wales.
If thou call forth a hundred men of name,
Of lords, knights, squires, and English gentlemen,
And with thyself and those kneel at his feet,
He straight will fold his bloody colours up
And ransom shall redeem lives forfeited:
If not, this day shall drink more English blood
Than e'er was buried in [y]our British earth.
What is the answer to his proffer'd mercy?

Pr. Ed. This heaven that covers France contains the mercy
That draws from me submissive orisons;
That such base breath should vanish from my lips,
To urge the plea of mercy to a man,
The Lord forbid! Return, and tell the king,
My tongue is made of steel and it shall beg
My mercy on his coward burgonet;
Tell him, my colours are as red as his,
My men as bold, our English arms as strong,
Return him my defiance in his face.

Her. I go.   [*Exit.*]

Enter another.

Pr. Ed.   What news with thee?
Her. The Duke of Normandy, my lord and master,
Pitying thy youth is so engirt with peril,
By me hath sent a nimble-jointed jennet,
As swift as ever yet thou didst bestride,
And therewithal he counsels thee to fly;
Else, death himself hath sworn that thou shalt die.
Pr. Ed. Back with the beast unto the beast that sent him;
Tell him, I cannot sit a coward's horse.
Bid him to-day bestride the jade himself;
For I will stain my horse quite o'er with blood
And double-gild my spurs, but I will catch him.
So tell the carping boy, and get thee gone.

[*Exit Herald.*]

Enter another.

Her. Edward of Wales, Philip, the second son
    To the most mighty Christian King of France,
    Seeing thy body's living date expir'd,
    All full of charity and Christian love,
    Commends this book, full fraught with prayers,
    To thy fair hand, and, for thy hour of life,
    Entreats thee that thou meditate therein
    And arm thy soul for her long journey towards.
    Thus have I done his bidding, and return.

Pr. Ed. Herald of Philip, greet thy lord from me;
    All good, that he can send, I can receive:
    But think'st thou not the unadvised boy
    Hath wrong'd himself in thus far tend'ring me?
    Haply, he cannot pray without the book;
    I think him no divine extemporal:
    Then render back this commonplace of prayer,
    To do himself good in adversity.
    Besides, he knows not my sin's quality
    And therefore knows no prayers for my avail;
    Ere night his prayer may be, to pray to God
    To put it in my heart to hear his prayer;
    So tell the courtly wanton, and be gone.

Her. I go.   [*Exit.*]

Pr. Ed. How confident their strength and number makes
    them!—
    Now, Audley, sound those silver wings of thine,
    And let those milk-white messengers of time
    Show thy time's learning in this dangerous time;
    Thyself art bruis'd and bit with many broils,
    And stratagems forepast with iron pens
    Are texted in thine honourable face;
    Thou art a married man in this distress,
    But danger woos me as a blushing maid:
    Teach me an answer to this perilous time.

Aud. To die is all as common as to live;
    The one in choice, the other holds in chase:
    For from the instant we begin to live

We do pursue and hunt the time to die:
First bud we, then we blow, and after seed;
Then, presently, we fall; and, as a shade
Follows the body, so we follow death.
If then we hunt for death, why do we fear it?
If we fear it, why do we follow it?
If we do fear, how can we shun it?
If we do fear, with fear we do but aid
The thing we fear to seize on us the sooner:
If we fear not, then no resolved proffer
Can overthrow the limit of our fate:
For, whether ripe or rotten, drop we shall,
As we do draw the lottery of our doom.

Pr. Ed. Ah, good old man, a thousand thousand armours
These words of thine have buckled on my back.
Ah, what an idiot hast thou made of life,
To seek the thing it fears! and how disgrac'd
The imperial victory of murd'ring death!
Since all the lives, his conquering arrows strike,
Seek him, and he not them, to shame his glory.
I will not give a penny for a life,
Nor half a halfpenny to shun grim death,
Since for to live is but to seek to die,
And dying but beginning of new life.
Let come the hour when he that rules it will!
To live, or die, I hold indifferent.   *Exeunt.*

[SCENE V

The Same. The French Camp.]

Enter King John and Charles.

K. John. A sudden darkness hath defac'd the sky,
The winds are crept into their caves for fear,
The leaves move not, the world is hush'd and still,
The birds cease singing, and the wand'ring brooks
Murmur no wonted greeting to their shores;
Silence attends some wonder and expecteth

That heaven should pronounce some prophecy:
Where or from whom proceeds this silence, Charles?

Char. Our men with open mouths and staring eyes
  Look on each other, as they did attend
  Each other's words, and yet no creature speaks;
  A tongue-tied fear hath made a midnight hour
  And speeches sleep through all the waking regions.

K. John. But now the pompous sun, in all his pride,
  Look'd through his golden coach upon the world,
  And on a sudden, hath he hid himself;
  That now the under earth is as a grave,
  Dark, deadly, silent, and uncomfortable.

                                        A clamour of ravens.

Hark! what a deadly outcry do I hear!

Char. Here comes my brother Philip.

K. John.   All dismayed:—

                    Enter Philip.

What fearful words are those thy looks presage?

Phil. A flight, a flight!

K. John. Coward, what flight? thou liest, there needs no
    flight.

Phil. A flight!

K. John. Awake thy craven powers, and tell on
  The substance of that very fear indeed,
  Which is so ghastly printed on thy face:
  What is the matter?

Phil.   A flight of ugly ravens
  Do croak and hover o'er our soldiers' heads,
  And keep in triangles and corner'd squares
  Right as our forces are embattled;
  With their approach there came this sudden fog
  Which now hath hid the airy floor of heaven
  And made at noon a night unnatural
  Upon the quaking and dismayed world:
  In brief, our soldiers have let fall their arms
  And stand like metamorphos'd images,
  Bloodless and pale, one gazing on another.

K. John. Ay, now I call to mind the prophecy;
But I must give no entrance to a fear.—
Return, and hearten up these yielding souls;
Tell them, the ravens seeing them in arms—
So many fair against a famished few—
Come but to dine upon their handiwork
And prey upon the carrion that they kill:
For when we see a horse laid down to die,
Although not dead, the ravenous birds
Sit watching the departure of his life;
Even so these ravens, for the carcases
Of those poor English that are mark'd to die,
Hover about, and, if they cry to us,
'Tis but for meat that we must kill for them.
Away, and comfort up my soldiers,
And sound the trumpets; and at once despatch
This little business of a silly fraud.   *Exit Philip.*

Another noise. Salisbury brought in by a French Captain.

Cap. Behold, my liege, this knight, and forty mo,—
Of whom the better part are slain and fled,—
With all endeavour sought to break our ranks,
And make their way to the encompass'd prince;
Dispose of him as please your majesty.
K. John. Go, and the next bough, soldier, that thou seest,
Disgrace it with his body presently:
For I do hold a tree in France too good
To be the gallows of an English thief.
Sal. My Lord of Normandy, I have your pass
And warrant for my safety through this land.
Char. Villiers procur'd it for thee, did he not?
Sal. He did.
Char. And it is current, thou shalt freely pass.
K. John. Ay, freely to the gallows to be hang'd,
Without denial or impediment:—
Away with him.
Char. I hope, your highness will not so disgrace me
And dash the virtue of my seal-at-arms:

He hath my never-broken name to show,
Character'd with this princely hand of mind;
And rather let me leave to be a prince
Than break the stable verdict of a prince:
I do beseech you, let him pass in quiet.

K. John. Thou and thy word lie both in my command;
What canst thou promise, that I cannot break?
Which of these twain is greater infamy,
To disobey thy father, or thyself?
Thy word, nor no man's, may exceed his power;
Nor that same man doth never break his word
That keeps it to the utmost of his power:
The breach of faith dwells in the soul's consent:
Which if thyself without consent do break,
Thou art not charged with the breach of faith.—
Go, hang him; for thy licence lies in me:
And my constraint stands the excuse for thee.

Char. What, am I not a soldier in my word?
Then, arms adieu, and let them fight that list:
Shall I not give my girdle from my waist
But with a guardian I shall be controll'd,
To say, I may not give my things away?
Upon my soul, had Edward Prince of Wales
Engag'd his word, writ down his noble hand,
For all your knights to pass his father's land,
The royal king, to grace his warlike son,
Would not alone safe-conduct give to them,
But with all bounty feasted them and theirs.

K. John. Dwell'st thou on precedents? Then be it so.—
Say, Englishman, of what degree thou art.

Sal. An earl in England though a prisoner here;
And those that know me call me Salisbury.

K. John. Then, Salisbury, say whither thou art bound.

Sal. To Calice, where my liege, King Edward, is.

K. John. To Calice, Salisbury? Then to Calice pack;
And bid the king prepare a noble grave
To put his princely son, black Edward, in.
And as thou travell'st westward from this place,

Some two leagues hence there is a lofty hill,
Whose top seems topless, for the embracing sky
Doth hide his high head in her azure bosom;
Upon whose tall top when thy foot attains,
Look back upon the humble vale beneath,
(Humble of late, but now made proud with arms)
And thence behold the wretched Prince of Wales,
Hoop'd with a band of iron round about.
After which sight to Calice spur amain,
And say, the prince was smother'd and not slain:
And tell the king, this is not all his ill,
For I will greet him ere he thinks I will.
Away, begone; the smoke but of our shot
Will choke our foes, though bullets hit them not.

[*Exeunt.*]

[SCENE VI

The Same. A Part of the Field of Battle.]

Alarum. Enter Prince Edward and Artois.

Art. How fares your grace? are you not shot, my lord?
Pr. Ed. No, dear Artois; but chok'd with dust and smoke
    And stepp'd aside for breath and fresher air.
Art. Breathe then, and to't again: the amazed French
    Are quite distract with gazing on the crows;
    And, were our quivers full of shafts again,
    Your grace should see a glorious day of this:—
    O, for more arrows! Lord! that's our want.
Pr. Ed. Courage, Artois! a fig for feathered shafts
    When feathered fowls do bandy on our side!
    What need we fight and sweat and keep a coil
    When railing crows out-scold our adversaries?
    Up, up, Artois! the ground itself is arm'd
    [With] fire-containing flint; command our bows
    To hurl away their pretty-colour'd yew,
    And to't with stones: away, Artois, away;
    My soul doth prophesy we win the day.   *Exeunt.*

Alarum. Enter King John.

[*K. John.*] Our multitudes are in themselves confounded,
    Dismayed and distraught; swift-starting fear
    Hath buzz'd a cold dismay through all our army,
    And every petty disadvantage prompts
    The fear-possessed abject soul to fly:
    Myself, whose spirit is steel to their dull lead
    (What with recalling of the prophecy
    And that our native stones from English arms
    Rebel against us) find myself attainted
    With strong surprise of weak and yielding fear.

Enter Charles.

[*Char.*] Fly, father, fly! the French do kill the French;
    Some that would stand let drive at some that fly:
    Our drums strike nothing but discouragement,
    Our trumpets sound dishonour and retire;
    The spirit of fear, that feareth nought but death,
    Cowardly works confusion on itself.

Enter Philip.

[*Phil.*] Pluck out your eyes and see not this day's shame!
    An arm hath beat an army; one poor David
    Hath with a stone foil'd twenty stout Goliahs:
    Some twenty naked starvelings with small flints
    Have driven back a puissant host of men,
    Array'd and fenc'd in all accomplements.
K. John. Mordieu, they quoit at us and kill us up;
    No less than forty thousand wicked elders
    Have forty lean slaves this day ston'd to death.
Char. O, that I were some other countryman!
    This day hath set derision on the French,
    And all the world will blurt and scorn at us.
K. John. What, is there no hope left?
Phil. No hope but death, to bury up our shame.
K. John Make up once more with me; the twentieth part
    Of those that live are men enough to quail
    The feeble handful on the adverse part.

Char. Then charge again: if Heaven be not oppos'd,
  We cannot lose the day.
K. John.   On, away.   [*Exeunt.*

   Enter Audley, wounded, and rescued by two squires.

First Esq. How fares my lord?
Aud.   Even as a man may do,
  That dines at such a bloody feast as this.
Second Esq. I hope, my lord, that is no mortal scar.
Aud. No matter, if it be; the count is cast,
  And, in the worst, ends but a mortal man.
  Good friends, convey me to the princely Edward,
  That, in the crimson bravery of my blood,
  I may become him with saluting him;
  I'll smile and tell him that this open scar
  Doth end the harvest of his Audley's war.   *Exeunt.*

[SCENE VII

The Same. The English Camp.]

*Enter Prince Edward, King John, Charles, and all, with
ensigns spread.*

Pr. Ed. Now, John in France, and lately John of France,
  Thy bloody ensigns are my captive colours;
  And you, high-vaunting Charles of Normandy,
  That once to-day sent me a horse to fly,
  Are now the subjects of my clemency.
  Fie, lords! is't not a shame that English boys,
  Whose early days are yet not worth a beard,
  Should in the bosom of your kingdom thus,
  One against twenty, beat you up together?
K. John. Thy fortune, not thy force, hath conquer'd us.
Pr. Ed. An argument that Heaven aids the right.—

       [*Enter Artois, with Philip.*]

  See, see, Artois doth bring with him along
  The late good-counsel-giver to my soul!—

Welcome, Artois, and welcome, Philip, too:
Who now, of you or I, have need to pray!
Now is the proverb verified in you,
Too bright a morning breeds a louring day,—

Sound trumpets. Enter Audley.

But, say, what grim discouragement comes here!
Alas, what thousand armed men of France
Have writ that note of death in Audley's face?—
Speak, thou that woo'st death with thy careless smile
And look'st so merrily upon thy grave
As if thou wert enamour'd on thine end,
What hungry sword hath so bereav'd thy face
And lopp'd a true friend from my loving soul?

Aud. O prince, thy sweet bemoaning speech to me
Is as a mournful knell to one dead-sick.

Pr. Ed. Dear Audley, if my tongue ring out thy end.
My arms shall be thy grave: what may I do,
To win thy life, or to revenge thy death?
If thou wilt drink the blood of captive kings
Or that it were restorative, command
A health of king's blood, and I'll drink to thee:
If honour may dispense for thee with death,
The never-dying honour of this day
Share wholly, Audley, to thyself, and live.

Aud. Victorious prince,—that thou art so, behold
A Cæsar's fame in king's captivity,—
If I could hold dim death but at a bay,
Till I did see my liege thy royal father,
My soul should yield this castle of my flesh,
This mangled tribute, with all willingness
To darkness, consummation, dust and worms.

Pr. Ed. Cheerly, bold man! thy soul is all too proud
To yield her city for one little breach
Should be divorced from her earthly spouse
By the soft temper of a Frenchman's sword.
Lo, to repair thy life, I give to thee
Three thousand marks a year in English land.

Aud. I take thy gift, to pay the debts I owe.
    These two poor squires redeem'd me from the French,
    With lusty and dear hazard of their lives;
    What thou hast given me, I give to them;
    And, as thou lov'st me, prince, lay thy consent
    To this bequeath in my last testament.
Pr. Ed. Renowned Audley, live, and have from me
    This gift twice doubled, to these squires and thee:
    But, live or die, what thou hast given away,
    To these and theirs shall lasting freedom stay.—
    Come, gentlemen, I'll see my friend bestow'd
    Within an easy litter; then we'll march
    Proudly toward Calice with triumphant pace
    Unto my royal father, and there bring
    The tribute of my wars, fair France's king.   *Exeunt.*

[ACT V

SCENE I

Picardy. The English Camp before Calais.]

Enter King Edward, Queen Philip, Derby, soldiers.

K. Ed. No more, Queen Philip, pacify yourself;
    Copland, except he can excuse his fault,
    Shall find displeasure written in our looks.—
    And now unto this proud resisting town:
    Soldiers, assault; I will no longer stay,
    To be deluded by their false delays;
    Put all to sword, and make the spoil your own.

*Enter six citizens in their shirts, bare foot, with halters about
their necks.*

Cit. Mercy, King Edward! mercy, gracious lord!
K. Ed. Contemptuous villains! call ye now for truce?
    Mine ears are stopp'd against your bootless cries:—

Sound, drums' alarum; draw, threat'ning swords!

1 *Cit.* Ah, noble prince, take pity on this town,
And hear us, mighty king!
We claim the promise that your highness made;
The two days' respite is not yet expir'd,
And we are come with willingness to bear
What torturing death or punishment you please,
So that the trembling multitude be sav'd.

K. Ed. My promise? well, I do confess as much:
But I require the chiefest citizens,
And men of most account, that should submit.
You peradventure are but servile grooms
Or some felonious robbers on the sea,
Whom, apprehended, law would execute,
Albeit severity lay dead in us:
No, no, ye cannot overreach us thus.

2 *Cit.* The sun, dread lord, that in the western fall
Beholds us now low brought through misery,
Did in the orient purple of the morn
Salute our coming forth, when we were known;
Or may our portion be with damned fiends.

K. Ed. If it be so, then let our covenant stand,
We take possession of the town in peace:
But, for yourselves, look you for no remorse;
But, as imperial justice hath decreed,
Your bodies shall be dragg'd about these walls
And after feel the stroke of quartering steel:
This is your doom;—go, soldiers, see it done.

Queen. Ah, be more mild unto these yielding men!
It is a glorious thing, to stablish peace;
And kings approach the nearest unto God,
By giving life and safety unto men.
As thou intendest to be King of France,
So let her people live to call thee king;
For what the sword cuts down or fire hath spoil'd
Is held in reputation none of ours.

K. Ed. Although experience teach us this is true,
That peaceful quietness brings most delight

When most of all abuses are controll'd,
Yet, insomuch it shall be known that we
As well can master our affections
As conquer other by the dint of sword,
Philip, prevail; we yield to thy request;
These men shall live to boast of clemency,—
And, tyranny, strike terror to thyself.

Cit. Long live your highness! happy be your reign!

K. Ed. Go, get you hence, return unto the town;
And if this kindness hath deserv'd your love,
Learn then to reverence Edward as your king.—

Exeunt.

Now, might we hear of our affairs abroad,
We would, till gloomy winter were o'er-spent,
Dispose our men in garrison a while.
But who comes here?

Enter Copland and King David.

Der. Copland, my lord, and David King of Scots.

K. Ed. Is this the proud presumptuous squire o' the
   north
That would not yield his prisoner to my queen?

Cop. I am, my liege, a northern squire, indeed,
But neither proud nor insolent, I trust.

K. Ed. What moved thee then to be so obstinate
To contradict our royal queen's desire?

Cop. No wilful disobedience, mighty lord,
But my desert and public law of arms:
I took the king myself in single fight;
And, like a soldier, would be loath to lose
The least pre-eminence that I had won:
And Copland straight upon your highness' charge
Is come to France and with a lowly mind
Doth vail the bonnet of his victory.
Receive, dread lord, the custom of my fraught,
The wealthy tribute of my labouring hands;
Which should long since have been surrender'd up,
Had but your gracious self been there in place.

Queen. But, Copland, thou didst scorn the king's com-
    mand,
  Neglecting our commission in his name.
Cop. His name I reverence, but his person more;
  His name shall keep me in allegiance still,
  But to his person I will bend my knee.
K. Ed. I pray thee, Philip, let displeasure pass;
  This man doth please me and I like his words:
  For what is he that will attempt great deeds
  And lose the glory that ensues the same?
  All rivers have recourse unto the sea;
  And Copland's faith, relation to his king.—
  Kneel therefore down; now rise, King Edward's knight:
  And, to maintain thy state, I freely give
  Five hundred marks a year to thee and thine.—

Enter Salisbury.

Welcome, Lord Salisbury: what news from Britain?
Sal. This, mighty king: the country we have won;
  And John de Mountford, regent of that place,
  Presents your highness with this coronet,
  Protesting true allegiance to your grace.
K. Ed. We thank thee for thy service, valiant earl;
  Challenge our favour, for we owe it thee.
Sal. But now, my lord, as this is joyful news,
  So must my voice be tragical again
  And I must sing of doleful accidents.
K. Ed. What, have our men the overthrow at Poitiers?
  Or is our son beset with too much odds?
Sal. He was, my lord: and as my worthless self,
  With forty other serviceable knights,
  Under safe-conduct of the Dauphin's seal
  Did travel that way, finding him distress'd,
  A troop of lances met us on the way,
  Surpris'd, and brought us prisoners to the king;
  Who, proud of this and eager of revenge,
  Commanded straight to cut off all our heads:
  And surely we had died, but that the duke,

More full of honour than his angry sire,
Procur'd our quick deliverance from thence:
But, ere we went, 'Salute your king,' quoth he,
'Bid him provide a funeral for his son,
To-day our sword shall cut his thread of life;
And, sooner than he thinks, we'll be with him,
To quittance those displeasures he hath done':
This said, we passed, not daring to reply;
Our hearts were dead, our looks diffus'd and wan.
Wand'ring, at last we climb'd unto a hill;
From whence, although our grief were much before,
Yet now to see the occasion with our eyes
Did thrice so much increase our heaviness:
For there, my lord, O, there we did descry
Down in a valley how both armies lay.
The French had cast their trenches like a ring;
And every barricado's open front
Was thick emboss'd with brazen ordinance.
Here stood a battle of ten thousand horse;
There twice as many pikes, in quadrant-wise:
Here cross-bows and deadly-wounding darts:
And in the midst, like to a slender point
Within the compass of the horizon,—
As't were a rising bubble in the sea,
A hazel-wand amidst a wood of pines,
Or as a bear fast chain'd unto a stake,—
Stood famous Edward, still expecting when
Those dogs of France would fasten on his flesh.
Anon, the death-procuring knell begins:
Off go the cannons, that, with trembling noise,
Did shake the very mountain where they stood;
Then sound the trumpets' clangour in the air,
The battles join: and, when we could no more
Discern the difference 'twixt the friend and foe,
(So intricate the dark confusion was)
Away we turn'd our wat'ry eyes, with sighs
As black as powder fuming into smoke.
And thus, I fear, unhappy have I told

The most untimely tale of Edward's fall.

Queen. Ah me! is this my welcome into France?
  Is this the comfort that I look'd to have
  When I should meet with my beloved son?
  Sweet Ned, I would thy mother in the sea
  Had been prevented of this mortal grief!

K. Ed. Content thee, Philip: 'tis not tears will serve
  To call him back if he be taken hence:
  Comfort thyself, as I do, gentle queen,
  With hope of sharp, unheard-of, dire revenge.—
  He bids me to provide his funeral;
  And so I will: but all the peers in France
  Shall mourners be and weep out bloody tears
  Until their empty veins be dry and sere:
  The pillars of his hearse shall be their bones;
  The mould that covers him, their cities' ashes;
  His knell, the groaning cries of dying men;
  And, in the stead of tapers on his tomb,
  An hundred fifty towers shall burning blaze,
  While we bewail our valiant son's decease.

After a flourish, sounded within, enter a Herald.

Her. Rejoice, my lord; ascend the imperial throne!
  The mighty and redoubted Prince of Wales,
  Great servitor to bloody Mars in arms,
  The Frenchman's terror and his country's fame,
  Triumphant rideth like a Roman peer:
  And, lowly at his stirrup, comes afoot
  King John of France together with his son
  In captive bonds; whose diadem he brings
  To crown thee with and to proclaim thee king.

K. Ed. Away with mourning, Philip, wipe thine eyes;—
  Sound, trumpets, welcome in Plantagenet!

Enter Prince Edward, King John, Philip, Audley, Artois.

  As things, long lost, when they are found again,
  So doth my son rejoice his father's heart,
  For whom, even now, my soul was much perplex'd!

Queen. Be this a token to express my joy,   *Kiss.*
    For inward passions will not let me speak.
Pr. Ed. My gracious father, here receive the gift,

[*Presenting him with King John's crown.*]

This wreath of conquest and reward of war,
Got with as mickle peril of our lives
As e'er was thing of price before this day;
Install your highness in your proper right:
And, herewithal, I render to your hands
These prisoners, chief occasion of our strife.

K. Ed. So, John of France, I see you keep your word.
    You promis'd to be sooner with ourself
    Than we did think for, and 'tis so indeed:
    But, had you done at first as now you do,
    How many civil towns had stood untouch'd
    That now are turn'd to ragged heaps of stones?
    How many people's lives might'st thou have sav'd
    That are untimely sunk into their graves?

K. John. Edward, recount not things irrevocable;
    Tell me what ransom thou requir'st to have.

K. Ed. Thy ransom, John, hereafter shall be known.
    But first to England thou must cross the seas
    To see what entertainment it affords;
    Howe'er it falls, it cannot be so bad
    As ours hath been since we arriv'd in France.

K. John. Accursed man! of this I was foretold,
    But did misconster what the prophet told.

Pr. Ed. Now, father, this petition Edward makes,—
    To thee, [*kneels*] whose grace hath been his strongest
        shield,
    That, as thy pleasure chose me for the man
    To be the instrument to show thy power,
    So thou wilt grant, that many princes more,
    Bred and brought up within that little isle,
    May still be famous for like victories!—
    And, for my part, the bloody scars I bear,
    The weary nights that I have watch'd in field,

The dangerous conflicts I have often had,
The fearful menaces were proffer'd me,
The heat and cold and what else might displease,
I wish were now redoubled twenty-fold;
So that hereafter ages, when they read
The painful traffic of my tender youth,
Might thereby be inflamed with such resolve
As not the territories of France alone,
But likewise Spain, Turkey, and what countries else
That justly would provoke fair England's ire,
Might, at their presence, tremble and retire!

K. Ed. Here, English lords, we do proclaim a rest,
An intercession of our painful arms:
Sheathe up your swords, refresh your weary limbs,
Peruse your spoils; and, after we have breath'd
A day or two within this haven-town,
God willing, then for England we'll be shipp'd;
Where, in a happy hour, I trust, we shall
Arrive, three kings, two princes, and a queen.

[Exeunt]

WOODSTOCK

(Anonymous)

[DRAMATIS PERSONÆ:

THOMAS OF WOODSTOCK, Duke of Gloucester and Lord
    Protector of England.

JOHN OF GAUNT, Duke of Lancaster.

EDMUND OF LANGLEY, Duke of York.

EARL OF ARUNDEL, Lord Admiral of England.

EARL OF SURREY.

SIR THOMAS CHEYNEY.

KING RICHARD II.

SIR HENRY GREENE, a favourite of King Richard's.

SIR EDWARD BAGOT, another favourite.

SIR WILLIAM BUSHY, another favourite.

SIR THOMAS SCROOPE, another favourite.

SIR ROBERT TRESILIAN, a lawyer.

NIMBLE, a lawyer's devil.

CROSSBY, a law officer.

FLEMING, a law officer.

RICHARD EXTON, Lord Mayor of London.

SIMON IGNORANCE, Bailiff of Dunstable.

COWTAIL, a grazier.

CYNTHIA, a personage in a masque.

SHERIFF OF KENT.

SHERIFF OF NORTHUMBERLAND.

LAPOOLE, Governor of Calais.

THE GHOST OF THE BLACK PRINCE.

THE GHOST OF KING EDWARD III.

ANNE OF BOHEMIA, Queen of England.

DUCHESS OF GLOUCESTER, wife of Thomas of Woodstock.

DUCHESS OF IRELAND.

Also Servants, Maids, Courtiers, Law-officers, Soldiers,
             Archers, Knights.]

WOODSTOCK

[ACT I]

SCENE I [*A house near London*]

Enter hastily at several doors: DUKE OF LANCASTER, DUKE OF YORK, *the* EARLS OF ARUNDEL *and* SURREY, *with napkins on their arms and knives in their hands, and* SIR THOMAS CHEYNEY, *with others bearing torches, and some with cloaks and rapiers.*

ALL. Lights, lights, bring torches knaves!

LANC.   Shut to the gates;
  Let no man out until the house be searched.

YORK. Call for our coaches, let's away good brother;
  Now by th' blest saints—I fear we are poisoned all.

ARUND. Poisoned my lord?

LANC. Ay, ay, good Arundel, 'tis high time, begone.
  May heaven be blest for this prevention.

YORK. God for thy mercy! Would our cousin king
  So cozen us, to poison us in our meat?

LANC. Has no man here some helping antidote
  For fear already we have ta'en some dram?
  What thinkst thou, Cheyney; thou first broughtst the
    tidings,
  Are we not poisoned, think'st thou?

CHEY.   Fear not, my lords.
  That mischievous potion was as yet unserved;
  It was a liquid bane dissolved in wine,
  Which after supper should have been caroused
  To young King Richard's health.

LANC. Good i'faith! Are his uncles' deaths become
  Health to King Richard? How came it out?
  Sir Thomas Cheyney, pray resolve us.

CHEY. A Carmelite friar, my lord, revealed the plot
  And should have acted it, but, touched in conscience,

He came to your good brother, the Lord Protector,
And so disclosed it; who straight sent me to you.

YORK. The Lord protect him for it, ay, and our cousin king:
High Heaven be judge, we wish all good to him.

LANC. A heavy charge, good Woodstock, hast thou had,
To be protector to so wild a prince,
So far degenerate from his noble father,
   Whom the trembling French the Black Prince called,
   Not of a swart and melancholy brow
   (For sweet and lovely was his countenance)
   But that he made so many funeral days
   In mournful France; the warlike battles won
   At Crecy Field, Poitiers, Artoise and Maine
   Made all France groan under his conquering arm.
But heaven forestalled his diadem on earth
To place him with a royal crown in heaven.
Rise may his dust to glory! Ere he'd 'a done
A deed so base unto his enemy,
Much less unto the brothers of his father,
He'd first have lost his royal blood in drops,
Dissolved the strings of his humanity,
And lost that livelihood that was preserved
To make his (unlike) son a wanton king.

YORK. Forbear, good John of Gaunt; believe me, brother,
We may do wrong unto our cousin king:
I fear his flattering minions more than him.

LANC. By the blest Virgin, noble Edmund York
I'm past all patience. Poison his subjects,
His royal uncles! Why, the proud Castilian[s]
Where John of Gaunt writes King and Sovereign,
Would not throw off their vile and servile yoke
By treachery so base. Patience, gracious heaven!

ARUND. A good invoke, right princely Lancaster,
Calm thy high spleen. Sir Thomas Cheyney here
Can tell the circumstance; pray give him leave.

LANC. Well, let him speak.

CHEY. 'Tis certainly made known, my reverend lords,
To your loved brother, and the good Protector,

That not King Richard but his flatterers,
Sir Henry Greene, joined with Sir Edward Bagot,
And that sly machiavel Tresilian,
Whom now the king elects for Lord Chief Justice,
Had all great hands in this conspiracy.

LANC. By blessed Mary I'll confound them all.

YORK. Your spleen confounds yourself.

LANC. By kingly Edward's soul, my royal father,
    I'll be revenged at full on all their lives.

YORK. Nay, if your rage break to such high extremes
    You will prevent yourself, and lose revenge.

LANC. Why Edmund, canst thou give a reason yet
    Though we, so near in blood, his hapless uncles,
    (His grandsire Edward's sons; his father's brothers)
    Should thus be made away, why might it be
    That Arundel and Surrey here should die?

SURR. Some friend of theirs wanted my earldom sore.

ARUND. Perhaps my office of the Admiralty—
    If a better and more fortunate hand could govern it
    I would 'twere none of mine—
    Yet thus much can I say; and make my praise
    No more than merit: a wealthier prize
    Did never yet take harbour in our roads
    Than I to England brought. You all can tell,
    Full threescore sail of tall and lusty ships
    And six great carracks fraught with oil and wines
    I brought King Richard in abundance home
    So much, that plenty hath so staled our palates
    As that a tun of high-priced wines of France
    Is hardly worth a mark of English money.
    If service such as this done to my country
    Merit my heart to bleed, let it bleed freely.

LANC. We'll bleed together, warlike Arundel.
    Cousin of Surrey, princely Edmund York,
    Let's think on some revenge: if we must die
    Ten thousand souls shall keep us company.

YORK. Patience, good Lancaster. Tell me, kind Cheyney,
    How does thy master, our good brother Woodstock,

Plain Thomas, for by th' rood so all men call him
For his plain dealing, and his simple clothing:
Let others jet in silk and gold, says he,
A coat of English frieze best pleaseth me.
How thinks his unsophisticated plainness
Of these bitter compounds? Fears he no drug
Put in his broth? shall his healths be secure?

CHEY. 'Faith my lord, his mind suits with his habit
Homely and plain: both free from pride and envy
And therein will admit distrust to none.

Enter THOMAS OF WOODSTOCK *in frieze. The mace [afore]
him. The* LORD MAYOR EXTON, *and others with lights afore
them.*

And see, his grace himself is come to greet you.
By y'r leave there: room for my Lord Protector's grace!

YORK. ⎫
LANC. ⎭ Health to your grace.

WOOD. I salute your healths good brothers, pray pardon me;
I'll speak with you anon. Hie thee, good Exton;
Good Lord Mayor, I do beseech ye prosecute
With your best care a means for all our safeties.
Mischief hath often double practices;
Treachery wants not his second stratagem;
Who knows but steel may hit, though poison fail?
Alack-the-day, the night is made a veil
To shadow mischief; set, I beseech,
Strong guard and careful to attend the City.
Our Lady help, we know not who are friends,
Our foes are grown so mighty, pray be careful.

L. MAY. Your friends are great in London, good my lord.
I'll front all dangers, trust it on my word.   [*Exit*]

WOOD. Thanks from my heart I swear. Afore my God,
    I know not which way to bestow myself,
    The time's so busy and so dangerous too.
Why, how now, brothers? how fares good John o'
    Gaunt?
Th'art vexed I know; thou griev'st, kind Edmund York;

Arundel and Surrey, noble kinsmen
I know ye all are discontented much;
But be not so. Afore my God, I swear
King Richard loves you all; and, credit me,
The princely gentleman is innocent
Of this black deed and base conspiracy.
Speak, speak, how is't with princely Lancaster?

LANC. Sick Gloster, sick. . . We all are weary,
And fain we would lie down to rest ourselves
But that so many serpents lurk i' th' grass—
We dare not sleep.

WOOD.   Enough, enough;
Good brother, I have found out the disease:
When the head aches, the body is not healthful.
King Richard's wounded with a wanton humour,
Lulled and secured by flattering sycophants;
But 'tis not deadly yet, it may be cured:
Some vein let blood where the corruption lies,
And all shall heal again.

YORK. Then lose no time, lest it grow ulcerous.
The false Tresilian, Greene, and Bagot
Run naught but poison, brother; spill them all.

LANC. They guide the nonage king; 'tis they protect him.
You wear the title of protectorship
But like an under-officer, as though
Yours were derived from theirs; 'faith, you're too plain.

WOOD. In my apparel, you'll say.

LANC.   Good faith, in all.
The Commons murmur 'gainst the dissolute king.
Treason is whispered at each common table
As customary as their thanks to heaven.
Men need not gaze up to the sky to see
Whether the sun shine clear or no; 'tis found
By the small light should beautify the ground.
Conceit you me, a blind man thus much sees:
He wants his eyes to whom we bend our knees.

ARUND. You all are princes of the royal blood,
Yet like great oaks ye let the ivy grow

To eat your hearts out with his false embraces.
Ye understand, my lord?

WOOD. Ay, ay, good coz, as if ye plainly said,
'Destroy those flatterers and tell King Richard
He does abase himself to countenance them.'
Soft, soft!
Fruit that grows high is not securely plucked;
We must use ladders and by steps ascend
Till by degrees we reach the altitude.
You conceit me too?—Pray be smooth awhile.
Tomorrow is the solemn nuptial day
Betwixt the king and virtuous Anne a Beame
The Emperor's daughter, a right gracious lady
That's come to England for King Richard's love.
Then, as you love his grace—and hate his flatterers—
Discountenance not the day with the least frown;
Be ignorant of what ye know. Afore my God,
I have good hope this happy marriage, brothers,
Of this so noble and religious princess,
Will mildly calm his headstrong youth to see
And shun those stains that blur his majesty.
If not, by good King Edward's bones, our royal father,
I will remove those hinderers of his health,
Tho't cost my head.

YORK. ⎫
LANC. ⎬ On these conditions, brother, we agree.

ARUND. And I.

SURR.   And I.

LANC. To hide our hate is soundest policy.

YORK. And brother Gloster, since it is your pleasure
To have us smooth our sullen brows with smiles,
We'd have you suit your outside to your heart,
And like a courtier cast this country habit
For which the coarse and vulgar call your grace
By th' title of Plain Thomas: yet we doubt not
Tomorrow we shall have good hope to see
Your high protectorship in bravery.

WOOD. No, no, good York, this is as fair a sight;

My heart in this plain frieze sits true and right.
In this I'll serve my king as true and bold
As if my outside were all trapped in gold.

LANC. By Mary, but you shall not, brother Woodstock!
What, the marriage-day to Richard and his Queen,
And will ye so disgrace the state and realm?
We'll have you brave, i'faith!

WOOD.   Well, well,
For your sakes, brothers, and this solemn day,
For once I'll sumpter a gaudy wardrobe, but 'tis more
Than I have done (I vow) these twenty years.
Afore my God, the king could not have entreated me
To leave this habit, but your wills be done.
Let's hie to court; you all your wishes have:
One weary day, Plain Thomas will be brave.   *Exeunt*

SCENE 2 [*A house near London*]

Enter GREENE, BAGOT *and* TRESILIAN, *in rage.*

TRES. Nay, good Sir Henry, King Richard calls for you.

BAGOT. Prithee, sweet Greene,
Visit his highness and forsake these passions.

GREEN. 'Sblood I am vexed, Tresilian, mad me not,
Thyself and I and all are now undone.
The lords at London are secured from harm,
The plot's revealed. Black curses seize the traitor!

BAGOT. Eternal torments whip that Carmelite!

TRES. A deeper hell than Limbo Patrum hold him,
A fainting villain, confusion crush his soul!

BAGOT. Could the false slave recoil, and swore their
deaths!

GREEN. Mischief devour him! Had it but ta'en effect
On Lancaster and Edmund Duke of York,
(Those headstrong uncles to the gentle king)
The third brother, Plain Thomas, the Protector,
Had quickly been removed; but since 'tis thus
Our safeties must be cared for, and 'tis best

To keep us near the person of the king.
Had they been dead, we had ruled the realm and him.
BAGOT. So shall we still, so long as Richard lives.
I know he cannot brook his stubborn uncles.
Come, think not on't; cheer thee, Tresilian,
Here's better news for thee: we have so wrought
With kingly Richard, that by his consent
You are already mounted on your footcloth
(Your scarlet or your purple, which ye please)
And shortly are to underprop the name—
Mark me, Tresilian—of Lord Chief Justice of England.
TRES. Hum, hum, hum. Legit or non legit? Methinks
    already
I sit upon the bench with dreadful frowns
frighting the lousy rascals,
and when the jury once cries 'Guilty' could pronounce
'Lord have mercy on thee', with a brow
as rough and stern as surly Rhadamanth;
or when a fellow talks, cry 'Take him, jailor,
clap bolts of iron on his heels and hands!'
Chief Justice, my lords! Hum, hum, hum.
I will wear the office in his true ornament.
GREEN. But good your honour, as twill shortly be,
You must observe and fashion to the time
The habit of your laws. The king is young,
Ay, and a little wanton—so perhaps are we;
Your laws must not be beadles then, Tresilian,
To punish your benefactors, look to that.
TRES. How sir, to punish you, the minions to the king,
The jewels of his heart, his dearest loves?
Zounds, I will screw and wind the subtle law
To any fashion that shall like you best.
It shall be law, what I shall say is law,
And what's most suitable to all your pleasures.
BAGOT. Thanks to your lordship which is yet to come!
GREEN. Farewell Tresilian, still be near the court.
    Anon King Richard shall confirm thy state.
    We must attend his grace to Westminster

To the high nuptials of fair Anne a Beame,
That must be now his wife and England's queen.

Exeunt GREENE *and* BAGOT

TRES. So; let them pass; Tresilian, now bethink thee.
Hum, Lord Chief Justice; methinks already
I am swelled more plump than erst I was.
Authority's a dish that feeds men fat,
An excellent delicate: yet best be wise,
No state's secure without some enemies.
The Dukes will frown; why, I can look as grim
As John of Gaunt and all that frown with him.
But yet until mine office be put on
By kingly Richard, I'll conceal myself;
Framing such subtle laws that Janus-like
May with a double face salute them both.
I'll search my brain and turn the leaves of law:
Wit makes us great, greatness keeps fools in awe.
My man there ho! Where's Nimble?

[Enter] NIMBLE

NIMB. As Nimble as an eel, sir. Did ye call, sir?

TRES. Sir!—Look out some better phrase: salute again.

NIMB. I know no other, sir, unless you'll be frenchified, and
let me lay the Monsieur to your charge, or Sweet Signior.

TRES. Neither. 'Tis higher yet. Nimble, thou buckram scribe,
think once again.

NIMB. Neither Sir: nor Monsieur: nor Signior. What should
I call him? Troth, he's monstrously translated suddenly!
At first, when we were schoolfellows then I called him
Sirrah, but since he became my master I pared away the
Ah and served him with the Sir. What title he has got
now, I know not, but I'll try further. . . .
Has your worship any employment for me?

TRES. Thou gross uncaput, no, thou speak'st not yet.

NIMB. My mouth was open I'm sure. . . . If your honour
would please to hear me . . .

TRES. Ha, honour sayst thou? Ay, now thou hitt'st it,
Nimble.

NIMB. I knew I should wind about ye till I had your honour.

TRES. Nimble, bend thy knee. . . .
  The Lord Chief Justice of England speaks to thee.

NIMB. The Lord be praised! we shall have a flourishing commonwealth, sir.

TRES. Peace, let me speak to thee.

NIMB. Yes, anything—so your honour pray not for me, I care not; for now you're Lord Chief Justice, if ever ye cry, Lord have mercy upon me, I shall hang for't, sure!

TRES. No. Those fearful words shall not be pronounced against thee, Nimble.

NIMB. Thank ye, my lord. Nay, an you'll stand between me and the gallows, I'll be an arrant thief, sure. If I cannot pick up my crumbs by the law quickly, I'll cast away my buckram bags and be a highway lawyer now, certainly.

TRES. Canst thou remember, Nimble, how by degrees I rose, since first thou knew'st me? I was first a school-boy . . .

NIMB. Ay, saving your honour's speech, your worshipful tail was whipped for stealing my dinner out of my satchel. You were ever so crafty in your childhood, that I knew your worship would prove a good lawyer.

TRES. Interrupt me not. Those days thou knewst, I say,
  From whence I did become a plodding clerk,
  From which I bounced, as thou dost now, in buckram
  To be a pleading lawyer (and there I stayed)
  Till by the king I was Chief Justice made.
  Nimble, I read this discipline to thee
  To stir thy mind up still to industry.

NIMB. Thank your good lordship.

TRES. Go to thy mistress; 'Lady' you now must call her:
  Bid her remove her household up to London,
  Tell her our fortunes, and with how much peril
  We have attained this place of eminence.
  Go and remove her.

NIMB. With a Habeas Corpus or a Certiorari, I assure ye. And so I leave your lordship, always hoping of your wonted favour:

That when I have passed the London Bridge of Affliction
I may arrive with you at the Westminster Hall of Pro-
motion.
And then I care not.

TRES. Thou shalt: thou hast an executing look
And I will put the axe into thy hand.
I rule the law: thou by the law shalt stand.

NIMB. I thank your lordship, and a fig for the rope then!

Exeunt

[SCENE 3: *London, the Court*]

Sound a sennet. Enter in great state KING RICHARD *and*
QUEEN ANNE, *crowned*: LANCASTER, YORK, ARUNDEL, SURREY,
GREENE, BAGOT; *and* WOODSTOCK *very brave; the* DUCHESS
OF GLOSTER *and the* DUCHESS OF IRELAND.

KING. Bagot and Greene, next to the fair Queen Anne
Take your high places, by King Richard's side,
And give fair welcome to our queen and bride.
Uncles of Woodstock, York, and Lancaster,
Make full our wishes, and salute our queen:
Give all your welcomes to fair Anne a Beame.

LANC. I hope sweet prince, her grace mistakes us not
To make our hearts the worser part of us:
Our tongues have in our English eloquence
(Harsh though it is) pronounced her welcomes many
By oaths and loyal protestations,
To which we add a thousand infinites;
But in a word, fair queen, for ever welcome!

WOOD. Let me prevent the rest, for mercy's sake!
If all their welcomes be as long as thine
This health will not go round this week, by th' Mass!
Sweet queen, and cousin—now I'll call you so—
In plain and honest phrase, welcome to England!
Think they speak all in me—and you have seen
All England cry with joy, 'God bless the Queen'—
And so afore my God I know they wish it.

Only I fear my duty not misconstr'd—
Nay, nay, King Richard, 'fore God I'll speak the truth!
—Sweet queen, you've found a young and wanton choice,
A wild-head: yet a kingly gentleman;
A youth unsettled: yet he's princely bred;
Descended from the royal'st bloods in Europe,
The kingly stock of England and of France.
Yet he's a harebrain, a very wag i'faith,
But you must bear, madam: 'las, he's but a blossom;
But his maturity I hope you'll find
True English-bred, a king loving and kind.

KING. I thank ye for double praise, good uncle.

WOOD. Ay, ay, good coz, I'm Plain Thomas; by th' rood,
I'll speak the truth.

QUEEN. My sovereign lord, and you true English peers,
Your all-accomplished honours have so tied
My senses by a magical restraint
In the sweet spell of these your fair demeanours,
That I am bound and charmed from what I was;
My native country I no more remember
But as a tale told in my infancy,
The greatest part forgot: and that which is,
Appears to England's fair Elysium
Like brambles to the cedars, coarse to fine,
Or like the wild grape to the fruitful vine,
And, having left the earth where I was bred
And English made, let me be englishèd:
They best shall please me shall me English call.
My heart, great king to you: my love to all.

KING. Grammercy, Nan, thou highly honour'st me.

YORK. And blest is England in this sweet accord.

WOOD. Afore my God, sweet queen, our English ladies
And all the women that this isle contains
Shall sing in raise of this your memory,
And keep records of virtuous Anne a Beame,
Whose discipline hath taught them womanhood.
What erst seemed well by custom, now looks rude;
Our women, till your coming, fairest cousin,

Did use like men to straddle when they ride,
But you have taught them now to sit aside.
Yet (by y'r leave) young practice often reels:
I have seen some of your scholars kick up both their
    heels!

DUCH. GL. What have you seen, my lord?

WOOD.   Nay, nay, nothing, wife.
I see little without spectacles, thou knowst.

KING. Trust him not, aunt, for now he's grown so brave
He will be courting; ay, and kissing too.
Nay, uncle! now I'll do as much for you—
And lay your faults all open to the world!

WOOD. Ay, ay, do, do.

KING. I'm glad you're grown so careless: now by my crown
I swear, good uncles York and Lancaster,
When you this morning came to visit me
I did not know him in this strange attire.
How comes this golden metamorphosis
From homespun housewifery? Speak, good uncle;
I never saw you hatched and gilded thus.

WOOD. I am no stoic, my dear sovereign cousin,
To make my plainness seem canonical,
But to allow myself such ornaments
As might be fitting for your nuptial day
And coronation of your virtuous queen;
But were the eye of day once closed again
Upon this back they never more should come.

KING. You have much graced the day. But, noble uncle,
I did observe what I have wondered at;
As we, today, rode on to Westminster,
Methought your horse, that's wont to tread the ground
And pace as if he kicked it, scornfully,
Mount and curvet, like strong Bucephalus,
Today he trod as slow and melancholy
As if his legs had failed to bear his load.

WOOD. And can ye blame the beast? Afore my God,
He was not wont to bear such loads indeed!
A hundred oaks upon these shoulders hang

To make me brave upon your wedding-day,
And more than that; to make my horse more tire,
Ten acres of good land are stiched up here.
You know, good coz, this was not wont to be.

KING. In your tother hose, uncle?

GREEN. No, nor his frieze coat neither!

WOOD. Ay, ay, mock on. My tother hose, say ye?
There's honest plain dealing in my tother hose.
Should this fashion last I must raise new rents,
Undo my poor tenants, turn away my servants,
And guard myself with lace; nay, sell more land
And lordships too, by th' rood. Hear me, King Richard:
If thus I jet in pride, I still shall lose;
But I'll build castles in my tother hose.

QUEEN. The king but jests, my lord; and you grow angry.

WOOD. Tother hose! did some here wear that fashion
They would not tax and pill the Commons so!

YORK [*aside*]. 'Sfoot, he forewarned us, and will break out
himself.

LANC. [*aside*]. No matter; we'll back him, though it grow
to blows.

WOOD. Scoff ye my plainness, I'll talk no riddles,
Plain Thomas will speak plainly: there's Bagot there, and
Greene—

GREEN.
BAGOT. } And what of them, my lord?

WOOD. Upstarts, come down, you have no places there:
Here's better men to grace King Richard's chair,
If't pleased him grace them so.

KING.   Uncle, forbear.

WOOD. These cut the columns that should prop thy house.
They tax the poor, and I am scandalled for it;
That by my fault those late oppressions rise
To set the Commons in a mutiny
That London even itself was sacked by them.
And who did all these rank commotions point at?
Even at these two: Bagot here, and Greene,
With false Tresilian, whom your grace we hear

Hath made Chief Justice: well, well, be it so;
Mischief on mischief sure will shortly flow.
Pardon my speech, my lord. Since now we're all so brave,
To grace Queen Anne, this day we'll spend in sport.
But in my tother hose, I'll tickle them for't.

GREEN. Come, come, ye dote, my lord.

LANC. Dote, sir? Know ye to whom ye speak?

KING. No more, good uncles. Come, sweet Greene, ha'
done.
(I'll wring them all for this, by England's crown).
—Why is our Lord Protector so outrageous?

WOOD. Because thy subjects have such outrage shown them
By these thy flatterers. Let the sun dry up
What th' unwholesome fog hath choked the ground with.
Here's Arundel, thy ocean's admiral,
Hath brought thee home a rich and wealthy prize,
Ta'en three score sail of ships, and six great carracks
All richly laden; let those goods be sold
To satisfy those borrowed sums of coin
Their pride hath forced from the needy Commons:
To salve which inconvenience, I beseech your grace
You would vouchsafe to let me have the sale
And distribution of those goods.

KING. Our word, good uncle, is already passed,
Which cannot with our honour be recalled:
Those wealthy prizes already are bestowed
On these our friends.

ALL THE LORDS.   On them, my lord?

KING. Yes. Who storms at it?

WOOD.   Shall cankers eat the fruit
That planting and good husbandry hath nourished?

GREEN. ⎱
BAGOT. ⎰ Cankers?!

YORK. ⎱
ARUND. ⎰ Ay, cankers! caterpillars!

LANC.   Worse than consuming
fires
That eat up all their fury falls upon.

KING. Once more be still.
   Who is't that dares encounter with our will?
   We did bestow them. Hear me, kind uncles:
   We shall ere long be past protectorship
   Then will we rule ourself. And even till then
   We let you know those gifts are given to them:
   We did it, Woodstock—

WOOD. Ye have done ill, then.

KING.   Ha, dare ye say so?

WOOD. Dare I? Afore my God, I'll speak, King Richard,
   Were I assured this day my head should off;
   I tell ye, Sir, my allegiance stands excused
   In justice of the cause. Ye have done ill.
   The sun of mercy never shine on me
   But I speak truth. When warlike Arundel—
   Beset at sea—fought for those wealthy prizes,
   He did with fame advance the English cross,
   Still crying, 'Courage in King Richard's name.'
   For thee he won them, and do thou enjoy them;
   He'll fetch more honours home. But had he known
   That kites should have enjoyed the eagle's prize,
   The fraught had swum unto thine enemies.

KING. So, sir. We'll soothe your vexèd spleen, good uncle,
   And mend what is amiss. To those slight gifts
   Not worth acceptance, thus much more we add;
   Young Henry Greene shall be Lord Chancellor,
   Bagot, Lord Keeper of our privy seal,
   Tresilian, learned in our kingdom's laws,
   Shall be Chief Justice: by them and their directions
   King Richard will uphold his government.

GREENE. Change no more words, my lord; ye do deject
   Your kingly majesty to speak to such
   Whose homespun judgements, like their frosty beards,
   Would blast the blooming hopes of all your kingdom.
   Were I as you, my lord—

QUEEN. O gentle Greene, throw no more fuel on,
   But rather seek to mitigate this heat.
   Be patient, kingly Richard, quench this ire.

Would I had tears of force to stint this fire!

KING. Beshrew the churls that make my queen so sad.
But by my grandsire Edward's kingly bones,
My princely father's tomb, King Richard swears
We'll make them weep these wrongs in bloody tears.
Come, fair Queen Anne a Beame: Bagot and Greene,
Keep by King Richard's side; but as for you,
We'll shortly make your stiff obedience bow.

Exeunt KING *and* QUEEN

BAGOT. Remember this, my lords:
We keep the Seal: our strength you all shall know. *Exit*

GREEN. And we are Chancellor: we love you well, think so.
Exit

YORK. God for His mercy! Shall we brook these braves,
Disgraced and threatened thus by fawning knaves?

LANC. Shall we, that were great Edward's princely sons,
Be thus outbraved by flattering sycophants?

WOOD. Afore my God and holy saints I swear,
But that my tongue hath liberty to show
The inly passions boiling in my breast,
I think my overburdened heart would break.
What then may we conjecture? what's the cause
Of this remiss and inconsiderate dealing
Urged by the king and his confederates,
But hate to virtue—and a mind corrupt
With all preposterous rude misgovernment?

LANC. These prizes ta'en by warlike Arundel
Before his face are given those flatterers.

SURR. It is his custom to be prodigal
To any but to those do best deserve.

ARUND. Because he knew you would bestow them well,
He gave it such as for their private gain
Neglect both honour and their country's good.

Wind horns within

LANC. How now, what noise is this?

YORK. Some post, it seems: pray heaven the news be good.

Enter CHEYNEY

WOOD. Amen, I pray, for England's happiness.
　Speak, speak, what tidings, Cheyney?
CHEY. Of war, my lord . . . and civil dissension:
　The men of Kent and Essex do rebel.
WOOD. I thought no less; and always feared as much.
CHEY. The shrieves in post have sent unto your grace
　That order may be ta'en to stay the Commons
　For fear rebellion rise in open arms.
WOOD. Now, headstrong Richard, shalt thou reap the fruit
　Thy lewd licentious wilfulness hath sown.
　I know not which way to bestow myself!
YORK. There is no standing on delay, my lords,
　These hot eruptions must have some redress
　Or else in time they'll grow incurable.
WOOD. The Commons, they rebel: and the king all careless.
　Here's wrong on wrong to stir more mutiny.
　Afore my God I know not what to do.
LANC. Take open arms. Join with the vexèd Commons
　And hale his minions from his wanton side.
　Their heads cut off, the people's satisfied.
WOOD. Not so, not so! alack the day, good brother,
　We may not so affright the tender prince.
　We'll bear us nobly, for the kingdom's safety
　And the king's honour. Therefore list to me.
　You, brother Gaunt, and noble Arundel
　Shall undertake, by threats or fair entreaty,
　To pacify the murmuring Commons' rage;
　And whilst you there employ your service hours,
　We presently will call a parliament
　And have their deeds examined thoroughly;
　Where, if by fair means we can win no favour
　Nor make King Richard leave their companies,
　We'll thus resolve, for our dear country's good,
　To right her wrongs, or for it spend our blood.
LANC. About it then, we for the Commons, you for the
　court.

WOOD. Ay, ay. Good Lancaster, I pray be careful.
  Come, brother York, we soon shall right all wrong,
  And send some headless from the court ere long.

Exeunt

ACT II

[SCENE 1: *Westminster*]

Trumpets sound. Enter KING RICHARD, GREENE, BAGOT,
BUSHY, SCROOPE, TRESILIAN, *and others.*

KING. Thus shall King Richard suit his princely train
  Despite his uncles' pride. Embrace us, gentlemen.
  Sir Edward Bagot, Bushy, Greene, and Scroope,
  Your youths are fitting to our tender years
  And such shall beautify our princely throne.
  Fear not my uncles, nor their proudest strength,
  For I will buckler ye against them all.
GREENE. Thanks, dearest lord, let me have Richard's love
  And like a rock unmoved my state shall stand,
  Scorning the proudest peer that rules the land.
BUSH. Your uncles seek to overturn your state,
  To awe ye like a child—that they alone
  May at their pleasures thrust you from the throne.
SCROO. As if the sun were forced to decline
  Before his dated time of darkness comes.
BAGOT. Sweet king, set courage to authority
  And let them know the power of majesty.
GREEN. May not the lion roar, because he's young?
  What are your uncles but as elephants
  That set their aged bodies to the oak?
  You are the oak against whose stock they lean:
  Fall from them once, and then destroy them ever.
  Be thou no stay, King Richard, to their strength,
  But as a tyrant unto tyranny,
  And so confound them all eternally.
TRES. Law must extend unto severity

When subjects dare to brave their sovereign.

KING. Tresilian, thou art Lord Chief Justice now,
  Who should be learned in the laws but thee?
  Resolve us therefore what thou thinkst of them
  That under title of protectorship
  Seek to subvert their king and sovereign.

TRES. As of the king's rebellious enemies:
  As underminers of his sacred state;
  Which, in the greatest prince or mightiest peer
  That is a subject to your majesty,
  Is nothing less than treason capital,
  And he a traitor that endeavours it.

[BUSHY *reads a book*]

KING. Attaint them then, arrest them and condemn them.

GREEN. Hale them to th' block and cut off all their heads,
  And then, King Richard, claim the government.

KING. See it be done, Tresilian, speedily.

TRES. That course is all too rash, my gracious lord.

ALL. Too rash for what?

TRES. It must be done with greater policy
  For fear the people rise in mutiny.

KING. Ay, there's the fear: the Commons love them well
  And all applaud the wily Lancaster,
  The counterfeit, relenting Duke of York,
  Together with our fretful Uncle Woodstock,
  With greater reverence than King Richard's self.
  But time shall come, when we shall yoke their necks
  And make them bend to our obedience.
  How now, what readst thou, Bushy?

BUSH. The monument of English Chronicles,
  Containing acts and memorable deeds
  Of all your famous predecessor kings.

KING. What findst thou of them?

BUSH. Examples strange and wonderful, my lord.
  The end of treason even in mighty persons:
  For here 'tis said your royal grandfather,
  Although but young, and under government,
  Took the Protector then, proud Mortimer,

And on a gallows fifty foot in height
He hung him for his pride and treachery.

KING. Why should our proud Protector then presume
  And we not punish him, whose treason's viler far
  Than ever was rebellious Mortimer?
  Prithee read on: examples such as these
  Will bring us to our kingly grandsire's spirit.
  What's next?

BUSH. The battle full of dread and doubtful fear
  Was fought betwixt your father and the French.

KING. Read on, we'll hear it.

BUSH. Then the Black Prince, encouraging his soldiers,
  being in number but 7,750, gave the onset to the French
  king's puissant army, which were numbered to 68,000,
  and in one hour got the victory, slew 6,000 of the French
  soldiers; took prisoners of dukes, earls, knights and
  gentlemen to the number of 1,700, and of the common
  sort 10,000; so the prisoners that were taken were twice
  so many as the Englishmen were in number. Besides, the
  thrice-renowned Prince took with his own hand King
  John of France and his son prisoners. This was called the
  battle of Poitiers, and was fought on Monday the 19th of
  September 1356, my lord.

KING. A victory most strange and admirable.
  Never was conquest got with such great odds.
  O princely Edward, had thy son such hap,
  Such fortune and success to follow him,
  His daring uncles and rebellious peers
  Durst not control and govern as they do.
  But these bright shining trophies shall awake me,
  And as we are his body's counterfeit,
  So will we be the image of his mind,
  And die but we'll attain his virtuous deeds.
  What next ensues? Good Bushy, read the rest.

BUSH. Here is set down, my princely sovereign,
  The certain time and day when you were born.

KING. Our birthday sayst thou? is that noted there?

BUSH. It is, my lord.

KING.   Prithee let me hear't,
  For thereby hangs a secret mystery,
  Which yet our uncle strangely keeps from us.
  On, Bushy.
BUSH. Upon the 3rd of April 1365 was Lord Richard, son to
  the Black Prince, born at Bordeaux.
KING. Stay; let me think awhile. Read it again.
BUSH. Upon the 3rd of April 1365 was Lord Richard, son to
  the Black Prince, born at Bordeaux.
KING. 1365. . . . . What year is this?
GREEN: 'Tis now, my lord, 1387.
KING. By that account, the third of April next
  Our age is numbered two and twenty years.
  O treacherous men that have deluded us,
  We might have claimed our right a twelvemonth since!
  Shut up thy book, good Bushy: Bagot, Greene,
  King Richard in his throne will now be seen.
  This day I'll claim my right, my kingdom's due.
  Our uncles well shall know they but intrude:
  For which we'll smite their base ingratitude.

    [*A knock within.* BAGOT *to the door and returns*]

BAGOT. Edmund of Langley, Duke of York, my lord,
  Sent from the Lord Protector and the peers,
  Doth crave admittance to your royal presence.
KING. Our uncle Edmund, so. Were it not he
  We would not speak with him; but go admit him.
  Woodstock and Gaunt are stern and troublesome
  But York is gentle, mild and generous;
  And therefore we admit his conference.

       Enter YORK

BAGOT. He comes, my lord.
KING. Methinks 'tis strange, my good and reverend uncle,
  You, and the rest, should thus malign against us,
  And every hour with rude and bitter taunts
  Abuse King Richard and his harmless friends.
  We had a father—that once called ye brother:

A grandsire too—that titled you his son;
But could they see how you have wronged King
    Richard
Their ghosts would haunt ye; and in dead of night
Fright all your quiet sleeps with horrid fears.
I pray, stand up, we honour reverend years
In meaner subjects. Good uncle, rise and tell us:
What further mischiefs are there now devised
To torture and afflict your sovereign with?

YORK. My royal lord, even by my birth I swear,
My father's tomb, and faith to heaven I owe,
Your uncles' thoughts are all most honourable.
And to that end the good Protector sends me
To certify your sacred majesty
The peers of England now are all assembled
To hold a parliament at Westminster,
And humbly crave your highness would be there
To sit in council touching such affairs
As shall concern your country's government.

KING. Have they so soon procured a parliament?
Without our knowledge, too; 'tis somewhat strange.
Yet say, good uncle, we will meet them straight.

YORK. The news to all will be most wished and welcome.
I take my leave, and to your grace I swear,
As I am subject loyal, just and true,
We'll nothing do to hurt the realm nor you.

KING. We shall believe you, uncle. Go attend him—

Exit YORK

Yes, we will meet them,—but with such intent
As shall dismiss their sudden parliament
Till we be pleased to summon and direct it.
Come, sirs, to Westminster, attend our state.
This day shall make you ever fortunate.
The third of April—Bushy, note the time—
Our age accomplished, crown and kingdom's mine.

Exeunt

[SCENE 2: *Westminster*]

Flourish [of trumpets]. Enter LANCASTER, ARUNDEL, SURREY: *the* QUEEN *and* DUCHESS OF GLOSTER: WOODSTOCK [*with*] *petitions and the mace:* CHEYNEY. YORK *meets them in haste.*

WOOD. Now, brother York: what says King Richard, ha?

YORK. His highness will be here immediately.

WOOD. Go, cousin Surrey, greet the parliament,
Tell them the king is coming, give these petitions
To the knights and burgesses o' the lower house,
Sent from each several shire of all the kingdom.
These copies I will keep and show his highness.
Pray make haste.

SURR.   I will, my lord.   *Exit*

QUEEN. Pity King Richard's youth, most reverend uncles,
And in your high proceedings gently use him.
Think of his tender years; what's now amiss
His riper judgement shall make good and perfect
To your, and to the kingdom's, benefit.

YORK. Alack, sweet queen, you and our lord the king
Have little cause to fear our just proceedings.
We'll fall beneath his feet, and bend our knees
So he cast off those hateful flatterers
That daily ruinate his state and kingdom.

WOOD. Go in, sweet ladies, comfort one another.
This happy parliament shall make all even
And plant sure peace betwixt the king and realm.

QUEEN. May heaven direct your wisdoms to provide
For England's honour, and King Richard's good.

YORK. Believe no less, sweet queen. Attend her highness.
      Flourish [of trumpets]. Exeunt [QUEEN *and* DUCHESS]

ARUND. The king is come, my lords.

WOOD. Stand from the door then: make way, Cheyney.

[*Trumpets*] *sound a flourish. Enter* KING, BAGOT, BUSHY, GREENE, SCROOPE *and others.*

GREEN. Yonder's your uncles, my lord.

KING.   Ay, with our plain Protector!

Full of complaints, sweet Greene, I'll wage my crown.

BAGOT. Give them fair words, and smooth awhile:
    The toils are pitched, and you may catch them quickly.

KING. Why, how now, uncle? What, disrobed again
    Of all your golden rich habiliments?

WOOD. Ay, ay, good coz, I'm now in my tother hose,
    I'm now myself, Plain Thomas, and by th' rood
    In these plain hose I'll do the realm more good
    Than these that pill the poor, to jet in gold.

KING. Nay, be not angry, uncle.

WOOD. Be you then pleased, good coz, to hear me speak,
    And view thy subjects' sad petitions.
        See here King Richard; whilst thou liv'st at ease,
        Lulling thyself in nice security,
        Thy wronged kingdom's in a mutiny.
    From every province are the people come
    With open mouths exclaiming on the wrongs
    Thou and these upstarts have imposed on them.
    Shame is deciphered on thy palace gate,
    Confusion hangeth o'er thy wretched head,
    Mischief is coming and in storms must fall:
    Th' oppression of the poor to heaven doth call.

KING. Well, well, good uncle, these your bitter taunts
    Against my friends and me will one day cease;
    But what's the reason you have sent for us?

LANC. To have your grace confirm this parliament
    And set your hand to certain articles
    Most needful for your state and kingdom's quiet.

KING. Where are those articles?

ARUND. The states and burgesses o' the parliament
    Attend with duty to deliver them.

YORK. Please you ascend your throne, we'll call them in.

KING. We'll ask a question first, and then we'll see them:
    For trust me, reverend uncles, we have sworn
    We will not sit upon our royal throne
    Until this question be resolved at full.
    Reach me that paper, Bushy. Hear me, princes:
    We had a strange petition here delivered us.

A poor man's son, his father being deceased,
Gave him in charge unto a rich man's hands
To keep him and the little land he had
Till he attained to one-and-twenty years.
The poor revenue amounts but to three crowns,
And yet th' insatiate churl denies his right
And bars him of his fair inheritance.
Tell me, I pray: will not our English laws
Enforce this rich man to resign his due?

WOOD. There is no let to bar it, gracious sovereign.
Afore my God, sweet prince, it joys my soul
To see your grace in person thus to judge his cause.

YORK. Such deeds as this will make King Richard shine
Above his famous predecessor kings
If thus he labour to establish right.

KING. The poor man then had wrong, you all confess?

WOOD. And shall have right, my liege, to quit his wrong.

KING. Then, Woodstock, give us right; for we are wronged.
Thou art the rich, and we the poor man's son;
The realms of England, France, and Ireland
Are those three crowns thou yearly keep'st from us.
Is't not a wrong when every mean man's son
May take his birthright at the time expired,
And we, the principal, being now attained
Almost to two and twenty years of age,
Cannot be suffered to enjoy our own
Nor peaceably possess our father's right?

WOOD. Was this the trick, sweet prince! Alack the day,
You need not thus have doubled with your friends.
The right I hold, even with my heart I render
And wish your grace had claimed it long ago;
Thou'dst rid my age of mickle care and woe.
And yet I think I have not wronged your birthright:
For if the times were searched, I guess your grace
Is not so full of years till April next.
But be it as it will. Lo, here, King Richard,
I thus yield up my sad Protectorship:

Gives the Mace up

A heavy burden hast thou ta'en from me:
Long mayst thou live in peace and keep thine own
That truth and justice may attend thy throne.

KING. Then in the name of heaven we thus ascend it,
  And here we claim our fair inheritance
  Of fruitful England, France, and Ireland,
  Superior Lord of Scotland, and the rights
  Belonging to our great dominions.
  Here, uncles, take the crown from Richard's hand
  And once more place it on our kingly head:
  This day we will be new enthronisèd.

WOOD. With all our hearts, my lord. Trumpets, be ready.

A Flourish

ALL. Long live King Richard, of that name the second,
  The sovereign lord of England's ancient rights!

KING. We thank ye all, so. Now we feel ourself.
  Our body could not fill this chair till now,
  'Twas scanted to us by protectorship.
  But now we let ye know King Richard rules
  And will elect and choose: place and displace
  Such officers as we ourself shall like of.
  And first, my lords, because your age is such
  As pity 'twere'ye should be further pressed
  With weighty business of the common weal,
  We here dismiss ye from the council-table
  And will that you remain not in our court.
  Deliver up your staves. And hear ye, Arundel,
  We do discharge ye of the Admiralty.
  Scroope, take his office and his place in Council.

SCROO. I thank your highness.

YORK. Here, take my staff, good cousin. York thus leaves thee:
  Thou lean'st on staves that will at length deceive thee.

LANC. There lie the burden of old Lancaster;
  And may he perish that succeeds my place!

KING. So, sir: we will observe your humour.
  Sir Henry Greene, succeed our uncle York—
  And Bushy take the staff of Lancaster.

BUSH. I thank your grace: his curses fright not me;
    I'll keep it to defend your majesty.

WOOD. What transformation do mine eyes behold
    As if the world were topsy-turvey turned!
    Hear me, King Richard.

KING.   Plain Thomas, I'll not hear ye.

GREEN. Ye do not well to move his majesty.

WOOD. Hence flatterer, or by my soul I'll kill thee!
    Shall England, that so long was governed
    By grave experience of white-headed age,
    Be subject now to rash unskilful boys?
    Then force the sun run backward to the east,
    Lay Atlas' burden on a pygmy's back,
    Appoint the sea his times to ebb and flow;
    And that as easily may be done as this.

KING. Give up your council-staff, we'll hear no more.

WOOD. My staff, King Richard? See, coz, here it is:
    Full ten years' space within a prince's hand,
    A soldier and a faithful counsellor,
    This staff hath always been discreetly kept;
    Nor shall the world report an upstart groom
    Did glory in the honours Woodstock lost;
    And therefore, Richard, thus I sever it.
       There, let him take it, shivered, cracked and broke,
    As will the state of England be ere long
    By this rejecting true nobility.
    Farewell King Richard. I'll to Plashey; brothers,
    If ye ride through Essex, call and see me.
    If once the pillars and supporters quail,
    How can the strongest castle choose but fail?

LORDS. And so will he ere long. Come, come, let's leave
    them.

BUSH. Ay, ay, your places are supplied sufficiently.
                 Exeunt the Lords [*with* ARUNDEL]

SCROO. Old doting graybeards!
    Fore God, my lord, had they not been your uncles
    I'd broken my council-staff about their heads.

GREEN. We'll have an act for this: it shall be henceforth

counted high treason for any fellow with a gray beard to
come within forty foot of the court gates.

BAGOT. Ay, or a great-bellied doublet: we'll alter the kingdom presently.

GREEN. Pox on't, we'll not have a beard amongst us; we'll
shave the country and the city too, shall we not, Richard?

KING. Do what ye will, we'll shield and buckler ye.
We'll have a guard of archers to attend us;
And they shall daily wait on us and you.
Send proclamations straight in Richard's name
T' abridge the laws our late Protector made.
Let some be sent to seek Tresilian forth.

BAGOT. Seek him! Hang him, he lurks not far off I warrant
[you]; an this news come abroad once, ye shall have him
here presently.

KING. Would he were come. His counsel would direct you
well.

GREEN. Troth, I think I shall trouble myself but with a
few counsellors. What cheer shall we have to dinner, King
Richard?

KING. No matter what today. We'll mend it shortly.
The hall at Westminster shall be enlarged
And only serve us for a dining-room,
Wherein I'll daily feast ten thousand men.

GREEN. An excellent device: the Commons have murmured
[against us] a great while, and there's no such means as
meat to stop their mouths.

SCROO. 'Sfoot, make their gate wider: let's first fetch their
money and bid them to dinner afterwards.

GREEN. 'Sblood, and I were not a Councillor, I could find in
myself to dine at a tavern today, sweet king.
Shall's be merry?

SCROO. We must have money to buy new suits, my lord;
The fashions that we wear are gross and stale.
We'll go sit in council to devise some new.

ALL. A special purpose to be thought upon!
It shall be the first thing we'll do.

KING. Come, wantons, come. If Gloster hear of this,

He'll say our Council guides us much amiss.
Dismiss the parliament our uncles called,
And tell the peers it is our present pleasure
That each man parts unto his several home.
When we are pleased, they shall have summons sent
And with King Richard hold a parliament.
Set forward.

GREEN. You of the Council march before the king:
I will support his arm.

KING.   Grammercy, Greene.

Trumpets sound [a] flourish. Exeunt

[SCENE 3: *The Queen's apartment, Westminster*]

Enter the QUEEN, *the* DUCHESS OF GLOSTER, *the* DUCHESS OF
IRELAND, *and other maids with shirts and bands and other
linen.*

QUEEN. Tell me, dear aunt, has Richard so forgot
The types of honour and nobility
So to disgrace his good and reverend uncles?

D. GLO. Madam, 'tis true. No sooner had he claimed
The full possession of his government
But my dear husband and his noble brethren
Were all dismissèd from the council-table,
Banished the court, and even before their faces
Their offices bestowed on several grooms.

D. IRE. My husband, Ireland—that unloving lord—
(God pardon his amiss, he now is dead)
King Richard was the cause he left my bed,

QUEEN. No more, good cousin. Could I work the means,
He should not so disgrace his dearest friends.
Alack the day! though I am England's queen,
I meet sad hours and wake when others sleep.
He meets content, but care with me must keep.

Distressèd poverty o'erspreads the kingdom:
In Essex, Surrey, Kent, and Middlesex
Are seventeen thousand poor and indigent
Which I have numbered; and to help their wants
My jewels and my plate are turned to coin
And shared amongst them. O riotous Richard,
A heavy blame is thine for this distress,
That dost allow thy polling flatterers
To gild themselves with others' miseries.

[D. GLO.] Wrong not yourself with sorrow, gentle queen,
    Unless that sorrow were a helping means
    To cure the malady you sorrow for.

[QUEEN.] The sighs I vent are not mine own, dear aunt;
    I do not sorrow in mine own behalf,
    Nor now repent with peevish frowardness
    And wish I ne'er had seen this English shore,
    But think me happy in King Richard's love.
    No, no, good aunt, this troubles not my soul;
    'Tis England's subjects' sorrow I sustain:
    I fear they grudge against their sovereign.

[D. GLO.] Fear not that, madam, England's not mutinous:
    'Tis peopled all with subjects, not with outlaws.
    Though Richard (much misled by flatterers)
    Neglects, and throws his sceptre carelessly,
    Yet none dares rob him of his kingly rule.

[D. IRE.] Besides, your virtuous charity, fair queen,
    So graciously hath won the Commons' love
    As only you have power to stay their rigour.

[QUEEN.] The wealth I have shall be the poor's revenue
    As sure as 'twere confirmed by parliament.
    This mine own industry—and sixty more
    I daily keep at work—is all their own.
    The coin I have, I send them; would 'twere more.
    To satisfy my fears, or pay those sums
    My wanton lord hath forced from needy subjects,
    I'd want myself. Go, let those trunks be filled
    With those our labours to relieve the poor.
    Let them be carefully distributed.

Enter CHEYNEY

For those that now shall want, we'll work again,
    And tell them ere two days we shall be furnished.
[CHEY.] What, is the court removing? Whither goes that
    trunk?
[D. IRE.] 'Tis the queen's charity, sir, of needful clothing
    To be distributed amongst the poor.
[CHEY.] Why, there's one blessing yet, that England hath
    A virtuous queen, although a wanton king.
    Good health, sweet princess. Believe me, madam,
    You have quick utterance for your housewifery.
    Your grace affords good pennyworths sure, ye sell so
        fast!
    Pray heaven your getting quit you swift return.
[QUEEN.] Amen: for 'tis from heaven I look for recompense.
[CHEY.] No doubt, fair queen, the righteous powers will
        quit you
    For these religious deeds of charity.
    But to my message:—
[*To* DUCH. OF GLOSTER]   Madam, my lord the duke
    Entreats your grace prepare with him to horse:
    He will this night ride home to Plashey House.
D. GLOS. Madam, ye hear I'm sent for.
QUEEN.   Then begone:
    Leave me alone in desolation.
D. IRE. Adieu, good aunt, I'll see ye shortly there:
    King Richard's kindred are not welcome here.
QUEEN. Will ye all leave me then? O woe is me,
    I now am crowned a queen of misery.
D. GLO. Where didst thou leave my husband, Cheyney?
        speak!
CHEY. Accomp'nied with the Dukes of York and Lancaster
    Who, as I guess, intend to ride with him,
    For which he wished me haste your grace's presence.
D. GLO. Thou seest the passions of the queen are such
    I may not too abruptly leave her highness;
    But tell my lord I'll see him presently.

QUEEN. Sawst thou King Richard, Cheyney? Prithee tell me:
    What revels keep his flattering minions?
CHEY. They sit in council to devise strange fashions,
    And suit themselves in wild and antic habits
    Such as this kingdom never yet beheld:
    French hose, Italian cloaks, and Spanish hats,
    Polonian shoes with peaks a hand full long,
    Tied to their knees with chains of pearl and gold.
    Their plumèd tops fly waving in the air
    A cubit high above their wanton heads.
    Tresilian with King Richard likewise sits
    Devising taxes, and strange shifts for money
    To build again the hall at Westminster
    To feast and revel in; and when abroad they come,
    Four hundred archers in a guard attend them.
QUEEN. O certain ruin of this famous kingdom!
    Fond Richard! thou buildst a hall to feast in
    And starv'st thy wretched subjects to erect it.
    Woe to those men that thus incline thy soul
    To these remorseless acts and deeds so foul!

Flourish [*within*]

[D. GLO. The] trumpets tell us that King Richard's coming.
    I'll take my leave, fair queen; but credit me,
    Ere many days, again I'll visit ye.
D. IRE. I'll home to Langley, with my uncle York,
    And there lament alone my wretched state.
                   Exeunt both the DUCHESSES
QUEEN. Blest heaven conduct ye both. Queen Anne alone
    For Richard's follies still must sigh and groan.
                       Exit QUEEN

[ACT III

SCENE 1: *London: the Court*]

Sound a sennet. Enter KING RICHARD, BAGOT, BUSHY, GREENE *and* SCROOPE, *very richly attired in new fashions; and* TRESILIAN, *whispering with the* KING. *A guard of archers after them.*

KING. Come, my Tresilian.
　Thus like an emperor shall King Richard reign,
　And you so many kings attendant on him.
　Our guard of archers, keep the doors, I charge ye:
　Let no man enter to disturb our pleasures.
　Thou toldst me, kind Tresilian, thou'dst devised
　Blank Charters, to fill up our treasury,
　Opening the chests of hoarding cormorants
　That laugh to see their kingly sovereign lack.
　Let's know the means, we may applaud thy wit.

TRES. See here, my lord; only with parchment, innocent
　sheepskins. Ye see here's no fraud; no clause, no deceit in
　the writing.

ALL. Why, there's nothing writ!

TRES. There's the trick on't!
　These blank charters shall be forthwith sent
　To every shrieve through all the shires of England,
　With charge to call before them presently
　All landed men, freeholders, farmers, graziers,
　Or any else that have ability.
　Then in your highness' name they shall be charged
　To set their names, and forthwith seal these blanks;
　That done, these shall return to court again,
　But cartloads of money soon shall follow them.

SCROO. Excellent Tresilian!

BUSH. 　　　　　　　　　　Noble Lord Chief Justice!

BAGOT. Where should his grace get such a councillor!

GREEN. Not if his beard were off! Prithee Tresilian, off
　with it.
　'Sfoot, thou seest we have not a beard amongst us!

Thou send'st our barbers there to poll the whole country,
'Sfoot, let some shave thee!

BUSH. 'Twould become thee better, faith, and make thee
look more grim when thou sit'st in judgement.

TRES. I tell ye, gallants; I will not lose a hair of my lordship
And King Richard's favour for the Pope's revenues.

Enter the QUEEN

GREEN. By y'r leave, there! Give way to the Queen!

KING. Now Anne a Beame: how cheers my dearest queen?
Is't holiday, my love? Believe me, lords,
'Tis strange to take her from her sempstery:
She and her maids are all for housewifery.
Shalt work no more, sweet Nan—now Richard's king,
And peers and people all shall stoop to him.
We'll have no more protecting uncles, trust me!
Prithee look smooth and bid these nobles welcome.

QUEEN. Whom my lord favours must to me be welcome.

KING. These are our councillors, I tell ye, lady,
And these shall better grace King Richard's court
Than all the doting heads that late controlled us.
Thou seest already we begin to alter
The vulgar fashions of our homespun kingdom.
I tell thee, Nan, the states of Christendom
Shall wonder at our English royalty.
We held a Council to devise these suits:
Sir Henry Greene devised this fashion shoe,
Bushy this peak: Bagot and Scroope set forth
This kind coherence, twixt the toe and knee,
To have them chained together lovingly;
And we as sovereign did confirm them all.
Suit they not quaintly, Nan? Sweet queen, resolve me.

QUEEN. I see no fault that I dare call a fault.
But would your grace consider with advice
What you have done unto your reverend uncles?
(My fears provoke me to be bold, my lord)
They are your noble kinsmen: to revoke the sentence
    were—

KING. —An act of folly, Nan! King's words are laws;
    If we infringe our word we break our law.
    No more of them, sweet queen.

TRES. Madam, what's done was with advice enough;
    The king is now at years, and hath shook off
    The servile yoke of mean protectorship.

BUSH. His highness can direct himself sufficient.
    Why should his pleasures then be curbed by any
    As if he did not understand his state?

KING. They tell thee true, sweet love. Come, ride with me
    And see today my hall at Westminster
    Which we have builded now to feast our friends.

GREEN. Do, do, good madam. Prithee sweet king, let's ride
    somewhither an it be but to show ourselves. 'Sfoot, our
    devices here are like jewels kept in caskets, or good faces
    in masks, that grace not the owners, because they're
    obscured. If our fashions be not published, what glory's
    in the wearing?

KING. We'll ride through London only to be gazed at.
    Fair Anne a Beame, you shall along with us:
    At Westminster shalt see my sumptuous hall,
    My royal tables richly furnished
    Where every day I feast ten thousand men:
    To furnish out which feast I daily spend
    Thirty fat oxen and three hundred sheep,
    With fish and fowl in numbers numberless.
    Not all our chronicles shall point a king
    To match our bounty, state, and royalty.
    Or let all our successors yet to come
    Strive to exceed me; and if they forbid it,
    Let records say, only King Richard did it.

QUEEN. O but my lord 'twill tire your revenues
    To keep this festival a year together!

KING. As many days as I write England's king
    We will maintain that bounteous festival.
    Tresilian: look to your blank charters speedily,
    Send them abroad with trusty officers;
    And Bagot, see a messenger be sent

To call our uncle Woodstock home to th' court:
Not that we love his meddling company,
But that the ragged Commons love his plainness;
An should grow mutinous about these blanks,
We'll have him near us. Within his arrow's length,
We stand secure; we can restrain his strength.
See it be done. Come, Anne, to our great hall
Where Richard keeps his gorgeous festival.

[Trumpets] sound. Exeunt. Manet TRESILIAN

TRES. Within there, ho!

Enter CROSSBY *and* FLEMING

CROSS. Your lordship's pleasure?

TRES. What, are those blanks despatched?

FLEM. They're all trussed up, my lord, in several packets.

TRES. Where's Nimble? Where's that varlet?

Enter NIMBLE [*in peaked shoes with knee-chains*]

NIMB. As nimble as a morris-dancer, now my bells are
      on:
      How do ye like the rattling of my chains, my lord?

TRES. O villain, thou wilt hang in chains for this.
      Art thou crept into the court fashion, knave?

NIMB. Alas my lord! ye know I have followed your lordship
      without e'er a rag since ye run away from the court once;
      and I pray let me follow the fashion a little, to show myself
      a courtier.

TRES. Go spread those several blanks throughout the king-
      dom,
      And here's commission with the Council's hands
      With charge to every shrieve and officer
      T'assist and aid you, and when they're sealed and signed,
      See ye note well such men's ability
      As set their hands to them. Inquire what rents
      What lands, or what revenues they spend by th' year,
      And let me straight receive intelligence.
      Besides, I'd have you use yourselves so cunningly
      To mark who grudges, or but speaks amiss

Of good King Richard, myself, or any of his new
    councillors.
Attach them all for privy whisperers
And send them up; I have a trick in law
Shall make King Richard seize into his hands
The forfeiture of all their goods and lands.
Nimble, take thou these blanks, and see you take especial
    note of them.

NIMB. I'll take the ditty, sir, but you shall set a note to't, for
if any man shall speak but an ill word of anything that's
written here—

TRES. Why, ass, there's nothing.

NIMB. And would ye have them speak ill of nothing? That's
strange. But I mean, my lord, if they should but give this
paper an ill word, as to say, 'I will treat this paper', or,
worse, 'I will rend this paper', or fouler words than that,
as to say, 'I will bumfiddle your paper'; if there be any
such I have a black book for them, my lord, I warrant ye.

TRES. Be it your greatest care to be severe.
Crossby and Fleming, pray be diligent.

CROSS. We shall, my lord.

NIMB. But how if we meet with some ignoramus fellows,
my lord, that cannot write their minds: what shall they
do?

TRES. If they but set to their marks, 'tis good.

NIMB. We shall meddle with no women in the blanks, shall
we?

TRES. Rich widows, none else; for a widow is as much as man
and wife.

NIMB. Then a widow's a hermaphrodite, both cut and long-
tail.
And if she cannot write, she shall set her mark to it?

TRES. What else, sir?

NIMB. But if she have a daughter, she shall set her mother's
mark to't?

TRES. Meddle with none but men and widows, sir, I charge ye.

NIMB. Well, sir, I shall see a widow's mark then; I ne'er saw
none yet!

TRES. You have your lessons perfect: now begone:
Be bold and swift in execution.

Exit TRESILIAN

NIMB. Goodbye, my lord . . . We will domineer over the
vulgar, like so many St Georges over the poor dragons.
Come sirs: we are like to have a flourishing common
wealth i'faith! *Exeunt*

[SCENE 2: *Plashey House, Essex*]

Enter WOODSTOCK, LANCASTER *and* YORK, *at Plashey*.

WOOD. Come, my good brothers, here at Plashey House
I'll bid you welcome with as true a heart
As Richard with a false, and mind corrupt,
Disgraced our names and thrust us from his court.

LANC. Beshrew him that repines, my lord, for me:
I lived with care at court, I now am free.

YORK. Come, come, let's find some other talk, I think not
on it:
I ne'er slept soundly when I was amongst them
So let them go. This house of Plashey, brother,
Stands in a sweet and pleasant air, i'faith:
'Tis near the Thames, and circled round with trees
That in the summer serve for pleasant fans
To cool ye; and in winter strongly break
The stormy winds that else would nip ye too.

WOOD. And in faith, old York,
We have all need of some kind wintering;
We are beset (heaven shield!) with many storms.
And yet these trees at length will prove to me
Like Richard and his riotous minions;
Their wanton heads so oft play with the winds,
Throwing their leaves so prodigally down,
They'll leave me cold at last; and so will they
Make England wretched; and, i' th' end, themselves.

LANC. If Westminster Hall devour as it has begun,
'Twere better it were ruined lime and stone.

WOOD. Afore my God, I late was certified
  That at one feast was served ten thousand dishes.
YORK. He daily feasts, they say, ten thousand men,
  And every man must have his dish, at least.
WOOD. Thirty fat oxen and three hundred sheep
  Serve but one day's expenses.
LANC. A hundred scarcely can suffice his guard;
  A camp of soldiers feeds not like those bowmen.
WOOD. But how will these expenses be maintained?
YORK. O they say there are strange tricks come forth
  To fetch in money; what they are, I know not.
WOOD. You've heard of the fantastic suits they wear?
  Never was English king so habited.
LANC. We could allow his clothing, brother Woodstock,
  But we have four kings more, are equalled with him:
  There's Bagot, Bushy, wanton Greene, and Scroope
  In state and fashion without difference.
YORK. Indeed, they're more than kings; for they rule him.
WOOD. Come, come, our breaths reverberate the wind.
  We talk like good divines, but cannot cure
  The grossness of the sin: or shall we speak
  Like all-commanding wise astronomers,
  And flatly say, such a day shall be fair?
  And yet it rains, whether he will or no.
  So may we talk; but thus will Richard do.

Enter CHEYNEY, *with blanks*

LANC. How now, Cheyney, what drives thee on so fast?
CHEY. If I durst, I would say (my lord)
  Tresilian drives me, on behalf so ill:
  I'm still the pursuivant of unhappy news:
  Here's blank charters, my lords. I pray, behold them,
  Sent from King Richard and his councillors.
WOOD. Thou mak'st me blank at very sight of them!
  What must these?
LANC. They appear in shape of obligations.
CHEY. They are no less—the country's full of them.
  Commissions are come down to every shrieve

To force the richest subjects of the land
To set their hands, and forthwith seal these blanks,
And then the bond must afterwards be paid:
That shall confirm a due debt to the king
As much or little as they please to point it.

LANC. O strange unheard-of vile taxation!

WOOD. Who is't can help my memory a little?
Has not this e'er been held a principle:
'There's nothing spoke or done that has not been'?

YORK. It was a maxim ere I had a beard.

WOOD. 'Tis now found false. An open heresy!
This is a thing was never spoke nor done.
Blank charters call ye them? If any age
Keep but a record of this policy
(I phrase it too too well!)—flat villainy—
Let me be chronicled Apostata,
Rebellious to my king and country both!

LANC. How do the people entertain these blanks?

CHEY. With much dislike, yet some for fear have signed
them:
Others there be, refuse and murmur strongly.

WOOD. Afore my God, I cannot blame them for it:
He might as well have sent defiance to them.
O vulture England, wilt thou eat thine own?
Can they be rebels called, that now turn head?
I speak but what I fear: not what I wish.
This foul oppression will withdraw all duty,
And in the Commons' hearts hot rancours breed
To make our country's bosom shortly bleed.

LANC. What shall we do to seek for remedy?

YORK. Let each man hie him to his several home
Before the people rise in mutiny,
And, in the mildest part of lenity,
Seek to restrain them from rebellion—
For what can else be looked for? Promise redress:
That eloquence is best in this distress.

LANC. York counsels well. Let's haste away;
The time is sick. We must not use delay.

YORK. Let's still confer by letters.

WOOD.   Content, content:
  So friends may parley, even in banishment.
  Adieu, good brothers. Cheyney, conduct them forth.

                     Exeunt all but WOODSTOCK
  Adieu, good York and Gaunt, farewell for ever.
  I have a sad presage comes suddenly
  That I shall never see these brothers more:
  On earth, I fear, we never more shall meet.
  Of Edward the Third's seven sons, we three are left
  To see our father's kingdom ruinate.
  I would my death might end the misery
  My fear presageth to my wretched country.
  The Commons will rebel, without all question,
  And fore my God, I have no eloquence
  To stay this uproar; I must tell them plain
  We all are struck—but must not strike again.

Enter a Servant

  How now? what news?

SERVANT. There's a horseman at the gate, my lord,
  He comes from the king, he says, to see your grace.

WOOD. To see me, sayst thou? A God's name, let him
  come [so]
  He brings no blank charters with him.
  Prithee, bid him 'light and enter.

SERV. I think he dares not for fouling on his feet, my lord;
  I would have had him 'light, but he swears as he's a
  courtier, he will not off on's horse-back till the inner gate
  be open.

WOOD. Passion of me, that's strange. I prithee, give him
  satisfaction, open the inner gate. What might this fellow
  be?

SERV. Some fine fool: he's attired very fantastically, and talks
  as foolishly——

WOOD. Go let him in; and when you have done, bid Cheyney
  come and speak with me.

SERV. I will, my lord.

Enter a spruce Courtier on horseback

Come on, sir, ye may ride into my lord's cellar now, an ye will, sir.

COUR. Prithee, fellow, stay and take my horse.

SERV. I have business for my lord, sir, I cannot.   *Exit*

COUR. A rude swain, by heaven, but stay, here walks another. Hear'st-ta, thou!—fellow—is this Plashey House?

WOOD. Ye should have asked that question before ye came in, sir. But this is it.

COUR. The hinds are all most rude and gross. I prithee walk my horse.

WOOD. I have a little business, sir.

COUR. Thou shalt not lose by't. I'll give thee a tester for thy pains.

WOOD. I shall be glad to earn money, sir.

COUR. Prithee, do—and know thy duty. Thy head's too saucy.

WOOD. Cry ye mercy, I did not understand your worship's calling.

COUR. The Duke of Gloster lies here, does he not?

WOOD. Marry does he, sir.

COUR. Is he within?

WOOD. He's not far off, sir; he was here even now.

COUR. Ah, very good: walk my horse well I prithee, he's travelled hard and he's hot i'faith. I'll in and speak with the Duke, and pay thee presently.

Exit Courtier

WOOD. I make no doubt, sir. O strange metamorphosis! Is't possible that this fellow that's all made of fashions should be an Englishman? No marvel if he know not me, being so brave, and I so beggarly.

Well, I shall earn money to enrich me now,
and tis the first I earned, by th' rood, this forty year.
Come on sir, you have sweat hard about this haste,
yet I think you know little of the business. Why so, I say?
You're a very indifferent beast; you'll follow any man that

will lead you. Now truly sir, you look but e'en leanly on't;
you feed not in Westminster Hall adays, where so many
sheep and oxen are devoured. I'm afraid they'll eat you
shortly, if you tarry amongst them. You're pricked more
with the spur than the provender, I see that. I think your
dwelling be at Hackney when you're at home, is't not?
You know not the duke neither, no more than your master;
and yet I think you have as much wit as he. Faith, say
a man should steal ye, and feed ye fatter, could ye run
away with him lustily? Ah, your silence argues a consent,
I see. By th' Mass, here comes company: we had both
been taken if we had, I see.

Enter CHEYNEY, *Courtier, and Servants*

CHEY. Saw ye not my lord at the gate, say ye?
    Why, I left him there but now.

COUR. In sooth I saw no creature, sir, only an old groom I
    got to walk my horse.

CHEY. A groom, say ye! 'Sfoot, 'tis my lord—the Duke.
    What have ye done? This is somewhat too coarse your
    grace should be an ostler to this f[ellow]!

COUR. I do beseech your grace's pardon. The error was in
    the mistake [that] your plainness did deceive me. Please
    it your grace to redeliver—

WOOD. No, by my faith. I'll have my money first: promise
    is a [promise].

COUR. I know your grace's goodness will refuse it.

WOOD. Think not so nicely of me; indeed I will not.

COUR. If you so please, there is your tester.

WOOD. If you so please, there is your horse, sir.
    Now pray you tell me, is your haste to me?

COUR. Most swift and serious, from His Majesty.

WOOD. What, from King Richard, my dear lord and kins-
    man? Go, sirrah, take you his horse, lead him to the
    stable, meat him well—I'll double his reward: there's
    twelve pence for ye.

SERV. I thank your grace.   *Exit with the horse*

WOOD. Now sir, your business.

COUR. His majesty commends him to your grace—

WOOD. This same's a rare fashion you have got at court.
Of whose devising was't, I pray?

COUR. I assure your grace, the king his council sat three days
about it.

WOOD. By my faith, their wisdoms took great pains, I assure
ye.
The state was well employed the while, by th' rood.
Then this at court is all the fashion now?

COUR. The king himself doth wear it,
Whose most gracious majesty sent me in haste.

WOOD. This peak doth strangely well become the foot.

COUR. This peak the king doth likewise wear, being a
Polonian peak;
and me did his highness pick from forth the rest—

WOOD. He could not have picked out such another, I assure
ye.

COUR. I thank your grace that picks me out so well;
But as I said, his highness would request—

WOOD. But this most fashionable chain, that links as 'twere
The toe and knee together—

COUR. In a most kind coherence, so it like your grace;
For these two parts, being in operation and quality differ-
ent, as for example: the toe a disdainer, or spurner: the
knee a dutiful and most humble orator; this chain doth,
as it were, so toeify the knee and so kneeify the toe, that
between both it makes a most methodical coherence, or
coherent method.

WOOD. 'Tis most excellent, sir, and full of art. Please ye
walk in.

COUR. My message tendered, I will tend your grace.

WOOD. Cry ye mercy, have you a message to me?

COUR. His majesty, most affectionately, and like a royal
kinsman,
Entreats your grace's presence at the court.

WOOD. Is that your message sir? I must refuse it, then.
My English plainness will not suit that place;
The court's too fine for me. My service here

Will stand in better stead, to quench the fire
Those blanks have made—I would they were all burnt,
Or he were hanged that first devised them, sir,
They stir the country so; I dare not come,
And so excuse me, sir. If the king think it ill,
He thinks amiss: I am Plain Thomas still.
The rest I'll tell ye as ye sit at meat.
Furnish a table, Cheyney: call for wine.
Come, sir, ye shall commend me to the king;
Tell him I'll keep these parts in peace to him.

Exeunt

[SCENE 3: *The market square, Dunstable*]

Enter MASTER IGNORANCE *the Bailey of Dunstable*, CROSSBY,
FLEMING, *and* NIMBLE, *with blanks.* [*Officers with bills in
attendance.*]

CROSS. Despatch, good Mr Bailey, the market's almost done,
you see; 'tis rumoured that the blanks are come, and the
rich choughs begin to flock out o' the town already. You
have seen the high shrieve's warrant and the Council's
commission, and therefore I charge ye, in the king's name,
be ready to assist us.

BAIL. Nay, look ye sir. Be not too pestiferous, I beseech ye.
I have begun myself and sealed one of your blanks already,
and by my example there's more shall follow. I know my
place and calling, my name is Ignorance and I am Bailey
of Dunstable; I cannot write nor read, I confess it, no
more could my father, nor his father nor none of the
Ignorants this hundred year, I assure ye.

NIMB. Your name proclaims no less, sir, and it has been a
most learned generation.

BAIL. Though I cannot write, I have set my mark: ecce
signum: read it I beseech ye.

NIMB. The mark of Simon Ignorance, the Bailey of Dunstable: being a sheephook with a tarbox at end on't.

BAIL. Very right. It was my mark ever since I was an innocent; and therefore, as I say, I have begun and will assist ye; for here be rich whoresons i' the town, I can tell ye, that will give ye the slip an ye look not to it.

FLEM. We therefore presently will divide ourselves: you two shall stay here while we, Mr Ignorance, with some of your brethren, the men of Dunstable, walk through the town, noting the carriage of the people. They say there are strange songs and libels cast about the market-place against my lord Tresilian and the rest of the king's young councillors. If such there be, we'll have some aid and attach them speedily.

BAIL. Ye shall do well, sir, and for your better aiding, if you can but find out my brother, Mr Ignoramus, he will be most pestiferous unto ye, I assure ye.

CROSS. I'm afraid he will not be found, sir; but we'll inquire. Come fellow Fleming; and Nimble, look to the whisperers I charge ye. *Exeunt* CROSSBY *and* FLEMING

NIMB. I warrant ye; come, Mr Bailey, let your billmen retire till we call them. And you and I will here shadow ourselves and write down their speeches.

BAIL. Nay, you shall write and I will mark, sir.

Enter a Farmer, a Butcher, and a Grazier, very hastily

BAIL. And see, see: here comes some already, all rich chubs by the Mass, I know them all sir.

FARM. Tarry, tarry, good neighbours, take a knave with ye! What a murrain! Is there a bear broke loose i' the town, that ye make such haste from the market?

GRAZ. A bear? no, nor a lion baited neither. I tell ye, neighbour, I am more afraid of the bee than the bear; there's wax to be used today, and I have no seal about me. I may tell you in secret, here's a dangerous world towards. Neighbour, you're a farmer, and I hope here's none but God and good company—we live in such a state, I am e'en almost weary of all, I assure ye. Here's my other neighbour, the butcher, that dwells at Hackley, has heard his landlord tell strange tidings. We shall be all hoisted an we tarry here, I can tell ye.

NIMB. They begin to murmur. I'll put them down all for whisperers. Mr Bailey, what's he that talks so?

BAIL. His name is Cowtail, a rich grazier, and dwells here hard by at Leighton Buzzard.

NIMB. [*writing*] Cow—tail—a grazier, dwelling at Leighton —Buzzard, Mr Bailey?

BAIL. Right, sir. Listen again sir.

FARM. Ah, sirrah? and what said the good knight your land-lord, neighbour?

BUTCH. Marry, he said, but I'll not stand to anything, I tell ye that aforehand; he said that King Richard's new Councillors (God amend them) had crept into honester men's places than themselves were; and that the king's uncles and the old lords were all banished the court; and he said flatly we should never have a merry world so long as it was so.

NIMB. Butcher, you and your landlord will be both hanged for't.

BUTCH. And then he said that there's one Tresilian—a lawyer —that has crept in amongst them and is now a lord, for-sooth, and he has sent down into every country of England a sort of Black Chapters.

FARM. Black Chapters? A God's name, neighbour, out of what Black Book were they taken?

GRAZ. Come, come. They are blank charters, neighbours. I heard of them afore, and therefore I made such haste away. They're sent down to the high shrieve with special charge that every man that is of any c[redit] or worship i' the country must set their hands and seal to them, for what intent I know not. I say no more. I smell something.

FARM. Well, well, my masters. Let's be wise. We are not all one man's [sons]. They say there are whispering knaves abroad; let's hie us home, for I assure ye, 'twas told me where I broke my fast this after[noon] that there were above three score gentlemen in our shire that had set their hands and seals to those blank charters already.

GRAZ. Now God amend them for it; they have given an ill example we shall be forced to follow.

BUTCH. I would my wife and children were at Jerusalem with all the wealth! I'd make shift for one, I warrant them. Come, neighbours, let's begone.

NIMB. Step forward with your bills, Mr Bailey. Not too fast, sirs! I charge ye i' the king's name to stand till we have done with ye.

GRAZ. ⎫
FARM. ⎬ Saint Benedicite, what must we do now tro'?
BUTCH. ⎭

BAIL. Be not so pestiferous, my good friends and neighbours: you are men of wealth and credit in the country; and therefore as I myself and others have begun, I charge ye in his highness' name presently to set your hands and seals to these blank charters.

GRAZ. Jesu receive my soul, I'm departed!

FARM. I'm e'en struck to at heart too.

BUTCH. Alas sir, we are poor men, what should our hands do?

BAIL. There's no harm I warrant ye; what need you fear, when ye see Bailey Ignorance has sealed before ye?

GRAZ. I pray ye, let's see them sir.

NIMB. Here, ye bacon-fed pudding-eaters, are ye afraid of a sheepskin?

GRAZ. Mass! 'tis somewhat darkly written.

FARM. Ay, ay, twas done i' the night, sure.

GRAZ. Mass, neighbours! Here's nothing that I see.

BUTCH. And can it be any harm, think ye, to set your hands to nothing? These blank charters are but little pieces of parchment—let's set our marks to them, and be rid of a knave's company.

FARM. As good at first as last: we can be but undone.

GRAZ. Ay, and our own hands undoes us, that's the worst on't. Lend's your pen, sir.

BUTCH. We must all venture, neighbours, there's no remedy.

NIMB. They grumble as they do it. I must put them down for whisperers and grumblers. Come, have you done yet?

GRAZ. Ay sir. (Would you and they were sodden for my swine!)

NIMB. Here's wax, then. I'll seal them for ye, and you shall severally take them off, and then deliver them as your deeds. *Seal them.* Come you boar's grease, take off this seal here; so: this is your deed.

FARM. Faith, sir, in some respect it is and it is not.

NIMB. And this is yours.

GRAZ. Ay sir; against my will, I swear.

NIMB. Ox-jaw, take off this seal: you'll deliver your deed with a good conscience?

BUTCH. There 'tis, sir: against my conscience, God's my witness. I hope ye have done with us now, sir.

NIMB. No, ye caterpillars, we have worse matters against ye yet. Sirrah, you know what your landlord told ye, concerning my lord Tresilian, and King Richard's new favourites, and more than that: you know your own speeches; and therefore, Mr Bailey, let some of your bill-men away with them to the high shrieve's presently, either to put in bail, or be sent up to th' court for privy whisperers.

BAIL. Their offences are most pestiferous. Away with them.

ALL. Now out, alas, we shall all to hanging, sure!

NIMB. Hanging? nay that's the least on't, ye shall tell me that a twelvemonth hence else.

Exeunt Officers with the three men

Stand close, Mr Bailey; we shall catch more of these traitors presently.

BAIL. You shall find me most pestiferous to assist ye; and so, I pray ye, commend my service to your good lord and master. Come, sir, stand close; I see——

Enter a Schoolmaster and a Serving-man

SERV. Nay, sweet Mr Schoolmaster, let's hear't again, I beseech ye.

S-M. Patientia. You're a serving-man, I'm a scholar. I have shown art and learning in these verses, I assure ye; and yet if they were well searched they're little better than libels. But the carriage of a thing is all, sir: I have covered them rarely.

SERV. 'Sfoot, the country's so full of intelligencers that two men can scarce walk together but they're attached for whisperers.

S-M. This paper shall wipe their noses, and they shall not boo to a goose for't; for I'll have these verses sung to their faces by one of my schoolboys, wherein I'll tickle them all i'faith. Shalt hear else. But first let's look there be no pitchers with ears, nor needles with eyes about us.

SERV. Come, come, all's safe I warrant ye.

S-M. Mark then. Here I come over them for their blank charters; sha't hear else:—

> Will ye buy any *Parchment* knives?
> We sell for little gain:
> Whoe'er are weary of their lives
> They'll rid them of their pain.
>
> *Blank charters* they are called,
> A vengeance on the villain,
> I would he were both flayed and bald:
> God bless my lord Tresilian.

Is't not rare?

NIMB. O rascals! They are damned three hundred fathom deep already!

S-M. Nay, look ye sir, there can be no exceptions taken, for this last line helps all, wherein with a kind of equivocation I say, 'God bless my lord Tresilian'. Do ye mark, sir? Now here, in the next verse I run o'er all the flatterers i' the court by name. Ye shall see else:—

> A poison may be green,
> But bushy can be no faggot:
> God mend the king and bless the queen,
> And 'tis no matter for Bagot.
>
> For Scroope, he does no good;
> But if you'll know the villain,
> His name is now to be understood:
> God bless my lord Tresilian.

How like ye this, sir?

SERV. Most excellent i'faith, sir.

NIMB. O traitors! Mr Bailey, do your authority.

BAIL. Two most pestiferous traitors. Lay hold of them, I charge ye.

SERV. What mean ye, sir?

NIMB. Nay, talk not; for if ye had a hundred lives they were all hanged. Ye have spoken treason in the ninth degree.

S-M. Treason?! Patientia, good sir, we spoke not a word.

BAIL. Be not so pestiferous. Mine ears have heard your examinations, wherein you uttered most shameful treason, for ye said 'God bless my lord Tresilian.'

S-M. I hope there's no treason in that, sir.

NIMB. That shall be tried. Come, Mr Bailey: their hands shall be bound under a horse's belly and sent up to him presently; they'll both be hanged, I warrant them.

SERV. Well, sir, if we be, we'll speak more ere we be hanged, in spite of you.

NIMB. Ay, ay, when you're hanged, speak what you will, we care not. Away with them.

Exeunt Schoolmaster and Serving-man [with Officer]
Ye see, Mr Bailey, what knaves are abroad now you are here; 'tis time to look about, ye see.

BAIL. I see there are knaves abroad indeed, sir: I pick for mine own [part]. I will do my best to reform the pestiferousness of the time, and as for example I have set my mark to the charters, so will I set mine eyes to observe these dangerous cases.

Enter one a-whistling

NIMB. Close again, Mr Bailey: here comes another whisperer, I see by some——O villain! he whistles treason! I'll lay hold of him myself.

WHISTLER. Out, alas, what do ye mean, sir?

NIMB. A rank traitor, Mr Bailey; lay hold on him, for he has most erroneously and rebelliously whistled treason.

WHIST. Whistled treason! alas, sir, how can that be?

BAIL. Very easily, sir. There's a piece of treason that flies up and down the country in the likeness of a ballad, and this being the very tune of it, thou hast whistled treason.

WHIST. Alas, sir, ye know I spake not a word.

NIMB. That's all one; if a man whistles treason 'tis as ill as speaking it. Mark me, Mr Bailey: the bird whistles that cannot speak. And yet there be birds in a manner that can speak too; your raven will call ye [rascal] your crow will call ye knave, Mr Bailey: ergo, he that can whistle can speak, and therefore this fellow hath both spoke and whistled treason. How say you, Bailey Ignorance?

BAIL. Ye have argued well, sir, but ye shall hear me sift him nearer, for I do not think but there are greater heads in this matter, and therefore my good fellow, be not pestiferous, but say and tell the truth: who did set you a-work? or who was the cause of your whistling? or did any man say to you, 'Go whistle'?

WHIST. Not any man, woman, or child, truly sir.

BAIL. No? How durst you whistle, then? or what cause had ye to do so?

WHIST. The truth is, sir, I had lost two calves out of my pasture, and being in search of them, from the top of the hill I might spy you two at th' bottom here, and took ye for my calves, sir; and that made me come whistling down for joy, in hope I had found them.

NIMB. More treason yet! He take a courtier and a Bailey for two calves! To limbo with him; he shall be quartered and then hanged.

WHIST. Good Mr Bailey, be pitiful.

BAIL. Why, [look] ye sir! he makes a pitiful fellow of a Bailey too! Away with him! Yet stay a while; here comes your fellows, sir.

Enter CROSSBY *and* FLEMING

[FLEM.] Now Mr Bailey, are your blanks sealed yet?

BAIL. They are, sir; and we have done this day most strange and pestiferous service, I assure ye sir.

FLEM. Your care shall be rewarded. Come, fellow Nimble, we must to court about other employments: there are already thirteen thousand blanks signed and returned to the shrieves, and seven hundred sent up to th' court for

whisperers, out of all which my lord will fetch a round
sum, I doubt it not. Come, let's away.

NIMB. Ay, ay. We'll follow. Come, ye sheepbiter. Here's
a traitor of all traitors that not only speaks, but has
whistled treason. Come, come, sir, I'll spoil your whistle
I warrant ye!   *Exeunt*

ACT IV

[SCENE 1: *London*]

Enter TRESILIAN *with writings, and a man with bags of money.*

TRES. Sirrah, are the bags sealed?

SERV. Yes, my lord.

TRES. Then take my keys; and lock the money in my study,
safe bar and make sure, I charge ye. So. Begone.

SERV. I will, my lord.   *Exit Servant*

TRES. So. Seven thousand pounds
From Bedford, Buckingham, and Oxford shires
These blanks already have returned the king,
So then there's four for me and three for him.
Our pains in this must needs be satisfied;
Good husbands will make hay while the sun shines,
And so must we, for thus conclude these times:
So men be rich enough, they're good enough.
Let fools make conscience how they get their coin.
I'll please the king and keep me in his grace,
For princes' favours purchase land apace.
These blanks that I have scattered in the realm
Shall double his revenues to the crown.

Enter BUSHY *and* SCROOPE

SCROO. Now, Lord Tresilian, is this coin come yet?

BUSH. King Richard wants money; you're too slack,
Tresilian.

TRES. Some shires have sent; and more, my lords, will
follow.

These sealed blanks I now have turned to bonds,
And these shall down to Norfolk presently.
The choughs with much ado have signed and sealed,
And here's a secret note my men have sent
Of all their yearly 'states amount unto,
And by this note I justly tax their bonds.
Here's fat whoreson in his russet slops
And yet may spend three hundred pounds by th' year:
The third of which the hogsface owes the king.
Here's his bond for't, with his hand and seal,
And so by this I'll sort each several sum:
The thirds of all shall to King Richard come.
How like you this, my lords?

SCROO. Most rare, Tresilian. Hang 'em, codsheads,
Shall they spend money and King Richard lack it?

BUSH. Are not their lives and lands and livings his?
—Then rack them thoroughly.

TRES. O my lords, I have set a trick afoot for ye; an ye follow
it hard and get the king to sign it, you'll be all kings by it.

BUSH. The farming out the kingdom? Tush, Tresilian, 'tis
half granted already, and had been fully concluded, had
not the messenger returned so unluckily from the Duke
of Gloster, which a little moved the king at his uncle's
stubbornness. But to make all whole, we have left that
smooth-faced flattering Greene to follow him close; and
he'll never leave till he has done it, I warrant ye.

SCROO. There's no question on't: King Richard will betake
himself to a yearly stipend, and we four by lease must
rent the kingdom.

Enter BAGOT

BUSH. Rent it, ay, and rack it too, ere we forfeit our leases,
an we had them once. How now, Bagot, what news?

BAGOT. All rich and rare; the realm must be divided presently, and we four must farm it—the leases are a-making,
and for £7,000 a month the kingdom is our own, boys.

BUSH. 'Sfoot, let's differ for no price; an it were £70,000 a
month we'll make somebody pay for't.

SCROO. Where is his highness?

BAGOT. He will be here presently to seal the writings. He's
a little angry that the duke comes not, but that will vanish
quickly. On with your soothest faces, ye wenching rascals,
humour him finely, and you're all made by it.

Enter KING RICHARD, GREENE, *and others*

BUSH. See, see! he comes; and that flattering hound, Greene,
close at's elbow.

SCROO. Come, come, we must all flatter if we mean to live
by it.

KING. Our uncle will not come, then.

GREEN. That was his answer, flat and resolute.

KING. Was ever subject so audacious?

BAGOT. And can your grace, my lord, digest these wrongs?

KING. Yes, as a mother that beholds her child
    Dismembered by a bloody tyrant's sword.
    I tell thee, Bagot, in my heart remains
    Such deep impressions of his churlish taunts
    As nothing can remove the gall thereof
    Till with his blood mine eyes be satisfied.

GREEN. 'Sfoot, raise powers, my lord, and fetch him thence
    perforce.

KING. I dare not, Greene, for whilst he keeps i' the country
    There is no meddling; he's so well beloved
    As all the realm will rise in arms with him.

TRES. 'Sfoot, my lord, an you'd fain have him, I have a trick
    shall fetch him from his house at Plashey in spite of all
    his favourites.

GREEN. Let's ha't, Tresilian, thy wit must help or all's
    dashed else.

TRES. Then thus, my lord:—While the duke securely revels
    i' the country, we'll have some trusty friends disguise
    themselves like maskers and this night ride down to
    Plashey, and in the name of some near adjoining friends,
    offer their sports to make him merry, which he no doubt
    will thankfully accept. Then in the mask we'll h[ave] it
    so devised, the dance being done and the room voided,

then upon some occasion single the duke alone, thrust him
in a masking-suit, clap a vizard on his face, and so convey
him out o' the house at pleasure.

SCROO. How if he cry, and call for help?

TRES. What serves your drums [for], but to drown his cries?
And, being in a mask, 'twill never be suspected.

GREEN. Good, and to help it, my lord, Lapoole, the Governor of Calais, is new come over, who, with a troop of
soldiers closely ambushed in the woods, near the house,
shall shroud themselves till the mask be ended, then, the
duke being attached, he shall be there ready to receive
him, hurry him away to the Thames side, where a ship
shall be laid ready for his coming, so clap him under
hatches, hoist sails, and secretly convey him out o' the
realm to Calais. And so by this means ye shall prevent all
mischief, for neither of your uncles nor any of the kingdom shall know what's become of him.

KING. I like it well, sweet Greene; and by my crown,
We'll be in the mask ourself, and so shall you.
Get horses ready: this night we'll ride to Plashey;
But see ye carry it close and secretly,
For whilst this plot's a-working for the duke,
I'll set a trap for York and Lancaster.
Go, Tresilian, let proclamations straight be sent
Wherein thou shalt accuse the dukes of treason,
And then attach, condemn, and close imprison them.
Lest the commons should rebel against us,
We'll send unto the King of France for aid,
And in requital we'll surrender up
Our forts of Guisnes and Calais to the French.
Let crown and kingdom waste, yea life and all,
Before King Richard see his true friends fall!
Give order our disguises be made ready,
And let Lapoole provide the ship and soldiers:
We will not sleep, by heaven, till we have seized him.

BUSH. 'Sfoot, urge our suit again, he will forget it else.

KING. These traitors once surprised, then all is sure:
Our kingdom's quiet, and your state's secure.

GREEN. Most true, sweet king; and then your grace, as you
promised, farming out the kingdom to us four, shall not
need to trouble yourself with any business—this old
turkeycock Tresilian shall look to the law, and we'll
govern the land most rarely.

KING. So, sir. The love of thee and these, my dearest Greene,
    Hath won King Richard to consent to that
    For which all foreign kings will point at us.
    And of the meanest subject of our land
    We shall be censured strangely, when they tell
    How our great father toiled his royal person
    Spending his blood to purchase towns in France;
    And we his son, to ease our wanton youth
    Become a landlord to this warlike realm,
    Rent out our kingdom like a pelting farm
    That erst was held, as fair as Babylon,
    The maiden conqueress to all the world.

GREEN. 'Sfoot, what need you care what the world talks?
You still retain the name of king, and if any disturb ye, we
four come presently from the four parts of the kingdom,
with four puissant armies to assist you.

KING. You four must be all then, for I think nobody else
will follow you, unless it be to hanging!

GREEN. Why Richard, King Richard, will ye be as good as
your word, and seal the writings? 'Sfoot, an thou dost
not and I do not join with thine uncles and turn traitor,
would I might be turned to a toadstool!

KING. Very well, sir: they did well to choose you for their
orator, that has King Richard's love and heart in keeping.
Your suit is granted, sir: let's see the writings.

ALL. They're here, my lord.

KING. View them, Tresilian, then we'll sign and seal them.
Look to your bargain, Greene, and be no loser, for if ye
forfeit or run behindhand with me—I swear I'll both
imprison and punish ye soundly.

GREEN. Forfeit, sweet king? 'Sblood, I'll sell their houses
ere I'll forfeit my lease, I warrant thee.

KING. If they be stubborn, do, and spare not; rack them

soundly and we'll maintain it. Remember ye not the proviso enacted in our last parliament, that no statute, were it ne'er so profitable for the commonwealth, should stand in any force against our proceedings?

GREEN. 'Tis true, my lord: then what should hinder ye to accomplish anything that may best please your kingly spirit to determine?

KING. True, Greene, and we will do it in spite of them. Is't just, Tresilian?

TRES. Most just, my liege. These gentlemen here, Sir Henry Greene, Sir Edward Bagot, Sir William Bushy, and Sir Thomas Scroope, all jointly here stand bound to pay your majesty, or your deputy, wherever you remain, seven thousand pounds a month for this your kingdom; for which your grace, by these writings, surrenders to their hands all your crown lands, lordships: manors, rents: taxes, subsidies, fifteens, imposts; foreign customs, staples for wool, tin, lead, and cloth: all forfeitures of goods or lands confiscate; and all other duties that do, shall, or may appertain to the king or crown's revenues; and for non-payment of the sum or sums aforesaid, your majesty to seize the lands and goods of the said gentlemen above named, and their bodies to be imprisoned at your grace's pleasure.

KING. How like you that, Greene? Believe me, if you fail, I'll not favour ye a day.

GREEN. I'll ask no favour at your hands, sir: ye shall have your money at your day, and then do your worst, sir!

KING. 'Tis very good. Set to your hands and seals. Tresilian, we make you our deputy to receive this money. Look strictly to them, I charge ye.

TRES. If the money come not to my hands at the time appointed, I'll make them smoke for't.

GREEN. Ay, ay, you're an upright justice, sir, we fear ye not. Here my lord: they're ready, signed and sealed.

TRES. Deliver them to His Majesty all together, as your special deeds.

ALL. We do, with humble thanks: unto His Majesty
  That makes us tenants to so rich a lordship.

KING. Keep them, Tresilian; now will we sign and seal to
  you. Never had English subjects such a landlord.

GREEN. Nor ever had English king such subjects as we four,
  that are able to farm a whole kingdom and pay him rent
  for't.

KING. Look that ye do. We shall expect performance
  speedily. There's your indenture, signed and sealed,
  which as our kingly deed we here deliver.

GREEN. Thou never didst a better deed in thy life; sweet
  bully, thou mayst now live at ease, we'll toil for thee, and
  send thy money in tumbling.

KING. We shall see your care, sir.
  Reach me the map, we may allot their portions,
  and part the realm amongst them equally.
  You four shall here by us divide yourselves
  into the nine-and-thirty shires and counties of my king-
    dom parted thus:—
  (Come stand by me and mark those shires assigned ye)
  Bagot, thy lot
  betwixt the Thames and sea thus lies: Kent, Surrey,
  Sussex, Hampshire, Berkshire, Wiltshire, Dorsetshire,
  Somersetshire, Devonshire, Cornwall; those parts are
    thine
  As amply, Bagot, as the crown is mine.

BAGOT. All thanks, love, duty, to my princely sovereign.

KING. Bushy from thee shall stretch his government over
  these [lands] that lie in Wales, together
  with our counties of Gloster, Wo'ster, Hereford, Shrop-
  shire, Staffordshire, and Cheshire: there's thy lot.

BUSH. Thanks to my king that thus hath honoured me.

KING. Sir Thomas Scroope. From Trent to Tweed thy lot
  is parted thus: all Yorkshire, Derbyshire, Lancashire,
  Cumberland, Westmorland, and Northumberland.
  Receive thy lot, thy state and government.

SCROO. With faith and duty to your highness' throne.

KING. Now, my Greene, what have I left for thee?

GREEN. 'Sfoot, an you'll give me nothing, then goodnight
landlord! Since ye have served me last, an I be not the
last shall pay your rent, ne'er trust me!

KING. I kept thee last to make thy part the greatest.
See here sweet Greene:—
Those shires are thine, even from the Thames to Trent;
Thou here shalt lie, i' the middle of my land.

GREEN. That's best i' the winter. Is there any pretty wenches
in my government?

KING. Guess that by this; thou hast London, Middlesex,
Essex, Suffolk, Norfolk, Cambridgeshire,
Hertfordshire, Bedfordshire, Buckinghamshire,
Oxfordshire, Northamptonshire,
Rutlandshire, Leicestershire, Warwickshire, Huntingdon-
shire,
And Lincolnshire—there's your portion, sir.

GREEN. 'Slid, I will rule like a king amongst them,
And thou shalt reign like an emperor over us.

KING. Thus have I parted my whole realm amongst ye.
Be careful of your charge and government.
And now to attach our stubborn uncles.
Let warrants be sent down, Tresilian,
For Gaunt and York, Surrey and Arundel,
Whilst we this night at Plashey suddenly
Surprise Plain Woodstock; being parted thus
We shall with greater ease arrest and take them.
Your places are not sure while they have breath,
Therefore pursue them hard; those traitors gone,
The staves are broke the people lean upon,
And you may guide and rule then at your pleasures.
Away to Plashey, let our mask be ready.
Beware Plain Thomas, for King Richard comes
Resolved with blood to wash all former wrongs.

Exeunt

[SCENE 2: *Plashey House, Essex*]

Enter WOODSTOCK *and his* DUCHESS, *with a gentleman,*
CHEYNEY *and others.*

WOOD. The queen so sick! Come, come, make haste, good
    wife,
  Thou'lt be belated, sure, 'tis night already!
  On with thy cloak and mask! To horse, to horse!

DUCH. Good troth, my lord, I have no mind to ride.
  I have been dull and heavy all this day,
  My sleeps were troubled with sad dreams last night,
  And I am full of fear and heaviness.
  Pray let me ride tomorrow.

WOOD. What, and the queen so sick? Away for shame!
  Stay for a dream? Thou'st dreamt I'm sure ere this!

DUCH. Never so fearful were my dreams till now.
  Had they concerned myself, my fears were past;
  But you were made the object of mine eye,
  And I beheld you murdered cruelly.

WOOD. Ha, murdered?
  Alack, good lady. Didst thou dream of me?
  Take comfort, then, all dreams are contrary.

DUCH. Pray God it prove so, for my soul is fearful;
  The vision did appear so lively to me.
  Methought as you were ranging through the woods,
  An angry lion with a herd of wolves
  Had in an instant round encompassed you;
  When to your rescue, gainst the course of kind,
  A flock of silly sheep made head against them,
  Bleating for help; 'gainst whom the forest king
  Roused up his strength, and slew both you and them.
  This fear affrights me.

WOOD. Afore my God thou'rt foolish; I'll tell thee all thy
    dream.
  Thou knowst last night we had some private talk
  About the blanks the country's taxed withal,
  Where I compared the state (as now it stands,—
  Meaning King Richard and his harmful flatterers)

Unto a savage herd of ravening wolves,
The Commons to a flock of silly sheep
Who, whilst their slothful shepherd careless stood,
Those forest thieves broke in, and sucked their blood.
And this thy apprehension took so deep
The form was portrayed lively in thy sleep.
Come, come, 'tis nothing. What, are the horses ready?

CHEY. They are, my lord.

WOOD. Where is the gentleman that brought this message?
    Where lies the queen, sir?

[GENT.] At Sheen, my lord: most sick, and so much altered
    As those about her fear her sudden death.

WOOD. Forfend it, heaven! Away, make haste, I charge ye.
    What, weeping now? Afore my God thou'rt fond!
    Come, come, I know thou art no augurer of ill;
    Dry up thy tears: this kiss, and part: farewell.

DUCH. That farewell from your lips to me sounds ill.
    Where'er I go, my fears will follow still.

WOOD. See her to horseback, Cheyney.

>   *Exeunt* DUCHESS *and the rest. Manet* WOODSTOCK
>   'Fore God, tis late

And, but th' important business craves such haste,
She had not gone from Plashey House tonight.
But woe is me the good queen Anne is sick
And (by my soul) my heart is sad to hear it:
So good a lady, and so virtuous,
This realm for many ages could not boast of.
Her charity hath stayed the Commons' rage
That would ere this have shaken Richard's chair
Or set all England on a burning fire.
And—'fore my God—I fear, when she is gone
This woeful land will all to ruin run.

> *Enter* CHEYNEY

How now Cheyney, what, is thy lady gone yet?

CHEY. She is, my lord: with much unwillingness,
    And 'tis so dark I cannot blame her grace;
    The lights of heaven are shut in pitchy clouds

And flakes of fire run tilting through the sky
Like dim ostents to some great tragedy.

WOOD. God bless good Anne a Beame. I fear her death
Will be the tragic scene the sky foreshows us.
When kingdoms change, the very heavens are troubled.
Pray God King Richard's wild behaviour
Force not the powers of heaven to frown upon us.
My prayers are still for him: what think'st thou, Cheyney;
May not Plain Thomas live a time to see
This state attain her former royalty?
'Fore God I doubt it not: my heart is merry,
And I am suddenly inspired for mirth.
Ha! what sport shall we have tonight, Cheyney?

CHEY. I'm glad to see your grace addicted so,
For I have news of sudden mirth to tell ye,
Which, till I heard ye speak, I durst not utter;
We shall have a mask tonight, my lord.

WOOD. Ha, a mask say'st thou? what are they, Cheyney?

CHEY. It seems, my lord, some country gentlemen,
To show their dear affection to your grace,
Proffer their sports tonight to make you merry;
Their drums have called for entrance twice already.

WOOD. Are they so near? I prithee let them enter.
Tell them we do embrace their loves most kindly.
Give order through the house that all observe them.

Exit CHEYNEY

We must accept their loves, although the times
Are no way suited now for masks and revels.
What ho, within there!

Enter Servants

SERV. My lord?

WOOD. Prepare a banquet: call for lights and music.

[Exit a Servant]

They come in love—and we'll accept it so;
Some sport does well, we're all too full of woe.

Enter CHEYNEY

CHEY. They're come, my lord.

WOOD. They all are welcome, Cheyney. Set me a chair;
 We will behold their sports in spite of care.

Flourish [of] cornets. Then a great shout and winding of
horns. Then enter CYNTHIA.

CYNTH. From the clear orb of our ethereal Sphere
 Bright Cynthia comes to hunt and revel here.
 The groves of Calydon and Arden Woods
 Of untamed monsters, wild and savage herds,
 We and our knights have freed, and hither come
 To hunt these forests, where we hear there lies
 A cruel tuskèd boar, whose terror flies
 Through this large kingdom, and with fear and dread
 Strikes her amazèd greatness pale and dead.
 And, having viewed from far these towers of stone,
 We heard the people midst their joy and moan
 Extol to heaven a faithful prince and peer
 That keeps a court of love and pity here.
 Reverend and mild his looks; if such there be,
 This state directs, great prince, that you are he;
 And ere our knights to this great hunting go,
 Before your grace they would some pastime show
 In sprightly dancing. Thus they bade me say
 And wait an answer to return or stay.

WOOD. Nay, for heaven's pity let them come, I prithee.
 Pretty device, i'faith! Stand by, make room there!
 Stir, stir, good fellows, each man to his task!
 We shall have a clear night, the Moon directs the mask.

Music. Enter KING, GREENE, BUSHY, BAGOT, *like Diana's*
knights, led in by four other knights, in green, with horns
about their necks and boarspears in their hands.

WOOD. Ha, country sports say ye? 'Fore God tis courtly.
 A general welcome, courteous gentlemen.
 And when I see your faces I'll give each man more par-
   ticular.
 If your entertainment fail your merit,
 I must ask pardon; my lady is from home,

And most of my attendants waiting on her,
But we'll do what we can to bid you welcome.
Afore my God, it joys my heart to see
Amidst these days of woe and misery
Ye find a time for harmless mirth and sport;
But 'tis your loves, and we'll be thankful for 't.
Ah sirrah, ye come like knights to hunt the boar indeed;
And heaven he knows we had need of helping hands,
So many wild boars root and spoil our lands
That England almost is destroyed by them.
I care not if King Richard heard me speak it:
I wish his grace all good, high heaven can tell,
But there's a fault in some, alack the day:
His youth is led by flatterers much astray.
But he's our king, and God's great deputy;
And if ye hunt to have me second ye
In any rash attempt against his state,
Afore my God, I'll ne'er consent unto it.
I ever yet was just and true to him,
And so will still remain; what's now amiss
Our sins have caused, and we must bide heaven's will.
I speak my heart: I am Plain Thomas still.
Come, come, a hall! and music there! Your dance being
    done,
A banquet stands prepared to bid you welcome.

*Music. They dance. Then a drum [heard] afar off; [and]
enter* CHENEY.

WOOD. How now, Cheyney, is this banquet ready?
CHEY. There is no time, I fear, for banqueting.
    My lord, I wish your grace be provident;
    I fear your person is betrayed, my lord:
    The house is round beset with armèd soldiers.
WOOD. Ha, soldiers?
    Afore my God, the Commons all are up, then;
    They will rebel against the king, I fear me,
    And flock to me to back their bold attempts.
    Go arm the household, Cheyney.   *Exit* CHENEY

                      Hear me, gentlemen,
(Fore God I do not like this whispering)
If your intents be honest, show your faces.

KING. Guard fast the doors and seize him presently!
This is the cave, that keeps the tuskèd boar
That roots up England's vineyards uncontrolled.
Bagot, arrest him! If for help he cry,
Drown all his words, with drums, confusedly.

WOOD. Am I betrayed?

BAGOT. Ye cannot 'scape, my lord; the toils are pitched
And all your household fast in hold ere this.
Thomas of Woodstock: Duke of Gloster,
Earl of Cambridge and of Buckingham:
I here arrest thee in King Richard's name
Of treason to the Crown, his State and Realm.

WOOD. I'll put in bail, and answer to the law.
Speak, is King Richard here?

ALL.   No, no, my lord.
Away with him!

WOOD.   Villains, touch me not!
I am descended of the royal blood,
King Richard's uncle,
His grandsire's son; his princely father's brother:
Becomes it princes to be led like slaves?

KING. Put on a vizard. Stop his cries.

WOOD. Ha, who bids them so? I know that voice full well.
Afore my God, false men, King Richard's here!
Turn thee, thou headstrong youth, and speak again.
By thy dead father's soul, I charge thee hear me.
So may heaven help me at my greatest need
As I have wished thy good and England's safety.

BAGOT. You're still deceived, my lord, the king's not here.

BUSH. On with his masking-suit, and bear him hence.
We'll lead ye fairly to King Richard's presence.

WOOD. Nay, from his presence to my death you'll lead me;
And I am pleased I shall not live to see
My county's ruin, and his misery.
Thou hear'st me well, proud king, and well may'st boast

That thou betray'dst me here so suddenly,
For had I known thy secret treachery
Nor thou, nor these thy flattering minions,
With all your strengths had wronged plain Woodstock
    thus.
But use your wills; Your uncles Gaunt and York
Will give you thanks for this, and the poor Commons,
When they shall hear of these your unjust proceedings—

KING. Stop's mouth I say: we'll hear no more.

WOOD. Good heaven, forgive me, pray ye forbear a wh[ile];
I'll speak but one word more, indeed I will.
Some man commend me to my virtuous wife;
Tell her her dreams have ta'en effect indeed:
By wolves and lions now must Woodstock bleed.

KING. Deliver him to Lapoole, the ship lies ready;
Convey him o'er to Calais speedily,
There use him as we gave directions.
Sound up your drums, our hunting sports are done,
And when y'are past the house, cast by your habits
And mount your horses with all swiftest haste:
The boar is taken, and our fears are past.

Exeunt

[SCENE 3: *Sheen House.*]

Enter CROSSBY, FLEMING, *and* NIMBLE

CROSS. Come sirs, attend, my lord is coming forth.
The high shrieves of Kent and Northumberland
With twenty gentlemen are all arrested
For privy whisperers against the state;
In which I know my lord will find some trick
To seize their goods; and then there's work for us.

NIMB. Nay, there will be work for the hangman first; then
we rifle the goods, and my lord seizes the lands. If these
seven hundred whisperers that are taken come off lustily,
he'll have the devil and all shortly.

Enter TRESILIAN, *with the Shrieves of Kent and Northumber-*
  land, with Officers.

FLEM. See, see, they're coming.

TRES. Call for a marshal there! Commit the traitors.

SHRIEVES. We do beseech your honour hear us speak.

TRES. Sir, we'll not hear ye. The proof's too plain against ye.
  Becomes it you, sir, being shrieve of Kent,
  To stay the blanks King Richard sent abroad,
  Revile our messengers, refuse the charters,
  And spurn like traitors gainst the King's decrees?

S. KENT. My lord, I plead our ancient liberties
  Recorded and enrolled in the king's Crown-office,
  Wherein the men of Kent are clear discharged
  Of fines, fifteens, or any other taxes:
  For ever given them by the Conqueror.

TRES. You're still deceived; those charters were not sent
  To abrogate your ancient privilege,
  But for his highness' use they were devised
  To gather and collect amongst his subjects
  Such sums of money as they well might spare,
  And he in their defence must hourly spend.
  Is not the subject's wealth at the king's will?
  What, is he lord of lives and not of lands?
  Is not his high displeasure present death?
  And dare ye stir his indignation so?

S. NOR. We are free-born, my lord, yet do confess
  Our lives and goods are at the king's dispose:
  But how, my lord?—like to a gentle prince
  To take or borrow what we best may spare;
  And not, like bondslaves, force it from our hands.

TRES. Presumptuous traitors, that will we try on you.
  Will you set limits to the king's high pleasure?
  Away to prison! Seize their goods and lands.

S. KENT. Much good may it do ye my lord. The care is ta'en.
  As good die there, as here abroad be slain.

S. NOR. Well, God forgive both you and us, my lord:
  Your hard oppressions have undone the state
  And made all England poor and desolate.

TRES. Why suffer ye their speech? To prison hie!
   There let them perish, rot, consume, and die!
                    Exeunt [Officers] with the Shrieves
   Art thou there, Nimble?

NIMB. I am here, my lord. And since your lordship is now
   employed to punish traitors, I am come to present myself
   unto you.

TRES. What, for a traitor?

NIMB. No, my lord, but for a discoverer of the strangest
   traitor that was ever heard of . . . For by the plain arith-
   metic of my capacity, I have found out the very words
   a traitor spoke that has whistled treason.

TRES. How is that? Whistle treason?

NIMB. Most certain, my lord, I have a trick for't: if a carman do but whistle, I'll find treason in't, I warrant ye.

TRES. Thou'rt a rare statesman. Nimble, thou'st a reaching
   head.

NIMB. I'll put treason into any man's head, my lord, let him
   answer it as he can. And then, my lord, we have got a
   schoolmaster, that teaches all the country to sing treason.
   And like a villain he says, 'God bless your lordship'.

TRES. Thou'rt a most strange discoverer. Where are these
   traitors?

NIMB. All in prison, my lord. Mr Ignorance, the Bailey of
   Dunstable, and I, have taken great pains about them.
   Besides, here's a note of seven hundred whisperers, most
   on 'em sleepy knaves, we pulled them out of Bedfordshire.

TRES. Let's see the note. Seven hundred whispering traitors:
   Monstrous villains! We must look to these:
   Of all the sort these are most dangerous,
   To stir rebellion gainst the king and us.
   What are they, Crossby? are the rebels wealthy?

CROSS. Fat choughs, my lord, all landed men. Rich farmers,
   graziers and such fellows, that having been but a little
   pinched with imprisonment, begin already to offer their
   lands for liberty.

TRES. We'll not be nice to take their offers, Crossby,

Their lands are better than their lives to us,
And without lands they shall not ransom lives.
Go sirs, to terrify the traitors more,
Ye shall have warrants straight to hang them all;
Then if they proffer lands, and put in bail
To make a just surrender speedily,
Let them have lives, and after, liberty.
But those that have nor lands nor goods to pay,
Let them be whipped, then hanged. Make haste away.

NIMB. Well, then: I see my whistle must be whipped; he has
but two calves to live on, and has lost them too; and for my
schoolmaster, I'll have him march about the market-
place with ten dozen of rods at's girdle the very day he
goes a-feasting, and every one of his scholars shall have
a jerk at him. Come sirs.

TRES. Away and leave us. Here comes Sir Edward Bagot.

Enter BAGOT. *Exeunt* NIMBLE, [CROSSBY, *and the others*]

BAGOT. Right happily met, my lord Tresilian.

TRES. You're well returned to court, Sir Edward,
To this sad house of Sheen, made comfortless
By the sharp sickness of the good Queen Anne.

BAGOT. King Richard's come and gone to visit her.
Sad for her weak estate: he sits and weeps.
Her speech is gone. Only at sight of him
She heaved her hands and closed her eyes again,
And whether alive, or dead, is yet uncertain.

Enter BUSHY

TRES. Here comes Sir William Bushy. What tidings, sir?

BUSH. The king's a widower, sir. Fair Anne a Beame
Hath breathed her last farewell to all the realm.

TRES. Peace with her soul, she was a virtuous lady.
How takes King Richard this her sudden death?

BUSH. Fares like a madman; rends his princely hair,
Beats his sad breast, falls grovelling on the earth
All careless of his state, wishing to die

And even in death to keep her company.
But that which makes his soul more desperate—
Amid this heat of passion, weeping comes
His aunt the duchess, Woodstock's hapless wife,
With tender love and comfort—
At sight of whom his griefs again redoubled,
Calling to mind the lady's woeful state,
As yet all ignorant of her own mishap.
He takes her in his arms, weeps on her breast,
And would have there revealed her husband's fall
Amidst his passions, had not Scroope and Greene
By violence borne him to an inward room,
Where still he cries to get a messenger
To send to Calais to reprieve his uncle.

BAGOT. I do not like those passions.
  If he reveal the plot we all shall perish.
  Where is the duchess?

BUSH. With much ado we got her leave the presence
  With an intent in haste to ride to Plashey.

TRES. She'll find sad comforts there. Would all were well.
  A thousand dangers round enclose our state.

BAGOT. And we'll break through, my lord, in spite of fate.
  Come come, be merry, good Tresilian.

Enter the KING *and* SCROOPE

SCROO. My dearest lord! Forsake these sad laments.
  No sorrows can suffice to make her live.

KING. Then let sad sorrow kill King Richard too,
  For all my earthly joys with her must die,
  And I am killed with cares eternally.
  For Anne a Beame is dead, for ever gone!
  She was too virtuous to remain with me,
  And heaven hath given her higher dignity.
  O God, I fear, even here begins our woe:
  Her death's but chorus to some tragic scene
  That shortly will confound our state and realm.
  Such sad events black mischiefs still attend,
  And bloody acts, I fear, must crown the end.

BAGOT. Presage not so, sweet prince, your state is strong.
Your youthful hopes with expectation crown,
Let not one loss so many comforts drown.

KING. Despair and madness seize me. O dear friends,
What loss can be compared to such a queen?
Down with this house of Sheen, go ruin all!
Pull down her buildings, let her turrets fall:
For ever lay it waste and desolate
That English king may never here keep court,
But to all ages leave a sad report,
When men shall see these ruined walls of Sheen
And sighing say, 'Here died King Richard's queen'.
For which we'll have it wasted lime and stone
To keep a monument of Richard's moan.
O torturing grief!

BUSH. Dear liege, all tears for her are vain oblations;
Her quiet soul rests in celestial peace:
With joy of that, let all your sorrows cease.

KING. Send post to Calais and bid Lapoole forbear
On pain of life, to act our sad decree.
For heaven's love, go, prevent the tragedy.
We have too much provoked the powers divine
And here repent thy wrongs, good uncle Woodstock:
The thought whereof confounds my memory.
If men might die when they would point the time,
The time is now King Richard would be gone;
For as a fearful thunder-clap doth strike
The soundest body of the tallest oak,
Yet harmless leaves the outward bark untouched,
So is King Richard struck. Come, come let's go:
My wounds are inward. Inward burns my woe.

Exeunt

[ACT V

SCENE 1: *The castle, Calais*]

Enter LAPOOLE *with a light, after him* TWO MURDERERS.

LAP. Come sirs, be resolute. The time serves well
To act the business you have ta'en in hand.
The duke is gone to rest, the room is voided,
No ear can hear his cries; be fearless, bold,
And win King Richard's love, with heaps of gold.
Are all your instruments for death made ready?

1ST M. All fit to the purpose. See my lord, here's first a towel
with which we do intend to strangle him; but if he
strive and this should chance to fail, I'll mall his old
mazzard with this hammer—knock him down like an ox,
and after cut's throat. How like ye this?

LAP. No, wound him not,
It must be done so fair and cunningly
As if he died a common natural death,
For so we must give out to all that ask.

2ND M. There is no way then, but to smother him.

LAP. I like that best; yet one thing let me tell ye:
Think not your work contrived so easily
As if you were to match some common man.
Believe me sirs, his countenance is such,
So full of dread and lordly majesty,
Mixed with such mild and gentle haviour
As will (except you be resolved at full)
Strike you with fear even with his princely looks.

1ST M. Not an he looked as grim as Hercules,
As stern and terrible as the devil himself!

LAP. 'Tis well resolved: retire yourselves awhile;
Stay in the next withdrawing-chamber there
And when occasion serves, I'll call ye forth.

2ND M. Do but beckon with your finger, my lord,
and like vultures we come flying and seize him presently.

Exeunt [*the*] TWO MURDERERS

LAP. Do so; now by my fairest hopes, I swear
  The boldness of these villains to this murder
  Makes me abhor them and the deed for ever.
      Horror of conscience, with the king's command,
      Fights a fell combat in my fearful breast.
  The king commands his uncle here must die,
  And my sad conscience bids the contrary
  And tells me that his innocent blood thus spilt
  Heaven will revenge; murder's a heinous guilt,
      A seven times crying sin. Accursed man!
      The further that I wade in this foul act
      My troubled senses are the more distract,
      Confounded and tormented past my reason.
  But there's no lingering: either he must die
  Or great King Richard vows my tragedy.
  Then 'twixt two evils 'tis good to choose the least:
  Let danger fright faint fools; I'll save mine own
  And let him fall to black destruction.

He draws the curtains. [WOODSTOCK *discovered in his bed*]

  He sleeps upon his bed: the time serves fitly.
  I'll call the murderers in. Sound music there,
  To rock his senses in eternal slumbers.

Music [*within*]

  Sleep, Woodstock, sleep; thou never more shalt wake.
  This town of Calais shall for ever tell,
  Within her castle walls Plain Thomas fell.   *Exit*

Thunder and lightning. Enter the GHOST OF THE BLACK PRINCE.

1ST GHO. Night-horror and th' eternal shrieks of death
  Intended to be done this dismal night
  Hath shook fair England's great cathedral,
  And from my tomb elate at Canterbury
  The ghost of Edward the Black Prince is come
  To stay King Richard's rage, my wanton son.
  Thomas of Woodstock, wake! Thy brother calls thee.
  Thou royal issue of King Edward's loins,
  Thou art beset with murder, rise and fly.

If here thou stay, death comes and thou must die.
Still dost thou sleep? O I am naught but air!
Had I the vigour of my former strength
When thou beheldest me fight at Crecy field
Where, hand-to-hand, I took King John of France
And his bold sons my captive prisoners,
I'd shake these stiff supporters of thy bed
And drag thee from this dull security.
O yet for pity, wake! prevent thy doom!
Thy blood upon my son will surely come:
For which, dear brother Woodstock, haste and fly,
Prevent his ruin and thy tragedy.

WOOD. Oh! *Thunder.*   *Exit* GHOST

Enter EDWARD THE THIRD'S GHOST.

2ND GHO. Sleepst thou so soundly and pale death so nigh?
Thomas of Woodstock, wake, my son, and fly!
Thy wrongs have roused thy royal father's ghost
And from his quiet grave King Edward's come
To guard thy innocent life, my princely son.
Behold me here: sometime fair England's lord;
Seven warlike sons I left, yet being gone,
No one succeeded: in my kingly throne,
Richard of Bordeaux, my accursed grandchild,
Cut off your titles to the kingly state,
And now your lives and all would ruinate;
Murders his grandsire's sons, his father's brothers,
Becomes a landlord to my kingly titles,
Rents out my crown's revenues, racks my subjects
That spent their lives with me in conquering France,
Beheld me ride in state through London streets,
And at my stirrup lowly footing by
Four captive kings to grace my victory.
Yet that nor this his riotous youth can stay
Till death hath ta'en his uncles all away.
Thou sixth of Edward's sons, get up and fly;
Haste thee to England, close and speedily!
Thy brothers York and Gaunt are up in arms,

Go join with them: prevent thy further harms.
The murderers are at hand: awake, my son!
This hour foretells thy sad destruction.   *Exit* GHOST
[WOOD.] O good angels guide me, stay thou blessed spirit,
Thou royal shadow of my kingly father,
Return again! I know thy reverend looks;
With thy dear sight once more recomfort me,
Put by the fear my trembling heart foretells
And here is made apparent to my sight
By dreams and visions of this dreadful night.
Upon my knees I beg it. Ha! Protect me, heaven!
The doors are all made fast! 'Twas but my fancy:
All's whist and still, and nothing here appears
But the vast circuit of this empty room.
Thou blessed hand of mercy, guide my senses!
Afore my God, methought as here I slept
I did behold in lively form and substance
My father Edward and my warlike brother
Both gliding by my bed, and cried to me
To leave this place, to save my life, and fly.
Lighten my fears, dear Lord. I here remain
A poor old man, thrust from my native country,
Kept and imprisoned in a foreign kingdom.
If I must die, bear record, righteous heaven,
How I have nightly wak'd for England's good,
And yet to right her wrongs would spend my blood.
Send thy sad doom, King Richard: take my life.

Enter LAPOOLE *and the* MURDERERS

I wish my death might ease my country's grief.
LAP. We are prevented: back retire again,
  He's risen from his bed. What fate preserves him?
  —My lord, how fare you?
WOOD.   Thou canst not kill me, villain!
  God's holy angel guards a just man's life
  And with his radiant beams as bright as fire
  Will guard and keep his righteous innocence.
  I am a prince. Thou dar'st not murder me.

LAP. Your grace mistakes, my lord—

WOOD.   What art thou, speak!

LAP. Lapoole my lord: this city's governor.

WOOD. Lapoole, thou art King Richard's flatterer.
    O you just gods! record their treachery,
    Judge their foul wrongs, that under show of friendship
    Betrayed my simple, kind intendiments!
    My heart misgave it was no time for revels
    When you, like maskers, came disguised to Plashey,
    Joined with that wanton king to trap my life
    —For that, I know's the end his malice aims at;
    This castle, and my secret sending hither
    Imports no less. Therefore I charge ye tell me:
    Even by the virtue of nobility,
    And partly, too, on that allegiance
    Thou ow'st the offspring of King Edward's house,
    If aught thou know'st to prejudice my life,
    Thou presently reveal, and make it known.

LAP. Nay, good my lord, forbear that fond suspicion.

WOOD. I tell thee, Poole, there is no less intended.
    Why am I sent thus from my native country,
    But here at Calais to be murdered?
    And that, Lapoole, confounds my patience.
    This town of Calais, where I spent my blood
    To make it captive to the English king,
    Before whose walls great Edward lay encamped
    With his seven sons almost for fourteen months,
    Where the Black Prince my brother, and myself,
    The peers of England, and our royal father,
    Fearless of wounds, ne'er left till it was won
    —And was't to make a prison for his son?
    O righteous heavens, why do you suffer it?

LAP. Disquiet not your thoughts, my gracious lord.
    There is no hurt intended, credit me,
    Although awhile your freedom be abridged.
    I know the king; if you would but submit
    And write your letters to his majesty,
    Your reconcilement might be easily wrought.

WOOD. For what should I submit, or ask his mercy?
  Had I offended, with all low submission
  I'd lay my neck unto the block before him
  And willingly endure the stroke of death.
  But if not so, why should my fond entreaties
  Make my true loyalty appear like treason?
  No, no, Lapoole, let guilty men beg pardons,
  My mind is clear, and I must tell ye, sir,
  Princes have hearts like pointed diamonds
  That will in sunder burst afore they bend,
  And such lives here! Though death King Richard send,
  Yet fetch me pen and ink; I'll write to him
  Not to entreat, but to admonish him
  That he forsake his foolish ways in time
  And learn to govern like a virtuous prince,
  Call home his wise and reverend councillors,
  Thrust from his court those cursed flatterers
  That hourly work the realm's confusion.
  This counsel if he follow may in time
  Pull down those mischiefs that so fast do climb.

LAP. Here's pen and paper, my lord; will't please ye
    write?

WOOD. Anon I will; shut to the doors and leave me.
  Goodnight, Lapoole, and pardon me I prithee
  That my sad fear made question of thy faith.
  My state is fear-full, and my mind was troubled
  Even at thy entrance, with most fearful visions;
  Which made my passions more extreme and hasty.
  Out of my better judgement I repent it,
  And will reward thy love. Once more, goodnight.

LAP. Good rest unto your grace. (I mean in death;
  This dismal night thou breath'st thy latest breath.
  He sits to write, I'll call the murderers in
  To steal behind and closely strangle him.)   *Exit*

WOOD. So help me heaven I know not what to write,
  What style to use, nor how I should begin.
  My method is too plain to greet a king.
  I'll nothing say to excuse or clear myself,

For I have nothing done that needs excuse;
But tell him plain though here I spend my blood,

Enter both the MURDERERS

I wish his safety . . . and all England's good.

1ST M. Creep close to his back, ye rogue, be ready with the towel, when I have knocked him down, to strangle him.

2ND M. Do it quickly whilst his back is towards ye, ye damned villain; if thou lett'st him speak but a word, we shall not kill him.

1ST M. I'll watch him for that; down on your knees and creep, ye rascal.

WOOD. Have mercy, God! my sight o' the sudden fails me;
I cannot see my paper,
My trembling fingers will not hold my pen,
A thick congealed mist o'erspreads the chamber.
I'll rise and view the room.

1ST M. Not too fast for falling!   *Strikes him*

WOOD. What villain hand . . . hath done a deed so bad . . .
To drench his black soul in a prince's blood?

1ST M. Do ye prate sir? take that and that, zounds put the towel about's throat and strangle him quickly ye slave, or by the heart of hell, I'll fell thee, too.

2ND M. 'Tis done ye damned slave; pull ye dog: and pull thy soul to hell in doing it, for thou hast killed the truest subject that ever breathed in England.

1ST M. Pull, rogue, pull; think of the gold we shall have for doing it, and then let him—and thee—go to the devil together. Bring in the feather-bed and roll him up in that till he be smothered and stifled, and life and soul pressed out together. Quickly ye hell-hound!

2ND M. Here, here, ye cannibal. Zounds, he kicks and sprawls, lie on's breast, ye villain!

1ST M. Let him sprawl and hang. He's sure enough for speaking. Pull off the bed now—smooth down his hair and beard. Close his eyes and set his neck right: why, so. All fine and cleanly: who can say that this man was murdered now?

[Re-enter LAPOOLE]

LAP. What, is he dead?

2ND M. As a door-nail my lord. What will ye do with his body?

LAP. Take it up gently, lay him in his bed.
Then shut the door, as if he there had died.

1ST M. It cannot be perceived otherwise, my lord;
Never was murder done with such rare skill.
At our return we shall expect reward, my lord.

LAP. 'Tis ready told.
Bear in the body, then return and take it.

Exeunt [MURDERERS] with the body

Within there ho!

[Enter Soldiers]

[SOLD.] My lord?

LAP. Be ready with your weapons, guard the room;
There's two false traitors entered the duke's chamber,
Plotting to bear him thence, betray the castle,
Deliver up the town and all our lives
To the French forces that are hard at hand
To second their attempts. Therefore stand close,
And as they enter, seize them presently.
Our will's your warrant: use no further words
But hew them straight in pieces with your swords.

SOLD. I warrant ye my lord. An their skins were scaled with brass,
We have swords will pierce them. Come sirs, be ready.

[Re-enter the TWO MURDERERS]

1ST M. Come, ye miching rascal, the deed's done and all things performed rarely; we'll take our reward, steal close out o' the town, buy us fresh geldings, spur, cut, and ride till we are past all danger, I warrant thee.

LAP. Give their reward there! Quick, I say!

SOLDS. Down with the traitors! Kill the villains!

1ST M. } Hell and the devil!. Zounds! hold, ye rascals!
2ND M. }

They kill the MURDERERS

LAP. Drag hence their bodies, hurl them in the sea:
    The black reward of death's a traitor's pay.

Exeunt Soldiers with their bodies

So. This was well performed. Now who but we
Can make report of Woodstock's tragedy?
Only he died a natural death at Calais;
So we must give it out, or else King Richard
Through Europe's kingdoms will be hardly censured.
His headstrong uncles, York and Lancaster,
Are up, we hear, in open arms against him;
    The gentlemen and Commons of the realm,
    Missing the good old duke, their plain protector,
    Break their allegiance to their sovereign lord
    And all revolt upon the barons' side;
To help which harm, I'll o'er to England straight,
And with th' old troops of soldiers, ta'en from Calais,
I'll back King Richard's power, for should he fail,
And his great uncles get the victory,
His friends are sure to die; but if he win,
They fall, and we shall rise, whilst Richard's king.

Exit [LAPOOLE]

[SCENE 2: *Open country*]

Drums. March within. Enter TRESILIAN *and* NIMBLE *with armour.*

TRES. These proclamations we have sent abroad,
    Wherein we have accused the dukes of treason,
    Will daunt their pride; and make the people leave them.
    I hope no less, at least. Where art thou, Nimble?
NIMB. So loaden with armour I cannot stir, my lord.
TRES. Whose drums were those that beat even now?
NIMB. King Richard's drums, my lord; the young lords are
    pressing soldiers.
TRES. O, and do they take their press with willingness?
NIMB. As willing as a punk, that's pressed on a feather-bed,
    they take their pressing apiece with great patience. Marry,

the lords no sooner turn their backs, but they run away
like sheep, sir.

TRES. They shall be hanged like dogs for't.
What, dare the slaves refuse their sovereign?

NIMB. They say the proclamation's false, my lord;
And they'll not fight against the king's friends.

TRES. So; I feared as much, and since 'tis come to this,
I must provide betimes and seek for safety,
For now the king and our audacious peers
Are grown to such a height of burning rage
As nothing now can quench their kindled ire
But open trial, but the sword and lance;
And then I fear King Richard's part will fail.
Nimble: our soldiers run away thou say'st?

NIMB. Ay, by my troth, my lord. And I think 'tis our best
course to run after them; for if they run now, what will
they do when the battle begins? If we tarry here and the
king's uncles catch us, we are sure to be hanged.
My lord, have ye no trick of law to defend us? No demur
or writ of error to remove us?

TRES. Nimble, we must be wise.

NIMB. Then let's not stay to have more wit beaten into our
heads; I like not that, my lord.

TRES. I am a man for peace, and not for war.

NIMB. And yet they say you've made more wrangling i' the
land
Than all the wars ha' done these seven years.

TRES. This battle will revenge their base exclaims.
But hear'st thou, Nimble, I'll not be there today.
One man amongst so many is no maim,
Therefore, I'll keep aloof, till all be done.
If good, I stay; if bad, away I run.
Nimble, it shall be so. I'll neither fight nor die;
But, thus resolved, disguise myself and fly.   *Exit*

NIMB. 'Tis the wisest course, my lord;
And I'll go put off mine armour that I may run lustily too.
                                                       Exit

[SCENE 3: *Open country*]

Enter with Drum and Colours, YORK, LANCASTER, ARUNDEL,
SURREY, *with the* DUCHESS OF GLOSTER, CHEYNEY, *and*
SOLDIERS.

LANC. Go to our tents, dear sister, cease your sorrows.
We will revenge our noble brother's wrongs;
And force that wanton tyrant to reveal
The death of his dear uncle, harmless Woodstock,
So traitorously betrayed.

YORK.   Alack, good man,
It was an easy task to work on him,
His plainness was too open to their view;
He feared no wrong, because his heart was true.
Good sister, cease your weeping: there's none here
But are as full of woe, and touched as near.
Conduct and guard her, Cheyney, to the tent.
Expect to hear severest punishment
On all their heads that have procured his harms,
Struck from the terror of our threatening arms.

DUCH. May all the powers of heaven assist your hands,
And may their sins sit heavy on their souls
That they in death, this day, may perish all
That traitorously conspired good Woodstock's fall.

                                    Exeunt CHEYNEY *and the* DUCHESS

LANC. If he be dead, by good King Edward's soul
We'll call King Richard to a strict account
For that and for his realm's misgovernment.
You peers of England, raised in righteous arms
Here to re-edify our country's ruin,
Join all your hearts and hands never to cease
Till with our swords we work fair England's peace.

                                    Drums

ARUND. Most princely Lancaster, our lands and lives
Are to these just proceedings ever vowed.

SURR. Those flattering minions that o'erturn the state
This day in death shall meet their endless fate!

YORK. Never such vipers were endured so long
To grip and eat the heart of all the kingdom.

LANC. This day shall here determinate all wrongs.
The meanest man taxed by their foul oppressions
Shall be permitted freely to accuse,
And right they shall have to regain their own;
Or all shall sink to dark confusion.

[Drum]s sound[ed with]in

[YORK.] How now, what drums are these?

Enter CHEYNEY

CHEY. To arms, my lords, the minions of the king
Are swiftly marching on to give ye battle.

LANC. They march to death then, Cheyney. Dare the traitors
Presume to brave the field with English princes?

YORK. Where is King Richard? he was resolved but lately
To take some hold of strength, and so secure him.

CHEY. Knowing their states were all so desperate,
It seems they have persuaded otherwise,
For now he comes with full resolve to fight.
Lapoole this morning is arrived at court
With the Calais soldiers and some French supplies,
To back this now intended enterprise.

LANC. Those new supplies have spurred their forward hopes
And thrust their resolutions boldly on
To meet with death and sad destruction.

YORK. Their drums are near. Just heaven, direct this deed
And, as our cause deserves, our fortunes speed.

[Drums, and They] march about

Enter with Drum and Colours, the KING, GREENE, BUSHY,
BAGOT, SCROOPE, LAPOOLE, *and* SOLDIERS. *They march about.*

KING. Although we could have easily surprised,
Dispersed, and overthrown your rebel troops
That draw your swords against our sacred person,
The highest God's anointed deputy,
Breaking your holy oaths to heaven and us,

Yet of our mild and princely clemency
We have forborne; that by this parliament
We might be made partaker of the cause
That moved ye rise in this rebellious sort.

LANC. Hast thou, King Richard, made us infamous?
By proclamations false and impudent
Hast thou condemned us in our absence too
As most notorious traitors to the crown?
Betrayed our brother Woodstock's harmless life,
And sought base means to put us all to death?
And dost thou now plead doltish ignorance
Why we are banded thus in our defence?

GREEN. Methinks your treasons to His Majesty,
Raising his subjects gainst his royal life,
Should make ye beg for mercy at his feet.

KING. You have forgotten, uncle Lancaster,
How you in prison murdered cruelly
A friar carmelite, because he was
To bring in evidence against your grace
Of most ungracious deeds and practices.

LANC. And you, my lord, remember not so well
That by that carmelite at London once,
When at a supper, you'd have poisoned us—

YORK. For shame, King Richard, leave this company
That like dark clouds obscure[s] the sparkling stars
Of thy great birth, and true nobility.

ARUND. Yield to your uncles. Who but they should have
The guidance of your sacred state and Council?

BAGOT. Yield first your heads, and so he shall be sure
To keep his person and his state secure.

KING. And by my crown, if still you thus persist,
Your heads and hearts ere long shall answer it.

ARUND. Not till ye send for more supplies from France,
For England will not yield ye strength to do it!

YORK. Thou well may'st doubt their loves that lost their
      hearts.
Ungracious prince, cannot thy native country
Find men to back this desperate enterprise?

LANC. His native country! why, that is France my lords!
  At Bordeaux was he born, which place allures
  And ties his deep affections still to France.
  Richard is English blood: not English born.
  Thy mother travailed in unhappy hours
  When she, at Bordeaux, left her heavy load.
  The soil is fat for wines, not fit for men,
  And England now laments that heavy time.
  Her royalties are lost; her state made base;
  And thou no king, but landlord now become
  To this great state that terrored Christendom.
KING. I cannot brook these braves. Let drums sound death,
  And strike at once to stop this traitor's breath.
BAGOT. Stay, my dear lord; and once more hear me, princes.
  The king was minded—ere this brawl began—
  To come to terms of composition—
LANC. Let him revoke the proclamations,
  Clear us of all supposed crimes of treason,
  Reveal where our good brother Gloster keeps,
  And grant that these pernicious flatterers
  May by the law be tried, to quit themselves
  Of all such heinous crimes alleged against them,
  And we'll lay down our weapons at thy feet.
[MINIONS.] Presumptuous traitors!
[ALL KING'S MEN.] Traitors!
KING. Again we double it: rebellious traitors!
  Traitors to Heaven and us. Draw all your swords
  And fling defiance to those traitorous lords.
KING'S MEN. Let our drums thunder and begin the fight.
LORDS' MEN. Just Heaven protect us, and defend the right.
                                        Exeunt [severally]

[SCENE 4: *Open country*]

Alarum. Enter GREENE. CHEYNEY *meets* [*him*] *armed*.

CHEY. Stand, traitor! for thou canst not scape my sword.
GREEN. What villain fronts me with the name of traitor?

Was't thou, false Cheyney? Now, by King Richard's love,
I'll tilt thy soul out for that base reproach.
I would thy master and the late Protector
With both his treacherous brothers, Gaunt and York,
Were all opposed, with thee, to try these arms:
I'd seal't on all your hearts.   *Alarum*

CHEY.   This shall suffice
To free the kingdom from thy villainies.

               They fight. [Then] enter ARUNDEL

ARUN. Thou hunt'st a noble game, right warlike Cheyney:
Cut but this ulcer off, thou heal'st the kingdom.
Yield thee, false traitor, most detested man,
That sett'st King Richard gainst his reverend uncles
To shed the royal blood and make the realm
Weep for their timeless desolation.
Cast down thy weapons, for by this my sword
We'll bear thee from this place, alive or dead.

GREEN. Come both then. I'll stand firm and dare your worst.
He that flies from it, be his soul accursed!

               [They fight and GREENE *is slain]*

ARUN. So may the foes of England fall in blood.
Most desolate traitor! Up with his body, Cheyney,
And hale it to the tent of Lancaster.

           [Enter KIN]G, BAGOT, BUSHY, SCROOPE *and Soldiers*

CHEY. Stand firm, my lord. Here's rescue.

ARUN.   Courage, then!
We'll bear his body hence in spite of them.

     They fight. To them enter LANCASTER, YORK, *and* SURREY,
     and beat them away. [Exeunt fighting, all but the KING]

KING. O princely youth, King Richard's dearest friend!
What heavy star this day had dominance
To cut off all thy flowering youthful hopes?
Prosper, proud rebels, as you dealt by him!
Hard-hearted uncles, unrelenting churls,
That here have murdered all my earthly joys!

O my dear Greene, wert thou alive to see
How I'll revenge thy timeless tragedy
On all their heads that did but lift a hand
To hurt this body, that I held so dear.
Even by this kiss and by my crown I swear——

Alarum. Enter BAGOT, BUSHY, *and* SCROOPE *to the* KING.

BAGOT. Away, my lord! stand not to wail his death:
   The field is lost; our soldiers shrink and fly:
   Lapoole is taken prisoner by the lords.
   Hie to the Tower. There is no help in swords.
SCROO. Still to continue war were childishness.
   Their odds a mountain, ours a molehill is.
BUSH. Let's fly to London, and make strong the Tower.
   Loud proclamations post throughout the camp
   With promise of reward to all that take us.
   Get safety for our lives, my princely lord;
   If here we stay, we shall be all betrayed.
KING. O my dear friends, the fearful wrath of heaven
   Sits heavy on our heads for Woodstock's death.
   Blood cries for blood; and that almighty hand
   Permits not murder unrevenged to stand.
   Come, come, we yet may hide ourselves from worldly
      strength;
   But Heaven will find us out, and strike at length.
   Each lend a hand to bear this load of woe
   That erst King Richard loved and tendered so.
                      Exeunt [*bearing the body of* GREENE]

[SCENE 5: *Open country*]

Enter TRESILIAN *disguised, and* NIMBLE

TRES. Where art thou, Nimble?
NIMB. As light as a feather, my lord. I have put off my shoes
   that I might run lustily. The battle's lost and [they're all]
   prisoners: what shall we do, my lord? Yonder's [a ditch],
   we may run along that, and ne'er be seen, I warrant.

TRES. I did suspect no less; and so 'tis fallen:
The day is lost; and dashed are all our hopes.
King Richard's taken prisoner by the peers.
O that I were upon some steepy rock
Where I might tumble headlong to the sea
Before those cruel lords do seize on me!

NIMB. O that I were transformed into a mouse, that I
[might creep] into any hole i' the house, an I cared
not—

TRES. Come Nimble, 'tis no time to use delay.
I'll keep me in this poor disguise awhile,
And so, unknown, prolong my weary life
In hope King Richard shall conclude my peace.

Sound Retreat

Hark, hark, the trumpets call the soldiers back,
Retreat is sounded, now the time serves fit
And we may steal from hence. Away, good Nimble.

NIMB. Nay, stay my lord! 'Slid, an ye go that way, [go by
yourself] but an you'll be ruled by me, I have thought of
a [trick] that ye shall scape them all most bravely—

TRES. Bethink thyself, good Nimble: quickly, man!

NIMB. I'll meditate, my lord; and then I'm for ye.
[*Aside*] Now, Nimble, show thyself a man of valour.
Think of thy fortunes: 'tis a hanging-matter if thou conceal him; besides, there's a thousand marks for him that
takes him, with the Duke's favours, and free pardon. Besides
he's but a coward, he would ne'er have run from the battle
else. St Tantony assist me, I'll set upon him presently.
[*To* TRESILIAN]—My lord, I have thought upon this trick;
I must take ye prisoner.

TRES. How? Prisoner?

NIMB. There's no way to scape else. Then must I carry ye to
the king's uncles, who presently condemn ye for a traitor:
send ye away to hanging, and then 'God bless my lord
Tresilian.'

TRES. Wilt thou betray thy master, villain?

NIMB. Ay, if my master be a villain. You think 'tis nothing

for a man to be hanged for his master? You heard not the
proclamation?

TRES. What proclamation?

NIMB. O sir, all the country's full of them: that whosoever
sees you [and] does not presently take ye—and bring ye
to the lords—shall be hanged for his labour, therefore no
more words, lest I raise the whole camp upon ye. Ye see
one of your own swords of justice drawn over ye. There-
for go quietly, lest I cut your head off and save the hangman a labour.

TRES. O villain!

NIMB. No more words. Away, sir! *Exeunt*

[SCENE 6: *Open country*]

*Sound a retreat then a flourish, [and] enter with Drums
and Colours* LANCASTER, CHEYNEY, ARUNDEL, SURREY *and*
SOLDIERS, *with* LAPOOLE, BUSHY, *and* SCROOPE [*as*]
prisoners.

LANC. Thus princely Edward's sons, in tender care
Of wanton Richard and their father's realm,
Have toiled to purge fair England's pleasant field
Of all those rancorous weeds that choked the grounds
And left her pleasant meads like barren hills.
Who is't can tell us which way Bagot fled?

ARUN. Some say to Bristowe, to make strong the castle.

LANC. See that the port's belayed. He'll fly the land,
For England hath no hold can keep him from us.
Had we Tresilian hanged, then all were sure.
Where slept our scouts that he escaped the field?

CHEY. He fled, they say, before the fight began.

LANC. Our proclamations soon shall find him forth:
The root and ground of all these vile abuses.

Enter NIMBLE, *with* TRESILIAN, *bound and guarded*

LANC. How now? What guard is that? What traitor's there?

NIMB. The traitor now is ta'en:
I here present the villain,

And if ye needs will know his name:
God bless my lord Tresilian.

CHEY. Tresilian, my lord: attached and apprehended by his
man!

NIMB. Yes, an it please ye, my lord: twas I that took him.
I was once a trampler in the law after him, and I thank
him he taught me this trick, to save myself from hanging.

LANC. Thou'rt a good lawyer; and hast removed the cause
from thyself fairly.

NIMB. I have removed it with a Habeas Corpus; and then I
took him with a Certiorari, and bound him in this bond to
answer it. Nay, I have studied for my learning, I can tell
ye my lord: there was not a stone between Westminster
Hall and Temple Bar but I have told them every morning.

ARUN. What moved thee, being his man, to apprehend him?

NIMB. Partly for these causes: first, the fear of the proclamation: for I have plodded in Plowden and can find no
law. . . . . . .

THE
CHRONICLE
HISTORIE
OF
PERKIN WARBECK.

A Strange Truth.

Acted (some-times) by the Queenes
MAIESTIES Servants at the
Phœnix in *Drurie* lane.

Fide Honor.

LONDON,
Printed by *T. P.* for *Hugh Beeston*, and are to
be sold at his Shop, neere the *Castle* in
Cornehill. 1634.

TO

THE RIGHTLY HONOURABLE

WILLIAM CAVENDISH,

EARL OF NEWCASTLE, VISCOUNT MANSFIELD,
LORD BOLSOVER AND OGLE

MY LORD,

OUT of the darkness of a former age, enlightened by a late both learned and an honourable pen, I have endeavoured to personate a great attempt, and in it a greater danger. In other labours you may read actions of antiquity discoursed; in this abridgment find the actors themselves discoursing, in some kind practised as well what to speak as speaking why to do. Your lordship is a most competent judge in expressions of such credit; commissioned by your known ability in examining, and enabled by your knowledge in determining, the monuments of time. Eminent titles may, indeed, inform who their owners are, not often what. To yours the addition of that information in both cannot in any application be observed flattery, the authority being established by truth. I can only acknowledge the errors in writing mine own; the worthiness of the subject written being a perfection in the story and of it. The custom of your lordship's entertainments—even to strangers—is rather an example than a fashion; in which consideration I dare not profess a curiosity, but am only studious that your lordship will please, amongst such as best honour your goodness, to admit into your noble construction

JOHN FORD.

THE SCENE:

The Continent of Great Britain.

The Persons Presented:

HENRY THE SEVENTH.
DAWBENEY.
SIR WILLIAM STANLEY.
OXFORD.
SURREY.
BISHOP OF DURHAM.
URSWICK, CHAPLAIN TO KING HENRY.
SIR ROBERT CLIFFORD.
LAMBERT SIMNEL.
HIALAS, a Spanish agent.
Constable, Officers, Serving-men and Soldiers.
JAMES THE FOURTH, KING OF SCOTLAND.
EARL OF HUNTLEY.
EARL OF CRAWFORD.
LORD DALYELL.
MARCHMONT, a Herald.
PERKIN WARBECK.
FRION, his secretary.
MAYOR OF CORK [John a-Water].
HERON, a mercer.
SKETON, a tailor.
ASTLEY, a scrivener.

Women:

LADY KATHERINE GORDON, wife to Perkin.
COUNTESS OF CRAWFORD.
JANE DOUGLAS, Lady Katherine's maid.

PROLOGUE.

STUDIES have of this nature been of late
So out of fashion, so unfollow'd, that
It is become more justice to revive
The antic follies of the times than strive
To countenance wise industry; no want
Of art doth render wit or lame or scant
Or slothful in the purchase of fresh bays;
But want of truth in them who give the praise
To their self-love, presuming to out-do
The writer, or—for need—the actors too.
But such this author's silence best befits,
Who bids them be in love with their own wits.
From him to clearer judgments we can say
He shows a history couch'd in a play;
A history of noble mention, known,
Famous, and true; most noble, 'cause our own;
Not forg'd from Italy, from France, from Spain,
But chronicled at home; as rich in strain
Of brave attempts as ever fertile rage
In action could beget to grace the stage.
We cannot limit scenes, for the whole land
Itself appear'd too narrow to withstand
Competitors for kingdoms; nor is here
Unnecessary mirth forc'd to endear
A multitude: on these two rests the fate
Of worthy expectation,—truth and state.

THE
CHRONICLE
HISTORY OF
PERKIN WARBECK.

ACTUS PRIMUS: SCŒNA PRIMA.

[Westminster. The royal presence-chamber.]

Enter King HENRY, DURHAM, OXFORD, SURREY, Sir WILLIAM
STANLEY, Lord CHAMBERLAIN, Lord DAWBENEY. *The
King supported to his throne by Stanley and Durham.*

K. Hen. Still to be haunted, still to be pursu'd,
Still to be frighted with false apparitions
Of pageant majesty and new-coin'd greatness,
As if we were a mockery king in state,
Only ordain'd to lavish sweat and blood,
In scorn and laughter, to the ghosts of York,
Is all below our merits; yet, my lords,
My friends and counsellors, yet we sit fast
In our own royal birthright; the rent face
And bleeding wounds of England's slaughter'd people
Have been by us, as by the best physician,
At last both throughly cur'd and set in safety;
And yet, for all this glorious work of peace,
Ourself is scarce secure.
  Dur.   The rage of malice
Conjures fresh spirits with the spells of York.
For ninety years ten English kings and princes,
Threescore great dukes and earls, a thousand lords
And valiant knights, two hundred fifty thousand
Of English subjects have in civil wars
Been sacrific'd to an uncivil thirst
Of discord and ambition; this hot vengeance

Of the just powers above to utter ruin
And desolation had rain'd on, but that
Mercy did gently sheathe the sword of justice,
In lending to this blood-shrunk commonwealth
A new soul, new birth, in your sacred person.

Daw. Edward the Fourth, after a doubtful fortune,
Yielded to nature, leaving to his sons,
Edward and Richard, the inheritance
Of a most bloody purchase: these young princes,
Richard the tyrant, their unnatural uncle,
Forc'd to a violent grave: so just is Heaven,
Him hath your majesty by your own arm
Divinely strengthen'd, pull'd from his boar's sty,
And struck the black usurper to a carcass.
Nor doth the house of York decay in honours,
Though Lancaster doth repossess his right;
For Edward's daughter is King Henry's queen,—
A blessèd union, and a lasting blessing
For this poor panting island, if some shreds,
Some useless remnant of the house of York
Grudge not at this content.

Oxf.   Margaret of Burgundy
Blows fresh coals of division.

Sur.   Painted fires,
Without or heat to scorch or light to cherish.

Daw. York's headless trunk, her father; Edward's fate,
Her brother, king; the smothering of her nephews
By tyrant Gloster, brother to her nature;
Nor Gloster's own confusion,—all decrees
Sacred in heaven,—can move this woman-monster,
But that she still, from the unbottom'd mine
Of devilish policies, doth vent the ore
Of troubles and sedition.

Oxf.   In her age—
Great sir, observe the wonder—she grows fruitful,
Who in her strength of youth was always barren;
Nor are her births as other mothers' are,
At nine or ten months' end; she has been with child

Eight, or seven years at least, whose twins being born,—
A prodigy in nature,—even the youngest
Is fifteen years of age at his first entrance,
As soon as known i' th' world; tall striplings, strong
And able to give battle unto kings,
Idols of Yorkish malice.

 [*Daw.*]   And but idols;
A steely hammer crushes 'em to pieces.

 K. Hen. Lambert, the eldest, lords, is in our service,
Preferr'd by an officious care of duty
From the scullery to a falconer; strange example!
Which shows the difference between noble natures
And the base-born: but for the upstart duke,
The new-reviv'd York, Edward's second son,
Murder'd long since i' th' Tower,—he lives again,
And vows to be your king.

 Stan.   The throne is fill'd, sir.

 K. Hen. True, Stanley; and the lawful heir sits on it:
A guard of angels and the holy prayers
Of loyal subjects are a sure defence
Against all force and counsel of intrusion.
But now, my lords, put case, some of our nobles,
Our great ones, should give countenance and courage
To trim Duke Perkin; you will all confess
Our bounties have unthriftily been scatter'd
Amongst unthankful men.

 Daw.   Unthankful beasts,
Dogs, villains, traitors!

 K. Hen.   Dawbeney, let the guilty
Keep silence; I accuse none, though I know
Foreign attempts against a state and kingdom
Are seldom without some great friends at home.

 Stan. Sir, if no other abler reasons else
Of duty or allegiance could divert
A headstrong resolution, yet the dangers
So lately pass'd by men of blood and fortunes
In Lambert Simnel's party must command
More than a fear, a terror to conspiracy.

The high-born Lincoln, son to De la Pole,
The Earl of Kildare, Lord Geraldine,
Francis Lord Lovell, and the German baron,
Bold Martin Swart, with Broughton and the rest,
Most spectacles of ruin, some of mercy,
Are precedents sufficient to forewarn
The present times, or any that live in them,
What folly, nay, what madness, 'twere to lift
A finger up in all defence but yours,
Which can be but imposturous in a title.

K. Hen. Stanley, we know thou lov'st us, and thy heart
Is figur'd on thy tongue; nor think we less
Of any's here. How closely we have hunted
This cub, since he unlodg'd, from hole to hole,
Your knowledge is our chronicle; first Ireland,
The common stage of novelty, presented
This gewgaw to oppose us; there the Geraldines
And Butlers once again stood in support
Of this colossic statue; Charles of France
Thence call'd him into his protection,
Dissembled him the lawful heir of England;
Yet this was all but French dissimulation,
Aiming at peace with us; which being granted
On honourable terms on our part, suddenly
This smoke of straw was pack'd from France again,
T'infect some grosser air; and now we learn—
Maugre the malice of the bastard Nevill,
Sir Taylor, and a hundred English rebels—
They're all retir'd to Flanders, to the dam
That nurs'd this eager whelp, Margaret of Burgundy.
But we will hunt him there too; we will hunt him,
Hunt him to death, even in the beldam's closet,
Though th' archduke were his buckler!

Sur.   She has styl'd him
'The fair white rose of England.'

Daw.   Jolly gentleman!
More fit to be a swabber to the Flemish
After a drunken surfeit.

Enter URSWICK [*with a paper*].

Urs.   Gracious sovereign,
Please you peruse this paper.   [*The king reads.*]
Dur.   The king's countenance
Gathers a sprightly blood.
Daw.   Good news; believe it.
K. Hen. Urswick, thine ear. Thou'st lodg'd him?
Urs.   Strongly safe, sir.
K. Hen. Enough; is Barley come too?
Urs.   No, my lord.
K. Hen. No matter—phew! he's but a running weed,
At pleasure to be pluck'd-up by the roots;
But more of this anon.—I have bethought me.
My lords, for reasons which you shall partake,
It is our pleasure to remove our court
From Westminster to the Tower: we will lodge
This very night there; give, Lord Chamberlain,
A present order for 't.
Stan.   The Tower!—I shall, sir.
K. Hen. Come, my true, best, fast friends: these clouds
    will vanish,
The sun will shine at full; the heavens are clearing.
                              Flourish. Exeunt.

[SCENE II. *Edinburgh. An apartment in* Lord
            HUNTLEY'S *house.*]

Enter HUNTLEY *and* DALYELL.

Hunt. You trifle time, sir.
Dal.   O, my noble lord,
You construe my griefs to so hard a sense,
That where the text is argument of pity,
Matter of earnest love, your gloss corrupts it
With too much ill-plac'd mirth.
Hunt.   Much mirth, Lord Dalyell?
Not so, I vow; observe me, sprightly gallant,

I know thou art a noble lad, a handsome,
Descended from an honourable ancestry,
Forward and active, dost resolve to wrestle
And ruffle in the world by noble actions
For a brave mention to posterity;
I scorn not thy affection to my daughter,
Not I, by good Saint Andrew, but this bugbear,
This whoreson tale of honour,—honour, Dalyell!—
So hourly chats and tattles in mine ear
The piece of royalty that is stich'd-up
In my Kate's blood, that 'tis as dangerous
For thee, young lord, to perch so near an eaglet
As foolish for my gravity to admit it;
I have spoke all at once.

    Dal.   Sir, with this truth
You mix such wormwood, that you leave no hope
For my disorder'd palate e'er to relish
A wholesome taste again: alas, I know, sir,
What an unequal distance lies between
Great Huntley's daughter's birth and Dalyell's fortunes;
She's the king's kinswoman, plac'd near the crown,
A princess of the blood, and I a subject.

    Hunt. Right, but a noble subject; put in that too.

    Dal. I could add more; and in the rightest line
Derive my pedigree from Adam Mure,
A Scottish knight, whose daughter was the mother
To him who first begot the race of Jameses,
That sway the sceptre to this very day.
But kindreds are not ours when once the date
Of many years have swallow'd up the memory
Of their originals; so pasture-fields
Neighbouring too near the ocean are swoop'd-up,
And known no more, for stood I in my first
And native greatness, if my princely mistress
Vouchsaf'd me not her servant, 'twere as good
I were reduc'd to clownery, to nothing,
As to a throne of wonder.

    Hunt. [aside]   Now, by Saint Andrew,

A spark of mettle! he has a brave fire in him:
I would he had my daughter, so I knew't not.
But ['t] must not be so, must not.—Well, young lord,
This will not do yet; if the girl be headstrong,
And will not hearken to good counsel, steal her,
And run away with her; dance galliards, do,
And frisk about the world to learn the languages:
'Twill be a thriving trade; you may set up by't.

Dal. With pardon, noble Gordon, this disdain
Suits not your daughter's virtue or my constancy.

Hunt. You're angry.—[*Aside*] Would he would beat me,
    I deserve it.—
Dalyell, thy hand; we're friends: follow thy courtship,
Take thine own time and speak; if thou prevail'st
With passion more than I can with my counsel,
She's thine; nay, she is thine: 'tis a fair match,
Free and allow'd. I'll only use my tongue,
Without a father's power; use thou thine;
Self do, self have: no more words; win and wear her.

Dal. You bless me; I am now too poor in thanks
To pay the debt I owe you.

Hunt.   Nay, thou'rt poor
Enough.—[*Aside*] I love his spirit infinitely.—
Look ye, she comes: to her now, to her, to her!

Enter KATHERINE *and* JANE.

Kath. The king commands your presence, sir.

Hunt.   The gallant—
This, this, this lord, this servant, Kate, of yours,
Desires to be your master.

Kath.   I acknowledge him
A worthy friend of mine.

Dal.   Your humblest creature.

Hunt. [*aside*] So, so! the game's a-foot; I'm in cold
    hunting;
The hare and hounds are parties.

Dal.   Princely lady,
How most unworthy I am to employ

My services in honour of your virtues,
How hopeless my desires are to enjoy
Your fair opinion, and much more your love,
Are only matter of despair, unless
Your goodness give large warrant to my boldness,
My feeble-wing'd ambition.

   Hunt. [*aside*]   This is scurvy.

   Kath. My lord, I interrupt you not.

   Hunt. [*aside*]   Indeed!
Now, on my life, she'll court him.—Nay, nay, on, sir.

   Dal. Oft have I tun'd the lesson of my sorrows
To sweeten discord and enrich your pity;
But all in vain: here had my comforts sunk,
And never risen again to tell a story
Of the despairing lover, had not now,
Even now, the earl your father—

   Hunt. [*aside*]   He means me, sure.

   Dal. After some fit disputes of your condition,
Your highness and my lowness, given a licence
Which did not more embolden than encourage
My faulting tongue.

   Hunt.   How, how? how's that? embolden!
Encourage! I encourage ye! d'ye hear, sir?—
A subtle trick, a quaint one:—will you hear, man?
What did I say to you? come, come, to th' point.

   Kath. It shall not need, my lord.

   Hunt.   Then hear me, Kate.—
Keep you on that hand of her, I on this—
Thou stand'st between a father and a suitor,
Both striving for an interest in thy heart;
He courts thee for affection, I for duty,
He as a servant pleads, but by the privilege
Of nature though I might command, my care
Shall only counsel what it shall not force.
Thou canst but make one choice; the ties of marriage
Are tenures not at will, but during life.
Consider whose thou art, and who; a princess,
A princess of the royal blood of Scotland,

In the full spring of youth and fresh in beauty.
The king that sits upon the throne is young,
And yet unmarried, forward in attempts
On any least occasion to endanger
His person, wherefore, Kate, as I am confident
Thou dar'st not wrong thy birth and education
By yielding to a common servile rage
Of female wantonness, so I am confident
Thou wilt proportion all thy thoughts to side
Thy equals, if not equal thy superiors.
My Lord of Dalyell, young in years, is old
In honours, but nor eminent in titles
[N]or in estate, that may support or add to
The expectation of thy fortunes. Settle
Thy will and reason by a strength of judgment;
For, in a word, I give thee freedom; take it.
If equal fates have not ordain'd to pitch
Thy hopes above my height, let not thy passion
Lead thee to shrink mine honour in oblivion;
Thou art thine own; I have done.

   Dal.   O, you're all oracle,
The living stock and root of truth and wisdom!

   Kath. My worthiest lord and father, the indulgence
Of your sweet composition thus commands
The lowest of obedience; you have granted
A liberty so large, that I want skill
To choose without direction of example:
From which I daily learn, by how much more
You take off from the roughness of a father,
By so much more I am engag'd to tender
The duty of a daughter. For respects
Of birth, degrees of title, and advancement,
I nor admire nor slight them; all my studies
Shall ever aim at this perfection only,
To live and die so, that you may not blush
In any course of mine to own me yours.

   Hunt. Kate, Kate, thou grow'st upon my heart like
     peace,

Creating every other hour a jubilee.

    Kath. To you, my Lord of Dalyell, I address
Some few remaining words; the general fame
That speaks your merit, even in vulgar tongues
Proclaims it clear, but in the best, a precedent.

    Hunt. Good wench, good girl, i'faith!

    Kath.   For my part, trust me,
I value mine own worth at higher rate
'Cause you are pleas'd to prize it; if the stream
Of your protested service—as you term it—
Run in a constancy more than a compliment,
It shall be my delight that worthy love
Leads you to worthy actions, and these guide ye
Richly to wed an honourable name,
So every virtuous praise in after-ages
Shall be your heir, and I in your brave mention
Be chronicled the mother of that issue,
That glorious issue.

    Hunt.   O, that I were young again!
She'd make me court proud danger, and suck spirit
From reputation.

    Kath.   To the present motion
Here's all that I dare answer; when a ripeness
Of more experience, and some use of time,
Resolves to treat the freedom of my youth
Upon exchange of troths, I shall desire
No surer credit of a match with virtue
Than such as lives in you; mean time my hopes are
Preser[v]'d secure in having you a friend.

    Dal. You are a blessèd lady, and instruct
Ambition not to soar a farther flight
Than in the perfum'd air of your soft voice.
My noble Lord of Huntley, you have lent
A full extent of bounty to this parley;
And for it shall command your humblest servant.

    Hunt. Enough; we are still friends, and will continue
A hearty love. O, Kate, thou art mine own!—
No more—my Lord of Crawford.

Enter CRAWFORD.

Craw. From the king
I come, my Lord of Huntley, who in council
Requires your present aid.

Hunt. Some weighty business?

Craw. A secretary from a Duke of York,
The second son to the late English Edward,
Conceal'd, I know not where, these fourteen years,
Craves audience from our master; and 'tis said
The duke himself is following to the court.

Hunt. Duke upon duke! 'tis well, 'tis well; here's bustling
For majesty! My lord, I will along with ye.

Craw. My service, noble lady!

Kath. Please ye walk, sir?

Dal. [*aside*] Times have their changes; sorrow makes men
wise;
The sun itself must set as well as rise;
Then, why not I?—Fair madam, I wait on ye.

Exeunt.

[SCENE III. *London. An apartment in the Tower.*]

Enter DURHAM, Sir ROBERT CLIFFORD, *and*
URSWICK. *Lights.*

Dur. You find, Sir Robert Clifford, how securely
King Henry, our great master, doth commit
His person to your loyalty; you taste
His bounty and his mercy even in this,
That at a time of night so late, a place
So private as his closet, he is pleas'd
To admit you to his favour. Do not falter
In your discovery; but as you covet
A liberal grace, and pardon for your follies,
So labour to deserve it by laying open
All plots, all persons that contrive against it.

Urs. Remember not the witchcraft or the magic,
The charms and incantations, which the sorceress

Of Burgundy hath cast upon your reason!
Sir Robert, be your own friend now, discharge
Your conscience freely; all of such as love you
Stand sureties for your honesty and truth.
Take heed you do not dally with the king;
He's wise as he is gentle.
    Clif.   I am miserable,
If Henry be not merciful.
    Urs.   The king comes.

Enter King HENRY.

    K. Hen. Clifford!
    Clif. [*kneels*] Let my weak knees rot on the earth,
If I appear as leperous in my treacheries
Before your royal eyes, as to mine own
I seem a monster by my breach of truth.
    K. Hen. Clifford, stand up; for instance of thy safety,
I offer thee my hand.
    Clif.   A sovereign balm
For my bruis'd soul, I kiss it with a greediness.
                  [*Kisses the King's hand, and rises.*]
Sir, you're a just master, but I—
    K. Hen.   Tell me,
Is every circumstance thou hast set down
With thine own hand within this paper true?
Is it a sure intelligence of all
The progress of our enemies' intents
Without corruption?
    Clif.   True, as I wish heaven,
Or my infected honour white again.
    K. Hen. We know all, Clifford, fully, since this meteor,
This airy apparition first discradled
From Tournay into Portugal, and thence
Advanc'd his fiery blaze for adoration
To th' superstitious Irish; since the beard
Of this wild comet, conjur'd into France,
Sparkled in antic flames in Charles his court;
But shrunk again from thence, and, hid in darkness,

Flourish

Enter King JAMES, HUNTLEY, CRAWFORD, DALYELL,
and other Noblemen.

K. Ja. The right of kings, my lords, extends not only
To the safe conservation of their own,
But also to the aid of such allies
As change of time and state hath oftentimes
Hurl'd down from careful crowns to undergo
An exercise of sufferance in both fortunes;
So English Richard, surnam'd Cœur-de-Lion,
So Robert Bruce, our royal ancestor,
Forc'd by the trial of the wrongs they felt,
Both sought and found supplies from foreign kings,
To repossess their own. Then grudge not, lords,
A much-distressèd prince; King Charles of France
And Maximilian of Bohemia both
Have ratified his credit by their letters;
Shall we, then, be distrustful? No; compassion
Is one rich jewel that shines in our crown,
And we will have it shine there.

Hunt.   Do your will, sir.

K. Ja. The young duke is at hand: Dalyell, from us
First greet him, and conduct him on; then Crawford
Shall meet him next; and Huntley, last of all,
Present him to our arms. [*Exit Dal.*]—Sound sprightly
    music,
Whilst majesty encounters majesty.   *Hautboys.*

DALYELL *goes out, brings in* PERKIN *at the door, where* CRAW-
FORD *entertains him, and from* CRAWFORD HUNTLEY *salutes
him, and presents him to the* KING: *they embrace,* PERKIN
*in state retires some few paces back, during which ceremony,
the noblemen slightly salute* FRION, HERON *a mercer,*
SKETON *a tailor,* ASTLEY *a scrivener, with* JOHN A WAT-
RING, *all Perkin's followers. Salutations ended: cease music.*

War. Most high, most mighty king! that now there stands
Before your eyes, in presence of your peers,

A subject of the rarest kind of pity
That hath in any age touch'd noble hearts,
The vulgar story of a prince's ruin
Hath made it too apparent; Europe knows,
And all the western world, what persecution
Hath rag'd in malice against us, sole heir
To the great throne of old Plantagenets.
How from our nursery we have been hurried
Unto the sanctuary, from the sanctuary
Forc'd to the prison, from the prison hal'd
By cruel hands to the tormentor's fury,
Is register'd already in the volume
Of all men's tongues; whose true relation draws
Compassion, melted into weeping eyes
And bleeding souls; but our misfortunes since
Have rang'd a larger progress through strange lands,
Protected in our innocence by heaven.
Edward the Fifth, our brother, in his tragedy
Quench'd their hot thirst of blood, whose hire to murder
Paid them their wages of despair and horror;
The softness of my childhood smil'd upon
The roughness of their task, and robb'd them farther
Of hearts to dare, or hands to execute.
Great king, they spar'd my life, the butchers spar'd it;
Return'd the tyrant, my unnatural uncle,
A truth of my dispatch; I was convey'd
With secrecy and speed to Tournay; foster'd
By obscure means, taught to unlearn myself:
But as I grew in years, I grew in sense
Of fear and of disdain; fear of the tyrant
Whose power sway'd the throne then; when disdain
Of living so unknown, in such a servile
And abject lowness, prompted me to thoughts
Of recollecting who I was, I shook off
My bondage, and made haste to let my aunt
Of Burgundy acknowledge me her kinsman,
Heir to the crown of England, snatch'd by Henry
From Richard's head; a thing scarce known i'th' world.

K. Ja. My lord, it stands not with your counsel now
To fly upon invectives: if you can
Make this apparent what you have discours'd
In every circumstance, we will not study
An answer, but are ready in your cause.

War. You are a wise and just king, by the powers
Above reserv'd, beyond all other aids,
To plant me in mine own inheritance,
To marry these two kingdoms in a love
Never to be divorc'd while time is time.
As for the manner, first of my escape,
Of my conveyance next, of my life since,
The means and persons who were instruments,
Great sir, 'tis fit I over-pass in silence;
Reserving the relation to the secrecy
Of your own princely ear, since it concerns
Some great ones living yet, and others dead,
Whose issue might be question'd. For your bounty,
Royal magnificence to him that seeks it,
We vow hereafter to demean ourself
As if we were your own and natural brother,
Omitting no occasion in our person
To express a gratitude beyond example.

K. Ja. He must be more than subject who can utter
The language of a king, and such is thine.
Take this for answer: be whate'er thou art,
Thou never shalt repent that thou hast put
Thy cause and person into my protection.
Cousin of York, thus once more we embrace thee;
Welcome to James of Scotland! for thy safety,
Know, such as love thee not shall never wrong thee.
Come, we will taste a while our court-delights,
Dream hence afflictions past, and then proceed
To high attempts of honour. On, lead on!—
Both thou and thine are ours, and we will guard ye.
Lead on!   *Exeunt, manent the Ladies above.*

Countess of C. I have not seen a gentleman
Of a more brave aspect or goodlier carriage;

His fortunes move not him.—Madam, y'are passionate.

Kath. Beshrew me, but his words have touch'd me home,
As if his cause concern'd me; I should pity him
If he should prove another than he seems.

Enter CRAWFORD.

Craw. Ladies, the king commands your presence
    instantly
For entertainment of the duke.

Kath.   The duke
Must then be entertain'd, the king obey'd;
It is our duty.

Countess of C. We will all wait on him.

[SCENE II. *London. The Tower.*]

Flourish. Enter KING HENRY, OXFORD, DURHAM, SURREY.

K. Hen. Have ye condemn'd my chamberlain?

Dur.   His treasons
Condemn'd him, sir; which were as clear and manifest
As foul and dangerous: besides, the guilt
Of his conspiracy press'd him so nearly,
That it drew from him free confession
Without an importunity.

K. Hen.   O, lord bishop,
This argu'd shame and sorrow for his folly,
And must not stand in evidence against
Our mercy and the softness of our nature:
The rigour and extremity of law
Is sometimes too, too bitter; but we carry
A chancery of pity in our bosom.
I hope we may reprieve him from the sentence
Of death; I hope we may.

Dur.   You may, you may;
And so persuade your subjects that the title
Of York is better, nay, more just and lawful,
Than yours of Lancaster! so Stanley holds;
Which if it be not treason in the highest,

Then we are traitors all, perjur'd and false,
Who have took oath to Henry and the justice
Of Henry's title; Oxford, Surrey, Dawbeney,
With all your other peers of state and church,
Forsworn, and Stanley true alone to heaven
And England's lawful heir!

 Oxf.   By Vere's old honours,
I'll cut his throat dares speak it.

 Sur.   'Tis a quarrel
T'engage a soul in.

 K. Hen.   What a coil is here
To keep my gratitude sincere and perfect!
Stanley was once my friend, and came in time
To save my life; yet, to say truth, my lords,
The man stay'd long enough t'endanger it:
But I could see no more into his heart
Than what his outward actions did present;
And for 'em have rewarded him so fully,
As that there wanted nothing in our gift
To gratify his merit, as I thought,
Unless I should divide my crown with him,
And give him half; though now I well perceive
'Twould scarce have serv'd his turn without the whole.
But I am charitable, lords; let justice
Proceed in execution, whiles I mourn
The loss of one whom I esteem'd a friend.

 Dur. Sir, he is coming this way.

 K. Hen.   If he speak to me,
I could deny him nothing; to prevent it,
I must withdraw. Pray, lords, commend my favours
To his last peace, which I with him will pray for;
That done, it doth concern us to consult
Of other following troubles.   [*Exit*]

 Oxf.   I am glad
He's gone: upon my life, he would have pardon'd
The traitor, had he seen him.

 Sur.   'Tis a king
Compos'd of gentleness.

Dur.   Rare and unheard of:
But every man is nearest to himself;
And that the king observes; 'tis fit he should.

Enter STANLEY, EXECUTIONER, URSWICK, *and* DAWBENEY.

Stan. May I not speak with Clifford ere I shake
This piece of frailty off?
Daw.   You shall; he's sent for.
Stan. I must not see the king?
Dur.   From him, Sir William,
These lords and I am sent; he bade us say
That he commends his mercy to your thoughts;
Wishing the laws of England could remit
The forfeit of your life as willingly
As he would in the sweetness of his nature
Forget your trespass; but howe'er your body
Fall into dust, he vows, the king himself
Doth vow, to keep a requiem for your soul,
As for a friend close treasur'd in his bosom.
Oxf. Without remembrance of your errors past,
I come to take my leave, and wish you heaven.
Sur. And I; good angels guard ye!
Stan.   O, the king,
Next to my soul, shall be the nearest subject
Of my last prayers. My grace Lord of Durham,
My Lords of Oxford, Surrey, Dawbeney, all,
Accept from a poor dying man a farewell.
I was as you are once, great, and stood hopeful
Of many flourishing years; but fate and time
Have wheel'd about, to turn me into nothing.

Enter CLIFFORD.

Daw. Sir Robert Clifford comes, the man, Sir William,
You so desire to speak with.
Dur.   Mark their meeting.
Clif. Sir William Stanley, I am glad your conscience
Before your end hath emptied every burthen
Which charg'd it, as that you can clearly witness

How far I have proceeded in a duty
That both concern'd my truth and the state's safety.
   Stan. Mercy, how dear is life to such as hug it!
Come hither; by this token think on me!
        Makes a cross on CLIFFORD'S *face with his finger.*
   Clif. This token! What! I am abus'd?
   Stan.   You are not.
I wet upon your cheeks a holy sign,
The cross, the Christian's badge, the traitor's infamy:
Wear, Clifford, to thy grave this painted emblem;
Water shall never wash it off; all eyes
That gaze upon thy face shall read there written
A state-informer's character; more ugly
Stamp'd on a noble name than on a base.
The heavens forgive thee! Pray, my lords, no change
Of words; this man and I have us'd too many.
   Clif. Shall I be disgrac'd
Without reply?
   Dur.   Give losers leave to talk;
His loss is irrecoverable.
   Stan.   Once more,
To all a long farewell! The best of greatness
Preserve the king! My next suit is, my lords,
To be remember'd to my noble brother,
Derby, my much-griev'd brother: O, persuade him
That I shall stand no blemish to his house
In chronicles writ in another age.
My heart doth bleed for him and for his sighs:
Tell him, he must not think the style of Derby,
Nor being husband to King Henry's mother,
The league with peers, the smiles of fortune, can
Secure his peace above the state of man.
I take my leave, to travel to my dust:
Subjects deserve their deaths whose kings are just.—
Come, confessor, on with thy axe, friend, on!
                        Exeunt.
   Clif. Was I call'd hither by a traitor's breath
To be upbraided? Lords, the king shall know it.

Enter King HENRY *with a white staff.*

K. Hen. The king doth know it, sir; the king hath heard
What he or you could say. We have given credit
To every point of Clifford's information,
The only evidence 'gainst Stanley's head:
A'dies for't; are you pleas'd?

Clif.   I pleas'd, my lord!

K. Hen. No echoes: for your service, we dismiss
Your more attendance on the court; take ease,
And live at home; but, as you love your life,
Stir not from London without leave from us.
We'll think on your reward: away!

Clif.   I go, sir.   *Exit.*

K. Hen. Die all our griefs with Stanley! Take this staff
Of office, Dawbeney; henceforth be our chamberlain.

Daw. I am your humblest servant.

K. Hen.   We are follow'd
By enemies at home, that will not cease
To seek their own confusion: 'tis most true
The Cornish under Audley are march'd on
As far as Winchester; but let them come,
Our forces are in readiness; we'll catch 'em
In their own toils.

Daw.   Your army, being muster'd,
Consists in all, of horse and foot, at least
In number six-and-twenty thousand; men
Daring and able, resolute to fight,
And loyal in their truths.

K. Hen.   We know it, Dawbeney:
For them we order thus; Oxford in chief,
Assisted by bold Essex and the Earl
Of Suffolk, shall lead on the first battalia;
Be that your charge.

Oxf.   I humbly thank your majesty.

K. Hen. The next division we assign to Dawbeney;
These must be men of action, for on those
The fortune of our fortunes must rely.
The last and main ourself commands in person;

As ready to restore the fight at all times
As to consummate an assurèd victory.

Daw. The king is still oraculous.

K. Hen. But, Surrey,
We have employment of more toil for thee,
For our intelligence comes swiftly to us,
That James of Scotland late hath entertain'd
Perkin the counterfeit with more than common
Grace and respect; nay, courts him with rare favours.
The Scot is young and forward; we must look for
A sudden storm to England from the north,
Which to withstand, Durham shall post to Norham,
To fortify the castle and secure
The frontiers against an invasion there.
Surrey shall follow soon, with such an army
As may relieve the bishop, and encounter
On all occasions the death-daring Scots.
You know your charges all; 'tis now a time
To execute, not talk: Heaven is our guard still.
War must breed peace; such is the fate of kings.

Exeunt.

[SCENE III. *Edinburgh. An apartment in the palace.*]

Enter CRAWFORD *and* DALYELL.

Craw. 'Tis more than strange; my reason cannot answer
Such argument of fine imposture, couch'd
In witchcraft of persuasion, that it fashions
Impossibilities, as if appearance
Could cozen truth itself; this dukeling mushroom
Hath doubtless charm'd the king.

Dal. He courts the ladies,
As if his strength of language chain'd attention
By power of prerogative.

Craw. It madded
My very soul to hear our master's motion:
What surety both of amity and honour

Must of necessity ensue upon
A match betwixt some noble of our nation
And this brave prince, forsooth!

    Dal.   'Twill prove too fatal;
Wise Huntley fears the threat'ning. Bless the lady
From such a ruin!

    Craw.   How the counsel privy
Of this young Phaëthon do screw their faces
Into a gravity their trades, good people,
Were never guilty of! the meanest of 'em
Dreams of at least an office in the state.

    Dal. Sure, not the hangman's; 'tis bespoke already
For service to their rogueships—silence!

          Enter King JAMES *and* HUNTLEY.

    K. Ja.   Do not
Argue against our will; we have descended
Somewhat—as we may term it—too familiarly
From justice of our birthright, to examine
The force of your allegiance,—sir, we have,—
But find it short of duty.

    Hunt.   Break my heart,
Do, do, king! Have my services, my loyalty,
Heaven knows untainted ever, drawn upon me
Contempt now in mine age, when I but wanted
A minute of a peace not to be troubled,
My last, my long one? Let me be a dotard,
A bedlam, a poor sot, or what you please
To have me, so you will not stain your blood,
Your own blood, royal sir, though mix'd with mine,
By marriage of this girl to a straggler.
Take, take my head, sir; whilst my tongue can wag,
It cannot name him other.

    K. Ja.   Kings are counterfeits
In your repute, grave oracle, not presently
Set on their thrones with sceptres in their fists.
But use your own detraction; 'tis our pleasure
To give our cousin York for wife our kinswoman,

The Lady Katherine: instinct of sovereignty
Designs the honour, though her peevish father
Usurps our resolution.

Hunt.   O, 'tis well,
Exceeding well! I never was ambitious
Of using congees to my daughter-queen—
A queen! perhaps a quean!—Forgive me, Dalyell,
Thou honourable gentleman;—none here
Dare speak one word of comfort?

Dal.   Cruel misery!

Craw. The lady, gracious prince, may be hath settled
Affection on some former choice.

Dal.   Enforcement
Would prove but tyranny.

Hunt.   I thank ye heartily.
Let any yeoman of our nation challenge
An interest in the girl, then the king
May add a jointure of ascent in titles,
Worthy a free consent; now he pulls down
What old desert hath builded.

K. Ja.   Cease persuasions.
I violate no pawns of faiths, intrude not
On private loves; that I have play'd the orator
For kingly York to virtuous Kate, her grant
Can justify, referring her contents
To our provision. The Welsh Harry henceforth
Shall therefore know, and tremble to acknowledge,
That not the painted idol of his policy
Shall fright the lawful owner from a kingdom.
We are resolv'd.

Hunt.   Some of thy subjects' hearts,
King James, will bleed for this.

K. Ja.   Then shall their bloods
Be nobly spent. No more disputes; he is not
Our friend who contradicts us.

Hunt.   Farewell, daughter!
My care by one is lessen'd, thank the king for't;
I and my griefs will dance now.

Enter WARBECK, *leading* KATHERINE, *complimenting*; Countess
    of CRAWFORD, JANE, FRION, MAYOR OF CORK, ASTLEY,
    HERON, *and* SKETON.

                    Look, lords, look;
Here's hand in hand already!
  K. Ja.   Peace, old frenzy!
How like a king he looks! Lords, but observe
The confidence of his aspect; dross cannot
Cleave to so pure a metal—royal youth!
Plantagenet undoubted!
  Hunt. [*aside*]   Ho, brave youth
But no Plantagenet, by'r lady, yet,
By red rose or by white.
  War.   An union this way
Settles possession in a monarchy
Establish'd rightly, as is my inheritance;
Acknowledge me but sovereign of this kingdom,
Your heart, fair princess, and the hand of providence
Shall crown you queen of me and my best fortunes.
  Kath. Where my obedience is, my lord, a duty,
Love owes true service.
  War.   Shall I?—
  K. Ja.   Cousin, yes,
Enjoy her; from my hand accept your bride;
                     [*He joins their hands.*]
And may they live at enmity with comfort
Who grieve at such an equal pledge of troths!
You are the prince's wife now.
  Kath.   By your gift, sir.
  War. Thus I take seizure of mine own.
  Kath.   I miss yet
A father's blessing. Let me find it; humbly
Upon my knees I seek it.
  Hunt.   I am Huntley,
Old Alexander Gordon, a plain subject,
Nor more nor less; and, lady, if you wish for
A blessing, you must bend your knees to heaven;
For heaven did give me you. Alas, alas,

What would you have me say? May all the happiness
My prayers ever su'd to fall upon you
Preserve you in your virtues!—Prithee, Dalyell,
Come with me; for I feel thy griefs as full
As mine; let's steal away, and cry together.

Dal. My hopes are in their ruins.

Exeunt HUNT. *and* DAL.

K. Ja.   Good, kind Huntley
Is overjoy'd: a fit solemnity
Shall perfect these delights. Crawford, attend
Our order for the preparation.

Exeunt. Manent FRION, MAYOR, ASTLEY, HERON, *and*
SKETON.

Fri. Now, worthy gentlemen, have I not follow'd
My undertakings with success? Here's entrance
Into a certainty above a hope.

Her. Hopes are but hopes; I was ever confident, when
I traded but in remnants, that my stars had reserved me to
the title of a viscount at least: honour is honour, though cut
out of any stuffs.

Sket. My brother Heron hath right wisely delivered his
opinion; for he that threads his needle with the sharp eyes
of industry shall in time go through-stitch with the new suit
of preferment.

Ast. Spoken to the purpose, my fine-witted brother
Sketon; for as no indenture but has its counterpane, no
noverint but his condition or defeasance; so no right but
may have claim, no claim but may have possession, any act
of parliament to the contrary notwithstanding.

Fri. You are all read in mysteries of state,
And quick of apprehension, deep in judgment,
Active in resolution; and 'tis pity
Such counsel should lie buried in obscurity.
But why, in such a time and cause of triumph,
Stands the judicious Mayor of Cork so silent?
Believe it, sir, as English Richard prospers,
You must not miss employment of high nature.

Mayor. If men may be credited in their mortality, which

I dare not peremptorily aver but they may or not be,
presumptions by this marriage are then, in sooth, of fruitful
expectation. Or else I must not justify other men's belief,
more than other should rely on mine.

Fri. Pith of experience! those that have borne office
Weigh every word before it can drop from them.
But, noble counsellors, since now the present
Requires in point of honour,—pray, mistake not,—
Some service to our lord, 'tis fit the Scots
Should not engross all glory to themselves
At this so grand and eminent solemnity.

Sket. The Scots! the motion is defied. I had rather, for
my part, without trial of my country, suffer persecution
under the pressing-iron of reproach; or let my skin be
punch'd full of eyelet-holes with the bodkin of derision.

Ast. I will sooner lose both my ears on the pillory of forgery.

Her. Let me first live a bankrupt, and die in the lousy Hole
of hunger, without compounding for sixpence in the pound.

Mayor. If men fail not in their expectations, there may
be spirits also that digest no rude affronts, Master Secretary
Frion, or I am cozened; which is possible, I grant.

Fri. Resolv'd like men of knowledge: at this feast, then,
In honour of the bride, the Scots, I know,
Will in some show, some masque, or some device,
Prefer their duties; now it were uncomely
That we be found less forward for our prince
Than they are for their lady; and by how much
We outshine them in persons of account,
By so much more will our endeavours meet with
A livelier applause. Great emperors
Have for their recreations undertook
Such kind of pastimes: as for the conceit,
Refer it to my study; the performance
You all shall share a thanks in: 'twill be grateful.

Her. The motion is allowed: I have stole to a dancing-
school when I was a prentice.

Ast. There have been Irish hubbubs, when I have made
one too.

Sket. For fashioning of shapes and cutting a cross-caper,
turn me off to my trade again.

Mayor. Surely there is, if I be not deceived, a kind of
gravity in merriment; as there is, or perhaps ought to be,
respect of persons in the quality of carriage, which is as it is
construed, either so or so.

Fri. Still you come home to me; upon occasion
I find you relish courtship with discretion;
And such are fit for statesmen of your merits.
Pray ye wait the prince, and in his ear acquaint him
With this design; I'll follow and direct ye.

                                    Exeunt, manet FRION.

O, the toil
Of humouring this abject scum of mankind,
Muddy-brain'd peasants! Princes feel a misery
Beyond impartial sufferance, whose extremes
Must yield to such abettors; yet our tide
Runs smoothly, without adverse winds: run on!
Flow to a full sea! time alone debates
Quarrels forewritten in the book of fates.   *Exit.*

ACTUS TERTIUS: SCŒNA PRIMA

[*Westminster. The palace.*]

Enter King HENRY, *his gorget on, his sword, plume of feathers,
leading-staff, and* URSWICK.

K. Hen. How runs the time of day?
Urs.   Past ten, my lord.
K. Hen. A bloody hour will it prove to some,
Whose disobedience, like the sons o'th' earth,
Throw[s] a defiance 'gainst the face of heaven.
Oxford, with Essex and stout De la Pole,
Have quieted the Londoners, I hope,
And set them safe from fear.

Urs.   They are all silent.

K. Hen. From their own battlements they may behold
Saint George's Fields o'erspread with armèd men;
Amongst whom our own royal standard threatens
Confusion to opposers. We must learn
To practise war again in time of peace,
Or lay our crown before our subjects' feet;
Ha, Urswick, must we not?

Urs.   The powers who seated
King Henry on his lawful throne will ever
Rise up in his defence.

K. Hen.   Rage shall not fright
The bosom of our confidence: in Kent
Our Cornish rebels, cozen'd of their hopes,
Met brave resistance by that country's earl,
George Abergeny, Cobham, Poynings, Guilford,
And other loyal hearts; now, if Blackheath
Must be reserv'd the fatal tomb to swallow
Such stiff-neck'd abjects as with weary marches
Have travell'd from their homes, their wives, and
    children,
To pay, instead of subsidies, their lives,
We may continue sovereign. Yet, Urswick,
We'll not abate one penny what in parliament
Hath freely been contributed; we must not;
Money gives soul to action. Our competitor,
The Flemish counterfeit, with James of Scotland,
Will prove what courage need and want can nourish,
Without the food of fit supplies: but, Urswick,
I have a charm in secret that shall loose
The witchcraft wherewith young King James is bound,
And free it at my pleasure without bloodshed.

Urs. Your majesty's a wise king, sent from heaven,
Protector of the just.

K. Hen.   Let dinner cheerfully
Be serv'd in; this day of the week is ours,
Our day of providence; for Saturday
Yet never fail'd in all my undertakings

To yield me rest at night. [*A flourish.*]—What means this
    warning?
Good fate, speak peace to Henry!

     Enter DAWBENEY, OXFORD, *and* Attendants.

  Daw.   Live the king.
Triumphant in the ruin of his enemies!
  Oxf. The head of strong rebellion is cut off,
The body hew'd in pieces.
  K. Hen.   Dawbeney, Oxford,
Minions to noblest fortunes, how yet stands
The comfort of your wishes?
  Daw.   Briefly thus:
The Cornish under Audley, disappointed
Of flatter'd expectation, from the Kentish—
Your majesty's right-trusty liegemen—flew,
Feather'd by rage and hearten'd by presumption,
To take the field even at your palace-gates,
And face you in your chamber-royal; arrogance
Improv'd their ignorance, for they, supposing,
Misled by rumour, that the day of battle
Should fall on Monday, rather brav'd your forces
Than doubted any onset; yet this morning,
When in the dawning I, by your direction,
Strove to get Deptford-Strand-bridge, there I found
Such a resistance as might show what strength
Could make; here arrows hail'd in showers upon us
A full yard long at least, but we prevail'd.
My Lord of Oxford, with his fellow peers
Environing the hill, fell fiercely on them
On the one side, I on the other, till, great sir,
Pardon the oversight, eager of doing
Some memorable act, I was engag'd
Almost a prisoner, but was freed as soon
As sensible of danger; now the fight
Began in heat, which quench'd in the blood of
Two thousand rebels, and as many more
Reserv'd to try your mercy, have return'd

A victory with safety.

    K. Hen.   Have we lost
An equal number with them?

    Oxf.   In the total
Scarcely four hundred. Audley, Flammock, Joseph,
The ringleaders of this commotion,
Railèd in ropes, fit ornaments for traitors,
Wait your determinations.

    K. Hen.   We must pay
Our thanks where they are only due; O, lords,
Here is no victory, nor shall our people
Conceive that we can triumph in their falls.
Alas, poor souls! let such as are escap'd
Steal to the country back without pursuit.
There's not a drop of blood spilt but hath drawn
As much of mine; their swords could have wrought wonders
On their king's part, who faintly were unsheath'd
Against their prince, but wounded their own breasts.
Lords, we are debtors to your care; our payment
Shall be both sure and fitting your deserts.

    Daw. Sir, will you please to see those rebels, heads
Of this wild monster-multitude?

    K. Hen.   Dear friend,
My faithful Dawbeney, no; on them our justice
Must frown in terror; I will not vouchsafe
An eye of pity to them. Let false Audley
Be drawn upon an hurdle from the Newgate
To Tower-hill in his own coat of arms
Painted on paper, with the arms revers'd,
Defac'd and torn; there let him lose his head,
The lawyer and the blacksmith shall be hang'd,
Quarter'd; their quarters into Cornwall sent
Examples to the rest, whom we are pleas'd
To pardon and dismiss from further quest.—
My Lord of Oxford, see it done.

    Oxf.   I shall, sir.

    K. Hen. Urswick!

    Urs.   My lord?

K. Hen.   To Dinham, our high-treasurer,
Say, we command commissions be new granted
For the collection of our subsidies
Through all the west, and that speedily.
Lords, we acknowledge our engagements due
For your most constant services.

Daw.   Your soldiers
Have manfully and faithfully acquitted
Their several duties.

K. Hen.   For it we will throw
A largess free amongst them, which shall hearten
And cherish-up their loyalties. More yet
Remains of like employment; not a man
Can be dismiss'd, till enemies abroad,
More dangerous than these at home, have felt
The puissance of our arms. O, happy kings
Whose thrones are raisèd in their subjects' hearts!

Exeunt.

[SCENE II. *Edinburgh. The palace.*]

Enter HUNTLEY *and* DALYELL.

Hunt. Now, sir, a modest word with you, sad gentleman:
Is not this fine, I trow, to see the gambols,
To hear the jigs, observe the frisks, be enchanted
With the rare discord of bells, pipes, and tabors,
Hotch-potch of Scotch and Irish twingle-twangles,
Like to so many quiristers of Bedlam
Trolling a catch! The feasts, the manly stomachs,
The healths in usquebaugh and bonny-clabber,
The ale in dishes never fetch'd from China,
The hundred-thousand knacks not to be spoken of,
And all this for King Oberon and Queen Mab,
Should put a soul into ye. Look ye, good man,
How youthful I am grown, but, by your leave,
This new queen-bride must henceforth be no more
My daughter; no, by'r lady, 'tis unfit,

And yet you see how I do bear this change,
Methinks courageously; then shake-off care
In such a time of jollity.

    Dal.   Alas, sir,
How can you cast a mist upon your griefs?
Which, howsoe'er you shadow, but present
To any judging eye the perfect substance,
Of which mine are but counterfeits.

    Hunt.   Foh, Dalyell!
Thou interrupt'st the part I bear in music
To this rare bridal-feast; let us be merry,
Whilst flattering calms secure us against storms.
Tempests, when they begin to roar, put out
The light of peace, and cloud the sun's bright eye
In darkness of despair; yet we are safe.

    Dal. I wish you could as easily forget
The justice of your sorrows as my hopes
Can yield to destiny.

    Hunt.   Pish! then I see
Thou dost not know the flexible condition
Of my apt nature. I can laugh, laugh heartily,
When the gout cramps my joints; let but the stone
Stop in my bladder, I am straight a-singing;
The quartan-fever, shrinking every limb,
Sets me a-capering straight; do but betray me,
And bind me a friend ever: what! I trust
The losing of a daughter, though I doted
On every hair that grew to trim her head,
Admits not any pain like one of these.
Come, thou'rt deceiv'd in me; give me a blow,
A sound blow on the face, I'll thank thee for't;
I love my wrongs: still thou'rt deceiv'd in me.

    Dal. Deceiv'd! O, noble Huntley, my few years
Have learnt experience of too ripe an age
To forfeit fit credulity; forgive
My rudeness, I am bold.

    Hunt.   Forgive me first
A madness of ambition; by example

Teach me humility, for patience scorns
Lectures, which schoolmen use to read to boys
Uncapable of injuries. Though old,
I could grow tough in fury, and disclaim
Allegiance to my king; could fall at odds
With all my fellow-peers that durst not stand
Defendants 'gainst the rape done on mine honour,
But kings are earthly gods, there is no meddling
With their anointed bodies; for their actions
They only are accountable to heaven.
Yet in the puzzle of my troubled brain
One antidote's reserv'd against the poison
Of my distractions; 'tis in thee t' apply it.

   Dal. Name it; O, name it quickly, sir!

   Hunt.   A pardon
For my most foolish slighting thy deserts;
I have cull'd out this time to beg it, prithee,
Be gentle; had I been so, thou hadst own'd
A happy bride, but now a castaway,
And never child of mine more.

   Dal.   Say not so, sir;
It is not fault in her.

   Hunt.   The world would prate
How she was handsome; young I know she was,
Tender, and sweet in her obedience,
But lost now; what a bankrupt am I made
Of a full stock of blessings! Must I hope
A mercy from thy heart?

   Dal.   A love, a service,
A friendship to posterity.

   Hunt.   Good angels
Reward thy charity! I have no more
But prayers left me now.

   Dal.   I'll lend you mirth, sir,
If you will be in consort.

   Hunt.   Thank ye truly:
I must; yes, yes, I must; here's yet some ease,
A partner in affliction: look not angry.

Dal. Good, noble sir!   [*Flourish.*]
Hunt.   O, hark! we may be quiet,
The King and all the others come; a meeting
Of gaudy sights: this day's the last of revels;
Tomorrow sounds of war; then new exchange;
Fiddles must turn to swords.—Unhappy marriage!

A Flourish. Enter King JAMES, WARBECK *leading* KATHERINE,
    CRAWFORD, COUNTESS, *and* JANE. HUNTLEY *and* DALYELL
    fall among them.

K. Ja. Cousin of York, you and your princely bride
Have liberally enjoy'd such soft delights
As a new-married couple could forethink;
Nor has our bounty shorten'd expectation:
But after all those pleasures of repose,
Of amorous safety, we must rouse the ease
Of dalliance with achievements of more glory
Than sloth and sleep can furnish; yet, for farewell,
Gladly we entertain a truce with time,
To grace the joint endeavours of our servants.
War. My royal cousin, in your princely favour
Th' extent of bounty hath been so unlimited,
As only an acknowledgment in words
Would breed suspicion in our state and quality.
When we shall, in the fulness of our fate,—
Whose minister, Necessity, will perfect,—
Sit on our own throne; then our arms, laid open
To gratitude, in sacred memory
Of these large benefits, shall twine them close,
Even to our thoughts and heart, without distinction.
Then James and Richard, being in effect
One person, shall unite and rule one people,
Divisible in titles only.
K. Ja.   Seat ye.
Are the presenters ready?
Craw.   All are entering.
Hunt. Dainty sport toward, Dalyell! sit; come, sit,
Sit and be quiet; here are kingly bug's-words!

Enter at one door Four Scotch Antics, *accordingly habited.*
Enter at another Four Wild Irish *in trowses, long-haired, and
accordingly habited. Music. The Masquers dance.*

K. Ja. To all a general thanks!
War. In the next room
Take your own shapes again; you shall receive
Particular acknowledgment. *[Exeunt the Masquers.]*
K. Ja. Enough
Of merriments. Crawford, how far's our army
Upon the march?
Craw. At Hedon-hall, great king;
Twelve thousand, well prepar'd.
K. Ja. Crawford, to-night
Post thither. We in person, with the prince,
By four o'clock to-morrow after dinner
Will be wi' ye; speed away!
Craw. I fly, my lord. *[Exit.]*
K. Ja. Our business grows to head now: where's your
secretary,
That he attends ye not to serve?
War. With Marchmont,
Your herald.
K. Ja. Good, the proclamation's ready;
By that it will appear how th' English stand
Affected to your title. Huntley, comfort
Your daughter in her husband's absence; fight
With prayers at home for us, who for your honours
Must toil in fight abroad.
Hunt. Prayers are the weapons
Which men so near their graves as I do use;
I've little else to do.
K. Ja. To rest, young beauties!
We must be early stirring; quickly part:
A kingdom's rescue craves both speed and art.
Cousins, good-night. *A flourish.*
War. Rest to our cousin-king.
Kath. Your blessing, sir.

Hunt. Fair blessings on your highness! sure, you need
   'em.
      Exeunt omnes. Manent WAR. *and* KATH. [*and* JANE].
  War. Jane, set the lights down, and from us return
To those in the next room this little purse;
Say we'll deserve their loves.
  Jane.   It shall be done, sir. [*Exit.*]
  War. Now, dearest, ere sweet sleep shall seal those eyes,
Love's precious tapers, give me leave to use
A parting ceremony; for to-morrow
It would be sacrilege t'intrude upon
The temple of thy peace: swift as the morning
Must I break from the down of thy embraces,
To put on steel, and trace the paths which lead
Through various hazards to a careful throne.
  Kath. My lord, I'd fain go wi' ye; there's small fortune
In staying here behind.
  War.   The churlish brow
Of war, fair dearest, is a sight of horror
For ladies' entertainment; if thou hear'st
A truth of my sad ending by the hand
Of some unnatural subject, thou withal
Shalt hear how I died worthy of my right,
By falling like a king; and in the close,
Which my last breath shall sound, thy name, thou fairest,
Shall sing a requiem to my soul, unwilling
Only of greater glory, 'cause divided
From such a heaven on earth as life with thee.
But these are chimes for funerals; my business
Attends on fortune of a sprightlier triumph,
For love and majesty are reconcil'd,
And vow to crown thee empress of the west.
  Kath. You have a noble language, sir; your right
In me is without question, and however
Events of time may shorten my deserts
In others' pity, yet it shall not stagger
Or constancy or duty in a wife.
You must be king of me; and my poor heart

Is all I can call mine.
    War.   But we will live,
Live, beauteous virtue, by the lively test
Of our own blood, to let the counterfeit
Be known the world's contempt.
    Kath.   Pray, do not use
That word; it carries fate in't. The first suit
I ever made, I trust your love will grant.
    War. Without denial, dearest.
    Kath.   That hereafter,
If you return with safety, no adventure
May sever us in tasting any fortune:
I ne'er can stay behind again.
    War.   You're lady
Of your desires, and shall command your will;
Yet 'tis too hard a promise.
    Kath.   What our destinies
Have rul'd-out in their books we must not search,
But kneel to.
    War.   Then to fear when hope is fruitless,
Were to be desperately miserable;
Which poverty our greatness dares not dream of,
And much more scorns to stoop to: some few minutes
Remain yet; let's be thrifty in our hopes.   *Exeunt.*

[SCENE III. *The palace at Westminster.*]

Enter King HENRY, HIALAS, *and* URSWICK.

    K. Hen. Your name is Pedro Hialas, a Spaniard?
    Hial. Sir, a Castilian born.
    K. Hen.   King Ferdinand,
With wise Queen Isabel his royal consort,
Write ye a man of worthy trust and candour.
Princes are dear to heaven who meet with subjects
Sincere in their employments; such I find
Your commendation, sir. Let me deliver
How joyful I repute the amity

With your most fortunate master, who almost
Comes near a miracle in his success
Against the Moors, who had devour'd his country,
Entire now to his sceptre. We, for our part,
Will imitate his providence, in hope
Of partage in the use on't; we repute
The privacy of his advisement to us
By you, intended an ambassador
To Scotland, for a peace between our kingdoms,
A policy of love, which well becomes
His wisdom and our care.

  Hial.   Your majesty
Doth understand him rightly.

  K. Hen.   Else
Your knowledge can instruct me; wherein, sir,
To fall on ceremony would seem useless,
Which shall not need; for I will be as studious
Of your concealment in our conference
As any council shall advise.

  Hial.   Then, sir,
My chief request is, that on notice given
At my dispatch in Scotland, you will send
Some learnèd man of power and experience
To join entreaty with me.

  K. Hen.   I shall do it,
Being that way well provided by a servant
Which may attend ye ever.

  Hial.   If King James,
By any indirection, should perceive
My coming near your court, I doubt the issue
Of my employment.

  K. Hen.   Be not your own herald:
I learn sometimes without a teacher.

  Hial.   Good days
Guard all your princely thoughts!

  K. Hen.   Urswick, no further
Than the next open gallery attend him.
A hearty love go with you!

Hial. Your vow'd beadsman.

Exeunt URS. *and* HIAL.

K. Hen. King Ferdinand is not so much a fox,
But that a cunning huntsman may in time
Fall on the scent: in honourable actions
Safe imitation best deserves a praise.

Enter URSWICK.

What, the Castilian's pass'd away?

Urs. He is,
And undiscover'd; the two hundred marks
Your majesty convey'd, he gently purs'd
With a right modest gravity.

K. Hen. What was't
He mutter'd in the earnest of his wisdom?
He spoke not to be heard; 'twas about——

Urs. Warbeck:
How if King Henry were but sure of subjects,
Such a wild runagate might soon be cag'd,
No great ado withstanding.

K. Hen. Nay, nay; something
About my son Prince Arthur's match.

Urs. Right, right, sir:
He humm'd it out, how that King Ferdinand
Swore that the marriage 'twixt the Lady Katherine
His daughter and the Prince of Wales your son
Should never be consummated as long
As any Earl of Warwick liv'd in England,
Except by new creation.

K. Hen. I remember
'Twas so, indeed: the king his master swore it?

Urs. Directly, as he said.

K. Hen. An Earl of Warwick!
Provide a messenger for letters instantly
To Bishop Fox. Our news from Scotland creeps;
It comes so slow, we must have airy spirits;
Our time requires dispatch.—[*Aside*] The Earl of Warwick!
Let him be son to Clarence, younger brother

To Edward! Edward's daughter is, I think,
Mother to our Prince Arthur. Get a messenger!   *Exeunt.*

[SCENE IV. *Before the castle of Norham.*]

Enter King JAMES, WARBECK, CRAWFORD, DALYELL,
HERON, ASTLEY, MAYOR, SKETON, *and soldiers.*

K. Ja. We trifle time against these castle-walls;
The English prelate will not yield: once more
Give him a summons.   *Parley* [*sounded*].

Enter above DURHAM *armed, a truncheon in his hand,
and Soldiers.*

War.   See, the jolly clerk
Appears, trimm'd like a ruffian!
K. Ja.   Bishop, yet
Set ope the ports, and to your lawful sovereign,
Richard of York, surrender up this castle,
And he will take thee to his grace; else Tweed
Shall overflow his banks with English blood,
And wash the sand that cements those hard stones
From their foundation.
Dur.   Warlike King of Scotland,
Vouchsafe a few words from a man enforc'd
To lay his book aside, and clap on arms
Unsuitable to my age or my profession.
Courageous prince, consider on what grounds
You rend the face of peace, and break a league
With a confederate king that courts your amity;
For whom too? for a vagabond, a straggler,
Not noted in the world by birth or name,
An obscure peasant, by the rage of hell
Loos'd from his chains to set great kings at strife.
What nobleman, what common man of note,
What ordinary subject hath come in,
Since first you footed on our territories,
To only feign a welcome? Children laugh at

Your proclamations, and the wiser pity
So great a potentate's abuse by one
Who juggles merely with the fawns and youth
Of an instructed compliment; such spoils,
Such slaughters as the rapine of your soldiers
Already have committed, is enough
To show your zeal in a conceited justice.
Yet, great king, wake not yet my master's vengeance;
But shake that viper off which gnaws your entrails.
I and my fellow-subjects are resolv'd,
If you persist, to stand your utmost fury,
Till our last blood drop from us.

  War.   O, sir, lend
No ear to this traducer of my honour!—
What shall I call thee, thou gray-bearded scandal,
That kick'st against the sovereignty to which
Thou ow'st allegiance? Treason is bold-fac'd
And eloquent in mischief: sacred king,
Be deaf to his known malice.

  Dur.   Rather yield
Unto those holy motions which inspire
The sacred heart of an anointed body.
It is the surest policy in princes
To govern well their own than seek encroachment
Upon another's right.

  Craw.   The king is serious,
Deep in his meditation[s].

  Dal.   Lift them up
To heaven, his better genius!

  War.   Can you study
While such a devil raves? O, sir!

  K. Ja.   Well, bishop,
You'll not be drawn to mercy?

  Dur.   Construe me
In like case by a subject of your own:
My resolution's fix'd: King James, be counsell'd,
A greater fate waits on thee. *Exit* DURHAM *cum suis.*

  K. Ja.   Forage through

The country; spare no prey of life or goods.

    War. O, sir, then give me leave to yield to nature;
I am most miserable. Had I been
Born what this clergyman would by defame
Baffle belief with, I had never sought
The truth of mine inheritance with rapes
Of women or of infants murder'd, virgins
Deflower'd, old men butcher'd, dwellings fir'd,
My land depopulated, and my people
Afflicted with a kingdom's devastation;
Show more remorse, great king, or I shall never
Endure to see such havoc with dry eyes;
Spare, spare, my dear, dear England!

    K. Ja.　　　　　　　　　　　You fool your piety,
Ridiculously careful of an interest
Another man possesseth. Where's your faction?
Shrewdly the bishop guess'd of your adherents,
When not a petty burgess of some town,
No, not a villager, hath yet appear'd
In your assistance; that should make ye whine,
And not your country's sufferance, as you term it.

    Dal. The king is angry.

    Craw.　　　　　　　And the passionate duke
Effeminately dolent.

    War.　　　　The experience
In former trials, sir, both of mine own
Or other princes cast out of their thrones,
Have so acquainted me how misery
Is destitute of friends or of relief,
That I can easily submit to taste
Lowest reproof without contempt or words.

                Enter FRION.

    K. Ja. An humble-minded man!

                          Now, what intelligence
Speaks Master Secretary Frion?

    Fri.　　　　　　　Henry
Of England hath in open field o'erthrown

The armies who oppos'd him in the right
Of this young prince.

    K. Ja.   His subsidies, you mean:
More, if you have it?

    Fri.   Howard, Earl of Surrey,
Back'd by twelve earls and barons of the north,
An hundred knights and gentlemen of name,
And twenty thousand soldiers, is at hand
To raise your siege. Brooke, with a goodly navy,
Is admiral at sea; and Dawbeney follows
With an unbroken army for a second.

    War. 'Tis false! they come to side with us.

    K. Ja.   Retreat;
We shall not find them stones and walls to cope with.
Yet, Duke of York, for such thou sayst thou art,
I'll try thy fortune to the height. To Surrey,
By Marchmont, I will send a brave defiance
For single combat; once a king will venture
His person to an earl, with condition
Of spilling lesser blood: Surrey is bold,
And James resolv'd.

    War.   O, rather, gracious sir,
Create me to this glory, since my cause
Doth interest this fair quarrel; valu'd least,
I am his equal.

    K. Ja.   I will be the man.
March softly off: where victory can reap
A harvest crown'd with triumph, toil is cheap.   *Exeunt.*

ACTUS QUARTUS: SCŒNA PRIMA.

[The English camp near Ayton, on the Borders.]

Enter SURREY, DURHAM, *Soldiers, with drums and colours.*

    Sur. Are all our braving enemies shrunk back,
Hid in the fogs of their distemper'd climate,
Not daring to behold our colours wave

In spite of this infected air? Can they
Look on the strength of Cundrestine defac'd?
The glory of Hedon-hall devasted? that
Of Edington cast down? the pile of Fulden
O'erthrown? and this, the strongest of their forts,
Old Ayton-castle, yielded and demolish'd?
And yet not peep abroad? The Scots are bold,
Hardy in battle; but it seems the cause
They undertake, considerèd, appears
Unjointed in the frame on't.

    Dur.   Noble Surrey,
Our royal master's wisdom is at all times
His fortune's harbinger, for when he draws
His sword to threaten war, his providence
Settles on peace, the crowning of an empire.

                                 Trumpet [within].

    Sur. Rank all in order: 'tis a herald's sound;
Some message from King James: keep a fix'd station.

    Enter MARCHMONT *and another Herald in their coats.*

    March. From Scotland's awful majesty we come
Unto the English general.

    Sur.   To me?
Say on.

    March. Thus, then; the waste and prodigal
Effusion of so much guiltless blood
As in two potent armies of necessity
Must glut the earth's dry womb, his sweet compassion
Hath studied to prevent; for which to thee,
Great Earl of Surrey, in a single fight
He offers his own royal person; fairly
Proposing these conditions only, that
If victory conclude our master's right,
The earl shall deliver for his ransom
The town of Berwick to him, with the fishgarths;
If Surrey shall prevail, the king will pay
A thousand pounds down present for his freedom,
And silence further arms: so speaks King James.

Sur. So speaks King James! so like a king he speaks.
Heralds, the English general returns
A sensible devotion from his heart,
His very soul, to this unfellow'd grace,
For let the king know, gentle heralds, truly,
How his descent from his great throne, to honour
A stranger subject with so high a title
As his compeer in arms, hath conquer'd more
Than any sword could do; for which—my loyalty
Respected—I will serve his virtues ever
In all humility; but Berwick, say,
Is none of mine to part with; in affairs
Of princes subjects cannot traffic rights
Inherent to the crown. My life is mine,
That I dare freely hazard; and—with pardon
To some unbrib'd vainglory—if his majesty
Shall taste a change of fate, his liberty
Shall meet no articles. If I fall, falling
So bravely, I refer me to his pleasure
Without condition; and for this dear favour,
Say, if not countermanded, I will cease
Hostility, unless provok'd.

   March.   This answer
We shall relate unpartially.

   Dur.   With favour,
Pray have a little patience.—[*Aside to Surrey*] Sir, you find
By these gay flourishes how wearied travail
Inclines to willing rest; here's but a prologue,
However confidently utter'd, meant
For some ensuing acts of peace. Consider
The time of year, unseasonableness of weather,
Charge, barrenness of profit, and occasion
Presents itself for honourable treaty,
Which we may make good use of. I will back,
As sent from you, in point of noble gratitude
Unto King James, with these his heralds; you
Shall shortly hear from me, my lord, for order
Of breathing or proceeding, and King Henry,

Doubt not, will thank the service.

Sur. [*aside to Dur.*]   To your wisdom,
Lord Bishop, I refer it.

Dur. [*aside to Sur.*] Be it so, then.

Sur. Heralds, accept this chain and these few crowns.

March. Our duty, noble general.

Dur.   In part
Of retribution for such princely love,
My lord the general is pleas'd to show
The king your master his sincerest zeal,
By further treaty, by no common man:
I will myself return with you.

Sur.   Y'oblige
My faithfullest affections t'ye, Lord Bishop.

March. All happiness attend your lordship!
                                   [*Exit with* Her.]

Sur.   Come, friends
And fellow-soldiers, we, I doubt, shall meet
No enemies but woods and hills to fight with;
Then 'twere as good to feed and sleep at home:
We may be free from danger, not secure.   *Exeunt.*

[Scene II. *The Scottish camp.*]

Enter Warbeck *and* Frion.

War. Frion, O, Frion, all my hopes of glory
Are at a stand! the Scottish king grows dull,
Frosty, and wayward, since this Spanish agent
Hath mix'd discourses with him; they are private,
I am not call'd to council now; confusion
On all his crafty shrugs! I feel the fabric
Of my designs are tottering.

Fri.   Henry's policies
Stir with too many engines.

War.   Let his mines,
Shap'd in the bowels of the earth, blow up
Works rais'd for my defence, yet can they never

Toss into air the freedom of my birth,
Or disavow my blood Plantagenet's;
I am my father's son still. But, O, Frion,
When I bring into count with my disasters
My wife's compartnership, my Kate's, my life's,
Then, then my frailty feels an earthquake. Mischief
Damn Henry's plots! I will be England's king,
Or let my aunt of Burgundy report
My fall in the attempt deserv'd our ancestors!

    Fri. You grow too wild in passion: if you will
Appear a prince indeed, confine your will
To moderation.

    War.   What a saucy rudeness
Prompts this distrust! If? If I will appear!
Appear a prince! death throttle such deceits
Even in their birth of utterance! cursèd cozenage
Of trust! Ye make me mad; 'twere best, it seems,
That I should turn impostor to myself,
Be mine own counterfeit, belie the truth
Of my dear mother's womb, the sacred bed
Of a prince murder'd and a living baffled!

    Fri. Nay, if you have no ears to hear, I have
No breath to spend in vain.

    War.   Sir, sir, take heed!
Gold and the promise of promotion rarely
Fail in temptation.

    Fri.   Why to me this?

    War.   Nothing.
Speak what you will; we are not sunk so low
But your advice may piece again the heart
Which many cares have broken; you were wont
In all extremities to talk of comfort:
Have ye none left now? I'll not interrupt ye.
Good, bear with my distractions! If King James
Deny us dwelling here, next whither must I?
I prithee, be not angry.

    Fri.   Sir, I told ye
Of letters come from Ireland; how the Cornish

Stomach their last defeat, and humbly sue
That with such forces as you could partake
You would in person land in Cornwall, where
Thousands will entertain your title gladly.

War. Let me embrace thee, hug thee; thou'st reviv'd
My comforts; if my cousin-king will fail,
Our cause will never.

      Enter MAYOR, HERON, ASTLEY, SKETON.

                 Welcome my tried friends!
You keep your brains awake in our defence.
Frion, advise with them of these affairs,
In which be wondrous secret; I will listen
What else concerns us here: be quick and wary.   *Exit.*

Ast. Ah, sweet young prince! Secretary, my fellow-counsellors and I have consulted, and jump all in one opinion directly; an if these Scotch garboils do not fadge to our minds, we will pell-mell run amongst the Cornish choughs presently and in a trice.

Sket. 'Tis but going to sea and leaping ashore, cut ten or twelve thousand unnecessary throats, fire seven or eight towns, take half a dozen cities, get into the market-place, crown him Richard the Fourth, and the business is finished.

Mayor. I grant ye, quoth I, so far forth as men may do, no more than men may do; for it is good to consider when consideration may be to the purpose, otherwise—still you shall pardon me—little said is soon amended.

Fri. Then you conclude the Cornish action surest?

Her. We do so, and doubt not but to thrive abundantly. Ho, my masters, had we known of the commotion when we set sail out of Ireland, the land had been ours ere this time.

Sket. Pish, pish! 'tis but forbearing being an earl or a duke a month or two longer. I say, and say it again, if the work go not on apace, let me never see new fashion more. I warrant ye, I warrant ye; we will have it so, and so it shall be.

Ast. This is but a cold phlegmatic country, not stirring enough for men of spirit. Give me the heart of England for my money!

Sket. A man may batten there in a week only, with hot loaves and butter, and a lusty cup of muscadine and sugar at breakfast, though he make never a meal all the month after.

Mayor. Surely, when I bore office I found by experience that to be much troublesome was to be much wise and busy: I have observed how filching and bragging has been the best service in these last wars; and therefore conclude peremptorily on the design in England. If things and things may fall out, as who can tell what or how—but the end will show it.

Fri. Resolv'd like men of judgment! Here to linger
More time is but to lose it: cheer the prince,
And haste him on to this; on this depends
Fame in success, or glory in our ends.   *Exeunt.*

[SCENE III. *Another part of the same.*]

Enter King JAMES, DURHAM, *and* HIALAS *on either side.*

Hial. France, Spain, and Germany combine a league
Of amity with England; nothing wants
For settling peace through Christendom, but love
Between the British monarchs, James and Henry.

Dur. The English merchants, sir, have been receiv'd
With general procession into Antwerp;
The emperor confirms the combination.

Hial. The King of Spain resolves a marriage
For Katherine his daughter with Prince Arthur.

Dur. France courts this holy contract.

Hial.   What can hinder
A quietness in England?

Dur.   But your suffrage
To such a silly creature, mighty sir,
As is but in effect an apparition,
A shadow, a mere trifle?

Hial.   To this union

The good of both the church and commonwealth
Invite ye.

 Dur. To this unity, a mystery
Of providence points out a greater blessing
For both these nations than our human reason
Can search into. King Henry hath a daughter,
The Princess Margaret; I need not urge,
What honour, what felicity can follow
On such affinity 'twixt two Christian kings
Inleagu'd by ties of blood; but sure I am,
If you, sir, ratify the peace propos'd,
I dare both motion and effect this marriage
For weal of both the kingdoms.

 K. Ja.   Dar'st thou, Lord Bishop?

 Dur. Put it to trial, royal James, by sending
Some noble personage to the English court
By way of embassy.

 Hial.   Part of the business
Shall suit my mediation.

 K. Ja.   Well, what heaven
Hath pointed out to be, must be; you two
Are ministers, I hope, of blessèd fate.
But herein only I will stand acquitted;
No blood of innocents shall buy my peace,
For Warbeck, as you nick him, came to me,
Commended by the states of Christendom,
A prince, though in distress; his fair demeanour,
Lovely behaviour, unappallèd spirit,
Spoke him not base in blood, however clouded.
The brute beasts have both rocks and caves to fly to,
And men the altars of the church; to us
He came for refuge: kings come near in nature
Unto the gods in being touch'd with pity.
Yet, noble friends, his mixture with our blood,
Even with our own, shall no way interrupt
A general peace; only I will dismiss him
From my protection, throughout my dominions,
In safety; but not ever to return.

Hial. You are a just king.
Dur.   Wise, and herein happy.
K. Ja. Nor will we dally in affairs of weight:
Huntley, Lord Bishop, shall with you to England,
Ambassador from us: we will throw down
Our weapons; peace on all sides! Now repair
Unto our council; we will soon be with you.
  Hial. Delay shall question no dispatch; heaven crown it!
                              Exeunt DUR. *and* HIAL.
  K. Ja. A league with Ferdinand! a marriage
With English Margaret! a free release
From restitution for the late affronts!
Cessation from hostility! and all
For Warbeck, not deliver'd, but dismiss'd!
We could not wish it better. Dalyell!

                    Enter DALYELL.

  Dal.   Here, sir.
  K. Ja. Are Huntley and his daughter sent for?
  Dal.   Sent for,
And come, my lord.
  K. Ja.   Say to the English prince,
We want his company.
  Dal.   He is at hand, sir.

  Enter WARBECK, KATHERINE, JANE, FRION, HERON,
          SKETON, MAYOR, ASTLEY.

  K. Ja. Cousin, our bounty, favours, gentleness,
Our benefits, the hazard of our person,
Our people's lives, our land, hath evidenc'd
How much we have engag'd on your behalf;
How trivial and how dangerous our hopes
Appear, how fruitless our attempts in war,
How windy, rather smoky, your assurance
Of party shows, we might in vain repeat;
But now obedience to the mother church,
A father's care upon his country's weal,
The dignity of state, direct our wisdom

To seal an oath of peace through Christendom
To which we're sworn already; it is you
Must only seek new fortunes in the world,
And find an harbour elsewhere. As I promis'd
On your arrival, you have met no usage
Deserves repentance in your being here,
But yet I must live master of mine own.
However, what is necessary for you
At your departure, I am well content
You be accommodated with, provided
Delay prove not my enemy.

    War.   It shall not,
Most glorious prince. The fame of my designs
Soars higher than report of ease and sloth
Can aim at; I acknowledge all your favours
Boundless and singular: am only wretched
In words as well as means to thank the grace
That flow'd so liberally. Two empires firmly
You're lord of, Scotland and Duke Richard's heart:
My claim to mine inheritance shall sooner
Fail than my life to serve you, best of kings;
And, witness Edward's blood in me, I am
More loth to part with such a great example
Of virtue than all other mere respects.
But, sir, my last suit is, you will not force
From me what you have given, this chaste lady,
Resolv'd on all extremes.

    Kath.   I am your wife;
No human power can or shall divorce
My faith from duty.

    War.   Such another treasure
The earth is bankrupt of.

    K. Ja.   I gave her, cousin,
And must avow the gift; will add withal
A furniture becoming her high birth
And unsuspected constancy; provide
For your attendance: we will part good friends.

                    Exit KING *and* DALYELL.

War. The Tudor hath been cunning in his plots;
His Fox of Durham would not fail at last.
But what? our cause and courage are our own;
Be men, my friends, and let our cousin-king
See how we follow fate as willingly
As malice follows us. Ye're all resolv'd
For the west parts of England?

 All.   Cornwall, Cornwall!

 Fri. Th' inhabitants expect you daily.

 War.   Cheerfully
Draw all our ships out of the harbour, friends;
Our time of stay doth seem too long, we must
Prevent intelligence; about it suddenly.

 All. A prince, a prince, a prince!

            Exeunt COUNSELLORS.

 War. Dearest, admit not into thy pure thoughts
The least of scruples, which may charge their softness
With burden of distrust. Should I prove wanting
To noblest courage now, here were the trial,
But I am perfect, sweet; I fear no change,
More than thy being partner in my sufferance.

 Kath. My fortunes, sir, have arm'd me to encounter
What chance soe'er they meet with.—Jane, 'tis fit
Thou stay behind, for whither wilt thou wander?

 Jane. Never till death will I forsake my mistress,
Nor then in wishing to die with ye gladly.

 Kath. Alas, good soul!

 Fri.   Sir, to your aunt of Burgundy
I will relate your present undertakings;
From her expect on all occasions welcome.
You cannot find me idle in your services.

 War. Go, Frion, go. Wise men know how to soothe
Adversity, not serve it. Thou hast waited
Too long on expectation; never yet
Was any nation read of so besotted
In reason as t'adore the setting sun.
Fly to the archduke's court; say to the duchess,
Her nephew, with fair Katherine his wife,

Are on their expectation to begin
The raising of an empire: if they fail,
Yet the report will never. Farewell, Frion!

Exit FRION.

This man, Kate, has been true, though now of late
I fear too much familiar with the Fox.

Enter HUNTLEY *and* DALYELL.

Hunt. I come to take my leave; you need not doubt.
My interest in this sometime child of mine;
She's all yours now, good sir. O, poor lost creature,
Heaven guard thee with much patience! if thou canst
Forget thy title to old Huntley's family,
As much of peace will settle in thy mind
As thou canst wish to taste but in thy grave.
Accept my tears yet, prithee; they are tokens
Of charity as true as of affection.

Kath. This is the cruell'st farewell!

Hunt.   Love, young gentleman,
This model of my griefs; she calls you husband;
Then be not jealous of a parting kiss,
It is a father's, not a lover's offering;
Take it, my last. [*Kisses her*] I am too much a child.
Exchange of passion is to little use,
So I should grow too foolish: goodness guide thee!

Exit HUNT.

Kath. Most miserable daughter!—Have you aught
To add, sir, to our sorrows?

Dal.   I resolve,
Fair lady, with your leave, to wait on all
Your fortunes in my person, if your lord
Vouchsafe me entertainment.

War. We will be bosom-friends, most noble Dalyell;
For I accept this tender of your love
Beyond ability of thanks to speak it.
Clear thy drown'd eyes, my fairest: time and industry
Will show us better days, or end the worst. *Exeunt.*

[SCENE IV. *The palace at Westminster.*]

Enter OXFORD *and* DAWBENEY.

Oxf. No news from Scotland yet, my lord?
   Daw.   Not any
But what King Henry knows himself; I thought
Our armies should have march'd that way: his mind,
It seems, is alter'd.
   Oxf.   Victory attends
His standard everywhere.
   Daw.   Wise princes, Oxford,
Fight not alone with forces. Providence
Directs and tutors strength; else elephants
And barbèd horses might as well prevail
As the most subtle stratagems of war.
   Oxf. The Scottish king show'd more than common
     bravery
In proffer of a combat hand to hand
With Surrey.
   Daw.   And but show'd it; northern bloods
Are gallant being fir'd, but the cold climate,
Without good store of fuel, quickly freezeth
The glowing flames.
   Oxf.   Surrey, upon my life,
Would not have shrunk an hair's-breadth.
   Daw.   May he forfeit
The honour of an English name and nature,
Who would not have embrac'd it with a greediness
As violent as hunger runs to food!
'Twas an addition any worthy spirit
Would covet, next to immortality,
Above all joys of life: we all miss'd shares
In that great opportunity.

Enter King HENRY *and* URSWICK *whispering.*

   Oxf.   The king!
See, he comes smiling.

Daw.   O, the game runs smooth
On his side, then, believe it; cards well shuffled
And dealt with cunning bring some gamester thrift:
But others must rise losers.

K. Hen.   The train takes?

Urs. Most prosperously.

K. Hen.   I knew it should not miss.
He fondly angles who will hurl his bait
Into the water 'cause the fish at first
Plays round about the line and dares not bite.
Lords, we may reign your king yet; Dawbeney, Oxford,
Urswick, must Perkin wear the crown?

Daw.   A slave!

Oxf. A vagabond!

Urs.   A glow-worm!

K. Hen.   Now, if Frion,
His practis'd politician, wear a brain
Of proof, King Perkin will in progress ride
Through all his large dominions; let us meet him,
And tender homage, ha, sirs? Liegemen ought
To pay their fealty.

Daw.   Would the rascal were,
With all his rabble, within twenty miles
Of London!

K. Hen. Farther off is near enough
To lodge him in his home; I'll wager odds,
Surrey and all his men are either idle
Or hasting back. They have not work, I doubt,
To keep them busy.

Daw.   'Tis a strange conceit, sir.

K. Hen. Such voluntary favours as our people
In duty aid us with, we never scatter'd
On cobweb parasites, or lavish'd out
In riot or a needless hospitality.
No undeserving favourite doth boast
His issues from our treasury; our charge
Flows through all Europe, proving us but steward
Of every contribution which provides

Against the creeping canker of disturbance.
Is it not rare, then, in this toil of state
Wherein we are embark'd, with breach of sleep,
Cares, and the noise of trouble, that our mercy
Returns nor thanks nor comfort? Still the West
Murmur and threaten innovation,
Whisper our government tyrannical,
Deny us what is ours, nay, spurn their lives,
Of which they are but owners by our gift;
It must not be.

    Oxf.   It must not, should not.

Enter a POST.

    K. Hen.   So then—
To whom?

    Messenger. This packet to your sacred majesty.

    K. Hen. Sirrah, attend without.   [*Exit* MESS.]

    Oxf. News from the North, upon my life.

    Daw.   Wise Henry
Divines aforehand of events; with him
Attempts and execution are one act.

    K. Hen. Urswick, thine ear. Frion is caught; the man
Of cunning is outreach'd: we must be safe.
Should reverend Morton, our archbishop, move
To a translation higher yet, I tell thee
My Durham owns a brain deserves that see;
He's nimble in his industry, and mounting:
Thou hear'st me?

    Urs.   And conceive your highness fitly.

    K. Hen. Dawbeney and Oxford, since our army stands
Entire, it were a weakness to admit
The rust of laziness to eat amongst them;
Set forward toward Salisbury: the plains
Are most commodious for their exercise.
Ourself will take a muster of them there;
And or disband them with reward, or else
Dispose as best concerns us.

    Daw.   Salisbury!

Sir, all is peace at Salisbury.

   K. Hen.   Dear friend,

The charge must be our own; we would a little

Partake the pleasure with our subjects' ease.

Shall I entreat your loves?

   Oxf.   Command our lives.

   K. Hen. Ye're men know how to do, not to forethink.

My bishop is a jewel tried and perfect;

A jewel, lords. The post who brought these letters

Must speed another to the Mayor of Exeter;

Urswick, dismiss him not.

   Urs.   He waits your pleasure.

   K. Hen. Perkin a king? a king!

   Urs.   My gracious lord,—

   K. Hen. Thoughts busied in the sphere of royalty

Fix not on creeping worms without their stings,

Mere excrements of earth. The use of time

Is thriving safety, and a wise prevention

Of ills expected. We're resolv'd for Salisbury.

                                       Exeunt.

[SCENE V. *The coast of Cornwall.*]

A general shout within. Enter WARBECK, DALYELL,
         KATHERINE, *and* JANE.

   War. After so many storms as wind and seas

Have threaten'd to our weather-beaten ships,

At last, sweet fairest, we are safe arriv'd

On our dear mother earth, ingrateful only

To heaven and us in yielding sustenance

To sly usurpers of our throne and right.

These general acclamations are an omen

Of happy process to their welcome lord;

They flock in troops, and from all parts with wings

Of duty fly to lay their hearts before us.

Unequall'd pattern of a matchless wife,

How fares my dearest yet?

Kath.   Confirm'd in health,
By which I may the better undergo
The roughest face of change; but I shall learn
Patience to hope, since silence courts affliction,
For comforts, to this truly noble gentleman,—
Rare unexampled pattern of a friend!—
And my belovèd Jane, the willing follower
Of all misfortunes.

Dal.   Lady, I return
But barren crops of early protestations,
Frost-bitten in the spring of fruitless hopes.

Jane. I wait but as the shadow to the body;
For, madam, without you let me be nothing.

War. None talk of sadness; we are on the way
Which leads to victory: keep cowards' thoughts
With desperate sullenness! The lion faints not
Lock'd in a grate, but loose disdains all force
Which bars his prey,—and we are lion-hearted,—
Or else no king of beasts.   *Another shout.*

                    Hark, how they shout,
Triumphant in our cause! bold confidence
Marches on bravely, cannot quake at danger.

Enter SKETON.

Sket. Save King Richard the Fourth! save thee, king
of hearts! The Cornish blades are men of mettle; have pro-
claimed, through Bodmin and the whole county, my sweet
prince Monarch of England: four thousand tall yeomen,
with bow and sword, already vow to live and die at the foot
of King Richard.

Enter ASTLEY.

Ast. The mayor, our fellow-counsellor, is servant for an
emperor. Exeter is appointed for the rendezvous, and nothing wants to victory but courage and resolution. *Sigillatum
et datum decimo Septembris, anno regni regis primo, et cætera;
confirmatum est.*[1] All's cock-sure.

    [1] 'Sealed and dated September the tenth, in the first year of the
king's reign, etc.; it is confirmed.'

War. To Exeter! to Exeter, march on!
Commend us to our people: we in person
Will lend them double spirits; tell them so.
    Sket. and Ast. King Richard, King Richard!
    War. A thousand blessings guard our lawful arms!
A thousand horrors pierce our enemies' souls!
Pale fear unedge their weapons' sharpest points!
And when they draw their arrows to the head,
Numbness shall strike their sinews! Such advantage
Hath Majesty in its pursuit of justice,
That on the proppers-up of Truth's old throne
It both enlightens counsel and gives heart
To execution; whiles the throats of traitors
Lie bare before our mercy. O, divinity
Of royal birth! how it strikes dumb the tongues
Whose prodigality of breath is brib'd
By trains to greatness! Princes are but men
Distinguish'd in the fineness of their frailty,
Yet not so gross in beauty of the mind;
For there's a fire more sacred purifies
The dross of mixture. Herein stand the odds,
Subjects are men on earth, kings men and gods.

                                              Exeunt.

ACTUS QUINTUS: SCŒNA PRIMA.

[Saint Michael's Mount, Cornwall.]

Enter KATHERINE *and* JANE *in riding-suits, with one Servant.*

    Kath. It is decreed; and we must yield to fate,
Whose angry justice, though it threaten ruin,
Contempt, and poverty, is all but trial
Of a weak woman's constancy in suffering.
Here, in a stranger's and an enemy's land,
Forsaken and unfurnish'd of all hopes

But such as wait on misery, I range,
To meet affliction wheresoe'er I tread.
My train and pomp of servants is reduc'd
To one kind gentlewoman and this groom.
Sweet Jane, now whither must we?

    Jane.   To your ships,
Dear lady, and turn home.

    Kath.   Home! I have none.
Fly thou to Scotland; thou hast friends will weep
For joy to bid thee welcome; but, O, Jane,
My Jane, my friends are desperate of comfort,
As I must be of them; the common charity,
Good people's alms and prayers of the gentle,
Is the revenue must support my state.
As for my native country, since it once
Saw me a princess in the height of greatness
My birth allow'd me, here I make a vow
Scotland shall never see me being fall'n
Or lessen'd in my fortunes. Never, Jane,
Never to Scotland more will I return.
Could I be England's queen,—a glory, Jane,
I never fawn'd on,—yet the king who gave me
Hath sent me with my husband from his presence,
Deliver'd us suspected to his nation,
Render'd us spectacles to time and pity;
And is it fit I should return to such
As only listen after our descent
From happiness enjoy'd to misery
Expected, though uncertain? Never, never!
Alas, why dost thou weep? and that poor creature
Wipe his wet cheeks too? let me feel alone
Extremities, who know to give them harbour;
Nor thou nor he has cause: you may live safely.

    Jane. There is no safety whiles your dangers, madam,
Are every way apparent.

    Serv.   Pardon, lady,
I cannot choose but show my honest heart;
You were ever my good lady.

Kath.   O, dear souls,
Your shares in grief are too, too much!

Enter DALYELL.

Dal.   I bring,
Fair princess, news of further sadness yet
Than your sweet youth hath been acquainted with.

Kath. Not more, my lord, than I can welcome; speak it,
The worst, the worst I look for.

Dal.   All the Cornish
At Exeter were by the citizens
Repuls'd, encounter'd by the Earl of Devonshire
And other worthy gentlemen of the country.
Your husband march'd to Taunton, and was there
Affronted by King Henry's chamberlain,
The king himself in person with his army
Advancing nearer, to renew the fight
On all occasions; but the night before
The battles were to join, your husband privately
Accompanied with some few horse, departed
From out the camp, and posted none knows whither.

Kath. Fled without battle given?

Dal.   Fled, but follow'd
By Dawbeney; all his parties left to taste
King Henry's mercy,—for to that they yielded,—
Victorious without bloodshed.

Kath.   O, my sorrows!
If both our lives had prov'd the sacrifice
To Henry's tyranny, we had fall'n like princes,
And robb'd him of the glory of his pride.

Dal. Impute it not to faintness or to weakness
Of noble courage, lady, but [to] foresight;
For by some secret friend he had intelligence
Of being bought and sold by his base followers.
Worse yet remains untold.

Kath.   No, no, it cannot.

Dal. I fear you are betray'd; the Earl of Oxford
Runs hot in your pursuit.

Kath.   He shall not need;
We'll run as hot in resolution gladly
To make the earl our jailor.
    Jane.   Madam, madam,
They come, they come!

                Enter OXFORD, *with Followers.*

    Dal.   Keep back! or he who dares
Rudely to violate the law of honour
Runs on my sword.
    Kath.   Most noble sir, forbear!
What reason draws you hither, gentlemen?
Whom seek ye?
    Oxf.   All stand off! With favour, lady,
From Henry, England's king, I would present
Unto the beauteous princess, Katherine Gordon,
The tender of a gracious entertainment.
    Kath. We are that princess, whom your master king
Pursues with reaching arms to draw into
His power; let him use his tyranny,
We shall not be his subject.
    Oxf.   My commission
Extends no further, excellentest lady,
Than to a service; 'tis King Henry's pleasure
That you, and all that have relation t'ye,
Be guarded as becomes your birth and greatness;
For, rest assur'd, sweet princess, that not aught
Of what you do call yours shall find disturbance,
Or any welcome other than what suits
Your high condition.
    Kath.   By what title, sir,
May I acknowledge you?
    Oxf.   Your servant, lady,
Descended from the line of Oxford's Earls,
Inherits what his ancestors before him
Were owners of.
    Kath.   Your king is herein royal,
That by a peer so ancient in desert

As well as blood commands us to his presence.

Oxf. Invites ye, princess, not commands.

Kath.   Pray use
Your own phrase as you list; to your protection
Both I and mine submit.

Oxf.   There's in your number
A nobleman whom fame hath bravely spoken.
To him the king my master bade me say
How willingly he courts his friendship; far
From an enforcement, more than what in terms
Of courtesy so great a prince may hope for.

Dal. My name is Dalyell.

Oxf.   'Tis a name hath won
Both thanks and wonder from report, my lord;
The court of England emulates your merit,
And covets to embrace ye.

Dal.   I must wait on
The princess in her fortunes.

Oxf.   Will you please,
Great lady, to set forward?

Kath.   Being driven
By fate, it were in vain to strive with heaven.   *Exeunt.*

[SCENE II. *Salisbury.*]

Enter King HENRY, SURREY, URSWICK, *and a guard of
Soldiers.*

K. Hen. The counterfeit, King Perkin, is escap'd:—
Escape so let him; he is hedg'd too fast
Within the circuit of our English pale
To steal out of our ports, or leap the walls
Which guard our land; the seas are rough and wider
Than his weak arms can tug with. Surrey, henceforth
Your king may reign in quiet; turmoils past,
Like some unquiet dream, have rather busied
Our fancy than affrighted rest of state.
But, Surrey, why, in articling a peace
With James of Scotland, was not restitution

Of losses which our subjects did sustain
By the Scotch inroads question'd?

Sur.   Both demanded
And urg'd, my lord; to which the king replied,
In modest merriment, but smiling earnest,
How that our master Henry was much abler
To bear the detriments than he repay them.

K. Hen. The young man, I believe, spake honest truth;
He studies to be wise betimes. Has, Urswick,
Sir Rice ap Thomas, and Lord Brook our steward,
Return'd the Western gentlemen full thanks
From us for their tried loyalties?

Urs.   They have;
Which, as if health and life had reign'd amongst 'em,
With open hearts they joyfully receiv'd.

K. Hen. Young Buckingham is a fair-natur'd prince,
Lovely in hopes, and worthy of his father;
Attended by an hundred knights and squires
Of special name he tender'd humble service,
Which we must ne'er forget: and Devonshire's wounds,
Though slight, shall find sound cure in our respect.

Enter DAWBENEY *with* WARBECK, HERON, JOHN A-WATER,
ASTLEY, *and* SKETON.

Daw. Life to the king, and safety fix his throne!
I here present you, royal sir, a shadow
Of majesty, but in effect a substance
Of pity; a young man, in nothing grown
To ripeness but th' ambition of your mercy:
Perkin, the Christian world's strange wonder.

K. Hen.   Dawbeney,
We observe no wonder; I behold, 'tis true,
An ornament of nature, fine and polish'd,
A handsome youth indeed, but not admire him.
How came he to thy hands?

Daw.   From sanctuary
At Bewley, near Southampton; register'd,
With these few followers, for persons privileg'd.

K. Hen. I must not thank you, sir; you were to blame
T'infringe the liberty of houses sacred:
Dare we be irreligious?

   Daw.   Gracious lord,
They voluntarily resign'd themselves
Without compulsion.

   K. Hen.   So? 'twas very well;
'Twas very, very well.—Turn now thine eyes,
Young man, upon thyself and thy past actions;
What revels in combustion through our kingdom
A frenzy of aspiring youth hath danc'd,
Till, wanting breath, thy feet of pride have slipt
To break thy neck!

   War.   But not my heart; my heart
Will mount till every drop of blood be frozen
By death's perpetual winter; if the sun
Of majesty be darken'd, let the sun
Of life be hid from me in an eclipse
Lasting and universal. Sir, remember
There was a shooting-in of light when Richmond,
Not aiming at a crown, retir'd, and gladly,
For comfort to the Duke of Bretaine's court.
Richard, who sway'd the sceptre, was reputed
A tyrant then; yet then a dawning glimmer'd
To some few wandering remnants, promising day
When first they ventur'd on a frightful shore
At Milford Haven—

   Daw.   Whither speeds his boldness?
Check his rude tongue, great sir.

   K. Hen.   O, let him range:
The player's on the stage still, 'tis his part;
He does but act. What follow'd?

   War.   Bosworth Field;
Where, at an instant, to the world's amazement,
A morn to Richmond, and a night to Richard,
Appear'd at once. The tale is soon applied;
Fate, which crown'd these attempts when least assur'd,
Might have befriended others like resolv'd.

K. Hen. A pretty gallant! Thus, your aunt of Burgundy,
Your duchess-aunt, inform'd her nephew; so,
The lesson prompted and well conn'd, was moulded
Into familiar dialogue, oft rehears'd,
Till, learnt by heart, 'tis now receiv'd for truth.

War. Truth, in her pure simplicity, wants art
To put a feignèd blush on; scorn wears only
Such fashion as commends to gazers' eyes
Sad ulcerated novelty, far beneath
The sphere of majesty: in such a court
Wisdom and gravity are proper robes,
By which the sovereign is best distinguish'd
From zanies to his greatness.

K. Hen.   Sirrah, shift
Your antic pageantry, and now appear
In your own nature, or you'll taste the danger
Of fooling out of season.

War.   I expect
No less than what severity calls justice,
And politicians safety; let such beg
As feed on alms, but if there can be mercy
In a protested enemy, then may it
Descend to these poor creatures, whose engagements,
To th' bettering of their fortunes, have incurr'd
A loss of all; to them if any charity
Flow from some noble orator, in death
I owe the fee of thankfulness.

K. Hen.   So brave!
What a bold knave is this! Which of these rebels
Has been the Mayor of Cork?

Daw.   This wise formality.—
Kneel to the king, ye rascals!   [*They kneel.*]

K. Hen.   Canst thou hope
A pardon, where thy guilt is so apparent?

Mayor. Under your good favours, as men are men, they
may err; for I confess, respectively, in taking great parts, the
one side prevailing, the other side must go down: herein the
point is clear, if the proverb hold, that hanging goes by

destiny, that it is to little purpose to say, this thing or that
shall be thus or thus; for, as the Fates will have it, so it must
be; and who can help it?

Daw. O, blockhead! thou a privy-counsellor?
Beg life, and cry aloud, 'Heaven save King Henry!'

Mayor. Every man knows what is best, as it happens; for
my own part, I believe it is true, if I be not deceived, that
kings must be kings and subjects subjects; but which is
which, you shall pardon me for that: whether we speak
or hold our peace, all are mortal; no man knows his
    end.

K. Hen. We trifle time with follies.

[*Her. Mayor Ast. Sket.*]   Mercy, mercy!

K. Hen. Urswick, command the dukeling and these
    fellows
To Digby, the Lieutenant of the Tower:
With safety let them be convey'd to London.
It is our pleasure no uncivil outrage,
Taunts or abuse be suffer'd to their persons;
They shall meet fairer law than they deserve.
Time may restore their wits, whom vain ambition
Hath many years distracted.

War.   Noble thoughts
Meet freedom in captivity: the Tower,
Our childhood's dreadful nursery!

K. Hen.   No more!

Urs. Come, come, you shall have leisure to bethink ye.

        Exit URS. *with* PERK. *and his* [*Followers.*]

K. Hen. Was ever so much impudence in forgery?
The custom, sure, of being styl'd a king
Hath fasten'd in his thought that he is such;
But we shall teach the lad another language:
'Tis good we have him fast.

Daw.   The hangman's physic
Will purge this saucy humour.

K. Hen.   Very likely;
Yet we could temper mercy with extremity,
Being not too far provok'd.

Enter OXFORD, KATHERINE *in her richest attire,* [DALYELL],
JANE, *and Attendants.*

Oxf.   Great sir, be pleas'd,
With your accustom'd grace to entertain
The Princess Katherine Gordon.
    K. Hen.   Oxford, herein
We must beshrew thy knowledge of our nature.
A lady of her birth and virtues could not
Have found us so unfurnish'd of good manners
As not, on notice given, to have met her
Half way in point of love. Excuse, fair cousin,
The oversight: O, fie! you may not kneel;
'Tis most unfitting: first, vouchsafe this welcome,
A welcome to your own; for you shall find us
But guardian to your fortune[s] and your honours.
    Kath. My fortunes and mine honours are weak cham-
        pions,
As both are now befriended, sir: however,
Both bow before your clemency.
    K. Hen.   Our arms
Shall circle them from malice—A sweet lady!
Beauty incomparable! here lives majesty
At league with love.
    Kath.   O, sir, I have a husband.
    K. Hen. We'll prove your father, husband, friend, and
        servant.
Prove what you wish to grant us. Lords, be careful
A patent presently be drawn for issuing
A thousand pounds from our exchequer yearly
During our cousin's life. Our queen shall be
Your chief companion, our own court your home,
Our subjects all your servants.
    Kath.   But my husband?
    K. Hen. By all descriptions, you are noble Dalyell,
Whose generous truth hath fam'd a rare observance.
We thank ye; 'tis a goodness gives addition
To every title boasted from your ancestry,
In all most worthy.

Dal.   Worthier than your praises,
Right princely sir, I need not glory in.

K. Hen. Embrace him, lords. Whoever calls you mistress
Is lifted in our charge. A goodlier beauty
Mine eyes yet ne'er encounter'd.

Kath.   Cruel misery
Of fate! what rests to hope for?

K. Hen.   Forward, lords,
To London. Fair, ere long I shall present ye
With a glad object, peace, and Huntley's blessing.

Exeunt.

[Scene III. *London. The Tower-hill.*]

Enter Constable *and* Officers, Warbeck, Urswick, *and*
Lambert Simnel *as a falconer. A pair of stocks.*

Const. Make room there! keep off, I require ye; and none
come within twelve foot of his majesty's new stocks,
upon pain of displeasure. Bring forward the malefactors. Friend,
you must to this gear, no remedy. Open the hole, and in with
his legs, just in the middle hole; there, that hole. [*Warbeck
is put in the stocks.*] Keep off, or I'll commit you all: shall not
a man in authority be obeyed? So, so, there; 'tis as it should
be: put on the padlock, and give me the key. Off, I say, keep
off!

Urs. Yet, Warbeck, clear thy conscience: thou hast
      tasted
King Henry's mercy liberally; the law
Has forfeited thy life; an equal jury
Have doom'd thee to the gallows; twice most wickedly,
Most desperately, hast thou escap'd the Tower,
Inveigling to thy party with thy witchcraft
Young Edward Earl of Warwick, son to Clarence,
Whose head must pay the price of that attempt;
Poor gentleman, unhappy in his fate,
And ruin'd by thy cunning! so a mongrel
May pluck the true stag down. Yet, yet, confess

Thy parentage; for yet the king has mercy.

   Lamb. You would be Dick the Fourth; very likely!
Your pedigree is publish'd; you are known
For Osbeck's son of Tournay, a loose runagate,
A landloper; your father was a Jew,
Turn'd Christian merely to repair his miseries:
Where's now your kingship?

   War.   Baited to my death?
Intolerable cruelty! I laugh at
The Duke of Richmond's practice on my fortunes;
Possession of a crown ne'er wanted heralds.

   Lamb. You will not know who I am?

   Urs.   Lambert Simnel,
Your predecessor in a dangerous uproar;
But, on submission, not alone receiv'd
To grace, but by the king vouchsaf'd his service.

   Lamb. I would be Earl of Warwick, toil'd and ruffled
Against my master, leap'd to catch the moon,
Vaunted my name Plantagenet, as you do;
An earl, forsooth! whenas in truth I was,
As you are, a mere rascal, yet his majesty,
A prince compos'd of sweetness,—Heaven protect him!—
Forgave me all my villainies, repriev'd
The sentence of a shameful end, admitted
My surety of obedience to his service,
And I am now his falconer, live plenteously,
Eat from the king's purse, and enjoy the sweetness
Of liberty and favour, sleep securely,
And is not this, now, better than to buffet
The hangman's clutches, or to brave the cordage
Of a tough halter which will break your neck?
So, then, the gallant totters! Prithee, Perkin,
Let my example lead thee: be no longer
A counterfeit; confess, and hope for pardon.

   War. For pardon! hold, my heart-strings, whiles contempt
Of injuries, in scorn, may bid defiance
To this base man's foul language! Thou poor vermin,
How dar'st thou creep so near me? Thou an earl!

Why, thou enjoy'st as much of happiness
As all the swing of slight ambition flew at.
A dunghill was thy cradle. So a puddle,
By virtue of the sunbeams, breathes a vapour
T' infect the purer air, which drops again
Into the muddy womb that first exhal'd it.
Bread and a slavish ease, with some assurance
From the base beadle's whip, crown'd all thy hopes,
But, sirrah, ran there in thy veins one drop
Of such a royal blood as flows in mine,
Thou wouldst not change condition, to be second
In England's state, without the crown itself.
Coarse creatures are incapable of excellence,
But let the world, as all to whom I am
This day a spectacle, to time deliver,
And by tradition fix posterity
Without another chronicle than truth,
How constantly my resolution suffer'd
A martyrdom of majesty.

    Lamb.   He's past
Recovery; a Bedlam cannot cure him.

    Urs. Away, inform the king of his behaviour.

    Lamb. Perkin, beware the rope! the hangman's coming.

    Urs. If yet thou hast no pity of thy body,
Pity thy soul!

                          Exit SIMNEL.

    Enter KATHERINE, JANE, DALYELL, *and* OXFORD.

    Jane.   Dear lady!

    Oxf.   Whither will ye,
Without respect of shame?

    Kath.   Forbear me, sir,
And trouble not the current of my duty.
O, my lov'd lord! can any scorn be yours
In which I have no interest? Some kind hand
Lend me assistance, that I may partake
Th' infliction of this penance. My life's dearest,
Forgive me; I have stay'd too long from tendering
Attendance on reproach; yet bid me welcome.

War. Great miracle of constancy! my miseries
Were never bankrupt of their confidence
In worst afflictions, till this; now I feel them.
Report and thy deserts, thou best of creatures,
Might to eternity have stood a pattern
For every virtuous wife without this conquest.
Thou hast outdone belief; yet may their ruin
In after-marriages be never pitied,
To whom thy story shall appear a fable!
Why wouldst thou prove so much unkind to greatness
To glorify thy vows by such a servitude?
I cannot weep; but trust me, dear, my heart
Is liberal of passion. Harry Richmond,
A woman's faith hath robb'd thy fame of triumph!
    Oxf. Sirrah, leave-off your juggling, and tie up
The devil that ranges in your tongue.
    Urs.   Thus witches,
Possess'd, even [to] their deaths deluded, say
They have been wolves and dogs, and sail'd in eggshells
Over the sea, and rid on fiery dragons,
Pass'd in the air more than a thousand miles,
All in a night; the enemy of mankind
Is powerful, but false, and falsehood confident.
    Oxf. Remember, lady, who you are; come from
That impudent impostor.
    Kath.   You abuse us,
For when the holy churchman join'd our hands,
Our vows were real then; the ceremony
Was not in apparition, but in act.
Be what these people term thee, I am certain
Thou art my husband, no divorce in heaven
Has been su'd-out between us; 'tis injustice
For any earthly power to divide us.
Or we will live or let us die together.
There is a cruel mercy.
    War.   Spite of tyranny
We reign in our affections, blessèd woman!
Read in my destiny the wreck of honour;

Point out, in my contempt of death, to memory
Some miserable happiness; since herein,
Even when I fell, I stood enthron'd a monarch
Of one chaste wife's troth pure and uncorrupted.
Fair angel of perfection, immortality
Shall raise thy name up to an adoration,
Court every rich opinion of true merit,
And saint it in the Calendar of Virtue,
When I am turn'd into the self-same dust
Of which I was first form'd.

    Oxf.   The lord ambassador,
Huntley, your father, madam, should he look on
Your strange subjection in a gaze so public,
Would blush on your behalf, and wish his country
Unleft for entertainment to such sorrow.

    Kath. Why art thou angry, Oxford? I must be
More peremptory in my duty.—Sir,
Impute it not unto immodesty
That I presume to press you to a legacy
Before we part for ever.

    War.   Let it be, then,
My heart, the rich remains of all my fortunes.

    Kath. Confirm it with a kiss, pray.

    War.   O, with that
I wish to breathe my last! upon thy lips,
Those equal twins of comeliness, I seal
The testament of honourable vows: [*Kisses her.*]
Whoever be that man that shall unkiss
This sacred print next, may he prove more thrifty
In this world's just applause, not more desertful!

    Kath. By this sweet pledge of both our souls, I swear
To die a faithful widow to thy bed;
Not to be forc'd or won: O, never, never!

Enter SURREY, DAWBENEY, HUNTLEY, *and* CRAWFORD.

    Daw. Free the condemnèd person; quickly free him!
What has he yet confess'd?

                [*Warbeck is taken out of the stocks.*]

Urs.   Nothing to purpose;
But still he will be king.

Sur.   Prepare your journey
To a new kingdom, then. Unhappy madam,
Wilfully foolish! See, my lord ambassador,
Your lady daughter will not leave the counterfeit
In this disgrace of fate.

Hunt.   I never pointed
Thy marriage, girl; but yet, being married,
Enjoy thy duty to a husband freely.
The griefs are mine. I glory in thy constancy;
And must not say I wish that I had miss'd
Some partage in these trials of a patience.

Kath. You will forgive me, noble sir?

Hunt.   Yes, yes;
In every duty of a wife and daughter
I dare not disavow thee. To your husband,—
For such you are, sir,—I impart a farewell
Of manly pity; what your life has pass'd through,
The dangers of your end will make apparent;
And I can add, for comfort to your sufferance,
No cordial, but the wonder of your frailty,
Which keeps so firm a station. We are parted.

War. We are. A crown of peace renew thy age,
Most honourable Huntley! Worthy Crawford!
We may embrace; I never thought thee injury.

Craw. Nor was I ever guilty of neglect
Which might procure such thought. I take my leave, sir.

War. To you, Lord Dalyell,—what? accept a sigh,
'Tis hearty and in earnest.

Dal.   I want utterance;
My silence is my farewell.

Kath.   O, O!

Jane   Sweet madam,
What do you mean?—My lord, your hand.   [*To Dal.*]

Dal.   Dear lady,
Be pleas'd that I may wait ye to your lodging.

                              Exeunt DAL. KATH. JANE.

Enter Sheriff *and* Officers, SKETON, ASTLEY, HERON, *and*
MAYOR, *with halters about their necks.*

Oxf. Look ye; behold your followers, appointed
To wait on ye in death!
War.   Why, peers of England,
We'll lead 'em on courageously: I read
A triumph over tyranny upon
Their several foreheads. Faint not in the moment
Of victory! our ends, and Warwick's head,
Innocent Warwick's head,—for we are prologue
But to his tragedy,—conclude the wonder
Of Henry's fears; and then the glorious race
Of fourteen kings, Plantagenets, determines
In this last issue male; Heaven be obey'd!
Impoverish time of its amazement, friends,
And we will prove as trusty in our payments
As prodigal to nature in our debts.
Death? pish! 'tis but a sound; a name of air;
A minute's storm, or not so much: to tumble
From bed to bed, be massacred alive
By some physicians, for a month or two,
In hope of freedom from a fever's torments
Might stagger manhood; here the pain is past,
Ere sensibly 'tis felt. Be men of spirit!
Spurn coward passion! so illustrious mention
Shall blaze our names, and style us Kings o'er Death.
Daw. Away, impostor beyond precedent!
                    [*Exeunt all Officers and Prisoners.*
No chronicle records his fellow.
Hunt.   I have
Not thoughts left; 'tis sufficient in such cases
Just laws ought to proceed.

Enter King HENRY, DURHAM, *and* HIALAS.

K. Hen.   We are resolv'd.
Your business, noble lords, shall find success
Such as your king impórtunes.

Hunt.   You are gracious.
  K. Hen. Perkin, we are inform'd, is arm'd to die;
In that we'll honour him. Our lords shall follow
To see the execution; and from hence
We gather this fit use,—that public states,
As our particular bodies, taste most good
In health when purgèd of corrupted blood.   *Exeunt.*

EPILOGUE.

HERE has appear'd, though in a several fashion,
The threats of majesty, the strength of passion,
Hopes of an empire, change of fortunes; all
What can to theatres of greatness fall,
Proving their weak foundations. Who will please,
Amongst such several sights, to censure these—
No births abortive, nor a bastard brood,
Shame to a parentage or fosterhood,—
May warrant by their loves all just excuses,
And often find a welcome to the Muses.

King Iohn

AND

MATILDA,

A

TRAGEDY.

As it was Acted with great Applause
by her *Majesties* Servants at the
Cock-pit in *Drury-lane*.

Written
by ROBERT DAVENPORT Gent.

LONDON,
Printed for *Andrew Pennycuicke*, in
the Year 1655.

To the Knowing Reader

A good reader helps to make a book: a bad injures it. The author of this had no mind to be a man in print; nor took he any care for a sculpture to illustrate the frontispiece by crowning himself with laurel. Neither did he write his own encomiums, and (to prejudicate the simple) say his friends forced them upon him; they may help to sell the book, not better the matter. And since this tragedy is come to tell its own tale, and to speak for itself, he will be glad to know it able to carry its own commendation, and (being an infant, newly delivered to the world from the womb of the press) he hopes the knowing reader will rather crown it by his candour than kill it in the cradle.

R. D.

To the Right Honourable *Montague Berty, Earl of Lindsey, Lord Willoughby of Eresby &c.*

You are no stranger to things of this nature, and therefore the dedication will not startle you; such there are (my lord) whose soules are confined to their chink, and these look squint-eyed upon a dedication, because they fear there is a spirit in it will separate them. But, my lord, your nobleness to learning and wit raiseth your estimate to so high an account among knowing men that from thence I have derived this boldness, which I hope is pardonable not only for that your justice calls upon me for a duty I long since owed your honour, but also in regard the thing presented is no sleight piece but such (my lord) as I presume will accord with your judgement and liking. It passed the stage with general applause (myself being the last that acted Matilda in it) and since, through the absurdity of times, it hath lain obscured. My lord, though it doth not appear in its ancient and full glory, yet it comes dressed; first, with an humble regard to your honour, and then a confidence of its naked worth, but both it and myself are willingly subjected unto your honour's sentence, which I hope will not be too heavy, especially upon

My Lord,
Your honour's
Honourer,
Andrew Pennycuicke

The names of the persons in the play, and of the actors that
first acted it on the stage, and often before their Majesties.

KING JOHN	Mr. Bowyer
FITZWATER	Mr. Perkins, whose action gave grace to the play.
OLD LORD BRUCE.	Mr. Turner.
YOUNG BRUCE	Mr. Sumner
CHESTER	Mr. Jackson
OXFORD	Mr. Goat
LEICESTER	Mr. Young
HUBERT	Mr. Clarke
PANDULPH	Mr. Allen
BRAND	Mr. Shirelock, who performed excellently well.

Other lords and gentlemen, attendants on the king.

Queen Isabel
Matilda
Ladies of honour
Lady Abbess.

KING JOHN AND MATILDA

ACTUS I. SCŒNA I

[I. i. *King John's Palace: the Garden.*]

Enter King, Queen, and Oxford.

King. They will not come?

Ox. They will not.

King. They had been better—
What was their answer?

Ox. Thus said Fitzwater, father of the faction,
That was general for the barons against your majesty:
Tell John—

King. John!

Ox. That was his epithet,
Alleging how you stood at Rome, put from
Your kingly office. Tell John, quoth he, and frown'd,
That here at Baynard's Castle we intend
A settled stay for private reformations
Of conceiv'd injuries, which by the peace
The King made with us, were not throughly search'd,
But like green wounds, clos'd with too swift a salve.
Upon your private ends are with more danger
Doubts and distracted difficulties again
Broke forth; but having drawn them to a head,
They would send them to you to be ratified,
And then give you their attendance.

King. This is grave;
Who was there else?

Ox. Richmond, imperious Leicester, and old Bruce,
(The second in this revolt), who sent the same return.

King. A nest of rebels; to try the truth of these fine
flourishes,
You with Lord Mowbray, post unto Guildford,
And being there, pretending a visit unto Bruce's Lady,

Wind into observation of the castle; so from her,
The engine upon which these factions move,
Discover the intent of their designs.

    Queen. Sure, sir, the lady is noble; but your majesty's
Injunction shall be obey'd.   *Exit. Enter Chester.*

    King. This not only advantages
Our meeting with Fitzwater's daughter,
(O how the thought startles my blood)
But likewise furthers our resolv'd proceedings;
Chester: the news?

    Chest. Conceal yourself sir,
I have trapp'd her with a snare.

    King. Again, then shall I see her— *Exit. Enter Matilda*

    Mat. You told me, Chester,
That the queen did earnestly request my attendance:
You said she was here i'th' garden,
But it seems you were misinform'd.

    Ches. Excellent innocence: how thou art trapp'd!
I must attend the king; please you walk, madam,
But towards the grove; I was told the queen and ladies
Retired there for shade.

    Mat. I shall.

    Ches. And I must vanish.   *Exit Chester. Enter King.*

    Mat. Oh heaven, the King!

    King. Thy friend.

    Mat. False Chester!

    King. Fair Matilda,
Mistress of youth and beauty, sweet as a spring,
And comely as the holy shining priest
Deck'd in his glorious sacerdotal vestment;
Yet hear the passions of a lovesick prince,
And crown thy too, too cruel heart with pity.

    Mat. Yet let fall your too, too passionate pleadings,
And crown your royal heart with excellent reason.

    King. Hear me.

    Mat. The queen will hear you.

    King. Speak but a word that—

    Mat. What?

King. That may sound like something,
That may but busy my strong labouring heart
With hope that thou wilt grant, and every morning
I will walk forth and watch the early lark,
And at her sweetest note I will protest
Matilda spoke a word was like that note.

Mat. Oh how you tempt: remember, pray, your vows
To my betroth'd, Earl Robert Huntington;
Did you not wish, just as the poison touch'd
His manly heart, if ever you again
Laid battery to the fair foot of my unvanquish'd
Virtue, your death might be like his untimely,
And be poison'd? O take heed, sir,
Saints stand upon heaven's silver battlements
When kings make vows, and lay their
Listening ears to princes' protestation.

King. So did Matilda swear to live and die a maid,
At which fair nature like a snail shrunk back,
As loath to hear from one so fair so foul
A wound: my vow was vain, made without
Recollection of my reason; and yours, oh, madness!
Maids have sure foresworn such vows.
For Huntington, he like a heap of summer's
Dust into his grave is swept; and bad vows
Still are better broke than kept.

Mat. Alas, great sir, your queen you cannot make me;
What is it then instructs your tongue? Oh sir!
In things not right,
Lust is but love's well-languag'd hypocrite.

King. Words shall convert to deeds then; I am the king.

Mat. Do but touch me,
And as I grasp steel in my trembling hand,
                              Offers violence, she draws a knife.
So sure the king shall see Matilda fall
A sacrifice to virtue.

King. Cruel maid,
Crueller than the kid that eans her young
On the rough bosom of a ragged flint:

Go get thee to the woods, for thou art wild
As flame or winter; wheresoe'er thou walk'st
May wild winds chide thee, and the reeling trees,
Like a confus'd fall of many waters,
Rail on thy rudeness; may the birds that build
Among the wanton branches, 'stead of teaching
Notes to their young, sing something like thy niceness:
And lastly, may the brooks, when thou shalt lie
And cast a pair of cruel busy eyes
Upon their subtle slidings, may the water
The troubled image of my passions war
With the stones, the matter of thy heart, that thou may'st learn
Thy hardness and my sufferings to discern;
And so whilst I (if it be possible) study to forget you,
May beasts, and birds, and brooks, and trees, and wind
Hear me, and call Matilda too unkind.   *Exit.*

Mat. I'll unto Baynard's Castle to my father;
Oh, she had a violent need of castles, where a king
Lays such violent siege; but, O truth,
Thou art whilst tenant in a noble breast,
A crown of crystal in an ivory chest.   *Exit.*

Enter King and Chester.

King. Shall I be dazzl'd with effeminate darings?
Ches. With a woman's word, a knife too.
King. Have I left her.
Ches. But here she is not now, sir.
King. Oh Chester, run, run as thou lov'st my peace,
Feather thy feet with lovers' wishes; let but my desires
Dwell in thy eyes, thou'lt find her, were she compass'd
With a Cimmerian mist.
Ches. I will do my best, sir.   *Exit.*
King. Thy best; do everything, do anything,
Do all things that may find her. Whither, love,
Leads thy dark labyrinth? Cannot kings be free
From thy impetuous buffets? I have desir'd
A hard'ned heart, obdurate to thy shafts,

And sometimes am so, when, in the very minute,
Calling to mind Matilda's tears, like drops
Continued upon marble, they pierce through,
And I am lost again. Hast found her?   *Ent. Chester.*

   Ches. No sir, she is by this in Baynard's Castle,
Where her father and the lords—

   King. Command our barge, we'll after her like lightning:
We must have pledges, Chester, for their faiths; if they
     refuse,
Thunder shall meet with thunder, and each eye
Shall see strange comets in this troubled sky.   *Exeunt.*

[I. ii. *London: Baynard's Castle.*]

*Enter Fitzwater, Old Bruce, Young Bruce, Richmond and
Leicester, as in Baynard's Castle.*

   Fitz. My noble lords and honourable friends,
Not to particularize (what need plain dealing
Be apparelled in particulars?) to a short supper,
Or a poor pittance rather, ye are all
Heartily welcome, very heartily; I must tell truth still.

   Old Bruce. Brother, we thank you.

   Fitz. I would we had my sister, your wife at Guildford,
     with us.

   Rich. Where are the ladies?

   Leic. Comforting Matilda, sad return'd from court.

   Young Bruce. Betray'd by Chester, and again escap'd
Like a chaste dove out of the fowler's net,
The lustful king.

   Fitz. Oh John, John, wilt thou never
Leave thy wag's tricks? But let it pass, 'tis best
Because indeed 'tis past.

   Leic. I wonder how he receiv'd our resolv'd answer.

   Young Bruce. No matter how, he's like to have no
     other;
Now by my blood, you vext my very soul
That you sent any.

Old Bruce. Son, have a tamer spirit.

Young Bruce. Yes, and like horses,
Be held by th' nose by frivolous respect,
Whilst he casts copperas into our sores, and searches
Past honour's patience.

Fitz. Nephew, nephew, hear me
Let's bear a little; 'faith, he is the king,
And though at Rome he does stand interdicted,
Yet now and then takes a good start or two
Towards regularity, till the fit comes on him;
And for your neat horse simile, observe me;
Richmond and you are young men, we three old,
But not too old to tell truth; the horse that will not
Stand still and endure searching, howe'er in summer
With warmth and pasture he may strike at flies,
And play the wanton in a wealthy meadow
For all his summer pastime, yet 'tis said
Winter will leave him but a lean scal'd jade;
Come, come, y'are fools, y'are fools.

Leic. Well, let us—bear then.

Young Bruce. Let us? Oh my blood!
Besides, our injuries in his breach of promise,
He made by stains and public grievances,
How in the flames of his adulterate heart
Pursues he my chaste cousin, by sleights gets her
Within his talon, and but this afternoon,
Had not her friendly knife enfranchis'd her,
Even in the face of heaven, in his own garden
He would have ravish'd her.

Old Bruce. Brother, we are bound in honour not to bear
    it.

Leic. Let him know our griefs, and if—

Fitz. Well, well, with 'ifs' and 'ands'
Mad men leave rocks, and leap into the sands;
But something shall be thought on.   *Ent. Richmond.*

Rich. The king, attended
Only with the Earl of Chester, Oxford, and some
Other gentlemen, is new landed on the stairs.

All. The king!

Young Bruce. Shut the stairs' gate.

Fitz. 'Twere better gate and stairs

Were floating through the bridge; we are safe, my choleric
    cousin,

As in a sanctuary; 'tis enough,

A man would think, to see a great prince thus,

'Cause we'd not go to him, to come to us;   *Ent. King,*

Indeed, indeed, you speak unkindly.   *Oxford, Chester,*

    King. Behold great lords,   *and other lords.*

The cedars of the kingdom, how the king

(A shrub) shrinks out of majesty,

And comes to you; here's a fine conventicle!

Are ye blowing up new fires? and must Fitzwater,

Plain-breasted as his unaffected habit,

Be general again, again be call'd

The marshal of heaven's army and the Church's?

Are you planet-struck? You cannot talk.

    Fitz. Your pardon, sir;

I led the barons, but 'twas when they could not
    choose

But choose a leader, and then me they chose;

And why so, think ye? they all lov'd your Grace,

And grieve, grieve very heartily, I tell you,

To see you by some state mice so misled:

These state mice that nibble so upon the land's impaired
    freedom,

That would not so play in the lion's ear,

But that by tickling him themselves to advantage;

This troubl'd us, and griev'd the body politic,

And this we sought to mend; I tell truth, John, I,

We are thy friends John, and if ye take from friendship

The liberty of modest admonition,

Ye leave no mark whereby to distinguish it

From the fawning passion of a dog-base flattery;

If I speak plain, this truth be my defence

A good man's comfort is his conscience:

And so much for plain Robin.

King. Fitzwater,   Bruce,   Richmond,   and   stubborn
    Leicester,
This is the last of our admonitions,
Either lay by those arms, those lawless arms,
Which you have lifted 'gainst your lord the king,
And give such pledges as we shall accept
For settling of your loyalties, or here
By the abused suffering of a king,
And by the unkind scars with which you have
Deform'd the face of England, misery
Shall overtake you in a shape shall fright
The iron heart of faction, and the king
Shall come, no more acquainted with compassion,
But call the bloodiest ends a righteous vengeance.

Leic. I will not leave mine arms,
Nor break my word to you,
Unless provok'd, and justly; you have my faith,
If you mislike that pledge—

King. We do.

Leic. And I reply that I can spare no other.

Ches. D'ye hear, sir?

Old Bruce. Already we have pawn'd the now scorn'd
    gage
Of our afflicted honours, which, refus'd,
Flies back again, and so we stand discharg'd.

Fitz. King John, King John,
Perform but the seal'd covenants you are fled from,
The Charter running thus, given by our hand
The seventeenth day of June, and in the year
1215, the whole realm being sworn to't,
And six and twenty peers and barons sworn
To the execution, who, if you fail, are perjur'd;
Do this, and like a plait of osier wands
We shall bow any way, and you shall work us
Into what fashion you shall fancy; but
If you be melancholy, love-sick John,
Or lion, unyok'd heifer, head-strong John,
As in the matter of the loss of Normandy,

When Anjou, Bretagne, Maine, Poitou, and Touraine
Were deliver'd up to Philip, you'll find your friends
Not facile willows, but abrupt brambles,
Whose intricate irregularity
Whilst you shall go about to rectify,
They'll prick your fingers, and with unkind scratches
Expose you to a late deplor'd experience:
Come, come, know this, when love in our side sings,
The unkindest wounds are those we take from kings;
I am plain Robin.

   King. A downright rebel.

   Fitz. Rebel!

   King. So are ye all.

   All. Rebels!

   King. Traitors.

   All. Traitors!

   King. Rebels and traitors. Chester, Oxford, gentlemen,
Stand on your guards; there's danger in the room.

   Old Bruce. You are too passionate; perform with us,
You shall walk over us; if not, we stand
Our injur'd country's justicers.

   King. Proud boaster.
This night shall raise a storm. Brav'd? With you, Bruce,
We will begin; and yet he is the brother   *Aside.*
Unto Matilda's father, but his insolence—
Oh love, a little while let revenge reign.
This night shall beget passages shall prove
Your king a lion, vext; as, pleas'd, a dove.   *Exit*

   Ox. Lights for the king there, gentlemen. *King's party.*

   Young Bruce. What will you do? a tempest curl'd his
     forehead
Into the fashion of an angry ocean
Made wild with winds.

   Rich. We must resolve on something.

   Old Bruce. And suddenly, for in his executions
He is swift as lightning; air is not more light.

   Leic. Pandulph, the Pope's stern legate, 'tis divulg'd,
Is again come over from the Pope to proffer

The king his readmission into the Church,
And take off his six years' interdiction
Upon some propositions yet conceal'd,
And this may busy the king yet.

    Young Bruce. This? The greyhound
Is not more eager at his flying game
Than I know King John is in his passions
Of love or anger.

    Old Bruce. Why, brother, is this a time to study?

    Fitz. Troth, I was thinking of—stay, stay, I have't,
I was thinking, brother Bruce,—now 'tis gone again,
And farewell it; let's ply our business now.
If you mark'd, he said he would begin with you;
I would have you tonight stay not for the sun,
Which sure will rise blushing at this night's brawling:
Do you and Richmond, with some score of men,
Post to your house—'tis but an hour's riding,
And something more—there fortify yourselves,
Your lady, and your pretty little son:
Poor knave, he dreams not of these thunderbolts.
You, my young madcap, with your coz my daughter,
Shall unto Hertford Castle: she is the brand
I fear will fire our Troy. Leicester and I
Will gather powers, and thither after you;
You two for Guildford, you two for Hertford,
And we two, whither was't we two must go?

    Leic. Go? we two must stay i'th' city.

    Fitz. Passion of me, where was my memory?
But come, come, when kings our dials retrograde do run,
We leave to look on them, and go by th' sun:
Lights, lights, good gentlemen.   *Exeunt.*

[I. iii. *Guildford Castle.*]

      Enter Queen, Lady Bruce, and Hubert.

    Queen. Good lady, take not on so; Oxford says all
Is very well at London.

Lady Bruce. Yes, very well;
Why then follow'd he your grace with a troop of horse,
A band of men? Why hath he seiz'd the castle,
Cashier'd my servants? Oh madame, can it be,
Your grace, the altar where I ever paid
A subject's devout love, should by a sleight,
A feign'd accidental visit, make
An entrance for hostility and terror?

Queen. Hubert, redeem you now this lady's faith,
And relate the truth.

Hub. Only, upon mine honour,
Was I sent to seize this lady's young son, George,
As a pledge to th' king for her lord's loyalty.

Lady Bruce. No, Hubert, my son is far enough from thee,
Thou fatal keeper of poor boys.

Hub. You mean
Concerning Arthur, the unfortunate son
Of Geoffrey Plantagenet; oh, mad rumour!
Who would trust thee but with so much reputation
An honest beggar boasts of?

Queen. In that, believe me, madame, report hath wronged him,
Which I can witness, lady.

Lady Bruce. The king come, too;   *Enter King and*
                          Chester.
Oh my sweet George, my joy; what wilt thou do?

King. All is to our desire; where's Bruce's son?

Hub. Convey'd to Wales, she affirms, sir.

Lady Bruce. Where thou shalt never see him, John.

King. Good Madam,
We'll speak with you anon. Queen Isabel,
Thou must be still an agent to secure
Me and my kingdom; straight with the Earl of Chester
Post thou to Hertford Castle, whither we are certified
Young Bruce is fled with old Fitzwater's daughter.
Try if by fair means thou canst win her to
Attend on thee at court; if we have not her
A pledge, as this, for her father's faith, we stand

The food of faction; get her any way.
If she deny, Chester with forces ready
Off from the castle, shall give them fierce assault,
And force them past entreaties; go, my love,
And play the Amazon; with her surprisal
Secure a kingdom.

    Queen. This craves haste and care; come, noble Chester,
You shall along; but, good my lord, forget not
That lady's kindness to me.

    King. Oh my sweet.   *Kiss. Exit.*

    Hub. What a fine thing he makes the queen; oh lust,
With what smooth craft thou creep'st to things unjust!

    King. Oh my Matilda, if power or policy
May get thee once more in these arms, I will hazard
Even to a kingdom for thee; come, madame, fear not;
I wear no frowns, I am all mirth; let's see your pretty
    son.

    Lady Bruce. I fear your mirth is like the porpoise' pas-
    times;
My son hath been in Wales this month.

    King. Hubert, see the gates lock'd, a guard upon the walls,
Whilst we take some to search.

    Lady Bruce. Where will you search, King John?
For heaven's sake, do not search.

    Hub. Nay, and 't be come to that.   *Exit.*

    King. Let me go,
In these proceedings the king's safety rests,
The lion must not bend to baser beasts.   *Exit.*

    Lady Bruce. Heaven, to thee I kneel, who affrighted
    mother am,
Oh from this lion's claws keep my poor lamb.   *Exit.*

[I. iv. *Outside Guildford Castle.*]

    Enter Old Bruce and Richmond, and, above, Oxford.

    Old Bruce. The castle gates are shut; swift-footed tyranny,
That canst when thou pursu'st thy wild desires,
Outrun the wanton roe; oh Richmond, Richmond,

[II. ii. *Before Hertford Castle.*]

Enter soldiers, and Young Bruce prisoner.

Ches. You are mine, sir.

Young Bruce. 'Tis false; I am fortune's.

Ches. This day to fortune then I sacrifice,
As to my mistress.

Young Bruce. A whore is then your mistress.

Ches. A whore!

Young Bruce. A rascal jade,
That takes with the dexterity she gives; tell me
Of your mistress and the devil. O, my stars!

Ches. O, sir, we have ways to tame you; you re-
member
You brav'd me in the presence of the king
At Baynard's Castle.

Young Bruce. Oh I am mad,
Yet not so mad, but I dare still, brave Chester,
And from the top of my affliction
Upon thy light-heel'd miss, wanton fortune,
Cast from the manly temper of my blood
A noble scorn.

Ches. You shall be fetter'd first.

Young Bruce. Fetter'd!

Ches. Yes, and sent
Up to the king as an arch rebel, to whom
Before we have by letters sent our happy fortune.

Young Bruce. Rebel!
By that boiling sea of blood which thou hast troubl'd,
Had my desires but bodies, I would burst
Fetters of steel, tear off thy canker'd flesh,
And with thy jaw-bone, thou honour-wounding man,
I would kill a thousand of these rascals.

Ches. Drag him
Into the castle; since your fortunes move you,
We'll force you to a madness.

Young Bruce. Fool, thou canst not;

Frost makes fire fervent; he that wisely knows
His wealthy fate, bravely becomes his woes.   *Charge.*
    Ches. Are you so arm'd? Away with him.   *Exit.*

[II. iii. *Hertford Castle.*]

*Enter the Queen, dragging in Matilda, her hair loose
and face bloody.*

    Queen. Come forward, fury, witch.
    Mat. Alas, why thus,
Great queen, do you misuse me? Credit me,
I do not fear to die; young infants do it:
Nor wish I life; the murderer enjoys it;
But let me know my trespass.
    Queen. I'm made your stale,
The king, the king, you strumpet; oh thou wretch,
The matter of my spleen!   *Tears her.*
    Mat. Hear me but speak.
    Queen. Yes I will hear thee speak,
That every syllable may serve instead
Of a fierce wind to blow my fiercer fury
Into the fashion of a punishment
Fitting the daring of thy trespass.
    Mat. Hear me:
By these red marks, registers of your rashness,
And by these tears, the fruits of my affliction,
That the king passionately pursues my love
Is truth uncontradicted; but if I
Did ever think you wrong, let mine honour be
Buried in dark oblivion.
    Queen. Sin's a sweet tame serpent; they must beguile
That clothe rude errors in a soft smooth style:
But, strumpet, thou shalt rue't.   *Charge. Enter Chester.*
    Ches. Shift for yourself, madame;
Richmond, escap'd from London with the powers
Levied by Leicester, and Fitzwater, who
Were stay'd by Winchester and the legate Pandulph,

Hath rescued Bruce, got again the castle, *Enter Young*
And make you now their search. *Exit. Bruce and Rich-*
  Rich. Seize on the queen; *mond with soldiers.*
Madame, you are our prisoner.
  Young Bruce. Keep Chester safe, good Richmond;
Ha! oh, what rude hand
Hath ras'd this book of beauty? a face where virtue
Intelligibly stood to charm the reader! Tell me, cousin,
And by the thousands of thy tears and fears,
No tittle, place, degree, the very grave
Shall not secure the offender.
  Queen. There is death in's angry eyes. *Aside.*
  Mat. The rude soldiers,
My noble cousin, hal'd me thus and tore me,
And would have sure done worse, but that the queen,
The wondrous kind queen in her royal person,
Came with a troop of well-appointed soldiers,
And rescued me.
  Queen. She mocks me, sure.
  Young Bruce. The queen so kind?
  Mat. O cousin, had you seen.
How good she was in her quick speed, how zealous
To relieve innocence, you would have thought
She'd kill'd them with her frowns e'er she came at them,
So lamentably miserable were my sufferings,
So excellently noble was her charity.
  Young Bruce. Now, by my life, 'twas honour in the
  highest
Because a foe, and, gracious madame, not
To be outbid in this brave mart of honour,
You shall have a safe convoy and of quality
Fitting your person, to convey with your freedom
To th' angry king our loves, that he may see
How plain to him we mean, and how nobly
Unto a goodness of so fair deservings
As this now shown; see there be present order
For her majesty's attendance, and, sweet coz,
Withdraw from the cold air. *Exit.*

Queen. Farewell, Matilda;
Oh, pardon me for heaven's sake; now I find
Thy soul is crystal.

Mat. Remember to the king,
Good madame, my great sorrows; and forget not
To tell him this, that woman in whose heart
Virtue and honour stand a pair of sentinels,
The sea may sooner flame, fire admit frost,
Ere such a woman fall from heaven. Oh she,
Who as a regular star keeps virtue's sphere,
Shows like a pearl hung in an angel's ear.

Queen. Thou noble soul of goodness.   *Exit.*

[II. iv. *King John's Palace.*]

A chair of state discover'd, tables and chairs responsible, a
guard making a lane. Enter between them King John, Pan-
dulph the Pope's legate, Oxford, and members of the king's
party. After them, Fitzwater, Leicester, and Bruce. The king,
holding the crown, kneeling on the left side of the chair,
Pandulph possessing it.[1]

King. Lo, in the sight of prelates, peers,
Of earth and heaven, of all that hear
My words, I, John Plantagenet,
With all submissive reverence, set
My crown at the most sacred foot
Of Innocent the Third; unto't
I join my kingdom, give them free
Unto his pious clemency:
And for the follies of my reign,
Heats of my youth, and the rough strain
Of riper years, my rebellions, my high hand,
My six year's interdiction, and

---

[1] The stage directions of the 1655 edition of the play include
Chester and Richmond among those present. As they are elsewhere, the directions have been amended accordingly.

All my misdoings, I this, and those,
Submit to the pope's power to disclose.

Pan. You have by times retracted, and your foot now
Beats out a certain path; in these lords' sights I do
Produce the letter drawn obligatory
From John of England to his Holiness;
Peruse it, sir: you are there oblig'd to pay,
As yearly from this day renting your kingdom,
To Innocent the Third, and to his successors,
A thousand marks per annum.

King. It runs so.

Pan. Yes, three hundred for Ireland, and seven for
England.

Fitz. Do not peruse it, John; though thou and we
Have had some bickerings, yet let me counsel thee,
This is my country's cause.

Pan. You and your country
Have cause in this cause to rejoice.

Fitz. Good, good Sir Pandulph,
Though in our filial love to our mother church,
By his Holiness' command, we stay'd from Hertford,
Yet let's have fair play; do not wrong that mother,
Apparelling her comely holy face
With a forehead full of frowns, plaited proceedings.

Pan. You rail.

Fitz. I do not rail;
Although I hold in reverence the chair
(We had been at Hertford else, and not at London),
Yet in a true breast we should nothing see
But holy, pure, unmix'd simplicity.

King. Give me the pen.

Leic. Will you then sign?

King. Yes, you rough sons of faction,
And hook your stubborn nostrils; this is rhubarb
To your smooth palates: give me the pen to write.

Fitz. Do not write, John.

King. Do not prate, fool.

Fitz. In sooth that write

Will wrong thee; children and fools tell truth:
Remember that.

Pan. There was no way like this
To beat a path out to your peace.

King. Right reverend   *Pandulph offers to descend.*
And holy sir, receive to the pope's use
His will and your own charge. Sir, descend not,
But ere you re-invest me, hear me tell
A tale of sorrow; behold here these lords,
Who had been now bruising the face of peace
With unkind buffets, but for Winchester,
Your strict compulsion, and their seeming fear
Of deserv'd interdiction; but, oh sprite,
No devil deceives like th' household hypocrite,
These of my court, with young Bruce now insconc'd
At Hertford, whither, it may be, hair-brain'd Richmond
Hath retir'd his discontents.

Old Bruce. We miss our hopes else.

King. These bandy faction with me, and with their
    drums,
Lewd linguists to interpret their disloyalties,
Brave me i'th' field, deform th' afflicted face
Of trembling England with foul bloody stains,
'Larums at hideous midnight; they break my sleeps,
Fill them with fearful dreams, terrible startings,
And with the grief of my unfriendly fears
Force me to pierce my pillow with my tears.

Pan. Unnatural cruelty,
Able to melt marble into compassionate tears.

Ox. Dainty dissembler.

Old Bruce. Now may it please you—

Pan. Peace, until his Holiness' command be finished;
Ascend your now true seat, sir, and from the hand   *Pan-*
Of myself, Pandulph, legate for the Pope,   *dulph gives John*
Observing the due payments specified,   *the chair.*
Receive your crown and kingdoms; and with them
We here pronounce your absolute readmission
Into the Church, and from his Holiness

We re-invest you with all powers, prerogatives,
Freedoms, communities, and in the strength of efficacy
That constantly adheres to lawful princes,
And an obedient son unto the Church;
Long life to John of England, Wales and Ireland,
The lawful king! *Flourish.*

    Leic. I am mad.

    Fitz. So, so, now we must suffer
The kingdom's ancient liberties, land, lives,
And all to run the course that he shall steer;
Good heaven that I were dead, what do I hear. *Weeps.*

    Old Bruce. But I'll not, ass-like, bear my country's
        wrongs,
Mine own at home, and like a court chameleon,
Give thanks unto mine injurer; hear me, King John.

    King. You shall hear us, sir, first; we have been
        clouded
Six years, but like the sun in his meridian,
We now again are glorious; thus in brief,
Leicester, we require strong pledge for your loyalty;
Bruce, call your mad son home from Hertford:
Your wife and son shall better speed at Guildford;
For Richmond, in our re-assumed power
We will proclaim him traitor; and Fitzwater,
Either give up Matilda for your faith, or hear
What we shall sentence.

    Leic. We must stand then
What thunder you shall throw; perform with us,
We kiss your royal hands.

    Old Bruce. If not, we stand
Rocks in our resolution.

    King. D'ye hear them now, sir?

    Fitz. Nay, nay, let him hear me, too, then,
Lord legate Pandulph; thus 'tis,
And thus you may inform his Holiness;
In a field call'd Running-mead 'twixt Staines and Windsor,
After some bloody noses on both sides,
I tell truth, I; there the king and barons

Met for discussion of conceiv'd wrongs
And indeed not misconceiv'd; our houses, honours,
Our fathers' freedoms, the land's ancient liberties,
Unjustly to increase some private coffers,
Felt daily diminution; there to covenants drawn,
Bearing the name and scuse of Magna Carta,
Which many hundred years may be seen hereafter,
King John subscrib'd, we swore him fealty.

   King. Which fealty they denied till our assoilment
Of our six years' interdiction, forcing us therefore
To seal unlawful liberties.

   Leic. Upon our honours,
They were but what antiquity prov'd lawful.

   Ox. Oh, but my lord—

   Fitz. Tut, tut, lord me no lords;
He broke, we parted—I tell plain truth I—
Yet fell into no relapse of hostility;
But wot ye what, he casts a covetous eye
Upon my daughter, passionately pursues her;
There had been no other pledges but our oaths else,
For heaven knows them he had, and, amongst the rest,
Matilda must be my pledge, for well be deem'd
They yielding theirs, shame would brand my denial.
But catch craft, when we put truth to trial;
Kings should have shining souls, and white desires
Inflamed with zeal, not parch'd by Paphian fires;
So shines the soul in which virtue doth shroud,
As a serene sky bespotted with no cloud,
But a copper conscience, whilst the head wears gold,
Is but a plain downright untruth well told;
Come, come, I cannot fawn.

   King. But in the passion
Of a dog, sir, you can snarl; have you bark'd all your
    words?

   Fitz. I have told truth, I.

   King. Then we will fall to deeds;
Oxford, command a guard, and presently
Take them to th' Tower; we can now talk and do.

Away with them, and muzzle those fierce mastiffs
That durst leap at the face of majesty,
And strike their killing fangs into honour's heart;
Are they not gone? We shall be passionate
In your delay.

    Old Bruce. Come, Leicester, let us wear
Our sufferings like a garland.

    Leic. Tempest nor death
Could never outdo Leicester, who dares die
Laughing at time's poison'd integrity.

    Fitz. Now, by my troth, 'twas very nobly spoken.
Shall I turn tail? No, no, no, let's go;
But how things will be carried; ha! are these tears?
Body of me, they are! Shall I go like a sheep
With this pair of lions? Ha, ha, ha!
I do laugh now, John, and I'll tell thee why;
Th'art yet in thy green May, twenty-seven summers
Set in our kalends, but when forty winters more
Shall round thy forehead with a field of snow,
And when thy comely veins shall cease to flow,
When those majestic eyes shall float in rheums,
When giant nature her own self consumes,
When thy swift pulses shall but slowly pant,
When thou art all a volume of my want,
That like a tale-spent fire thou shalt sink,
Then, John, upon this lesson thou wilt think:
He dies a happy old man whose sweet youth
Was a continued sacrifice to truth;
I must weep now indeed.

    King. Away with them.   *Exit.*

    Pan. Unto King John, the favour of his Holiness,
With peace and happiness.   *Exit.*

    King. Which we return
With all filial obedience—look up, Oxford,
The day breaks, and the sun shall chase the night
Out of our hemisphere.   *Enter a gentleman.*

    Ox. Your news, sir?

    Gen. Letters from the queen, sir.

King. Was the Earl Richmond there with any powers
Ere your departure?   *King reads.*
   Gen. No, may it please your majesty, we heard not of him,
But all on your part went fair and fortunate.
   King. Oh Oxford, now they have her; fly back like
      lightning:
Tell him this day we'll meet them all at Barnet. *Exit gentle-*
   Ox. But her father's and her friends' imprisonment *man.*
May obdurate her heart; they dare not, sure,
On the great peril of a curse, to fall
Into a relapse now you are absolute.
Faith, sir, try smooth paths to your ends; to release them
I hold the winning'st way to captivate
Their duties and Matilda to your wishes.
   King. Good; do not kill me, joy, before our going.
Instantly thou shalt fly with the lords' release.
We pine in our delays; O Cupid, swiftly
Fly into Paphos, and from thy mother's shrine
Catch but a nimble wanton flame, and cast it
Into the busy kingdom of my heart,
That it may teach my tongue the art of victory,
And every year unto thy well-spent quiver
I'll add a shaft, and call it Cupid's love dart;
Come, Oxford, I tread methinks on air,
Until I read that volume of sweet grace,
The well-writ story of Matilda's face.
   Ox. She yields at last, my life on't, sir.   *Exit.*

ACTUS III. SCŒNA I

[III. i. *Windsor Castle.*]

Enter Brand reading of a letter.

*Will Brand, these are to certify, that fortune, mistress of
changes, with my unlucky stars, hath rendered me a prisoner
to my most mortal enemy, young Bruce.*

Brand. That mad Tamburlaine!
My entreaty is none of the noblest, but direct against my blood,
my desires, and my deservings.

Brand. Oh that I had a leg of that young Bruce, but
minc'd and butter'd.
I am credibly possess'd, his majesty hath into your custody
committed his mother and her young son, George, whereby you
have occasion cast into your hand to parallel their sufferings
with my fortunes; not that I would have you banish humanity.

Brand. He need never have writ that. Bawds and serjeants
have sav'd me the labour.
Nor give too deep a wound to conscience.

Brand. Another labour sav'd too,
Usurers do it daily.
But as I let you understand how I am here accommodated, so
shape the duty of a servant to parallel in their persons your
vilified Mr. Ralph Chester.

Brand. Brave lord, the ladder of my fortunes, shalt thou
suffer on that side, and for humanity's sake, and thread-bare
conscience (a couple of cousin-germans, that thrice a week
know not where to get a supper); shall the friends of him
that stands lord of thy fortunes, and thy profess'd foe, fare
well here? Now I talk of fare; I receiv'd this letter yesterday,
and since they have neither eaten bite, nor drunk drop; nor
by these ten stealers shall not, till I hear again from my
lord. . . . Come out madame mother, and your young prating
brat. . . . They do look hungry already. *Enter lady and boy.*

Lady Bruce. What would our unkind jailor?

Boy. Sure, mother, Mr. Brand hath brought us victuals.

Brand. No, sirrah, I come to tell you today is fasting day.

Lady Bruce. Two days together,
Good Mr. Brand, 'tis not mine own want begs,
But my poor boy's; I have held him pretty pastime
To have him yet forget that wild wolf hunger,
And still the harmless soul would point each period
Of his sport, crying, 'Mother, give me bread'.

Brand. She has a winning way,
Her carriage and her person are both exquisite;

Faith, tell me, madame, what would you give for some vic-
    tuals
To give your son?
    Lady Bruce. Anything; set thou the price, thou shalt have
    gold.
    Boy. And truly, sir, if you'll but give me a cake,
Or a capon's leg, when I am a man
I'll give you twenty shillings to buy your boy fine things.
    Brand. If you dare lie with me,
You and your son shall both have sustenance.
    Lady Bruce. Hearken, good heaven; what says the
    man?
    Boy. He would lie with you, mother;
But then when I am a-bed, too, there
Will be no room for my father.
    Brand. Be as plain and brief as I was; dare ye do't?
    Lady Bruce. No, thou bad man, I dare not.
    Brand. Nobody shall see't, by this hand.
    Lady Bruce. Thou liest, thou fiend; shouldst thou i'th'
    castle do't,
The towers would tremble and turn intelligencers
To all the passengers; the walls would shudder,
The escutcheons, streamers, banners, and all the relics
Of fame and honour would fall down, to see
Honour and fame so wounded.
    Brand. See! I am asham'd to hear you.
If such sins could not be done without being seen,
Informers would have a fine trade on't; a parator's place
Would countervail five serjeants, Ha, ha! 'Seen', quotha?
Why, there would not be sheets enough in the land
For the penitent, and innocent beadles enough to correct
    the
Guilty. Come, come, we'll do't i'th' dark then.
    Lady Bruce. In the dark; said'st thou?
Oh, in the deepest darkness the white angels
Will stare upon thee, and with flaming eyes
Will make the room appear to thy wild conscience
Twice lighter than the sun.

'Tis a foul devil that insinuates to thee
The sour sweetness of a deluded minute;
He has borrowed a white robe; pluck it off from him,
And thou wilt see him a black hideous monster;
How with a slavish look he will creep from thee,
Displeas'd that thou art fall'n again in love
With holy goodness.

    Brand. How my conscience wambles.

    Boy. Do, do, good sir; think of it.
It will make you give's some bread,
And then you'll be a very honest man.

    Brand. I have heard you.

    Lady Bruce. And with a thirsty soul, I hope.

    Brand. Yes, as usurers hear sermons more for novelty
than integrity, I love good words when I pay nothing for
'em; what do you see in me that I should appear unworthy
of your grant?

    Lady Bruce. Because in that request,
Thou appear'st to me as ugly as a toad.

    Brand. A toad!

    Boy. Ay, and a frog, too, if you go to that;
Do not cry, mother.

    Brand. Get you both in; by this victorious sword,
And by the horrid odious comparison,
For such a one first sure made comparisons odious,
Ye get not a bite these seven days.

    Lady Bruce. By that time
My boy and I shall make a pair of happy ones
In yonder glorious kingdom; tell me, George,
Shall this bad man abuse thy father's bed?
Or shall we fast yet longer?

    Brand. The boy will consent, I warrant you;
The pages have instructed him.

    Boy. Indeed, I am very hungry.

    Brand. Did I not tell you so?

    Boy. But rather than this goat shall lie in my father's
      place,
Indeed I'll fast these seven years.

Lady Bruce. Ah, noble boy,
Sweet plant of goodness, thou hast prov'd it true;
Virtue will wish the good it cannot do.

    Brand. A terribly ugly toad.   *Exeunt.*

[III. ii. *Barnet.*]

Enter King, Queen, and Oxford.

    Ox. Good sir, ye must be patient.

    King. Patient!
Bitterness dwells with me if I do not put him
To an eternal patience that shall dare
To witch me into that dull fit of fools.
Matilda won and lost!

    Queen. Good sir—

    King. Away,
Struggle not with the tempest of my blood;
That will undo thee.

    Queen. Richmond, lion-like,
After we sent our letter, with the forces
The barons had prepar'd, clouded our day
And made our fortunes his.

    Ches. They out o'th' Tower, too,
Fitzwater, Bruce, and Leicester, with fresh powers
Are not a league hence.

    King. The lion Richmond! A hare had he met with any
But field-mice, rats, runaways, and weasels,
Frighted even with the waving of a flag.
They would have call'd a scarecrow stuff'd with straw
And bound upon a ten groats Irish garron,
The glorious Richmond 'pon his fiery steed.
Oh, there is nothing certain but our sorrows;
Our borrow'd bliss is but the shuttle-cock
Of a day's pastime.

    Queen. I have pastim'd her, if tearing be a pastime.
Let that comfort you,

I have torn her almost to death.

    King. Matilda?

    Queen. Yes.

    King. And would you have it comfort me?

    Queen. I know it does; call but up your troops

Bravely again, recover her, and read

Upon her face my fury.

    King. O, ye cruel one,

Crueller than the flame that turn'd to cinders

The fair Ephesian temple; wild as a wolf.

The bear is not so bloody; tear her hairs,

Which when they took their pastime with the winds

Would charm the astonish'd gazer; tear that face,

Lovely as is the morning, in whose eyes

Stands writ the history of her heart, enticing

The ravish'd reader to run on, 'pon whose eye-lids

Discretion dwells, which when a wild thought

Would at those casements like a thief steal in,

Plays her heart's noble friend, and shuts out sin.

    Queen. O, why then, sir, if she be such a volume

Of white unvanquish'd virtue, would you stain

And blot the fair leaves with your foul desires?

Chaste, frosty bosoms brook no lust-born fires.

    King. She has put me to my sophistry.

    Queen. I knew I was made

Your stale for her obtaining.

Oh why

Raise you so high a pyramis to her praise,

And prostrate your own virtue? If she be

Such a book of goodness, with bad desires

Why do you read her? He no truth intends,

Seeks to corrupt that text which he commends.

Good sir, consider it.   *Enter Hubert.*

    King. Well, I will think on't, and you will have done.

    Hub. Now is the time, my lord,

If e'er you would be fortunate in your desires;

Richmond, young Bruce, Matilda,

With the Earl of Chester prisoner, and a slight convoy

But of some threescore horse and two hundred archers
Are now i'th' valley crossing of the county,
'Tis thought for Essex.

   King. Where are their main forces?

   Hub. Ensconc'd in Hertford Castle. Our forces yet
Not so diminish'd or in rout for want
Of their lost general, but, if you please,
We dare with hope assail them.

   King. I will be general;
Order the powers you have for present on set.

   Queen. My lord, you said you would consider.

   King. I am considering bravely how to charge
The foe just in the face. Matilda, I am now thy soldier;
Friend of my heart, the king himself comes for thee,
Who shall in this day's doings amply prove
Honour takes fire from the flame of love.

   Hub. Good fortune on our side, sir.   *Exeunt. Manet*

   Queen. Hear not that prayer,   *Queen.   A charge afar off.*
Good heaven; oh, tempt not virtue to adorn
A foul cause with fair fortunes. Hark, hark, they meet,
And now pell-mell the angry lords do lift
Unnatural swords. Good heaven, keep safe the king,
But let his cause miscarry. I will not stay
To see him so pursue those wild desires
Which cannot sure end well; I'll to the lords
So near at hand, and with Matilda's father
Accommodate my griefs, and let there be
Her fears, my tears, the king's infirmity.   *Exit.*

[III. iii. *Open country near Barnet.*]

      Enter King, Oxford, and Matilda.

   King. Oxford she,'s now the king's.

   Mat. Most miserable maid.

   King. Most excellent Matilda, all are thy friends;
Imperious love sat on my lance just then,
When on the panting breast of daring Richmond,

Who like a melancholy sullen cloud
Eclips'd thy chariot, thou didst see me point
My restless passion. Oxford, keep my happiness
Just with that care thou wouldst preserve that pair
Of precious things, thine eyes. Chester's engaged
Deep in the chase and we must fetch him on;
Pardon me, honour, that I plac'd love first;
My doings now are thine. *Exit.*

 Ox. Keep near the king, gentlemen;
His unbounded spirit may lose him else. Good madame,
Do not lament so. Though your friends are scatter'd,
Y'are in a sphere of happiness.

 Mat. Oh, that great power
That many times out of this toil hath taken me,
Deliver me again, because again
Virtue hath made me miserable. *Enter Young Bruce.*

 Young Bruce. Oh, that necessity
Should force us unto flight, base flight, repugnant
To man and honour. Ha! Happy flight now,
That brought me this way.

 Mat. Cousin!

 Young Bruce. Oxford, either give back
That pure unspotted dove from the killing talon
Of the forgetful king, or thou and I
Must never see him more.

 Ox. That to our fortunes;
I must not fail the king, sir.

 Young Bruce. I must not fail then *Enter Richmond.*
To get her as I can, sir. *Fight, Oxford falls.*

 Rich. We are scatter'd now,
Past making head again.

 Young Bruce. But I have made shift to get my coz again,
  sir.

 Rich. Let us not stay now to expostulate; necessity
Directs us to our friends, not a league distant;
If we not fly we are lost.

 Mat. Good coz, let's fly:
'Tis no disgrace to obey necessity.

Young Bruce. Oh, I could stamp and tear that hog, necessity.
Bitter necessity, thou scourge of things,
That forces lions to wear swallows' wings. *Exe. Manet Ox.*
    Ches. You have play'd the soldier, sir. *To him enter King,*
    King. The soldier, Chester! I am so light with joy *Chester,*
I could do anything.   *& others.*
    Ches. Troth, sir, would it might please you then to grace
Me with the presidentship of Picardy,
Fall'n in this last rebellion from the Lord
Bruce unto your crown.
    King.   'Tis thine as certain
As Matilda is the king's. Oh, Chester, now Matilda
Is in the king's power.
    Ox. No, sir, she is in heaven's.
    Ches. Who's this? Oxford! Let's help to raise him up.
    King. What say'st thou, man? Matilda, where is Matilda?
    Ox. Young Bruce in his flight happening upon this way
For her recovery gave me fierce assault;
I did stand for you, sir, as much as man could,
Till my misfortune found me, then I fell.
To him came Richmond, and with all speed possible
They have carried her to th' lords on t'other side the heath.
    King. Oh, villain, villain;
Suppose he had cut thy heart-strings, hadst thou cast
Thy dying eye upon Matilda's face
She would have shot another spirit into thee
More daring than the first, at least more fortunate.
    Ches. Let him be convey'd to th' town and dressed.
Our best course is now to withdraw; the lords
Are strong, and may give us dangerous chase else.
    King. What are our hopes?
Like garlands 'pon affliction's forehead worn,
Kiss'd in the morning, and at evening torn!   *Exit.*

[III. iv. *London: Baynard's Castle.*]

A table and chairs set out.

*Enter Fitzwater, Old Bruce, Young Bruce, Richmond,
and Leicester.*

Old Bruce. The day is then the king's.

Rich. White victory
Clapp'd on her silver wings, with a sullen face
Took leave of us, and pitched upon his tent,
Where she sat smiling while necessity
Enforced our flight.

Young Bruce. Oh, that witch necessity.

Fitz. Well, well, away with the witch.
'Tis well you brought Matilda off. Come, come.   *Sit to*
And brother Bruce you have a wife and son   *Council*
Unjustly detained from you. I am injur'd;
I pray you set our feet into the path
Of our proceedings.

Young Bruce. Let's with our powers
Raze Windsor walls.

Fitz. Now you are i'th' field straight,
Give old men leave; you would raze! What would you
raze?
Your reputation with your rash proceedings;
Come, come, hear your father.

Young Bruce. Why let him speak then.

Old Bruce. First let us take up our affronts in order,
And fix by ours the general's[1] grievances,
The crying groans of England, whose blubber'd cheeks
Are stiff with tears to see their privileges
Daily impair'd.

Rich. What's to be done?

Leic. Let's send to the French king,
Proffer him our assistance to transfer
The crown from John to him, if at such a day
He will put over a strong navy royal

---

[1] i.e. the people's.

With an army for the attempt, with which our
Forces making one body both at sea and land,
We bid fair for our freedoms.

    Fitz. I do not like it.

    Young Bruce. S'foot, you will like nothing;
Let us be ring'd and noos'd.

    Old Bruce. Besides, being assoil'd of his six years'
      interdiction;
Those that before fled from him as a leper
Will now flock to him.

    Rich. They begin already,
Although we seek (with our own) their good, to censure
And call hostility plain faction.

    Leic. This is my resolve; I say there is no way
To fix our freedoms but to call in Philip
And make him king.   *Exit Richmond.*

    All. So think we all.

    Fitz. Ay, but I think not so;
Though y'are all wise for Philip, he'll be a gainer,
But what will you get by 't? They run on rocks and shelves,
Can counsel others, not secure themselves.

    Young Bruce. We must and will do something.

    Fitz. You will send to Philip:
Instruct him to proceed: it may be, furnish
His navy with our pilots: he lands, we proffer
Change John for Philip; oh, can you think
That we can undergo a heavier stroke
From a natural than from a foreign stroke?
Go to, go to, who in no estate can rest,
They may change oft, but seldom comes the best.

    Old Bruce. I am diverted.

    Leic. Which way would you steer then?

    Fitz. By the same compass, but not upon this parallel;
I do not like the line, but this we'll do:
We'll send for Lewis—Philip's son, the dolphin—
And to him, seemingly, prefer the proffer.
A crown will fire him; maybe he shall land,
But with no more force than we please; and it may be

He shall take a fisher town, for every nation
Can take away their trading as the time goes.
Our main force being ready, we will hover
'Twixt John and Lewis; if John deny an oath
To redress our griefs and become regular,
And hostage for the keeping it, we join
With the French and fright him further; if he consent,
We fall on his part then, expulse Lewis,
And send him to the seas again. The dolphin
Is young and may be wrought on, but old Philip
Is dangerously politic; with foot ashore,
He'll brook no juggling: both ease and safety
We work on willows, but when we strike at oaks,
We sweat, and sometimes hurt with our own strokes.

    All. It should be thus effected.

    Leic. But let report divulge his landing
With more eminent danger than we will let him practise.

    Fitz. For this time,   *Enter Queen, Matilda, and ladies.*
Rise then. See the queen and ladies;
Good madame, cast off sadness:
Matilda, we are all here i'th' city safe;
The very hearts o' the citizens, men injur'd
In their privileges as we are, they are ours;
What should we fear then?   *Enter Richmond.*

    Mat. You are all such friends;
I am poor in my well-meaning thankfulness.

    Rich. A barge with divers youthful citizens,
Apparell'd rich like masquers, is now landed
Upon the stairs, hearing the queen was here
With all this meeting of their noble friends,
Proffer their loves and duties to conclude
And grace the evening with their revels.

    Fitz. In the hall we'll meet them. Did not I tell you
These citizens were noble lads, our friends?
Wait on the ladies, lord; I am here your grace's servant.
By my troth, I thank 'em; they will crown our feast
And credit me, having such a princely guest.   *Exeunt.*
                                   Loud Music.

[III. v. *The hall of Baynard's Castle.*]

*Enter at one door, Fitzwater, Old Bruce, Young Bruce,
Leicester, Matilda, and ladies; at the other door, the King,
Chester, Oxford, Masquers.*

A Dance.

Fitz. Now by my troth they are gallants:
Citizens, said you? Now I remember, too,
Ye do so gallant in your shops; no wonder then
If in masques you cut it. I remember, gentlemen,
Your fathers wore a kind of comely habit,
Comely, because it well became the reverend name of
    citizens,
But now let a knight walk with you in your shops—
And I commend you for't, ye keep the fashion—
We know not which is which . . . How my tongue ranges,
And night grows old: mad times must have mad changes;
Come, come, a hall, a hall!   *The masquers take the ladies,*
  Queen. Believe me you have done well.   *and fall to the*
                                    dance.
  Young Bruce. Pox o' these cats' guts, how they squeak.
Methinks a rattling sheep-skin lustily box'd
Would thunder brave amongst them.   *One of the torch-*
  Mat. I can dance no more indeed, sir.   *bearers takes*
  Fitz. I am deceiv'd if that fellow did not carry *Matilda*
A torch e'en now;
Will you shame the gentleman?
Dance when I bid you.
  Mat. Oh me, that grasp was like the kings!
  Old Bruce. Dance, coz.
  Fitz. In good deed, dance,
Or you will make me angry.   *The king pulls her violently.*
Body of me, that's too much for a torch-bearer!
You, sir Jack, sir Jack, she is no whit-leather;
She will not stretch, I assure you; if you come hither
For love, so 'tis.
  King. For love.
  Fitz. But if you and your company

Put on forgetful rudeness, pray take your Cupid yonder,
Your thing of feathers, and your barge stands ready
To bear ye all aboard the ship of fools.
I am plain Robin—passion of me!
Look if he do not threaten me! I will see thee,
Wert thou King John himself.   *Pulls off his vizard.*

All. The king!

Mat. Oh, which way shall I fly?

Queen. I would not leave so sweet a chaste companion.
         Exeunt Queen, Matilda, Richmond, and ladies. In the
         bustle Fitzwater drops one of his gloves; Hubert takes it
         up, and goes after the ladies.

Hub. What's this, one of her father's gloves?
This shall be drawn upon the lucky hand of a thriving plot.

King. Behold thy king; thine, Bruce, one of the fathers
Of these retir'd factions: Richmond, thy king;
And thine, rough Leicester. Is this still your nest
Wherein to hatch another scorpion's egg
To string the affected bosom of your country,
To bruise her sides with the earth-wounding hoofs
Of war-apparell'd horses, whose dreadful neighings
May fright her pale face to a bloody blush,
And again make her groan.

Fitz. Your pardon, sir;
By my good sword, I knew ye not.

Ches. No; if you had,
Your dangerous brother Bruce and you had laid
Some plot for his sacred person, then pleaded ignorance;
That ye took him as he seem'd, a saucy stranger.

Young Bruce. Chester, thou art not noble in thy censure,
And fawn'st thyself into the abus'd favour
Of the too credulous king.

Ches. O, temptation, what a devil art thou!
Now, by my blood, young man, you court my spleen
In a vainglorious shape. Chester fawn!
Just heaven forbid it.

Young Bruce. An axe upon your neck, the just heavens
     give you!

And that in heaven were justice—

Old Bruce. Son, y'are too full of choler.

Young Bruce. Choler? Halter!

Fitz. By the mass, that's near the choler.

King. Upon your lives, no more! The king is here.

Fitzwater, I did not come to quarrel with thee;

I would have such a good man ever near me.

And for a flourish to the rest, of whom,

As of old Bruce we have, we will require strict pledges, and,

Fitzwater, let thy daughter live at court; she shall be kept

I'th' custody of the queen, but as no pledge.

Fitz. The queen is gracious.

King. Come, to their ruins leave these turbulent lords.

Fitz. But suppose the queen should ride abroad to hunt,

And leave Matilda solitary at home,

I think the king would come and comfort her.

King. I am of thy mind; I think he would.

Fitz. Would he so?—I would have no one hear.

                                        Takes the king aside.

King. They cannot, man.

Fitz. Pray tell the king I'll keep my girl at home,

And comfort her myself.

King. You will?

Fitz. John, John, now I speak out;

You made your masque for this a masque indeed,

And well-a-day! that it should prove a cover

For such a night of tempests, such wild affections,

Such an ill-favour'd night—   *Enter Hubert.*

King. Hubert, is't done?

Hub. Past expectation; I have better'd your plot

And got the queen, too,

And will bring them early in the morning to th' court.

King. Have the torch-bearers given fire to the plot?

Hub. They mix'd with opportunity.   *Enter Richmond.*

Fitz. I do not like this whispering;

Where are the ladies and Matilda?

Rich. The ladies are at the further side the castle,
But by a glove you sent by a gentleman
That said he serv'd Earl Leicester, that with him
She and the queen should fly for safety whither
You had directed him, glad of any 'scape
They took a barge; another leapt in after them,
But who he was I know not: *Exit.*

Old Bruce. Sent you a glove?

Fitz. A glove indeed I miss, but I sent none.

Leic. This is a riddle.

King. I will play Oedipus, and expound it for you.
As Hubert has infus'd, you dropp'd your glove;
Ingenious Hubert found it, and, though we
Had directed otherwise, he employ'd a gentleman
Of our own chamber, one unknown to Matilda,
To bring it as your close intelligence
For her flight with him; he that leapt into th' barge
As they put off, was Oxford: now we have her,
Never again to lose her.

Leic. By my vex'd blood,
King John, this is not honourable.   *Enter Richmond.*

Rich. We are betray'd!
All that bore torches in the masque tonight
Were of the guard, who upon a receiv'd watchword,
Fell to their arms, beat down all oppos'd them,
And are shaping their course this way.

Young Bruce. Let's meet 'em;
We have an injur'd patience. Come death in whirlwinds,
I'll be the first shall front him. To thy prayers, John;
Pray heartily that thy friends' fatal points
May pierce these hearts, for if they miss, 't shall prove
The bloodiest beauty story ever told
To fright the readers' souls. A purple cloud
Shall shadow England; the whole land shall reel.
The centre groans; thy very crown shall stand
Trembling upon thy temples till it fall,
A mourner at thy fame's black funeral.   *Exit.*

Fitz. Oh noble nephew!   *Exeunt barons.*

King. Ha, ha, ha! Let em' rave on. Ingenious Hubert!
That couldst so swiftly apprehend a smooth
Path to th' possession of Matilda!
Quit Oxford from her charge; unto thy care
The king commends the mistress of his heart;
I'th' morning let me see her.

Hub. She shall wait upon you, sir.

Ches. The barons threaten high, sir.

King. Let them burst.
Come, gentlemen, to th' barge, and so to th' court;
To clip our wishes, perils appear sport.   *Exeunt.*

ACTUS IV. SCŒNA I

[IV. i. *Windsor Castle.*]

Enter Brand.

Brand. I wonder how my pair of prisoners fadge?
I am something dogged, too, a t'other side,
That thus long have not seen them; nor have they eat,
I am sure, since they came in. In yon madame's eye
I am as ugly as a toad. I will see her
And contemn her: you and your brat come out! *Enter Lady*
Here's meat; I am sure you are hungry.   *and boy.*

Boy. O mother, will you be sick now?
Mr. Brand hath brought us meat.

Lady Bruce. Oh, on my knee, sir,
I thank you, not for my want, for I feel
Nature almost quite vanquish'd, but for my son;
He may live long to thank you.

Boy. Give but my mother
A little piece of bread, and if I live,
As yet I may do, if you can be merciful,
I will tell my father such good things of you,
He shall return your kindness treble back
To your honest bosom. Oh, mother, for some bread!

KING JOHN AND MATILDA

Brand. Some bread?
Why, to have an honest bosom, as the world goes,
Is the next way to want bread. I'faith, tell me,
How have you pass'd the time you wanted victuals?

Lady Bruce. Very hardly;
And still the poor boy, sighing, would say, 'Mother,
You look very hungry', I did think straight how hard
Your heart was, then we both did fall a-weeping,
Cling'd our lean arms about each other's neck,
And sat a pair of mourners.

Brand. Delicate pastime; toads love no other.
Look ye, here is bread.

Boy. Oh, if you be a good man, give me but a bit
To give my mother; poor soul, how she looks!
Indeed, she's very hungry.

Brand. Yes, so is my dog;   *Puts it up again.*
I must keep this for his breakfast.

Lady Bruce. Give but my boy one bit,
And the saints sure will look how good you are;
They will be glad to see you charitable,
And call it excellent compassion.

Brand. No; coming from a toad, 'twill poison him.

Boy. It will not, sir; indeed, I am so hungry
I could eat rats or mice.

Brand. Your t'other hare-brain,
Your wild mad son, retains my lord a prisoner,
Uses him basely, and you must suffer for't.

Lady Bruce. Give me but paper, pen, and ink, I'll write
And charge him to fall down and lick the dust
Thy lord shall set his foot on; I will conjure him
And woo away his wildness by the groans
I suffer'd for him. I'll threaten his denial
With a mother's family-confounding curse;
This will I do, or anything that may
But purchase my poor boy one bite of bread.

Brand. No.

Lady Bruce. O, harder than the rocks, more merciless
Than the wild ravening wolf.   *Falls.*

Boy. Mother, do not die!
For heaven's sake, help my mother! Mother, look up,
And ye shall see me dance, and then the gentleman
Will sure bestow a piece of bread upon us.

Lady Bruce. Look here, thou iron-hearted man, upon
A pair of piercing miseries.

Brand. A scene of mirth.
I am all hard; the heat of lust withstood
To clip revenge, we stem a stream of blood.   *Exit.*

Boy. How do ye, mother?

Lady Bruce. How doth my boy?

Boy. Very sick indeed; but I warrant you are more
    hungry
Than I a great deal, are you not?

Lady Bruce. Oh no;
Thou art weak, and famine plays the tyrant with thee;
Look here, my boy: bite on thy mother's arm;
The blood will nourish thee.

Boy. Will your blood nourish me?

Lady Bruce. Yes, yes, I prithee try.

Boy. Why should not mine then nourish you? 'Tis the
    same.
Good mother, eat my arm, bite but a bite;
Truly, I shall hurt you if I bite yours.
I warrant you'll be better presently.

Lady Bruce. I shall, my son, and so shalt thou. Come
    near me;
Let us go hand in hand to heaven.

Boy. Oh mother, something pinch'd my very heart,
And I shall die, my dear, dear mother.   *Dies.*

Lady Bruce. Art thou gone, my son?
My soul shall overtake thee. Oh friendly death,
That gav'st that gripe, sure when thou kill'st the guilty
Frowns curl thy angry forehead, but when thou steal'st
Towards innocents, their pale fears to beguile *Enter Brand.*
Thou deck'st thy lean face with a lovely smile. (*Dies*) *reading*

Brand. My lord recover'd by the valiant king!   *a letter.*
In all his battles he is fortunate;

And now they shall have meat; ha! meat, said I?
I have made them worms' meat.
Oh, what a talking is within me! If I stay,
The building sure will crush me. I'll haste to th' court;
My lord here intimates the king's observance of me.
I must hence. Oh, guilt, thou draw'st death's image horrid!
When we begin to like our ills, how sweet a face hath sin,
Which but pass'd by, a cheater she appears:
Joys are her promise, but she pays us fears.   *Exit.*

[IV. ii. *London.*]

    Enter Hubert, Queen, and Matilda, a gentleman.

    Hub. Your care in the conveyance of Matilda
To this appointed place, the king shall recompense.
Withdraw yourself.
    Gent. I shall, my lord.   *Exit.*
    Queen. Matilda, where's that spirit that kept thy virtue
Valiant and bold?
    Mat. If virtue so ill pay us,
Who would be virtuous?
    Hub. Virtue! Pale poverty,
Reproach, disaster, shame sit on her forehead:
Despisings fill her sleeps: ill-favour'd injuries
Meet her at every turn: tears are her triumphs:
Her drink affliction: calumny attends her:
The unclean tongue of slander daily licks her
Out of her fashion; but if you be King John's friend—
    Mat. Oh, strong temptation.
    Queen. Matilda—
    Hub. You may, like
A nimble wind, play on the ruffling bosom
Of that fantastic wood, the world: your sleeps a paradise
Hung round with glittering dreams; then your dissem-
    blings
Will be call'd devotions, your rigged cold hypocrisy
Religion's holy heats. Mirth decks the court days,

The wanton minutes glide just like a stream
That clips the bosom of a wealthy mead
Till't get it great with child, a sweet green blessing.
Consider, 'tis the king.

   Mat. Ay, ay, the king.

   Queen. Trust not this tempter, lust's irreligious linguist.
Remember virtue is a holy flame,
A sacred inclination of the soul
To all things honest.

   Mat. I can resist no longer.
Oh Hubert, you are a victorious tempter

   Queen. Can this be possible?

   Hub. Forget not, at the beginning
Of this sweet race, honour holds out for you
A golden garland.

   Queen. Oh remember,
At the end of chastity's white race, an angel
Holds in his hand, shot through a silver cloud,
A crown for conquerors.

   Hub. Will ye lose the pleasures that—

   Mat. Ay, ay, those pleasures, Hubert; there is a voice
Of flesh and frailty in me that still cries,
'Matilda, take those pleasures', and I am now
The king's for ever.

   Queen. Let the queen then cut from earth
Such a dissembler.   *Offers violence to Matilda. Hubert*

   Hub. Nay, but you shall not.   *stays her.*

   Queen. Shame and death
Dwell with a goodness so short-liv'd, thou handsome hypo-
     crite,
Thou faith-defrauder; a religious qualm
Crossing the stomach of a seeming saint,
Which falls straight into humour, all thy devotions
Prove now but well-clad cheaters of time's charity.
Thy griefs and sighs are but sin's crafty games;   *Matilda*
Their soon-spent flashes play like holy flames.   *and Hubert*

   Hub. It shall be so; to some remote place, shut *whisper.*
From the danger of the angry queen I'll carry you,

And thither bring the king.

Mat. I long to see him.

Queen. Hubert, wilt thou play the court chameleon,
The perfum'd pander?

Hub. Yes, marry will I. Panders have need of perfumes.

Queen. O merry sin!
We smile towards hell, but howl when we are in.

Hub. Name but the place, madame, and religiously I vow,
By th' unstain'd honour of my name and house,
By the white reputation of a gentleman,
And as I wish for after-happiness, my care
Shall see it instantly in execution.

Mat. My cousin Bruce, Earl Richmond, with the convoy,
The king discomfited, they would madly have carried me
To Dunmow Abbey in fruitful Essex.

Hub. 'Sfoot, a thousand kings
Could not thence recover ye. But name the place
Whither I shall carry you; good madame, whither?

Mat. Good Hubert, thither.   *Falls on her knees.*

Hub. What, to a monastery?

Queen. Call her dissembling
No sin, good heaven, for she is still a saint.

Mat. Upon my knee I beg it, and every day
When I shall drop a bead, I'll strongly pray
That you may find a blessing.

Queen. Hark, Hubert.

Hub. There is something tells me there is honour in it,
To grant her good request.

Mat. Mark how your oath ran:
By the honour of your house,
By the white reputation of a gentleman;
And you wish for after-happiness,
You'd put my wish in speedy execution.
Oh Hubert, mark; he his house pulls down
That wounds his honours, though to please a crown.
By heralds he's a gentleman maintain'd
Whose reputation's whiteness stands unstain'd,
And he in after-happiness stands high,

O

That dares not with a sin buy sovereignty.

   Hub. Excellent oratory!

   Queen. Hubert, for truth's sake.

   Mat. Oh Hubert, for the glorious crown of chastity.

   Queen. For the victorious palm of wedlock faith.

   Mat. By the immaculate souls of holy maids.

   Queen. And by the unstain'd truth of honest wives.

   Mat. By the tears of virgins.

   Queen. By the truth of virtue.

   Mat. Oh, now to honour, Hubert, give thy name;
Sweet blooming virtue knows no blush of shame.

   Hub. The rareness of your souls has ravish'd me.
We'll change our course, steer through bridge, and so
For Essex and Dunmow. Victorious maid,
Rhetoric is poor in thy praise, whom a king
Nor sovereignty, the soul of women's longings,
Cannot corrupt! Oh women! Men-subduers!
Nature's extremes! No mean is to be had;
Excellent good, or infinitely bad!

   Both. Most noble Hubert.   *Exeunt.*

[IV. iii. *King John's Palace.*]

    Enter King, Fitzwater, Chester, and Oxford.

   King. 'Twas well yet that the trick has catch'd this old one;
Where are the rest?

   Ches. Richmond is gone for France:
Leicester escap'd to Windsor.

   King. How I thirst
To make mine arms wealthy with sweet Matilda!

   Fitz. Oh, if a father's prayers, an old man's tears,
An injur'd old man's tears, were ever prevalent,
Good heaven keep my girl a crystal fort,
Firm and unvanquish'd.

   King. Hubert my friend has her.
Will it please the mighty emperor of the barons,
The king may kiss Matilda; she will be here presently.

Then shall the great Fitzwater sit in state
And see Matilda and the poor king dally
And teach the winds to wanton. Hubert now has her,
The faithfull'st of my friends; from contrarieties
We will produce soft pleasures, sweet perfections.
Sirrah, Chester shall tell me when she frowns, and then
We'll court her cheeks into a comely smile;
If she but raise that milky hill, her breast,
With respirations, Oxford shall swear
It is a sigh, and I will seem to chide
His rashness, and protest love rais'd that gale
Just as her heart for my heart had set sail.

Fitz. Hear, heaven!

King. Chester shall watch her when she weeps, and tell me
They are Matilda's tears, when I will presently,
With a lover's pleasing fervency, protest
They are pearls by passion forc'd from Cupid's chest.

Ox. But what shall Hubert do,
Your bosom friend?

King. He shall with pretty thwarting passages,
To please Matilda, seem to make me angry,
And tell me 'tis impossible now t'obtain her;
Whereupon, impatient to illustrate love
With a new passion, oh how I will rave,
Misuse him strangely, and close up the scorn
Upon Matilda's lip.   *Enter a gentleman.*

Gent. Letters from th' Earl Hubert, sir.

King. His name but now,
Like a beloved passenger, took leave
Of my unwilling lips; he waits directions
Concerning her from me. Good Chester, read it;
I cannot read and rejoice too. Fitzwater,
Listen and rave.   *Chester reads.*

*May it please your excellent majesty, it hath pleas'd heaven so
throughly to captivate my reason by the potent pleadings of
your virtuous queen and unmatch'd Matilda, that I hold it now
impossible for your majesty ever to obtain her.*

King. Ha!

Fitz. That last was music.

King. Nay, kill us all, kill us all; will ye read on, sir?

Briefly, by that time these letters kiss your royal hands, she will
be cloister'd up in Dunmow Abbey, and end her days a vestal,
whither I could not choose but convey her, being thereunto
forcibly charmed by her tears and entreaties, and especially
forc'd by a secret command from heaven to mine own conscience.
I remain your most excellent majesty's transgressing servant,
                                                                    Hubert.

King. Most excellent villain!

Fitz. Observe, King John, ere heaven will virtue fail,
Contrary means, all winds, shall fill her sail.

Ches. How like a hare, the greyhound's chaps still at her,
Yet still she 'scapes! The king is full of tempest.

King. She's gone for ever.
Oh Hubert, let us never meet again,
Never more meet. Fitzwater, fetch her but back,
As from the first, so from this Isabel
We'll be divorc'd, marry and set Matilda
I'th' regal chair, the king's admired mistress.

Fitz. But will ye say and do, sir?

King. Yet there is hope! Now by my crown I will.
We shall be son and father; thou and I
Will walk upon our palace battlements,
And thou shalt carry up a covetous eye,
And thou shalt cast that covetous eye about
The fair, delightful, village-spotted valleys;
Thou shalt stand still, and think, and recollect
The troubl'd longings of thy large desires,
And whatsoever thou shalt ask the king,
Of all thou seest, the king shall give it thee.

Fitz. Well, let one ride before and certify
That we are coming.

King. Chester, put on wings.   *To himself.*
Thou good old man; the bird that croak'd now sings. *Exeunt.*

ACTUS V. SCŒNA I

[v. i. *Before Dunmow Abbey.*]

Enter King and Fitzwater, Oxford meeting them.

King. These are the abbey walls: Oxford, what news?

Ox. Matilda is afraid to venture forth,
But on yon battlements it was her promise *Enter Abbess and*
With the Lady Abbess to appear—and see, sir. *Matilda*

King. Give us leave. Oh were that habit *above.*
Not so unkind, a foe to fair increase,
I'd call it then celestial, and swear
A bright star mov'd in that immaculate sphere.
Matilda! Mistress of many graces!
And lovely as the blush that breaks the day!
Cast thy commanding eyes upon a king,
Whom love hath made a beggar!

Ab. Why hunts the king
With such a violent pursuit a chaste dove
That hath given up her name to heaven, and stands
White as her spotless vesture?

Fitz. Lady Abbess,
Pray give me leave, and hearken, my Matilda.
I bring thee golden news, my girl; we have cast
An ill-becoming calumny upon
The king's love all this while, for he protests
To be divorc'd from Isabel the queen,
And by marriage set thee in his bed,
A plant to spring and prosper. Women naturally
Do affect sovereignty; wilt thou run retrograde
In this fair zodiac? Though all ways yet
Have fail'd, this will take, I am sure. *To the king.*

Mat. Who hath taught my father
To turn apostate to that integrity
Slept in his noble breast? Through a divorce
I run to golden ruin; the king marry me?

King. And make thee queen of him and two large kingdoms.

The Christian world when they shall hear, shall wonder,
And magnify in their abundant praises,
The glory of our marriage.

Mat. Oh my lord, here I can call necessity
Excellent physic for a vast desire:
Our wants are holy waters cast on lust's fire.

Fitz. Oh brave, brave girl!
That I had thee here to buss thee;
Her very breath did smell of heaven.

King. Matilda!

Fitz. I have found thee gold, my girl;
These are glorious wrestlings,
Celestial strugglings; passion of me, that joy
Should carry April eyes!   *Weeps.*

King. Matilda, look upon thy sovereign courting
Thy cruelty with a pair of wooing eyes,
Labouring for mercy.

Fitz. No, no Matilda, look upon thy sovereign,
Tempting thy chastity with wanton eyes
Labouring in lust.

King. Thou man of rude defects, let me alone.

Fitz. Thou man of wild desires, let me alone.

King. Ha!

Fitz. Tut, tut, I know whose cause I have in hand,
And neither ha's nor hems can fright plain Robin.
The wound that foolish love-boy there (what call ye him?)
Had struck your heart with, because your smooth tongue
You could not come to supple it, as the dog does his
      foot,
With fair fine words you could lick me, and then
Lift me to stroke it and heal it by attorney.
He steers not steady that delights to roam,
Craft sets out swift, but ever comes short home;
I tell ye truth, I.

King. Abbess, deliver up Matilda,
Or with an army fill'd with ruffians, ravishers,
The very sons of darkness, we will level
This building to the bottom.

Ab. We know the king,
Being reconcil'd unto his mother Church,
Cannot conceive such outrage. [*John*] *appears passionate.*

Fitz. Now ye stamp, do ye?

Mat. Father, farewell; and to my lord my king,
The service of his most obsequious handmaid;
And good your majesty, be pleas'd to remember
How excellently-admirable your crown
Will then become ye, when ye shall cast off
The habit of your passions. I will pray for you, sir;
And, if't be possible, with prayers and tears
Quench your desires and fortify my fears.   *Exit.*

Fitz. A father's blessing, like a welcome cloud
With child of friendly showers, hover o'er thy goodness
And keep it ever green; she is gone, sir.

King. Go thou and run into the sea.

Fitz. Ha, ha; so the great emperor of the barons,
As you call'd him,
May come out again i'th' guts of a poor John!
No, no, I will live and laugh; you would have made her
The mistress of the king, and she is married
To the king's Master; oh, to the noblest king
Poor supplicant ever kneel'd to. To your King,
And her King, and to my King she's married;
Oh married, married, let the satyrs dance it,
The sweet birds sing it. Let the winds be wanton,
And as they softly with an evening whisper
Steal through the curl'd locks of the lofty wood,
Let them in their sweet language seem to say:
This, this was chaste Matilda's marriage day. *Exit Fitzwater.*

King. It is resolv'd, irrevocable; who waits? *Enter Chester.*

Ches. Sir?   *Enter Confessor.*

King. Have an eye upon that fox; where's our confessor?

Con. Attending, sir.

King. Your ear . . . do this.

Con. I shall, sir.

King. And hark you, without all expostulation, speedily
Make Brand the instrument.

Con. I shall not fail, sir.   *Exit.*
King. All my blood turns; she is now past all recovery.
Oh day, draw in thy light: time, do not keep
This deed for story: memory, fall asleep
In black oblivion's cavern; let this day
Still skip the kalend, and be wip'd away
From all discourse. Oh, let no chaste maid,
Rememb'ring how Matilda was betray'd,
With bitter tears curse the too cruel king;
No satyr dance this day, no sweet bird sing,
But let the raven and screech-owl cry,
Matilda the chaste maid must this day die.   *Exit.*

[v. ii. *Dunmow Abbey: the Garden.*]

Enter Brand and the Abbess reading a letter.

*Madam, These are to give you to understand that instantly and
without any the least expostulation you see convey'd into the
outward garden adjoining to the abbey your new votary Matilda,
that the bearer (this gentleman) may without the least inter-
ception have freedom of access to her. Let this from me be your
safety, and forget not, the wills of princes are indisputable.*
                              Eustace, Confessor to his Majesty.

Ab. No, no; no cloud of niceness, order, or regularity
Must intercept this mandate. Sir, the king's will,
The confessor's advertisement, and your hopes
Shall meet this minute; but virtue is, I hope,
The rudder of your voyage.
Brand. I tell you, madame, 'tis unspotted truth.
The king is chang'd so excellent, such a lover
Now of Matilda's noble constancy,
That therefore, as his confessor there certifies,
Your duty is expected
To work my admittance to her, which is only
To let her know how heartily his majesty
Admires and commends her.
Ab. 'Tis a joyful hearing;   *Enter Matilda.*

See where she walks; souls so heavenly simple
It seems the court digests not, and, being cloy'd,
Commends them to the cloister. *Exit.*

Brand. And she be so simple,
She's the fitter for the saints, things I ne'er think of,
Unless to stuff our similes. Excellent lady,
(There's such a deal of heaven in her face,
It makes my black soul tremble), excellent lady—

Mat. Your will, sir?

Brand. To let you understand the will of him,
Whose will the will of heaven hath new made.
Thus said King John in brief; tell that sweet saint,
(And there he wept as I do at the thought on't), *Weeps.*
The immaculate mistress of my dear devotions,
The king by this, with her eye not unacquainted,
Commends to her his hate of all that love,
The fervour of his blood contaminated.
Oh tell her—and he sigh'd there bitterly—
That as I was her tempter, I am now
Mine own despiser; as mine own despiser,
I will remain her virtue's strong admirer,
And there, just there, he kiss'd it. If't chance, quoth he,
Her gentle lip return the king's chaste meaning,
Mark but which place of this then happy glove
Receives that heavenly print, and bring it back,
That my lips there, like a pair of willing pilgrims,
May pay my heart's devotions. This was all;
And this, his glove, the token.

Mat. Excellent change!
Heaven now hath heard my prayers return his goodness;
I am sorry thou hast kiss'd the glove before me
For fear thy lips have lain where the king's did,
And cozen'd mine of that grace fell from them,
When he spake things thus good. Give me the glove.

Brand. Ha! *He looks towards the garden door, and whilst she turns herself that way, he changes the glove, and gives her the other poison'd.*

Mat. Thy looks made me believe that some were coming.

Brand. No, madame, I have cozen'd you; 'twas but the
wind.

Mat. No wind shall keep my duty from his majesty
With my observance. Say thus I return'd   *Kisses the poison'd*
My love of his great goodness, and if he ask thee   *glove.*
How I receiv'd the news of his rare change,
Say, as a teeming soil after a drought
Welcomes a wish'd-for flower. What a strange scent
Strongly beats up into my brains while I hold this glove
So near my breast! Thou art not honest, sure!

Brand. Near death we prophesy, and 'tis so, sure;
You cannot breathe three minutes.

Mat. Ha!

Brand. 'Tis nearly done, and there's no dallying;
I know 'tis strong and swift. As by a glove
You were carried from your father's to this cloister,
So by a glove you are from this cloister sent
To the chaste court of saints.

Mat. Heaven! Is this right?

Brand. No, 'twas a left-handed glove, look ye.
I kiss'd the right and cozen'd you,
So that a sinister act with a left-handed glove very prettily
Imports a wittiness in wickedness.

Mat. Thou art a merry murderer. The king was wont
To call me friend; oh, if he bestows
On's friends such gifts, what sends he to his foes?
Uncharitable love-token! Oh, what harsh hand
Temper'd this drain of death?

Brand. I could do't no better.

Mat. Merciless man, tigers to thee are tame!
Oh cozening crocodile, that with thy tears could take me!
How wilt thou howl
When thou and I meet next! When I shall sit
Above my sufferings, then will my blood be
A cloud betwixt eternity and thee.

Brand. Cloud(s)? Yes, much cloud(s).

Mat. There was the last call. To the king commend me,
And tell him, when in stories he shall stand,

When men shall read the Conqueror's great name,
Voluptuous Rufus, that unkind brother, Beauclerk,
Comely King Stephen, Henry the wedlock-breaker,
And lion-hearted Richard; when they shall come
Unto his name, with sighs it shall be said,
'This was King John—the murderer of a maid.'
Oh tell him I am past his strong temptations,
And though wild burning back'd his hot desire,
Like perfect gold I did outlive the fire.   *Dies.*

 Brand. She's dead and I must shift for one.
I hear some trampling.   *Enter Young Bruce.*
What's he has leap'd the garden walls? has a wenching look,
And should be a good vaulter. Guilty knaves make excellent
Eavesdroppers, and I love to sound strange bosoms. I will
  lie
To see and hear, and yet not heard nor seen.   *Stands aside.*

 Young Bruce. Here rumour gives my cousin, chaste
  Matilda,
To live a votary; ha! on the ground!
Murder'd most certainly, and so warm, that yet
The murderer at my approach may lurk
About the garden, for through the abbey 'tis
Impossible to pass; oh my griev'd blood,
Who made it so unfortunate to be good!

 Brand. He mùmbles something to himself.

 Young Bruce. This parallels my mother and my brother.
Ha! something stirs i'th' grove. Passion, I know thee not;
With a new art we must catch old bloodhounds. Well,
Although I am the king's well-wishing friend,
And have rais'd forces for his part at Windsor,
Yet with my heart I am glad a friendly hand
Hath made thee happy.

 Brand. 'Sfoot, this is one of our side,
But it seems he knows not 'twas the king's injunction.

 Young Bruce. Now business will be minded, state affairs
With vigilance effected, which before
Were so entangled in your hair forsooth,
Suitors could find no end of their beginnings.

Brand. By this light, I have done a good deed.

Young Bruce. Thou honest soul,
That by the heat of thy happy handiwork,
Canst not, I am sure, but be in hearing, if
My irregular start, upon private necessity,
Frighted thee off, be not asham'd to let
Thy unknown friend possess thee.

Brand. Oh brave young spark!

Young Bruce. Or if thy modesty must keep thee off,
So well I love thy work (and as I, the kingdom),
Let this purse of gold, this diamond fasten'd to't,
Tell thee thy friend was here. If thou'dst know him,
He is a kinsman to the Earl of Chester.
And because thou shalt not doubt thy friends' fair meanings,
I will return the way I came, although
With danger to my person.

Brand. Here is one, sir, wishes better to his friends.

                                             Shows himself.

Young Bruce. What art thou?

Brand. One that will take your honourable purse,
And yet pass suit at the common law.

Young Bruce. Wert thou the expert master of this piece?

Brand. You being kinsman to my lord and master,
Who ever hated this blood, I dare tell you
I practis'd first a business late at Windsor
Upon a mother and her son—

Young Bruce. Hold, heart; Old Bruce's lady
And the brat, her son?
Wert thou the happy instrument
To cut these houses down? didst thou do that?

Brand. It would deserve, well priz'd, another purse, sir.

Young Bruce. Gold must not part us; didst do't? *Gives him*

Brand. Both that and this, by this hand, sir.   *more gold.*

Young Bruce. Son of the devil, have I found thee?

Brand. [*Aside*] Sure he knows me.

Young Bruce. Fool, dost draw thy sword?
What a loud lie thou dost give heaven, to think
A sword can shield the guilty! Look here, villain,

Upon my horrid point, where death in tempest
And whirlwinds stares upon thee, thou murderer
Of my mother, brother, and my kinswoman.

Brand. 'Sfoot, here was a purse with a bob at the end on't;
Pray take your purse again.

Young Bruce. Toad, I will take thy heart first.

Brand. I deny nothing then:
Resolution crowns my craft. For those at Windsor
Let me free the king; I famish'd them because
Your mother was too coy: you may guess the rest.
For this, it was King John's injunction,
And I have done it daintily, by this light.

Young Bruce. By darkness and her angels,
Thy near kinsmen,
Thou shalt not live five minutes for't. *They fight, Brand
falls, Young Bruce keeps him down.*

Brand. O sir, what mean ye?

Young Bruce. To ask thee for a mother, a sweet brother,
A chaste kinswoman; oh, that thou couldst be
Ten days a-dying. Slave! I'll stick thy trunk
So thick with wounds, it shall appear a book
Full of red letters,
Characters of thy cruelty. *Stabs him.*

Brand. This is no bleeding month, sir.

Young Bruce. Thou liest; look yonder:
There lies mine almanac, a celestial body *Points to Matilda's*
Whose revolution, period, pale aspect *corpse,*
All tell me 'tis high time that thou shouldst bleed. *Stabs.*

Brand. Oh!

Young Bruce. Thy veins are all corruption;
Toads belch not fouler;
And should thy trunk be thrown upon a dunghill,
As it deserves no better burial,
The scent would poison swine; the very dogs
Would with howlings fly as from a midnight fiend,
And every raven that should feast upon't,
Would seek forsaken deserts, and there die
Full of infection. *Stabs.*

Brand. Oh, that last has finish'd me,
And where I go I know not; a bloody cloud
Hath hid heaven from me like a purple shroud.   *Dies.*

Young Bruce. Feast thou the crows.
This body I'll convey to Windsor, where my mother
And my sweet murther'd brother we'll expose
As spurs of righteous vengeance to all eyes:
Conscience and blood are strong incessant cries.   *Exit.*

[v. iii. *Before Windsor Castle.*]

*Enter King, Oxford, lords, and Fitzwater below: Old Bruce
and Leicester above.*

                                                  Charge.

King. You sons of death and disobedience,
Why is the king kept out?

Old Bruce. You shall know, sir;
Is't not enough the whole land's liberties
Lie yet a-gasping by your headstrong passions,
Wounded by your neglect, but through blood
D'ye chose your vast desires, my wife and son, sir?

King. Again as we are prince in our royal word,
The villain pass'd our precept.

Old Bruce. As you pass'd heaven's
In your bloody masquing night at Baynard's Castle,
When all the floors and the white walls were bloody,
Deep crimson blushes to behold a prince
In blood pursue his passions.

King. Barr'd out and brav'd,
You bate and chafe a lion. Bring old Fitzwater.
Thou, Bruce, and grumbling Leicester, either speedily
Give up the castle, and upon your knees
Fall to the mercy you have scorn'd, or here
Before a pair of minutes pass, the sword
Of incens'd justice shall even in your eyes
Leave this old rebel headless.

Fitz. Now, by the blood

I lost in holy Palestine with Richard,
(Oh that right royal soldier!), King John, I swear
That foul word 'rebel' has unriveted
The basis of reason and made me very angry.
Is to take truth's part to be a rebel?
To ease my groaning country, is that rebellion?
To preserve the unstain'd honour of a maid,
And that maid my daughter, to preserve your glory,
That you stand not branded in our chronicles
By the black name of wedlock-breaker; is this,
(Good heaven!) is this rebellion? Come, come, the axe;
Oh that wrong'd soul to death so falsely given,
                                        Enter Mowbray.
Flies sweetly singing her own truth to heaven!
    Mow. Stand on your guard, sir;
Young Bruce with twenty thousand
Strong able men from Cambridge and Essex,
With a speedy march, and with as dreadful threat'nings,
Comes thundering towards Windsor, all his ensigns
Crimson and black, which in their wanton wavings
Cry to the frighted country, as he marches,
Nothing but blood and death.
    Old Bruce. Oh noble son of a murdered mother.
    Leic. Honourable young man.
    King. Draw up our forces like a pair of angry winds
That have got a hollow cloud with child of tempests;
We'll make the valleys tremble.   *Enter Chester.*
    Ches. Resist now, sir,
Or the whole kingdom trembles; Lewis the dauphin,
By th' politic working of ingenious Richmond,
Who was sent for him, with six hundred sail
And fourscore flatboats is let in at Dover;
Subduing as they march, and the towns willingly
Giving them way, they have reach'd Rochester,
And if a speedy swift prevention meet not,
They will for London certainly.
    Leic. Now, John, thy crown sits quivering.
    Ches. These here so resolute—

Mow. Young Bruce so potent—

Ox. And, which strikes deep, a factious foreign foot
Upon our earth; 'tis a dangerous triplicity,
So that our forces were they three times trebl'd,
Distracted with a division thus triangular,
Cannot promise safety.

King. Take it in time, for now
The goodliest oak in the whole wood must bow.

Fitz. Oh that was very well said, sir, nor shall ye bow
But unto heaven and virtue, for kings have boasted
To be her servants; oh, in this tempest sir,
Give her the helm. Good brother Bruce, the king
Has faithfully acquitted him of the bloods
Of your wife and son; Leicester, the king now looks
Upon his passions with a displeased eye;
Trust to our faiths, sir; give the land her liberties,
And do but look upon my poor Matilda—

King. Oh, oh!

Fitz. With kingly chaste eyes and a holy soul.
My brother shall command his soul to obedience,
Leicester and he shall give ye up the castle,
We will call Richmond with his powers from Lewis,
We will be all one soul again, and force
The skipping French to put to sea again,
And you shall stand a king then absolute.
Good brother Leicester, sir, upon my knee
I urge your goodness now; shall we still stand
And chain our freedoms to a foreign hand?
When we shun seen rocks, then we safely sail;
Good, good King John, let the old man prevail.

King. Oh Chester, run to Dunmow, and if Brand yet
Have kept his hand white, bid that Brand forebear
For fear of burning everlastingly.

Ches. I shall, sir.   *Exit.*

King. Mowbray, with the bendings of the king.
Go meet that angry young man, Bruce, and tell him
Here's now no use for steel.

Mow. 'Twill be good news, sir.

King. Meet us at least, you stubborn men,
In our facile affections;
Why send ye not for Richmond? Must we fend, and
Beseech, too?

Leic. Pass but your royal promise
In the words of a king to perform what
Y'are fled from, the wind not with more swiftness
Shall fly to play with Richmond's lofty plume
Than shall be shown in his repeal.

King. 'Tis granted upon our kingly word—that time in
me
Shall read that giant's force, necessity!

Old Bruce. With all submissive reverence we descend,
And kiss your highness' hand.

Fitz. Right happy day;
My girl is safe, and all clouds blown away.   *Exeunt from
                                                    the walls.*

*Hoboys sound whilst the barons descend, each on his knee
kissing the king's hand; both parties joyfully embrace. Suddenly the hoboys cease, and a sad music of flutes heard. Enter
to the king and lords the Lady Abbess, ushering Matilda's
hearse, born by virgins, this motto fastened unto it—* To Piety
and Chastity. *The body of Matilda lying on the hearse and
attended by the queen, bearing in her hand a garland compos'd
of roses and lilies; after her, Young Bruce, Hubert, Chester,
and other gentlemen, all in mourning habits.*

The song in parts.

1. *Look what death hath done; here laid
   In one a martyr and a maid.*

2. *Angels crown those with just applause,
   Die in defence of virtue's laws.*

Chorus. *Such was her cause! Death, boast not of thy hand's
   Cruelty, since the vanquish'd victor stands.*

2. *Her chastity to time shall last
   Like laurel, which no lightning can blast.*

1. *Sweet maids, with roses deck her hearse,*
   Whose virtue stands above the reach of verse.

Chorus. *Heaven hath her pure part, whilst on earth her name*
   Moves in the sphere of a refulgent fame.

King. Hubert, interpret this apparition.
   Hub. Behold, sir,
A sad-writ tragedy so feelingly
Languag'd and cast, with such a crafty cruelty
Contriv'd and acted that wild savages,
Satyrs, and the rude rabble of the woods
Would weep to lay their ears to, and, admiring
To see themselves outdone, they would conceive
Their wildness mildness to this deed, and call
Men more than savage, themselves rational;
And thou, Fitzwater, reflect upon thy name,
And turn the son of tears; oh, forget
That Cupid ever spent a part upon thee,
That Hymen ever coupled thee, or that ever
The hasty, happy, willing messsenger
Told thee thou hadst a daughter; oh look here,
Look here, King John, and with a trembling eye   *Unveils*
Read your sad act, Matilda's tragedy.   *her face.*
   All. Matilda!
   Fitz. By the labouring soul of a much injur'd man,
It is my child Matilda.
   Queen. Oh cruel king, go sate thy bloody eye
With thy black command, which there lies executed.
   Old Bruce. Sweet niece.
   Leic. Chaste soul.
   Young Bruce. King, go and read thy cruelty.
   King. Do I stir, Chester?
Good Oxford, do I move? Stand I not still
To watch when the griev'd friends of dead Matilda
Will with a thousand stabs turn me to dust,
That in a thousand prayers they may be happy?
Will no one do't? then give a mourner room,   *Falls pas-*
A man of tears. Oh immaculate Matilda,   *sionately upon the*

These shed but failing heat drops, misting showers, *hearse*.
The faint dews of a doubtful April morning;
But from mine eyes ship-sinking cataracts,
Whole clouds of waters, wealthy exhalations
Shall fall into the sea of my affliction,
Till it amaze the mourners.

   Hub. Unmatch'd Matilda,
Celestial soldier that keep'st a fort of chastity
'Gainst all temptations.

   Fitz. Not to be a queen
Would she break her chaste vow; truth crowns your rede,
Unmatch'd Matilda was her name indeed.

   King. Oh take into your spirit-piercing praise
My scene of sorrow; I have well-clad woes,
Pathetic epithets to illustrate passion,
And steal true tears so sweetly from all these,
'T shall touch the soul, and at one pierce and please.

   Ches. What will he do? *The King takes the garland from*
        the Queen, and peruses the motto of the hearse.

   King. To piety and purity, and lilies mix'd with roses;
How well you have apparell'd woe! This pendant
To piety and purity directed
Insinuates a chaste soul in a clean body;
Virtue's white virgin, chastity's red martyr.
Suffer me then with this well-suited wreath
To make our griefs ingenious; let all be dumb.
Whilst the king speaks her epicedium.

   Ches. His very soul speaks sorrow.

   Ox. And it becomes him sweetly.

   King. Hail, maid and martyr! Lo, on thy breast,
Devotion's altar, chaste truth's chest,
I offer, as my guilt imposes,
Thy merit's laurel, lilies and roses;
Lilies, intimating plain
Thy immaculate life stuck with no stain;
Roses, red and sweet, to tell
How sweet red sacrifices smell; *Sets the garland on her*
Hang round then as you walk about this hearse,   *breast.*

The songs of holy hearts; sweet, virtuous verse.

Fitz. Bring Persian silks to deck her monument.

King. Arabian spices quick'ning by their scent.

Fitz. Numidian marble to preserve her praise.

King. Corinthian ivory her sweet shape to raise.

Fitz. And write in gold upon it: 'In this breast
Virtue sat mistress: passion but a guest.'

Old Bruce. My noble brother, I have lost a wife and
        son,
You a sweet daughter; look on the king's penitence,
His promise for the kingdom's peace: prefer
A public benefit. When it shall please,
Let heaven question him. Let us secure
And quit the land of Lewis.

Fitz. Do anything;
Do all things that are honourable, and the great King
Make you a good king, sir; and when your soul
Shall at any time reflect upon your follies,
Good King John, weep, weep very heartily.
It will become you sweetly; at your eyes
Your sin stole in: there pay your sacrifice.

King. Back unto Dunmow Abbey, where we'll pay
To sweet Matilda's memory and her sufferings
A monthly obsequy, which, sweet'ned by
The wealthy woes of a tear-troubl'd eye
Shall by those sharp afflictions of my face
Court mercy, and make grief arrive at grace.
Let my wild errors tell to time this truth;
Whilst passion holds the helm, reason and honour
Do suffer wrack: but they sail safe and clear
Who constantly by virtue's compass steer.

Song.

1. *Matilda! Now to take thy bed*
   In the dark dwellings of the dead.

2. *And rise in the great waking-day,*
   Sweet as incense, fresh as may.

1. *Rest thou chaste soul, fix'd in thy proper sphere,*
   Amongst heaven's fair ones; all are fair ones there.

Chorus. *Rest there, chaste soul, whilst we, here troubl'd, say:*
   Time gives us griefs, death take our joys away.

Exeunt omnes.

GLOSSARY

Abiram: see *Dathan*.

accomplements: military accoutrements.

affronted: confronted.

Almaine: Germany.

Ambrosians: users of the Ambrosian liturgy.

Anabaptists: an anarchical Protestant sect which sought reform through a literal interpretation of the Bible.

Anchors: Anchorites.

articles: restraints.

attach: arrest.

bane: poison.

Basels: order founded by St. Basil in the fourth century.

battalia: order of battle.

beadsman: well-wisher.

bearward: bearkeeper.

begging orders: monastic orders who lived on alms.

belayed: surrounded.

bendings: supplications.

Benno: the Bishop of Meissen who supported Pope Gregory VII in his famous dispute with Emperor Henry IV in the eleventh century.

Bernards: order founded by St. Bernard of Clairvaux about 1115.

bitchery: lewdness.

blemish: slander.

Blood of Hales: a fraudulent relic at the abbey of Hales in Gloucestershire, reputed to be visible only to those who had confessed themselves.

Boethius, Hector (1456?–1536): author of a history of Scotland.

Bonhams: 'Bons hommes', a name given to several monastic orders.

bonny-clabber: curds and whey.

braving: vaunting.

Bridgets: order founded by St. Bridget of Sweden in the fourteenth century.

Britain: often = Brittany.

British: often = Breton.

buckle for: struggle for.

buckram: conceited.

buckram bags: lawyer's bags.

bug's words: high-flown terms.

Bullen: Boulogne.

bumfiddle: make waste of.

burgonet: close-fitting helmet.

calk: make astrological calculations.

callet: lewd woman.

Camaldulsensers: the order of Camaldoli founded by St. Romuald in Italy in 1012.

cankers: canker worms.

carman: adult male.

case: skin.

Celestines: a reformed Bernardine order founded in 1254.

Certiorari: a writ sent from a superior to an inferior court.

chough: bumpkin.

chrismatory: vessel for sacramental oil.

Clarines: a sisterhood instituted in Italy by St. Clara and St. Francis in the early thirteenth century.

Cluniacs: a branch of the Benedictine order.

cockney: milksop.

coil: trouble.

common: confer.

conceit: idea.

conceited: imaginary.

congees: ceremonious bowings.

convent: summon.

conveyance: cunning contrivance.

copperas: vitriol.

crucifers: cross-bearers.

cuculled: cowled.

dane: don, master.

Darvel Gathiron: a huge wooden image of a saint, Derfel Gadarn, which was taken from North Wales and burned at Smithfield in 1538.

Dathan and Abiram: rebels against Moses who were swallowed up by the earth.

debatements: abatements.

defeasance: nullification.

determine: bring to an end.

disgests: aids digestion.

dodman: snail.

dolent: sorrowful.

Donates: a strict sect which ended in the seventh century.

dorter: dormitory.

draff: refuse.

eans: brings forth lambs.

earnest: pledge.

ecce signum: behold the sign.

Ehud: the slayer of Eglon, the Moabite king who invaded Israel.

elate: elevated.

Ember: the name given to each of the periods of fasting and prayer in the four seasons of the year.

emmets: ants.

engines: wiles.

ensifers: sword-bearers.

envir'd: surrounded.

Esdras: Ezra, who got permission from Cyrus to return to Jerusalem and rebuild parts which had been destroyed.

esterlings: invaders from the east.

expedient: speedy.

fadge: agree with.

fet, fetch: trick, contrivance.

fewte: fee.

fishgarths: fish-preserves.

flauns: custards or cheesecakes or pancakes.

foison: plenty.

fraught: freight.

froiter: refectory.

furniture: provision.

game: prize.

garboils: disturbances.

garron: hack, small horse.

gaud: prank.

gear: matter.

ghostly: spiritual.

Gilbertines: order of canons and nuns begun in Lincolnshire by Gilbert of Sempringham in the earlier twelfth century.

Giraldus Cambrensis (1146?–1220?): a Welsh divine who wrote topographical studies of Ireland and Wales.

glaive: broadsword.

Grandmontensers: followers of St. Stephen Grandmont who professed poverty and obedience.

gymold: double-ringed.

Habeas corpus: a writ requiring a person to be brought before a court or judge.

haggard: wild hawk.

Heli: the father of Joseph of Arimathea.

Helias: Elijah, who overthrew the worship of Baal among the Israelites.

hipocras: spiced wine.

Hole: one of the worst cells in the Counter jail.

hubbubs: merry-makings.

huckle bone: hip bone.

infused: insinuated.

intelligencers: informers.

interdict: ban ecclesiastical functions and privileges.

intoxicate: poisoned.

Ishbosheth: the son of King Saul. David slew his murderers.

Jacobites: French order of teaching friars.

jennet: small horse.

jet: strut.

Jeronimites: an order of hermits

established in Italy in the fourteenth century.

Kyrie: Lord.

landloper: adventurer.

Laternse: the Lateran church in Rome.

lawn: fine linen.

leathern: skin-clad.

Leland, John (1506?–52): a patriotic English antiquarian and historian.

Legit or non legit: 'he reads or does not read', referring to the test for exempting clerics from secular-laws.

let: hindrance.

liable to: subject to.

Limbo Patrum: a place on the borders of hell.

loller: heretic.

maim: disablement.

Major, John (1467–1550): a divine who published a history of Britain in 1521.

male: bag.

mall: batter.

manage: leadership.

Marshalsea: a London prison.

martialists: warriors.

masendewes: hospitals.

maugre: despite.

mazzard: head.

menys: means.

mesels: lepers.

miching: skulking.

Minors: Franciscan friars.

misconster: misconstrue.

mortmain: indisputable ecclesiastical ownership.

Nauclerus (d. 1510): a German jurist and historian.

New Learning: doctrines of the Reformation.

Newgate: a London prison.

niceness: fastidiousness.

nobles: gold coins.

nonage: under 21 years old.

noverint: writ.

orator: petitioner.

parator: apparitor, servant of a civil or ecclesiastical officer.

parel: peril.

Paris: Matthew (d. 1259): a monk whose *Chronica Majora* covers events from A.D. 1235 to 1259.

partage: share.

pastance: pastime.

pax: a representation of the Crucifixion kissed by priests and congregations at Mass.

peise: load.

pelting: paltry.

Phrigio, Paulus (1483?–1543): a German humanist and theologian.

pill: pillage.

Plowden, Edmund (1518–85): a lawyer, proverbial in the tag, 'The case is altered, quoth Plowden'.

Polydorus: Polydore Vergil (1470?–1555?), an Italian humanist whose history of England (1534) rejected patriotic legends and supported the Papacy.

Pomfret, Peter: a hermit of Wakefield who prophesied in 1212 that by the next Ascension Day, 23 May, King John's reign would be over.

Poor John: hake.

poppetly: puppet-like.

porpoise' pastimes: porpoises were believed to gambol when a storm was approaching.

portasse: breviary.

post: (adj.) haste: (noun) courier.

practice: conspiracy.

Premonstratensians: order founded by St. Norbert in 1119.

premye: gift.

pretended: alleged.

prime: hour of Divine Office appointed for 6 a.m. or sunrise.

principal: governor.

proctor: collector of church dues.

punk: whore.

Purgatorians: sellers of indulgences and pardons.

rack: drive.

religions: monastic orders.

rerage: arrears.

responsible: corresponding to.

resty-stiff: restively obstinate.

Rhodians: the Knights Hospitallers, who captured Rhodes in 1310.

runagate: vagabond.

Sacramentaries: deniers of the Real Presence in the bread and wine of the Eucharist.

St. Antony's hog: this animal symbolizes the demon of sensuality and gluttony vanquished by the saint during his temptations.

Saint Legard: St. Leger.

Saint Loy: St. Louis.

sallett: helmet.

Sanbenets: the third of the minor orders in the Roman Church.

scalacely: *scala cæli*. a special indulgence attached to certain churches and altars.

senys: signs, finger-language.

side-coats: great coats.

Sigebert of Gembloux (1030?–1112): a Belgian chronicler of the years A.D. 381–1111.

silly: simple.

skelp: slap.

skoymose: squeamish.

slaight: crafty.

soothest: most honest.

soothing: flattery.

Sophians: the eastern order of St. Sophia.

spear: close.

stacker: stagger.

stale: decoy.

stalls: installs.

stark: violent.

stealers: fingers.

stellifers: star-bearers.

sterracles: miracles.

stews: brothels.

straggler: vagabond.

sumpter: bear the burden of.

swabber: mopper-up.

swink: drink.

Swinsett Abbey: Swinstead Abbey, Lincolnshire, where King John is said to have been given poison by a monk.

'tach: attach, arrest.

Templars: a military order founded by the King of Jerusalem early in the twelfth century to protect pilgrims.

tendering: treating.

Tertians: an order intermediate between the world and the cloister, established by St. Francis in 1221.

tester: sixpence.

Teutonics: a military order founded about the end of the twelfth century.

timpany: tumour.

toils: snares.

towards: forward.

trains: stratagems.

travail, travel: endeavour.

Tree of Jesse: the family of Jesse, father of King David, from whom Christ was descended.

trentals: payments for requiem masses.

tro: in truth.

tyre: a strong sweet wine.

unappalled: undaunted.

upspear: shut.

ure: accustom.

usquebaugh: whisky.

vaward: vanguard.

via: away.

Vincent of Beauvais (1190?–1264?): the Dominican encyclopaedist.

wamble: totter.
ward: parrying.
waste: wear away.
wat: hare.
wedred: dressed in widow's weeds.
whinyard: short-sword.
whist: quiet.
whit-leather: tough, elastic leather.

White Carmes: Carmelites, White Friars.
wistly: attentively.
wit: intellect.
wits (bodily): the five senses.
witsave: vouchsafe.
worch: work.
wrack: destruction.

zanies: foils.

PRINTED IN GREAT BRITAIN
AT THE UNIVERSITY PRESS, OXFORD
BY VIVIAN RIDLER
PRINTER TO THE UNIVERSITY